外国语言文学学科
研究生核心课程教材

总主编 **查明建**

U0745337

外国语言学
研究方法

主　编　陈新仁

编　者　（按姓氏拼音排序）

曹　宁　　陈新仁　　胡旭辉　　李　民

马广惠　　乔丽婷　　王　玲　　王雪玉

吴诗玉　　徐翠芹　　徐锦芬　　徐晓东

杨　昆　　姚明鑫　　于国栋

上海外语教育出版社
外教社　SHANGHAI FOREIGN LANGUAGE EDUCATION PRESS

图书在版编目（CIP）数据

外国语言学研究方法 / 陈新仁主编；姚明鑫等编
. -- 上海：上海外语教育出版社，2024
外国语言文学学科研究生核心课程教材 / 查明建
总主编
ISBN 978-7-5446-8224-4

Ⅰ.①外… Ⅱ.①陈… ②姚… Ⅲ.①外语—语言学
—研究方法—研究生—教材 Ⅳ.①H3

中国国家版本馆CIP数据核字（2024）第104240号

出版发行：**上海外语教育出版社**
（上海外国语大学内） 邮编：200083
电　　话：021-65425300 (总机)
电子邮箱：bookinfo@sflep.com.cn
网　　址：http://www.sflep.com
责任编辑：陶　怡

印　　刷：启东市人民印刷有限公司
开　　本：710×1000　1/16　印张 23.75　字数 424千字
版　　次：2024年12月第1版　2024年12月第1次印刷

书　　号：ISBN 978-7-5446-8224-4
定　　价：65.00元

本版图书如有印装质量问题，可向本社调换
质量服务热线：4008-213-263

总 序

　　学科是以某一特定领域为对象建立起来的专门化的知识体系和学术体系。外语学科，就是以外语和语言对象国的语言、社会、历史、地理、文学、文化、哲学、思想、民族性、国民性等为对象的知识体系以及相应的学术体系和课程体系。

　　外语学科以前都是以外语语种作为专业来建设，专业意识强，学科意识薄弱，缺乏从一级学科层面来统筹、规划而进行有组织的学科建设。2013年，国务院学位委员会第六届外国语言文学学科评议组提出外语学科五大学科方向的方案，即外国语言学、外国文学、翻译学、比较文学与跨文化研究、国别和区域研究。2017年，国务院学位办公布的《学位授权审核申请基本条件（试行）》中，正式将外国语言文学一级学科下的十三个二级学科调整为五大学科方向。外语学科五大学科方向的确立，是中国高等外语教育史上第一次明确地界定外语学科的内涵和研究范围，并厘清了学科与专业的关系。这样就将原来按照外语语种划分、各自发展的二级学科、专业按五大方向统领了起来，并贯穿于二级学科的建设。五大方向既是外语学科知识体系、学术体系建设的核心内容，也是外语学科人才的培养方向，使二级学科、专业有了凝聚的向心力，从整体上形成学术资源共享、学术体系共建的合力，也极大地促进了研究生知识结构和学术能力的共育。

研究生培养是学科人才培养最高水平的体现。如果说本科阶段主要是建立专业基本知识结构，培养相应的专业能力，那么研究生阶段则注重问题意识、理论方法和研究能力的培养。国务院学位委员会组织各学科评议组编写了《学术学位研究生核心课程指南》（以下简称《课程指南》），其中《外国语言文学一级学科研究生核心课程指南》根据外语学科五大方向建设与发展的实际情况，提出了外国语言学、外国文学、翻译学等方向的核心课程，均涵盖理论和研究方法两个层面。

《课程指南》将理论、方法作为核心课程，这是因为理论、方法在学科领域人才培养中具有特殊的意义。

对刚进入研究生阶段学习的学生来说，如何发现问题，怎样开展研究，可能会有很多迷茫和困惑。在导师们"要有问题意识"的不断念叨和提醒声中，他们也学着去思辨、质疑、提问，并渐渐有了一些零碎的思想火花和片段式的想法、杂感。但如何将这些零碎、纷杂的思想火花凝聚成光束，聚焦成学术议题？如何判断自己那些片段式的想法和杂感是否有学术价值和意义，并继而建立富有学理性和学术深度的论述？这就需要理论和方法。

理论是从实践、经验和现象中提炼出问题，探讨事物的本质特征及其内在运行机制，提出一套系统性的认知模式。理论通过判断、演绎、推理等思维形式，以问题化、抽象化、概念化、命题化方式，对事物和现象提出认知和阐释框架。科学合理、有效地运用理论，就是研究方法。因此，我们也常将理论和方法并举或合为一体。

需要指出的是，运用理论不是学术研究的最终目的。无论理论多么"新颖""先进"，都只是思想工具，服务于所要探讨的问题。学术研究中，问题是第一位的。问题的学术价值和意义，决定了研究的价值和意义。研究生学术训练所强调的问题意识，不仅是指学术研究的出发点应该是问题，并且还内在地要求此问题是个值得探讨、富有学术价值和创新意义的问题。因此，不仅要有问题意识，更要有问题意义意识。

但另一方面，强调问题的首要性，并不是否定理论和方法的作用。理论为我们观察纷繁复杂的现象提供一个视角，为进入错综复杂的问题提供一把钥匙，为展开问题分析提供一个思路向导。运用理论的目的，是理性地、科学地、深度地分析研究对象，从纷繁复杂的表面现象发现其背后更深层次的问题。理论所指示的研究思路和方法，有助于避免问题思考和学术表达中的零散化、印象式、感性化倾向，从而保证论文写作的学理性、逻辑性和严谨性。

通常的学术论文写作，并不必特别说明运用了什么理论方法，理论方法应如盐溶于水，自然而然地蕴含在论文运思和具体论述之中。但研究生学位论文撰写，一般都要求说明"所运用的理论方法"。这是因为研究生阶段是学术研究规范养成的训练阶段，理论方法是学术研究的基本要求，将"所运用的理论方法"作为一个"规定动作"，意在检测，同时也是提醒研究生要有理论方法意识，论文写作的框架和研究思路要符合学术规范，论述上具有学理性、逻辑性和严谨性。

为此，我们参照《外国语言文学一级学科研究生核心课程指南》中对课程的描述、课程目标、课程内容、考核要求，组织相关专家根据外语学科的五大方向编写了"外国语言文学学科研究生核心课程教材"系列，包含《翻译学概论》《翻译研究方法》《外国语言学理论》《外国语言学研究方法》《外国文学理论》《外国文学研究方法》《比较文学理论与研究方法》《跨文化交际研究导论》《国别与区域研究导论》九种。这套教材以硕士研究生为主要使用对象，内容上注重基础理论知识和前沿性研究成果相结合，一方面帮助学生系统了解外语学科主要研究领域的理论、方法；另一方面，通过各章节设计的思考题，启发和鼓励学生"理论地"思考，从而提高理论修养和学术研究能力。

高质量发展已成为我国高等外语教育的新时代主题，外语学科的体系框架已经建立，而我们相信，"外国语言文学学科研究生核心课程教材"系列的编写出版，正是对外语学科知识体系和高端人才培养的进一步完善和探索，将为外国语言文学学科创新发展和中国式现代化建设做出贡献。

查明建

前　言

国务院学位委员会第七届学科评议组编写的《学术学位研究生核心课程指南（一）（试行）》（高等教育出版社，2020）规定，外国语言文学一级学科研究生核心课程包括六门课程，其中第四门为"外国语言学研究方法"。《外国语言学研究方法》一书就是根据该指南中关于这一核心课程的课程概述、课程目标、课程内容、考核要求编写而成的。

根据该指南，"外国语言学研究方法"是外国语言文学一级学科下属的外国语言学及应用语言学方向研究生核心课程，旨在帮助学生掌握并运用语言研究中的资料收集、整理、分析和评估的相关方法与技术，了解并熟悉语言研究的原理、逻辑和科学程序，培养学生以科学的方法认识、分析和解决实际问题的能力，培养学生的批判性思维、创新意识和科学精神，具备运用所学理论知识和方法独立完成学位论文撰写的能力以及独立从事所学外国语言或母语的理论和实践研究能力，为今后的语言研究打下坚实基础。该课程主要包括三个模块：语言学学位论文写作的基本范式，语言研究的定义、过程及常用技术手段，外国语言学研究的方法论，涉及方法论与基础理论、研究方法和研究技术三个层次，其中方法论包括定性和定量研究两个方面。

基于该指南关于"外国语言学研究方法"课程的描述，本教材将相关内容分解为 18 个单元，适用于一学期 16 周教学课时安排。除第 1 单元为全书导论外，第 2、3、4 单元为理论研究方法模块，第 5 到第 13 单元为实证研究方法模块（其中第 5、6、7、8、9 单元为定性研究方法子模块，第 10、11、12、13 单元为定量研究方法子模块），第 14、15、16 单元为统计方法模块，第 17、18 单元为论文写作规范与方法模块。除呈现方法论外，教材还在第 1 单元简要介绍了 NVivo、SPSS、Praat、AntConc、Python 等研究工具，在第 4 单元简要介绍了 CiteSpace（可视化知识图谱软件），在第 14、15 单元详细介绍了 SPSS（社会科学统计软件），在第 16 单元详细介绍了 R（社会科学统计软件）。此外，教材还在第 11 单元介绍了国内外多个大型语料库的基本信息。

相对于市面上现有关于语言学研究方法主题的编著或教材，本教材具有以下鲜明特色：

- **权威性：** 紧扣《学术学位研究生核心课程指南（一）（试行）》中关于"外国语言学研究方法"核心课程内容及要求的权威设定。不仅如此，本教材各单元由熟谙特定研究方法的名家或有丰富方法论实践的青年才俊担纲撰写。
- **全面性：** 与现有市面相关书籍不同，本教材几乎囊括了外国语言学研究中所有最常用的研究方法。
- **针对性：** 面向目标学生开展学术研究的实际需要，强调"应用""实用""够用"，确保科学性、可学性、可用性。
- **示范性：** 注重案例分析，精心选择来自硕博士论文、期刊论文的正反典型案例，展示特定研究方法应用范围、方式、要点、难点、误区等，同时结合论文撰写，提供相关方法的呈现方式。
- **操作性：** 面向课堂讲授，设计丰富、多样的课堂讨论与课外练习题目，在教学互动中促进研究方法的理解、吸收与运用，以不同形式的练习促进语言学研究方法论知识的掌握和研究能力的提升。
- **拓展性：** 推荐介绍相关方法的其他书籍以及使用相应方法的期刊文章。践行纸数融合的理念，立体化呈现教学内容。

本教材的编写工作分工如下：陈新仁负责整部教材的设计、统稿、审核、参考文献的制作，并与姚明鑫合作撰写了第 1 单元；胡旭辉负责编写第 2、3 单元；李民负责编写第 4 单元；徐翠芹负责编写第 5 单元；王玲负责编写第 6、8 单元；徐锦芬负责编写第 7 单元；王雪玉负责编写第 10 单元；于国栋负责编写第 9 单元；杨昆负责编写第 11 单元及附录 1；徐晓东负责编写第 12、13 单元；马广惠负责编写第 14、15 单元；吴诗玉负责编写第 16 单元；乔丽婷负责编写第 17 单元及附录 2、3、4；曹宁负责编写第 18 单元。

本教材的适用对象主要包括外国语言文学一级学科相关方向的硕士和博士研究生，其他语言研究相关学科方向的学生和研究者也可参考使用。

感谢上海外国语大学赵蓉晖教授对教材设计提出的宝贵意见，也对策划本教材的上海外语教育出版社杭海女士以及陶怡编辑谨致谢忱。由于水平有限，书中讹误在所难免，期望读者批评指正，以便修订更正。

陈新仁

目　录

第1单元
外国语言学研究方法概论

学习目标
- 了解外国语言学的定义与范围
- 知晓外国语言学的研究类型
- 了解外国语言学研究的常用方法
- 知晓外国语言学实证研究的常用工具

本单元简要介绍外国语言学的定义与范围、研究类型、常用研究方法及工具，以便读者初步了解外国语言学的研究方法，为接下来的阅读、学习或研究工作提供铺垫。

1.1　外国语言学的定义与范围

在了解外国语言学的定义之前，我们不妨先看看什么是语言学。对此，国内外学者有着不同的定义。胡壮麟（2002）认为语言学是语言的科学，或语言的科学研究。克里斯特尔（Crystal, 2010）在《剑桥语言百科全书》（*The Cambridge Encyclopedia of Language*）中指出，语言学的目的在于全面而明确地定义人类语言的本质。拉尔森（Larson, 2009）提出，语言学是考察语言知识的学科，是探究人们如何认识、习得以及使用语言的学科。总体来说，语言学是一门系统研究人类语言的科学，其研究范围涵盖人类语言的形式、意义、结构、功能、影响等各个方面。

我们常说的"外国语言学"，其实是"外国语言学及应用语言学"的缩略说法，是指相对于汉语及其方言研究的、侧重研究国外语言的"个别语言学"（如英语语言学、俄语语言学、日语语言学等）的概括说法（黄国文，2007），但也包括国外学者关于语言学流派、内部语言学、外部语言学、应用语言学等的研究。其中，内部语言学关注语言本体的结构、意义等，如语音学、音系学、形态学、句法学、语义学、语用学等；外部语言学关注语言与外部因素的互动，如社会语言学、心理语言学、神经语言学。接下来我们将对上述分支作简要的介绍。

语音学与音系学都是考察人类语言声音（speech sound）的语言学分支。语音学（phonetics）通常在生理的层面上研究说话人如何发出具体的声音以及听话人如何处理声音，而音系学（phonology）在抽象的层面上考察这些声音的组合规律（Clark & Yallop, 2000）。以元音 /a/ 为例，语音学家提出的问题有可能是"人类在发出 /a/ 的声音时，哪些发声器官在工作？声带是否震动？"，而音系学研究者则更多会考虑"/a/ 的前后通常出现哪些辅音？这些组合呈现什么样的规律？"。因此，这两个学科虽然都研究人类语言声音，考察的方面却大为不同。

形态学（morphology）的研究对象主要是词汇，包括词汇的内部结构、词汇的形成以及词汇形成的心理机制（Aronoff & Kudeman, 2011）。形态学的基本单位是词素（morpheme），也是词汇意义的最小构成单位。以英语为例，词素可包括组成词汇意义的词干和词缀，如 likeable 中的词干"like"和后缀

"-able"。形态学的重点研究方向之一，便是这些词素如何通过搭配组成词汇，并赋予其意义。同时，形态学的研究范围也包括词汇间的搭配、新词的产生和变化等与词汇形态相关的语言现象。

句法学（syntax）的研究主要集中在语法上，探究词汇或者特定表达如何在句子中进行排列组合，而这种排列组合又存在着什么样的规律。因此，句法学在研究方法上多注重对语法的形式描写。同时，句法学强调探究语言使用者大脑中的语法知识（Larson, 2009），如著名的句法学家乔姆斯基（Noam Chomsky）就曾提出具有普遍性意义的转换生成语法，以描写语法在人类大脑中生成的过程。该理论自提出起就引起了非常大的争议，几十年来争论不但没有停止，反而愈演愈烈。

语义学（semantics）是对语言意义的系统研究，其研究对象可包括词素、单词、短语、句子甚至文本等表达方式（Zimmermann & Sternefeld, 2013）。由此可见，语义学关注语言中的意义，如词汇意义的组成，或者不同意义之间的区别与联系。词汇的内涵及外延，或者一词多义现象也属于语义学的探讨范围。当然，语义学对意义的探讨不局限于词汇，它也探讨短语或者句子的意义。与句法学对句子在形式规则层面的考察不同，语义学对句子或短语的研究多在命题层面上进行。

语用学（pragmatics）可以简单理解为研究语言使用的语言学分支。具体而言，语用学从社会、文化、认知等功能角度（Verschueren, 1999）考察具体语境中的说话人意义，探讨支配语言使用（包括表达与理解）的原则与准则，考察影响语言使用的社会、文化、认知、心理、物理等因素，揭示语言使用的机制与规律（陈新仁, 2021）。语用学在一定程度上与语义学相似，即两者都研究语言的意义，但语用学更注重交际语境中的动态话语意义。因此，语用学研究离不开对交际语境中各种因素的考察，这其中涉及说话者（作家）对意义的传达以及听话人（读者）对意义的解读（Yule & Widdowson, 1996）。

社会语言学（sociolinguistics）研究语言与社会的关系。因此，我们可以将社会语言学纳入外部语言学的范畴。不同于内部语言学对语言内部系统的关注，社会语言学家关心的问题主要包括"为什么语言使用者在不同的社会环境中说话方式不同""语言具有什么样的社会功能"，或是"语言如何被用来传达社会意义"（Holmes, 2013: 1）。可以看出，社会语言学通过语言本体之外的视角，探讨社会语境中的语言使用。所以，在进行社会语言学研究时，研究者常常也需要考察不同社会因素对语言的影响，如媒体的作用、语言的社会规范、政策和法律等（Wardhaugh & Fuller, 2015）。

心理语言学（psycholinguistics）是探讨语言与心理的学科，属于心理学和语言学的交叉学科。具体地说，它研究人们使用语言（包括语言的理解、产生）和习得语言的心理过程和规律（冯志伟，2013）。其中，心理、思维和心智是心理语言学的核心研究对象，因此虽然该学科的研究客体是语言，但它本质上探究的仍然是语言使用者的心理运作过程和规律（陈晨、李秋杨，2011）。例如，心理语言学的一个重要研究方向就是儿童对语言的习得，这样的研究能够帮助我们理解人类如何加工和处理语言信息，反映人类语言活动的内在心理机制。

神经语言学（neurolinguistics）是现代语言学的一门新兴交叉学科，该学科集语言学、神经科学、心理学、认知科学等为一体，研究语言习得、生成和理解的神经机制，研究大脑如何产生、接收、存储和提取语言信息，从而探讨脑和语言的关系（杨亦鸣，2002）。神经语言学以探讨语言能力的神经基础和语言的生物本质为目标，涉及语言学的方方面面，如语法、语义、语音、语言习得与发展等方面的神经语言学研究。同时，需要指出的是，不同于语言的神经机制研究，神经语言学依旧扎根于语言学，其研究主旨是语言学的，即对语言神经机制的探索要以当代语言学理论为背景，并最终能够解释人类的语言能力，揭示语言本身的性质和规律，推动语言学的发展，而前者更多是从生物学的角度探求语言在大脑中的神经基础和加工机制（杨亦鸣、刘涛，2010）。

在外国语言学中，**应用语言学**（applied linguistics）有广义和狭义之分。广义的应用语言学包括言语治疗、翻译研究、语言与计算机的结合等涉及语言应用的诸多学科（Davies & Elder, 2008；冯志伟，1999）。狭义的应用语言学则多指以外语教学为主要研究对象（Davies & Elder, 2008；陈建平，2018），特别关注第二语言的教学、测试以及学习者的习得。

需要指出的是，**认知语言学**（cognitive linguistics）研究语言与认知的关系，更多被看作是一种研究视角或方法，而非一门分支学科。昂格尔里尔和施密德（Ungerer & Schmid, 2013: F36）在《认知语言学概论》（*An Introduction to Cognitive Linguistics*）中提到"认知语言学是一种研究语言现象的方法，它基于我们对外部世界的经验，以及对外部世界的感知和概念化的过程"。认知语言学的"认知"，指的是包括感知觉、知识表征、概念形成、范畴化、思维在内的大脑对客观世界及其关系进行处理从而能动地认识世界的过程（冯志伟，2013）。这个过程涉及人类的大脑与客观世界的互动，即我们如何通过大脑的认知活动对外部世界进行组织并将其概念化。例如，在认知语言学中，隐喻就不再被看作是一种修辞手段，而是我们的思维与外部世界进行互动并将其概念化的过程或方式。

同样需要指出的是，随着中外语言研究以及理论研究的交叉融合，本着文明互鉴、"西学为用"的宗旨，以外语教师为主体的外国语言学研究者不能仅仅满足于研究外国语言或外国语言理论，而应该与中国本土语言研究的实际相结合，其最终目标应该为中国的语言建设服务（潘文国，2007），与汉语界同行一起，共同探究人类语言的本质，同时也致力于服务我国的语言建设和外语教育。

1.2 外国语言学的研究类型

外国语言学研究从研究目的的角度看，可以分为理论研究和应用研究；从研究方法角度看，又可以分为思辨研究和实证研究。

理论研究（theoretical research）和**应用研究**（practical research）的研究目的不同。理论研究的主要目的是发展理论或者验证现有的理论（文秋芳，2004）。因此，理论研究不过多探讨具体的语言问题，而更多在抽象的层面上对语言现象进行系统的描写与阐释。应用研究则多是为了解决语言使用、语言生活中的具体问题。在应用语言学中，应用研究则是为了解决二语课堂和二语习得中的具体问题（文秋芳，2004）。理论研究和应用研究往往是相互补充的，理论研究为应用研究提供理论上的阐释框架，应用研究则提供具体的语言数据，充实理论的内涵并推动理论的发展。

思辨研究（theoretical research）和**实证研究**（empirical research）在方法上存在本质差异。思辨研究多服务于理论的建构和发展，提倡内省的批判性思维（critical thinking）。在思辨研究过程中，研究者往往不对某个具体语言问题进行详细的描写和分析，但可使用具体的语言使用实例来增加论证的充分性。实证研究则是对某个具体的语言现象进行具体观察和描写、分析的研究。在实证研究中，研究者需要进行系统的数据收集、观察与分析，研究者根据不同的研究目的和数据类型可以采用定性研究方法和定量研究方法。

1.3 外国语言学研究的常用方法

外国语言学的研究方法涵盖理论研究的方法和实证研究的方法。

在开展理论研究时，所采用的方法主要包括**归纳法**（induction）和**演绎法**（deduction）。归纳法具体运用于对具体语言现象的观察，并从中抽象出系统的规律或者法则，而演绎法则多基于典型的案例对语言现象进行推演。归纳法强调对语言事实的归纳，强调占有的语言材料越多越好，而演绎法则是利用逻辑推理，即使在掌握的语言材料有限的时候，也可以大胆假设，提出假说。归纳法往往只适用于能观察到的语言材料，无法穷尽复杂浩瀚的语言现象，因此理论体系的建设离不开演绎，即从一个最基本的出发点层层推导成一个理论体系。因此，在外国语言学的理论研究中，我们常常将归纳和演绎的方法相结合，通过系统的观察、描写、解释、推演来建立语言的理论体系。此外，理论研究还可以采用**对比研究法**、**理论逼近法**以及**比较研究法**（桂诗春、宁春岩，1997）。对比研究法的特点在于对比不同语言母语者的语言使用，从而帮助我们对语言建立普遍的理论模型。理论逼近法则强调基于对部分语言事实的观察，建立语言的理论模型，并对理论进行不断的检验和修正。比较研究法则重视在建立普遍的语言理论时，在不同的语言现实中寻找共性。

在开展实证研究时，所采用的研究方法可简单分为**定性研究方法**（qualitative research method）与**定量研究方法**（quantitative research method）。对于两者的区别，不同的学者给出了不同的解释。有的学者将两者的区别概述为研究数据是否为数字，即定量研究的研究数据都基于数字，而定性研究的数据是不基于数字的（Punch, 1998: 4）。也有学者认为两者的区别可以简单定义为回答什么样的问题，即定量方法面向封闭性的问题（如量化的假设），而定性方法更多回答开放性问题（如访谈）（Creswell & Creswell, 2018）。总体而言，定性研究方法之所以区别于定量研究方法，是因为两者在本质上揭示不同的语言规律。定性研究方法旨在系统性地考察语言现象的内部本质，而定量研究方法多依赖统计方法，旨在通过样本或者数据来揭示语言现象在统计学意义上的趋势或变化。

常见的定性研究方法包括**访谈法**、**有声思维法**、**观察法**、**行动研究法**、**扎根理论**、**主题分析法**、**民族志**、**话语分析法**、**会话分析法**等。例如，面对定性数据时，研究者常常需要对数据的内容进行不同维度的编码。比较常用的编码方法是扎根理论（grounded theory）（详见第 7 单元）。作为一种数据分析方法，扎根理论能够为我们提供一系列的指南，帮助我们系统、灵活地收集和分析定性数据（Charmaz, 2006）。最终，研究者可从系统的数据收集和分析过程中抽象出理论（Corbin & Strauss, 2014），即为扎根理论中的"理论"。扎根理论是一种自下而上的分析方法，该方法帮助研究者从数据中不断抽象、概括出新的概念或者理论。因此所谓"扎根"，即形成的理论植"根"于数据之上，一切的分析结果来源于对数据的系统性收集和分析。又如，主题分析法（thematic analysis）是分析定性数据的常用工具之一。这是一种从数据集（data set）中识别、分析、组织、描述并汇报主题（theme）

的方法（Braun & Clarke, 2006）。因此，主题分析法也是帮助研究者从定性数据中不断抽象出概念或主题的方法。研究者通常在不同的阶段对数据进行反复的分析和对比（Nowell et al., 2017），最后从杂乱的数据中抽象出不同的主题。因此，主题分析法在方法上与扎根理论具有相似之处。两者不同的地方在于，扎根理论的根本目的在于构建理论，而主题分析法更多强调对数据的整理和分析。

常见的定量研究方法则包括**问卷调查法**、**语料库分析法**、**实验研究法**等。例如，问卷调查法（survey）是外国语言学中常用的定量研究方法。研究者往往可以通过问卷（questionnaire）的方式广泛地收集样本。在设计问卷时，研究者通常需要注意问卷的信度（reliability）和效度（validity）。前者要求问卷在测量时需要具有一致性和稳定性，后者要求测量具有准确性。在进行问卷调查时，研究者可使用随机抽样或者方便抽样的方式进行数据采集。最后问卷数据可导入 SPSS、R 语言（详见第 16 单元）等统计处理软件进行分析。又如，语料库分析法（corpus analysis）（详见第 11 单元）是利用语料库处理软件开展研究的分析方法。该方法多用于对大规模语料的自动化检索及标注。常用的语料库分析法包括关键词检索（keywords search）、搭配词分析（collocate analysis）、索引行分析（concordance analysis）等。语料库分析法可以基于大量的真实语料，发现语言中反复出现的语言现象、模式或者规律，因此受到许多定量研究者的青睐。当然，研究者也可以基于语料库（corpus-based）或者从语料库中抽取数据（corpus-retrieved）开展定性分析。

1.4　外国语言学实证研究的常用工具

在上一节，我们简要讨论了定性、定量的研究方法。在开展定性或定量研究时，研究者常常会采用不同的研究工具。本节将简单介绍一些常见的定性与定量研究工具，包括常见定性分析工具 NVivo、常见统计工具 SPSS、常见声学分析工具 Praat、常见语料库分析工具 AntConc 等、常见编程语言 Python，以及常见的文献分析工具 CiteSpace。

NVivo 是一款由 QSR International 公司开发的定性分析工具。该软件功能强大且易于操作，是定性研究方法中常使用的工具。对于需要处理大量原始资料的质性研究而言，质性数据分析工具的运用在一定程度上有利于提高资料处理与分析的效率，而 NVivo 作为国际上主流的质性分析软件，能够有效地分析非结构化资料，其应用过程符合质性研究范式。因此，NVivo 能够帮助研究者有效地整理、分析定性数据，从而更加高效地进行定性数据的编码工作。在外国语言学研究中，我们通常也需要对大量的定性数据进行识别、分类和编码。这是一项耗时且具有挑战性的工作，NVivo 的出现能够在一定程度上为我们的编码工作提供助力。

SPSS 是外国语言学研究中常用的量化数据处理软件。该工具功能齐全，外国语言学研究中绝大部分的量化统计分析（如描述性统计、简单推理统计及多元统计）都可以在 SPSS 中完成。另外，使用该软件不需要研究者进行复杂的设置和操作，大部分的操作通过移动或者点击鼠标即可完成（文秋芳，2004）。

Praat 是由荷兰阿姆斯特丹大学的保罗·博尔斯马（Paul Boersma）教授与戴维·韦宁克（David Weenink）教授设计的一款语音处理工具。该软件提供了丰富的语音处理功能，如语音合成与编辑、语音数据统计分析、语音数据可视化等。由于该软件的操作便捷，人机界面也较为友好，因此非常适合作为英语语调教学的辅助工具。

语料库及语料库语言学的兴起为外国语言学研究带来了新的研究视角，同时也带来了大量的语料库处理工具。目前较为常用的语料库技术工具包括 **AntConc**、**WordSmith** 和 **LancsBox** 等。AntConc 是日本早稻田大学劳伦斯·安东尼（Laurence Anthony）教授于 2002 年开发的一款免费的单语语料库分析软件。该软件功能强大，能够进行索引检索（concordance）、搭配词检索（collocates）、主题词表分析（keyword list）等语料库常用操作。WordSmith 是由英国利物浦大学的迈克·斯科特（Mike Scott）于 1996 年开发的语料库处理软件，目前已经更新到第八代。WordSmith 整体来说与 AntConc 在功能上较为相似，也能满足关键词检索、搭配词检索和主题词分析这些基本功能。LancsBox 则是英国兰卡斯特大学的瓦茨拉夫·布热齐纳（Vaclav Brezina）团队于 2018 年开发的新一代语料库处理软件，该软件较之前的语料库处理软件来说，功能更加强大。LancsBox 不仅支持常规的语料库处理功能，还能够处理多语种多格式的语料，且具有更强大的检索、统计、数据处理和可视化功能。

随着学科的发展，主流的软件无法满足多层次的研究需求，这时编程工具逐渐出现在外国语言学研究中。通过编写自定义程序，研究者可实现对语料进行更深入的大规模挖掘，而类似的数据挖掘无法在 AntConc 或者 LancsBox 中完成。目前外国语言学研究中常见的编程语言主要是 **Python** 和 **R** 语言。其中，Python 在自然语言处理（natural language processing, NLP）技术应用中具有明显的优势，因此在外国语言学研究中 Python 常用于语料库的深度挖掘。

CiteSpace 是目前较受欢迎的文献计量分析软件，该工具可以用于文献检索，并具有强大的可视化分析功能。该技术工具可分析某科学领域在一定时期的发展热点和趋势，并生成相应的科学知识图谱。例如，夏秸、陈新仁（2021）年基于 Web of Science（WoS）数据库，借助 CiteSpace 对国外语言学领域 1980—2017 年间的立场研究英语文献进行了统计分析，并总结了立场研究的年度发文趋势、研究对象、研究话题、立场类别、语体、题材、高被引文献、高被引作者、高被引期刊等数据。通过 CiteSpace 的可视化分析，他们揭示了立场研究发文的增长趋势，总结了相关话题的学科互补和议题交叉特征，并为未来的立场研究指明了研究方向。由此可见，CiteSpace 的强大文献检索和分析功能能够有助于研究者梳理相关话题的文献，并以清晰的可视化方式呈现话题的发展和文献之间的联系。

课堂讨论

1. 定性研究方法和定量研究方法在诸多层面存在差异，除了本单元提到的差异，你认为定性研究方法和定量研究方法还有哪些区别？
2. 理论研究与应用研究有何区别？两者与思辨研究、实证研究又有何联系？我们常说的定性研究方法和定量研究方法属于以上哪一类研究的研究方法？
3. 民族志（ethnography）是外国语言学中常用的定性研究方法。该方法旨在研究自然、持续进行的环境中人们的行为，研究者聚焦于从文化角度去诠释这些行为（Watson-Gegeo, 1988）。因此，民族志研究者注重深入语言使用者的生活，观察其社会文化环境，并通过第一手记录的方式对语言及语言使用者进行描写和分析。下面的描述来自一篇运用民族志方法的文章。与同学讨论运用该方法需要注意哪些事项。

我国的不同语言，由于使用人口多少的不同，以及社会经济文化发展状况的差异，其功能也必然存在差异。在历史上，我国多民族分布的地区如新疆、广西、云南等地，都采取语言兼用的手段来弥补单一语言使用的不足。在当今不同民族广泛接触、交流的现代化进程中，少数民族只使用本族语言更是不够，还必须兼用别的语言特别是通用语汉语，实现语言交际功能的互补，以便更好地满足社会交际和发展文化教育的需要。在全国各民族地区，语言互补的现象比比皆是。比如云南省景洪县基诺乡的基诺族（共11400人），除了使用自己的母语外，还全民兼用汉语。基诺语在家庭内和村寨内使用，汉语在学校、机关、医院等场合使用。本族人在一起时说基诺语，若有其他民族在场就改说汉语。同当地其他民族在一起时说当地汉语，若与省外人则说普通话。

——戴庆厦（2008：3）

课外练习

1. 本单元简单介绍了外国语言学的定义、研究范围、研究方法和研究工具。完成下列练习以进一步巩固本单元所学的知识。练习包括单选题和多选题，其中第1至5题为单选题，第6至10题为多选题。

   (1) 外国语言学是研究 _____ 的学科。

   　　A.外国语言学理论　　　　　　B.人类语言本质和发展规律

   　　C.外国人如何说话

   (2) _____ 是内部语言学的一个分支。

   　　A.语用学　　　　　　　　　　B.应用语言学

   　　C.心理语言学

   (3) _____ 是外部语言学的一个分支。

   　　A.社会语言学　　　　　　　　B.音系学

   　　C.形态学

(4) 定性和定量研究是 _____ 的方法。

    A. 理论研究   B. 思辨研究

    C. 实证研究

(5) 会话分析主要用于对 _____ 的分析。

    A. 自然发生的口语语料   B. 学术文本

    C. 机构话语

(6) _____ 属于定性研究方法。

    A. 扎根理论   B. 主题分析法

    C. 问卷调查   D. 民族志

(7) _____ 属于定量研究方法。

    A. 问卷调查   B. 实验法

    C. 语料库分析   D. 话语分析

(8) _____ 既可以用于定量研究，又可以用于定性研究。

    A. 话语分析   B. 会话分析

    C. 语料库分析   D. 扎根理论

(9) 常用的语料库分析软件包括 _____。

    A. AntConc   B. SPSS

    C. WordSmith   D. CiteSpace

(10) 常用的编程语言包括 _____。

    A. Python   B. SPSS

    C. R 语言   D. LancsBox

2. 根据自己的研究兴趣，选择一篇已发表的外国语言学论文，从研究方法的角度探讨该论文属于思辨研究还是实证研究。再指出研究者在论文中使用了哪些研究方法。

3. 以小组为单位，选择一篇外国语言学论文，对其中的研究方法进行批判性的讨论，例如：使用的研究方法是否适合该研究？为何适合或不适合该研究？是否还有更合适的研究方法？

拓展阅读

Corbin, J., & Strauss, A. (2014). *Basics of qualitative research: Techniques and procedures for developing grounded theory.* London: Sage.

Creswell, J. W., & Creswell, J. D. (2018). *Research design: Qualitative, quantitative, and mixed methods approaches.* London: Sage.

Punch, K. F. (1998). *Introduction to social research: Quantitative and qualitative approaches.* London: Sage.

桂诗春、宁春岩. (1997). 语言学方法论. 北京：外语教学与研究出版社.

文秋芳. (2004). 应用语言学研究方法与论文写作. 北京：外语教学与研究出版社.

第 2 单元
理论语言学研究方法（一）

学习目标

- 了解理论语言学的核心、对象和目标
- 了解理论语言学研究的起点

本单元和下一单元聚焦于理论语言学（theoretical linguistics）的研究方法。理论语言学的研究方法需要建立在理解理论语言学的目标和本质的基础上，然后才能明确具体的科研方法背后的动因。因此，本单元首先对理论语言学做扼要的介绍，进而介绍理论语言学研究方法的要点。我们希望本单元所论述的理论语言学研究的思路和方法并不局限于某个流派，而是对理论语言学研究有普遍的意义。

2.1　理论语言学：核心、对象和目标

理论语言学是相对于应用语言学的语言学学科，所以其核心当然是"理论"。这个核心要求理论语言学的研究成果必须有理论层面的创新，即通过具体的语言研究归纳出抽象的理论层面的创新要素。我们由此需要提出的第一个问题是：我们为什么需要发展抽象的语言理论？回答这个问题需要了解当代语言学的本质。如果我们仅按字面意思将语言学理解为"有关语言的科学研究"，那么语言学就是任何有关语言研究的探索，这样的探索并不必然要求存在有关语言的一个自成一体的系统理论。假如我们认为语言就是语言社区约定俗成的一套系统，没有任何特别的内在机制，那么语言学的任务主要就是描述这个系统。

如果这样来看的话，语言学很容易失去核心的学科属性和领地。事实上，早在100多年前，弗迪南·德·索绪尔（Ferdinand de Saussure）在《普通语言学教程》[1]（*Course in General Linguistics*，下文简称《教程》）中就明确指出了这个问题。索绪尔（Saussure, 1916）指出，涉及语言的领域非常多，如社会学、心理学、人类学、语文学等，语言学研究的任务之一是界定语言学的学科范畴，因此必须将语言学与其他相关学科的边界厘清。在索绪尔看来，语言学的核心任务之一是研究具体语言（parole）背后的抽象语言系统（langue），即语言表象背后的本质。索绪尔认为这个语言的本质核心要素在于语言系统是一个特殊的具有心理和社会属性的符号系统，因此语言学家的任务是探索统辖这个符号系统的抽象规则是什么。如果我们把索绪尔有关语言属性的具体观点放置一边，那么可以说当代语言学的研究对象和目标基本沿袭了索绪尔的思路，即以人类语言作为研究对象，探索语言背后的核心机制，不同的只是各个学派对于这个核心机制的具体看法。譬如，生成学派认为语言背后的核心机制是先天的语言天赋，即普遍语法（Universal Grammar, UG），

1《普通语言学教程》并非索绪尔生前所作，而是其学生在他逝世后根据他的课堂讲义编撰而成。

而认知语言学和功能学派的语言学则认为语言背后的认知机制就是人类的普遍认知机制，并不存在专司语言的 UG。我们的核心在于讨论理论语言学的研究方法，因此不展开讨论这些具体的争议。

当我们把语言学的核心目标界定为探索人类语言背后的抽象机制，这也就意味着语言学本质上和其他理论科学（如物理学、生物学等）一样，是以解释性作为核心特征。这也是当代语言学与以莱昂纳德·布龙菲尔德（Leonard Bloomfield）为代表的美国结构主义语言学在学科属性上的本质差别。抛开种种技术细节和历史动因，美国结构主义语言学的核心任务是对语言的描述，其科学性不是体现在解释语言内在的机制，而是体现在描述方法上。这样说并非在贬低美国结构主义语言学所取得的重大成就和对后世重要的影响，而是想要强调当代语言学脱胎自对美国结构主义语言学的"反叛"，这个反叛的核心不在于否认语言描述的重要性，而在于强调当代语言学的目标不是止步于描述，而是要进一步解释。在某种程度上来说，从描述到解释，语言学的学科属性发生了巨大变化，将此说成是库恩（Kuhn, 1962）所谓的范式迁移（paradigm shift）也不为过。

在明确语言学学科属性和目标的基础上，我们可以聚焦于理论语言学的"理论"。理论之所以重要，是因为语言学的核心目标是解释语言背后的抽象机制，而任何学科（不局限于语言学）要具有科学意义上的解释力，必须要有一套严密的理论系统，并且在深入的研究中可以对这一套理论系统进行持续的改进。现在我们可以这样理解，理论之所以重要是因为需要有理论才能做真正的科学解释；理论需要不断改进，不是因为学者们喜欢摆弄术语，而是因为这是推进解释的要求。这不是理论语言的独特要求，而是当代理论科学的普遍特征。

2.2　理论语言学研究的起点

牛顿与苹果树的故事我们都耳熟能详。从习以为常的现象中发现令人困惑的问题，并以此为出发点，探索问题的答案，对现象做出解释。苹果从树上掉下来是一个人人皆知的现象，但是为什么苹果偏偏是往下掉而不是朝上呢？这事实上是一个非常令人困惑的问题，却往往被人忽视，而牛顿的理论物理研究则发现了万物运动背后的万有引力，不仅解释了苹果为什么下落，也被应用于解释宇宙天体的运行。

对于理论研究的学者来说，科研的起点可以说是好奇心，这种科研中的好奇心是需要培养的。当然，首先需要培养的是上面所说的意识，即面对常见的现象，我们不是认为这些现象理所当然，而是能从中发现让我们真正感到疑惑的要点。其次是专业的培养，因为专业的培养可以让我们知道去关注什么现象，也可以培养我们对表象的敏锐感。可以说，没有这样的起点，理论科学就失去了真正的内在驱动力。这也是为什么当代语言学家乔姆斯基说："能够让自己感到困惑的能力极具价值，值得我们认真培养"（The capacity to be puzzled is a valuable one to cultivate）（Chomsky, 2013: 37）。

当代理论语言学和其他科学一样，起点都是在常见的现象中发现"谜团"，科研人员因为这些谜团而感到困惑，进而通过学术研究试图来解开这些谜团。学科之间的差异在于面向的现象不同。语言学面向的对象自然就是语言现象。那么，理论语言学研究的起点在哪里呢？根据以上的论述，我们可以总结为如下的模式：

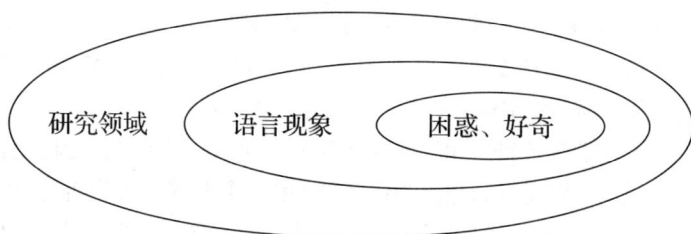

图2.1　理论语言学研究起点的思维模式

具体说来，当我们开始进入一项理论语言学研究时，首先必须有本研究领域的理论储备。这个理论储备的目的不是为了学一些理论术语来让我们的行文看上去有学术味道，而是通过这样的理论学习，我们可以明确自己的研究领域是什么，关注的理论核心问题是什么，这些问题是需要对什么现象做出解释。有了这些储备，我们就可以知道哪些现象是我们需要关注的。在此基础上，可以针对性地关注相关语言现象，将自己的观察结合理论背景，从中发现依然让人困惑的现象，找到自己的研究起点。从这个简单的模式描述中我们也可以发现，虽然研究的起点是自己的好奇心和困惑，但是科研的好奇心并非随机的突发奇想，而是在系统的理论储备和训练基础上，用自己的科研敏锐力去发现问题，这也是为什么乔姆斯基强调这样的能力是需要培养的。

如果以上这几个要素没有做好准备，那么往往在科研起点阶段就走错了方向。举例来说[1]：

---

1 本例内容纯属虚构，只是为了说明要点设计的虚拟场景。

假设有一位做语言学研究的学生 A，希望做和法律相关的语言学研究。为了这项研究，A 做了相当多的田野调查，发现某些法律尚不健全，某些特定人群的权益很容易受到伤害，大众针对某个问题的法律意识非常薄弱。因此，这位学生在他的开题设计中对这些法律问题做了详细的描述，其中也加入了他自己的田野调查的发现，最后提出希望自己的研究能够改善这个社会现状，维护某群体的利益，增强大众的法律意识。

　　以上案例的问题在于其描写对象完全不在语言学的范围之内。这个问题的根源在于没有认清自己所做研究的核心本质，从而无法识别自己的研究应该关注哪些现象。关注法律意识、公平正义、弱势群体权益这些当然没有错，但是如果确认自己是在做语言学研究，那么首先需要确认自己的研究对象和语言相关，既可以是语言本体，也可以是语言与外部要素的互动。究竟关注哪一类现象，则取决于自己对所处领域的研究。比如，如果关注法律语言学研究，可以在了解本领域的前提下，关注相关法律问题中有哪些与语言研究有关，如法律语言的话语分析、法律语音学研究的现状等。

　　下面我们会以当代语言学的几个著名案例来说明理论语言学研究的起点。生成语言学的研究起点可以简单归纳为一点，即语言有什么特别之处。从乔姆斯基最早期的研究至今，生成语言学研究的目的之一都是回答这个问题。生成语言学研究中著名的语言特殊现象是"柏拉图问题"（Plato's Problem），即，尽管语言系统如此复杂，为何儿童在普遍认知能力不发达且语言输入不系统的前提下，能早早掌握一门语言[1]。儿童并没有接受父母的系统训练，而且父母和周边人群给儿童的语言刺激往往都是碎片式、不成体系的，这就是所谓的刺激贫乏（poverty of stimulus）；可就是在这样的环境中，心智完全不成熟的儿童在 3–4 岁左右便基本能熟练讲自己的母语。这时候的儿童语言可能发音幼稚，讲话的内容也往往不着边际，但是他们的句子基本是符合语法的，这也是为什么我们能听懂他们的句子。以汉语为例，儿童可以熟练使用各类虚词（如"了""着""过"）。这些虚词的使用规则非常复杂，至今仍是语法学界争论的焦点，父母更不可能系统地教给儿童虚词的用法，但是儿童却能自然而然地掌握。更为重要的是，儿童讲出的话大部分都不是重复父母的话语，而是具备高度的创造性。这有力地推翻了以伯尔赫斯·弗雷德里克·斯金纳（Burrhus Frederic Skinner）为代表的行为主义（behaviourism）对儿童语言习得的看法。行为主义认为语言习得遵循外界刺激—个体反应—强

---

1 这里的"掌握"主要针对语法系统，不包括语言使用的适当性。如，4–5 岁的儿童基本可以用准确的语法结构来组织语言，但是往往会说出不合逻辑或语义/语用上令成人啼笑皆非的句子。

化—形成习惯的程序。这套程序无法充分解释上述儿童语言习得的特点。另一个与之相关的事实是，虽然世界语言表象差异巨大，但是儿童习得的时间段却是一致的，这也说明人类语言知识的内在本质是超越个体语言表象的内在先天（innate）机制。

我们再看从语言现象出发的具体例子。

例 2.1　a. Who do they think like each other?（他们认为谁相互喜欢对方？）
　　　　 b. Can the people who sing well also dance?（唱歌好的人是否也能跳舞？）

在例 2.1a 中，虽然 each other 在线性距离上和代词 they 靠得更近，但是却必须与线性距离更远的 who 共指；而在例 2.1b 中，虽然 sing 和 can 在线性距离上更近，但是与 can 有语义联系的却是动词 dance，也就是说，这句话中"能"指向的动作是"跳舞"而非"唱歌"。如果支配语言的能力完全来自普遍的认知能力，大脑解读句子时将会倾向于寻找线性距离最近的点以尽快完成认知处理（如以上例子中的指代、情态动词的动作限定），但是以上例子却表明，语言机制选择了在普遍认知能力上看似更复杂的基于层级（hierarchy）的运算。这些语言的特殊性并非来自晦涩难懂的语言现象，而都是基于看似平常的现象，深究后才让人感到困惑，而这样的困惑正是乔姆斯基为代表的生成语言学家的研究起点。前文介绍的语言现象的一个解释是，除了普遍的认知能力，人类还有一个负责语言的特殊认知机制，这个机制为人类先天具备，并且是将人类与动物区分开的重要特征。这个解释是乔姆斯基所开创的生成语言学的基本假设。

以上的例子是研究语言内部系统的例子，我们再以语用学为例。

例 2.2　Can you pass me the book?（能不能把书递给我？）

无论是英语还是汉语语境中，以上句子都是语言使用者习以为常的现象。但是语言哲学家和语言学家却从中发现了一个让人困惑不解的现象：明明语言形式是一个是非问句，为什么实际表达的却是一个命令？从语言学的视角来看，这个现象至少指向两个研究领域。第一是语言的意义研究，如果我们所表达的意义并不完全来自词汇意义和语法结构产生的组合意义，那么额外的意义又来自哪里？第二个是人类交际的认知机制，尤其是心智理论（theory of mind），因为我们需要解释，为什么当我们听到一个问句就可以立即明白对方是在向我们提出请求。由此，我们可以看到，一个看似简单常见的语言现象，触发的是当代理论语言学领域语义学和语用学的研究，也涉及语言哲学、认知科学及其与语言学的交叉研究。

具体到一篇研究性论文的写作，我们应该从具体的语言现象出发，将这个语言现象放置到本领域的宏观背景下，告诉读者：这个现象为什么给我们带来了困惑？需要我们回答什么样的问题？并由此告诉读者，对这个现象的解释不仅仅是解决了一个具体问题，同时也对本领域哪个理论要点做出了推进。我们以黄正德（Huang, 1982）和蔡维天（Tsai, 1994）的麻省理工学院（MIT）博士论文为例，这两项博士论文研究的起点之一是中英文特殊疑问句的差异：英语的特殊疑问词需要前置，而汉语的则不需要。

例 2.3　　a. What do you like?
　　　　　　b. 你喜欢什么？

以上例子是学习过英语的汉语使用者都知道的普通事实，但是当我们将这个差异放到理论背景下，则会发现其中的困惑。简单来说，如果要构成疑问句，需要两个要素，一个是疑问逻辑算子（Q-operator，以下简称"疑问算子"），一个是被疑问算子统辖的变量（variable）。所以对于例 2.3 中的问句，不论英语还是汉语，最终要表达的意思可以分解为：【你喜欢 x】；【（告诉我）x 是什么？】。其中 x 代表变量，第二个方括号的内容之所以可以推导出来，是因为第一个方括号的内容在一个疑问算子的统辖范围之内。对应到疑问句的句法中，我们需要问的是，变量、疑问算子及其结构关系在句法推导中是如何构建的。在早期的文献中（如 Chomsky, 1977），典型的研究结论是，特殊疑问词（如 what）包含了疑问算子，通过将特殊疑问词移动到句首位置，一方面移动后留下的语迹（trace）构成一个变量，同时这个变量又在句首疑问算子的管辖范围之内，因此带来了上面两个方括号里的内容，也意味着疑问句构建成功。按照这样的思路，在构建一个疑问句时，特殊疑问词必须要前置到句首位置。在这个背景下，我们习以为常的汉语特殊疑问句就带来了一个很大的困惑：宾语疑问词还在原来的位置，并没有移动到句首位置，为什么依然可以构建以上分析的疑问句语义信息。对于这个现象的研究，目的不仅仅是描述汉语疑问句的语法特征，而是要解释以上的理论问题，因此研究结果如果合理，则会推动我们对疑问句的普遍特征和跨语言差异的内在因素的理解，从而推动句法理论的发展。正是在这个问题上做出的开创性研究，使得黄正德和蔡维天各自的博士论文成为生成语言学领域的重要研究，至今仍然被广泛引用。

在一篇具体的论文中，研究的起点一般需要在引言部分阐述清楚。引言部分表面上只是全文的一个引子，但根据这一节的分析，我们知道，引言部分事关全局，决定了整个研究最根本的动因。因此，我们对理论语言学研究的引言部分可以有如下标准：（1）是否清晰展示了语言现象中引发困惑的具体要点；（2）是否勾勒出本研究的宏观理论背景，从而清晰告诉读者为什么这些现象会引发困惑，而对这些现象的解释又如何可以使现有理论得到潜在的发展。

在此需要强调的另外一个要点是，论文写作需要时刻遵循"读者友好"的原则，将上述内容清晰、明了地呈现在读者面前，而不是将这些要点散落在文章不同部分，期待读者自己通过层层分析才有可能明白。我们可以用以下的类比来说明。论文写作不应该像侦探、悬疑小说那样，要读者带着疑惑层层深入、不断猜测，到最后才明白作者的意图；相反，一篇论文应该像是一个案情分析，在最开始就要明确交代所有的要素和逻辑脉络，从而让读者在阅读文章的每一个阶段都明确知道我们的意图、核心逻辑、研究要点是什么。

基于前文内容，我们可以避免常见的引言部分的问题，如引言部分大谈理论，读者看完引言部分不知道全文的起点在哪里，要解决什么具体问题。另外一个常见现象是，在引言中罗列各种语言事实，但结构松散，读者无法知道这些语言事实为什么值得关注，可以对什么理论问题做出贡献。另外一个可以避免的问题是，读者无法通过引言部分了解文章的大致脉络。

课堂讨论

1. 语言学研究中常常涉及的现象包括语音、语义、句法结构以及语言与社会、文化等的关系，从这些角度出发，寻找一个让你感到好奇和困惑的语言现象，将这个现象陈述给你的同学，并解释为什么这个现象让你感到困惑。

2. 假如你要做一项语言学研究，关注对象是手机微信聊天中"呵呵"的使用。你会如何向非语言学专业的人解释这项研究的起点和意义？在思考这个问题时，联系本章内容，尤其是图 2.1 中的思维模式。

课外练习

1. 列举一个你关心的语言现象，分析如何用理论语言学的研究思路来研究这个现象。这个语言现象可以是课堂讨论第 1 题的内容。
2. 与同学交换阅读各自写的第 1 题的内容，列举优点和可改进的地方。

拓展阅读

Adger, D. (2021). On doing theoretical linguistics. *Theoretical Linguistics*, *47*(1–2), 33–45.

Haspelmath, M. (2021). General linguistics must be based on universals (or non-conventional aspects of language). *Theoretical Linguistics*, *47*(1–2), 1–31.

Saussure, F. de. (1916). *Cours de linguistique generale*. Paris: Payot. (中文版，高名凯（译）. (1980). 普通语言学教程. 北京：商务印书馆. 英文版, Bakin, W. (translate). (1959). *Course in general linguistics*. New York: Columbia University Press.)

胡旭辉等. (2023). 普通语言学研究新发展（第二章）. 北京：清华大学出版社.

第 3 单元
理论语言学研究方法（二）

学习目标
- 了解理论语言学研究中的现象描述
- 了解理论语言学研究中的假设
- 了解理论语言学研究中的论证

本单元承接上一单元内容，继续介绍理论语言学的研究方法。在上一单元，我们的核心是纵览理论语言学研究的本质，在此基础上分析了理论语言学研究的起点。本单元我们将介绍理论语言学研究中的两大核心要素，即描述与论证，这两者构成了理论语言学方法论的主体。

3.1 理论语言学研究中的描述

3.1.1 描述的充分性

科学研究需要具备系统的理论框架，推进理论的发展也是理论语言学研究的任务。作为科学研究的语言学理论，需要一套系统的理论框架，涵盖普遍、抽象、精准的原则，从而可以对语言现象做出深层的解释，并且这些理论要素都是可证伪的（falsifiable）。我们以生成语言学为例，乔姆斯基提出句法理论研究需要具备三个标准：观察充分性（observational adequacy）、描述充分性（descriptive adequacy）、解释充分性（explanatory adequacy）（Chomsky, 1964）。在句法研究中，观察充分性和描述充分性针对的都是某一个特定的语言现象；观察充分性的标准相对简单，只要观察到这个语言中正确的线性关系（语序）即可；描述充分性则是在此基础上要能够分析出这个语言线性语序背后的内在层级结构。解释充分性指的则是在前两个充分性的基础上，能够将特定语言的内在结构与人类语言的普遍共性结合起来，从而能够为这个语言内在结构之所以如此做出解释，同时也推动我们进一步了解语言共性与个体语言之间的关系。我们用一个简单的例子来说明问题。

例 3.1　a. This cup of coffee in my hand might have gone bad.

如果仅仅具备观察充分性，针对这句话，我们可以给出线性的语序：

b. This + cup + of + coffee + in + my + hand + might + have + gone + bad.

这里，我们无非是把一个个词逐个叠加了起来。我们这么呈现是因为我们观察到了表象的语序。如果止步于此，我们无法从语言现象中进一步探索语言的本质，因为这个观察得出的结构（如例 3.1c 所示）并没有真正总结出语言结构的模式：

c.

S (S for Sentence)

This　cup　of　coffee　in　my　hand　might　have　gone　bad.

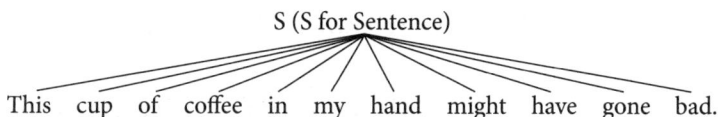

我们直觉上觉得 this cup of coffee in my hand 应该是构成了一个整体，比如可以用代词来替代这个整体：

d. It might have gone bad.

但是例 3.1c 的描述并不能呈现这个特点。这个描述说明，一个句子的内在结构并不是像例 3.1b 那样逐词叠加，而是先由单词组建成小的模块单元，再由这些单元合并组建更大的单元，直至构建成一个句子，大约的模式呈现如下：

e.

S
…　…
This cup of coffee in my hand might have gone bad.

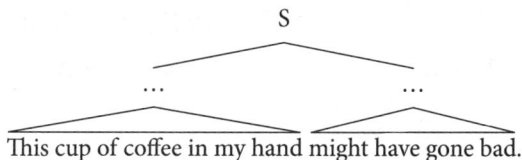

以上的描述已经超越了表象的逐词叠加的观察，而是粗略总结了线性语序背后的组建模式。这个描述为进一步的句法解释提供了基础，比如句法结构的层级关系（而不是例 3.1c 中纯粹的扁平结构）由此已经可以看出端倪。

下面我们用英汉自反代词的例子来说明描述充分性的要点。根据乔姆斯基约束理论（binding theory）中的约束原则 A（binding principle A），自反代词必须和同一个小句中对其成分统领（c-command）[1]的先行词同指（Chomsky, 1981）：

---

1 简单来说，在一个句法结构中，如果 X 和 Y 是句法上的姐妹关系（大致可以理解为双叉的两个节点），那么 X 成分统领 Y 以及 Y 下面的"子女"节点。需要注意的是，这是对成分统领非常简化的概括，包括这里的约束原则 A 的解释也是简单化的（比如"同一个小句"这个范围是需要精确界定的），相关的技术细节，读者可参考相关的句法学教材（如 Radford, 2009；Adger, 2003；Roberts, 2022；等等）。

例 3.2　a. John_i liked himself_i.

　　　　　b. John_j said Tim_j liked himself_{j/*i}.

以上句子中，下标 i 和 j 代表的是名词和自反代词的共指关系，星号 * 表示该共指关系不符合语法。例 3.2a 中，himself 必须和 John 共指，因为 John 和 himself 在同一个小句中且前者成分统领后者。例 3.2b 中，himself 只能和 Tim 同指，而不能和句子更前面的 John 共指，这是因为 Tim 和 himself 在同一个小句中，而 John 在 himself 所在的小句之外。因此，例 3.2 中的两个句子都满足约束原则 A。但是，下面的例子似乎说明汉语不受这条原则的制约：

例 3.3　a.张三说李四喜欢自己。

我们作为汉语母语者，应该都可以获得两个解读，即"自己"可以与"李四"共指，也可以与"张三"共指，究竟选择哪一个解读则由语境决定。观察到这一步，我们当然已经有了不少收获，上述讨论至少表明约束理论需要重新考量。但是，如果止步于此就得出结论，认为汉语的自反代词不受结构限制，纯粹由语境决定，就会走入误区。我们需要在描述上进一步深入，比如下面的例子：

　　　　　b.张三的哥哥说李四喜欢自己。

以上例子中，在不同语境下，"自己"可以与"李四"或者"张三的哥哥"共指，但无论提供怎样的语境信息，"自己"却无法与"张三"共指。究其原因，这与内在的结构相关：名词短语"张三的哥哥"和"李四"在结构上都成分统领"自己"，但是"张三"并没有成分统领"自己"。因此，要做到语言现象描述的充分，我们不能满足于表象，而需要进一步描述内在的抽象模式，由此我们才能为进一步的深入解释提供基础。譬如，基于这样的描述，我们可以得出的一个结论是，至少英汉的自反代词的指代在很大程度上受结构制约，这背后的原因是什么，这是理论解释要解决的问题。如果做不到描述的充分，我们连需要解释的问题都无法提出。

我们再看一个语用学的例子。以下例句来自斯波伯和威尔逊（Sperber & Wilson, 2015: 121）：

例 3.4　Passenger: What time is the next train to Oxford?

（旅客：下一班前往牛津的火车什么时候发车？）

Railway official: 12:48.

（铁路工作人员：12:48）

这是日常生活中常见的例子。如果铁路员工用正常语气说出发车时间，那么她的回答表达的就是"下一班火车将于 12:48 发车"。但是，如果她的语气非常紧急，那么她可能同时还希望传达"火车快开了"之类的信息。即使不做语言学研究，我们也可以完成这样的意义描述，但描述如果止步于此，则无法回答这句话为何能传达与字面不同的意义。在语用学理论背景下，我们还需要做进一步的描述并做相应的解释：话语所传达的意图并非总是一个完整精确的命题（即保尔·格莱斯［Herbert Paul Grice］所说的说话人意义），也可以表达并不能精准刻画的意义，斯波伯和威尔逊将这类意义称为"非确定性意义"（indeterminate meaning）。类似的现象还有《罗密欧与朱丽叶》中罗密欧的台词："Juliet is the sun"（朱丽叶是太阳）。两位学者引用贾维尔（Cavell, 1965/1976）的评论，指出罗密欧通过这句话要表达的信息无法用精确的命题信息刻画出来，因为这个意图表达的信息是比较模糊的，可以表达的含意存在多种可能性，例如：罗密欧世界中的温暖来自朱丽；罗密欧的每一天始于朱丽叶的出现，等等。在此基础上，我们将这类语言现象的描述归结为：当说话人表达意图时，这个意图可以是一个精确的命题，也可以是一个无法精确刻画的、有一定模糊性的信息。在这个描述充分的基础上，研究者才可以探讨相关的话题，比如：这样的非确定性意义是否属于语用学研究的范围（从而延伸至语用学的学科定位）？如果我们理解说话人意义（明确隐含的命题意义）是基于人类交际的机制，这个机制该如何解释这些非精确信息的生成呢（从而延伸至改进既往的理论或者提出新的理论框架）？

3.1.2 描述单一语言的可行性[1]

为理论语言学研究服务的语言描述，目标是推动语言学理论发展，进而探索语言本质。语言本质当然是语言的普遍属性，这是从索绪尔到当代生成语言学和认知语言学等理论语言学研究都认可的目标，所不同的只是对语言普遍属性的具体看法。在这个背景下，一个常见的针对理论语言学研究的批

| 1 本节是基于胡旭辉等（2023）第一章的部分内容。

评可以归纳如下：具体的语言学研究往往针对的是某一个语言，这样的研究如何可以得出语言的普遍属性？我们认为，任何一种人类语言的表象背后必然具有抽象的语言普遍属性。所以，逻辑上讲，从一门具体语言出发，抽象出语言背后的属性不无可能。

当然，这并不是说针对单一语言的研究必然可以抽象出语言的普遍属性，也不是说由此抽象出的属性一定是可靠的。基于有限语言的语言学研究要满足以下几个条件，才可能对探索语言普遍属性的理论语言学有所贡献。第一，研究者必须有探索语言普遍属性的目的。并不是所有的语言学研究都必须要为探索语言普遍属性服务。比如，如果研究汉语语法的目的是对外汉语教学，那么研究者需要做的便是精确归纳汉语语法的规律，并且以对外汉语教学实践为导向，在归纳中考虑如何呈现这些语法规律才能更好地为学生理解、接受和应用。但是，如果研究汉语的目标之一是通过探索汉语语法来呈现某些语言普遍属性，那么研究者必然会提出一些和语言普遍属性相关的问题并尝试做出解答。比如：汉语为什么有量词？量词是否实现了某种普遍的语言功能？

第二，研究者应该有跨语言比较的视角。即使不是基于大规模语料的类型学研究，也应该有比较的眼光。还是以汉语量词为例，我们可以问：为什么印欧语中没有量词？如果量词实现了某种普遍的功能，那么这个功能在印欧语中是如何实现的？这种比较的眼光，一方面会让具体语言的研究直接贡献于语言普遍属性的探索，也会帮助我们通过所聚焦的语言，发掘其他语言中被忽视的特点。

第三，研究者应该有开放的心态。虽然我们认为基于少数语言的研究也可以探索语言的普遍属性，但是与其他科学研究一样，这些研究的结论不是绝对的真理，我们需要通过持续的研究来验证、修正甚至否定已有的结论。比如，基于英语得出的某个普遍属性，可能在未来会因为汉语语料的分析而被推翻或进一步修正。语言学领域比较著名的例子是上一单元所说的有关wh- 词[1]移动的分析。乔姆斯基（Chomsky, 1977）指出，英语 wh- 词的移动是基于语言的普遍属性。一个句子要产生疑问句的解读，需要在句法推导过程中获得一个变量，同时需要有一个能管辖整句话的疑问算子，从而获得"这个变量是什么值"的解读。Wh- 词移动到句首就是为了满足这两个条件。移动后留下的痕迹（语迹）是一个变量，而 wh- 词本身带有疑问算子，放到

---

1 句法研究中，"wh- 词"等同于各语言中的疑问词，并不一定需要拼写出现"wh-"，包括下文涉及的汉语特殊疑问词。

句首可以管辖整个句子，最终获得疑问句的解读[1]。黄正德（Huang, 1982）的研究将汉语问句纳入疑问句的普通语言学研究视野中，对上述特殊疑问句的普遍属性提出了挑战，因为汉语的疑问词（如"什么""谁"）并不需要移动到句首。从研究方法来看，这项研究尤其值得我们重视的是，某项假设受到新的语言现象的挑战并不必然代表这项假设完全错误，另一个可能是这项假设的内核基本合理，但需要进一步修正。譬如，黄正德的研究表明乔姆斯基（Chomsky, 1977）有关 wh- 问句的核心理论假设并没有问题，只不过 wh- 词的移动在不同的语言中会发生在不同的阶段。在英语等语言中，wh- 词移动发生在语音可见的阶段，汉语中则发生在靠后的语音不可见的阶段[2]。基于汉语的疑问句研究并非仅限于此。在前人研究基础上，蔡维天（Tsai, 1994）认为汉语的 wh- 疑问句的特点来自 wh- 词的特殊属性：这些词项本身就是变量，因此不需要通过移动来制造变量。这类变量受各种语境中可及的逻辑算子的约束，因此在不同的话语中可充当被疑问算子约束的变量（如"你喜欢什么？"），也可充当被其他逻辑算子约束的变量（如"你也没吃什么，怎么就饱了呢？"）。根据蔡维天的解释，我们可以进一步推进有关疑问句的语言普遍属性：疑问句需要变量被疑问算子约束，且不同的语言可以通过不同的方式实现这种约束关系。赛托（Saito, 2017）对日语疑问句的研究某种程度上正是沿袭了这种思路，他指出日语疑问句的变量与约束关系来自另一个机制：疑问词依然是算子，需要移动来创造变量；同时疑问算子的具体内容未获得赋值，需要在句法中和相应的助词（particle）协同来获得。

第四，研究者应该有语言学理论的储备。单靠语言现象的描述、归纳以及对语言普遍属性的关注，是无法通过单一语言的某个现象进入到抽象的语言属性分析的。以前文所讨论的疑问句研究为例，如果没有一套有关句法移动、算子与变量的约束关系等句法和语义（及其互动的）理论，基本不可能从单一的语言现象中得出普遍的语言特征。再比如汉语的量词研究。博雷尔（Borer, 2005）基于一套有关谓词如何转化为可切分的实体的理论，指出汉语量词系统折射出了名词结构的普遍属性，即句法的功能结构中有一个负责切分（division）的节点，负责对谓词（此处为名词）进行切分。在此基础上，融入比较的视角，博雷尔指出这个节点的实现是语言的普遍需求，但如何实现则具有跨语言的差异，如英语大部分情况下是以复数标记 -s 来实现的。

---

1 这里是一个简单化的解释，具体的句法研究涉及相当多的技术细节，我们在此忽略。

2 为了不让读者感到困惑，我们也略去了相关的技术细节。这里需要强调的是，所谓的语音可见与不可见并非随意下的结论，是基于以往理论的构建和具体的论证。

3.2 理论语言学的核心：论证

3.2.1 归纳与演绎

前文已经指出，科学研究的终极目标是解释。解释要得以进行，其中关键的一步是归纳。归纳的核心是从特有的现象出发，最终发现普遍的规律。研究往往从观察现象起步，但是仅仅满足于观察与描述并不能达到科学研究的境界。我们还需要"归纳"这一关键的步骤。基于观察到的现象，科学研究人员从中归纳出普遍的抽象原则。任何科学研究都没有达到真正的终点，因此这些原则本质上都是假设。构建这些假设，也需要一套术语和概念，确保可以用清晰精确的方式呈现假设，并且也给同一研究领域的学术共同体提供一套通用的术语。而我们所说的理论，则是在某一个领域内，多个假设相互联系构建的一个复杂系统。以语用学为例，在语用学研究中我们有各种理论系统，比如，由奥斯汀（Austin, 1962）开创、塞尔（Searle, 1969, 1979）进一步发展的言语行为理论（speech act theory）首先有一套系统的假设，认为人类语言除了表达意义，也同时是在行事，即实现言语行为。在这个宏观假设下，还有一系列微观的假设，如言语行为的分类、言语行为的适切条件等。再比如，乔姆斯基的生成语言学理论在发展过程中构建了一套复杂的假设系统来解释名词的句法分布（格理论）、代词的指代（约束原则）、疑问词等移动的限制（毗邻原则）等。在此之上还有更为宏观的假设，如认为存在普遍语法，其核心内容是递归性合并（recursive merge）等。无论是宏观假设还是微观的具体假设，都是基于看似混乱复杂的语言事实归纳而得的。这里需要强调的是，这些归纳的结果之所以成为理论假设，是因为探索的是内在抽象的致使性机制（causal mechanism），超越了根据表象总结出的表层模式。举一个简单的例子：我们可以根据手握物体松手后的表象，归纳出一个表象的模式，即一旦松手，手里的物体就会掉落。这类基于表层总结出的模式，并没有触及本质，而物理学则对此归纳出抽象的致使性机制，如提出万有引力，解释究竟是什么致使万物如此运行。理论语言学也是如此：理论层面归纳的假设是为了探究语言背后的抽象机制，从而解释语言为何有这些特殊的属性，仅仅总结表层规律本质上并不算提出理论，至少不算是现代意义上的科学理论。无独有偶的是，著名物理学家爱因斯坦和语言学家乔姆斯基分别于1930年和2023年在美国《纽约时报》撰文向大众解释科学的本质，在这两篇文章（Einstein, 1930; Chomsky et al., 2023）中，两位作者都强调科学研究的核心目的是发现表象背后的致使性机制。读者可根据本书的参考文献查找这两篇文章进行阅读，相信会帮助加深对理论科学研究的理解。

理论的目的是解释现象。语言学理论当然是为了对更多的现象做出解释。以理论原则为出发点，对具体现象做出解释，这基本上属于演绎的范畴。在语言学研究中，演绎的过程一般涉及以下流程：从理论的普遍原则出发，构建针对某领域的具体假设，以此假设为前提，观察和收集语言现象来验证这个假设，最终对语言现象做出解释，并验证理论假设的合理性。应该说，大部分的理论科学，包括理论语言学研究，都处于一个中间状态，即，前人已经搭建了不同的理论框架，术语系统也已经比较完善，在此背景下，大部分的研究都是在一个理论框架下进行，此时归纳和演绎往往都要涉及。我们观察语言现象，从中归纳出一些规律，同时我们将这些规律和已有的语言学理论相结合，构建针对现象的新的假设，再进一步观察和分析更多的语言现象，以此验证假设的合理性。这个过程就涉及语言研究中极其重要的一个环节，即论证。下面我们将具体解释论证的相关要素。

3.2.2　假设的可证伪性

　　论证首先涉及如何构建假设的问题。波普（Popper, 1959）在著作《科学发现的逻辑》（*The Logic of Scientific Discovery*）中指出，科研工作包括提出假设，用观察或者实验的方法一步步验证这些假设。理论语言学研究的假设是研究的核心所在。合理的假设可以增进我们对某个现象背后本质的了解，也可以带来新的视角，为未来研究提供进一步的支持。本质上来说，我们撰写研究性论文、专著，目的就是向同行呈现我们的新结论，而要让同行接受我们的结论，就必须为结论提供扎实的论证。论证的方式在各类科学研究中都是一致的：需要基于逻辑和事实来证明假设的合理性。

　　前文已经提出，我们提出假设的起点是在看似普通的现象中看到令人困惑之处，从而提出假设来解释这些现象。因此，理论语言学科研中的假设首先是源于语言现象观察中产生的困惑。这个我们已经在前文具体论述，这里不再赘述。

　　其次，大部分的假设都是基于已有的知识而再往前迈进的。正是这样的叠加效应才能让人类不断加深对自我和世界的认识。在语言学领域，这要求我们对自己所做研究的领域有非常精确的了解，这个"了解"不但是包括知道观点，也包括知道这些观点得以构建的原因，包括采用的理论框架、事实以及在此基础上总结的假设。只有这样，我们才能知道，我们观察中发现的困惑是否已经有了（部分）答案，并且在我们自己提供答案的过程中能够精准使用系统的理论工具。这也提醒我们，理论语言学的方法背后是踏实的学习和批判性的分析，只有这样，才能在理论基础和思维能力上为构建新假设做好准备。

科研假设还有一个最重要的特点，即假设可以被验证（testable）和证伪，这也是波普对科学研究定性中的最核心的要素。当我们提出一个研究假设时，首先需要问自己，有什么方法可以去验证它的正确性，以及如果其他人想要推翻我的假设，是否可以有明确的路径。有关可证伪性，我们需要稍加说明以防误解。可证伪性是指一个假设的提出有明确的验证途径，只要沿着这个途径找到反例，就可以证伪这个假设。因此，可证伪性并不是说一个假设一定会被证伪，而只是说它的属性和呈现方式让潜在的证伪成为可能。这一点对于科学研究来说至关重要，因为如果没有这样的标准，我们就可能面临大量似是而非、含糊其词的假设，面对这样的假设，我们根本无法去验证和判断这个研究的合理性，也无法进行正常的学术辩论。

我们下面举一个非常简单的例子来说明问题。

例3.5　a. 我年轻时的偶像是于文华。
　　　　b. 这首歌的风格非常于文华。

基于例3.5，我们也许会得出如下的假设：

假设一：汉语词无定类，只要语境允许，一个词在汉语中可以获得不同词类，因此汉语词类的灵活性要高于英语。

比如例3.5a中的专有名词"于文华"在例3.5b中作为形容词使用，而这样的例子在英语中并不是很常见。

我们暂不讨论这个假设是否成立，而是关注这个假设是否满足前文所说的可证伪性。这需要看这个假设是否允许我们寻找证据来验证。我们如果要验证这个假设，就需要寻找更多的证据来证明是否汉语中的词语在词类上是灵活的。这个在现实中是可以做到的。所以，不论这个假设是否成立，从科学研究的可证伪标准来看，这是一个满足标准的假设。根据这个假设，我们可以寻找更多的证据，比如：

例3.6　a. 这首歌很**土**。
　　　　b. 这个人很**油**。

例3.6a中的"土"对应的英语名词不能作为其他词类使用。比如mud不能作形容词（得用muddy）。这进一步支持了前文的假设。

然而，作为研究者，我们需要进一步问，名词除了可以活用作形容词，是否也可用作动词？

例 3.7　a. John binned the paper.（约翰把纸扔到了垃圾桶里。）

b. Mary likes to bottle tap water.（玛丽喜欢把自来水用瓶子装起来。）

以上例子实际上反驳了前文的假设。首先，我们看到，汉语的词类虽然比较灵活，但并非绝对自由。比如，"（垃圾）桶""瓶"等名词一般不可以活用作动词。而且英语的例子也说明名词不可以作动词并非名词语义特殊造成的，因为英语中的名词用作动词并不少见。其次，认为汉语词类转换绝对比英语自由的论断也可能不正确，比如英语的名词活用作动词要比汉语灵活很多。

以上假设之所以能被推翻，是因为这是一个符合科学研究标准的假设，即这个假设本身存在可以被证伪的可能。我们再来看一个不合理的假设模式。同样根据上面"于文华"的例子，如果我们提出这个假设：

假设二：汉语的词类灵活性源于汉语独特的思维。

这一假设的问题在于，我们很难去验证这样的结论。首先，"汉语的思维"这一概念难以界定。其次，语法形式与具体某个文化的思维特征之间的关系也很难确定。这样的模糊性导致很难进一步推进相关研究[1]，因为我们没有办法根据这样的假设去寻找证据来精确验证。

3.2.3 反例

可能有不少人觉得，如果某一假设存在反例，它就要被彻底推翻。但是，在科学研究中，反例的存在并不一定意味着整个假设完全失效；另一种可能是，假设的总体精神依然可行，但相关细节需要改善。此时，反例的出现一方面有助于推进理论的发展，另一方面也可以帮助我们对现象有更好的了解。生成语言学研究在这一点上的绝佳例证是孤岛限制（island constraint）的提出与修正。简单来说，在英语等语言中，特殊疑问词需要移动到句首。比如：

例 3.8　What did she say he liked most?

她说他最喜欢什么？

但是，特殊疑问词并不能随意移动出来，比如：

---

1 我们并不是说思维方式与语法形式之间一定没有关系，而是强调，如果要研究这样的关系，必须要给出清晰可界定并且可以明确证伪的假设。

例 3.9　　*How have they known which song Mary should sing?
想要表达的意思：他们是否已经知道玛丽应该用什么方法唱哪首歌了？

乔姆斯基（Chomsky, 1973）提出毗邻条件（subjacency condition）对此进行解释。我们在此无须了解这个理论假设的技术细节，只需要明白，这个假设要求当一个成分从原始位置移动出来时，有一个句法结构的区域限制，这个区域之一是限定性的小句（我们称之为 S）。如果这个移动每次只跨越一个 S，那么就是符合语法的。例 3.9 不符合语法的内在原因在于 how 一次性跨越了两个 S（第一个 S 没有提供中途"歇脚"的位置，因为这个位置被"which song"占据了）。但是，里奇（Rizzi, 1978）指出，意大利语可以违反这个毗邻原则。里奇通过具体的语料分析发现，虽然意大利语违反了原始的毗邻原则，但特殊疑问词的移位也不是完全随意的，它们依然受到限制，只不过这个限制的范围不是 S，而是比 S 更大的区域 S'[1]。因此，里奇（Rizzi, 1978）依然承认毗邻原则的基本假设，只是增添了一个重要的细节，那就是：语言之间的差异可以体现在允许成分移位的区域的大小上。如果我们仅仅是因为意大利语的反例而推翻毗邻原则，那并不能增进我们对语言的认识，甚至还抛弃了原假设所发现的结论——特殊疑问词的移动有句法结构规律可循——这个很重要的发现。此外，里奇（Rizzi, 1978）通过反例的分析还推动了理论的发展，甚至超越了疑问词移动限制这个议题，上升到更高的理论高度，即跨语言的差异来自普遍宏观假设基础上具体细节的设定，即后来具有里程碑意义的"原则与参数"（principles and parameters）假设，这个假设成为 20 世纪 80 年代至今生成语言学研究跨语言差异的重要理论框架。

3.3　理论假设的不完美性

本单元反复出现的一个关键词是"假设"。在科学研究中，我们需要通过严谨的论证来筛选出合理的假设，但我们也需要了解一个前提，即任何假设都是不完美的。随着科学研究的不断推进和新现象的不断出现，一个假设随时可能被推翻或需要进一步修正，这也正是科学研究的魅力所在。如果我们

---

1 我们可以大致这样理解 S 和 S'：在"What do you like?"这个句子中，you like 占据的句法范围是 S 区域，而整个问句占据的是 S'。在目前的句法理论背景下，S 是 TP，S' 是 CP。但这些都是具体句法理论的细节，不做句法研究的读者可以不深究。

有了完美的假设和答案，那么进一步的研究也就没有了意义。纵观人类的科学发展史，我们可以发现科学的进步正是逐步改进假设的过程，这个过程反过来也让人们对世界有了更多的了解。以牛顿的万有引力理论和爱因斯坦的广义相对论为例。在引力比较弱的时候，比如地球上，牛顿的万有引力可以被认为是近似正确的，但是在引力很强的时候，比如黑洞，万有引力就不够精准以至于失效了，此时只有广义相对论能解释相关现象。但这显然并不削弱牛顿理论的任何意义，而是告诉我们，任何伟大的理论都只是假设，需要不断往前推进。这个前提在理论语言学研究中同样至关重要：在理论语言学研究中，不能盲信任何结论，要准备好通过我们自己的研究推进理论假设的发现。同时，这也告诉我们，在研究中，对待前人的假设要有宽容的态度，发现前人研究的不足固然是一个进步，但用完美主义的真理标准评价一个理论也是不合理的，我们可以基于证据和逻辑批评任何理论，但不能因为一个理论有不完美的地方就将其全盘否定。如果按照这种逻辑，人类科学研究中的所有理论可能都无法立足，科学就无从产生，更无法发展了。

课堂讨论

1. "语言学研究的目的是观察语言现象，所以理论并不重要，重要的是语言现象的描述，包括分类、记录等。"你如何看待这样的观点？请以实际的语言现象为例来陈述你的观点。
2. "汉语是一种没有屈折（inflection）标记的语言。"你是否赞同这一观点？请收集相关语言证据来支持你的观点。（提示：在论证过程中，先了解什么叫屈折变化，再关注汉语是否有屈折变化的标记，同时进一步讨论常见屈折标记［如"了""们"等虚词］是否算是真正意义上的屈折标记。）

课外练习

1. "英汉语在时间表达上的差异在于英语需要有时标记（tense marking），而汉语则不需要通过语法手段，只需通过语境即可确认时态（tense）。"你是否赞同这个论点？运用本章所论述的方法来支持你的观点，并反驳你的对立面观点。（提示：先看汉语表达时间是否有标记。当句中没有任何语法标记、只有语境［包括时间状语］时，再看汉语是否总能用符合语法的句子来精准地表达时间。最后，你还可以进一步分析英汉语在时间表达上更多的差异以及其中的原因。）
2. 寻找一篇关于汉语具有某种独特属性的文章，分析其观点的合理性及其论证的充分性。

拓展阅读

Adger, D. (2021). On doing theoretical linguistics. *Theoretical Linguistics*, *47*(1–2), 33–45.

Haegeman, L. (2006). *Thinking syntactically: A guide to argumentation and analysis*. Oxford: Blackwell.

Haspelmath, M. (2021). General linguistics must be based on universals (or non-conventional aspects of language). *Theoretical Linguistics*, *47*(1–2), 1–31.

Popper, K. (1959). *The logic of scientific discovery*. London: Routledge.

第 4 单元
文献研究法

学习目标

- 掌握文献研究法的基本概念及操作步骤
- 了解文献研究法与文献回顾的异同
- 熟悉 CiteSpace、VOSviewer 等常见的文献研究分析工具

4.1 基本概念

文献研究法是哲学、文学、史学、社会学等领域的常用方法。所谓文献研究法，是指根据研究需要，依据一定的标准和方法，对已经发表的文献资料（如论文、专著、报刊等）进行收集、整理、筛选、分析，形成科学认识的方法。借助文献研究法，可以丰富和深化研究者对某一领域或议题的认识，发现其研究特点，揭示其研究规律，并可能据此找到新的研究视角、新的研究方法或新的研究问题，为该领域或议题的研究注入新的活力。

文献研究法不能简单地等同于学术论文或著作中的文献回顾。一般来说，文献研究法有明确的文献收集和筛选标准。文献收集步骤明确，筛选标准科学，具有可重复性、可验证性，且所收集的文献一般有一定的数量。相比之下，我们常见的学术论文中的文献回顾，多与研究者的个人阅读经历有关，一般是研究者根据自己所阅读过的文献，依据一定的标准（比如按议题），对所读文献的主观梳理。文献回顾的过程尽管有一定的科学性，但主观性明显，例证痕迹明显，系统性不够。另外，文献回顾通常是学术论文的一个部分，而文献研究法既可用于做文献回顾，又可以单独用来考察、汇报特定话题或议题的研究状况，揭示其研究发展轨迹和各方面的特点。

4.2 基本步骤

文献研究法通常包括六个基本环节：提出课题或明确研究内容、进行研究设计、收集文献、整理文献、分析文献、综述文献。

所谓提出课题或假设，就文献研究法而言，主要是指在确定研究领域或课题的基础上（如"二语语用能力"），明确研究内容（如"国际二语语用学研究有何特点与趋势"）。

在研究设计阶段，需根据研究内容，确定文献收集的来源（如"SSCI来源期刊"）、明确需要收集的内容（如"作者""文章发表年度""关键词"）、确定所要使用的文献分析方法或工具（如 CiteSpace 和 VOSviewer）等。

收集和整理文献是指依据研究内容和一定的收集标准，进行文献收集和整理工作。文献的收集与整理看似简单，实际上非常重要，决定着后期文献分析的质量与水平。以在 Web of Science 收集关于语用能力研究的文献为例。在确定检索词时，因不同文献所用术语可能不同，所以仅检索 pragmatic competence 是不够的，还需要检索 pragmatic ability。这两个术语既可能出现在标题中，又可能出现在摘要、关键词中，所以 Web of Science 提供了两种选择：主题（含标题、摘要、关键词）和标题。前者检索范围较为宽泛，后者检索出的内容聚焦性很强，但检索结果也会骤减。要保证所获取文献的质量与水平，在选择数据库时可选择"Web of Science核心合集"，并且引文索引可进一步聚焦为"Social Science Citation Index"。通常情况下，检索的结果还可能存在不同程度的无关信息，这一过程可以通过"文献类型""类别"（基本对应于研究领域）"语种"等信息进行精炼，力求使收集到的文献与研究内容最大限度地相符。

就国内文献而言，文献数据的收集目前主要通过中国知网。语言学研究中比较常用的是中国知网中的"学术期刊""学位论文""学术辑刊"等。其中，"学术期刊"最为常用，可按"主题""篇关摘""篇名""关键词""摘要"等进行相应的检索。比如，若学生对"语用身份"这一议题感兴趣，选择"主题"，并在其后的空框内输入"语用身份"，就能得到与语用身份研究相关的文献了（选择"篇名"的话，搜索结果就会更为聚焦）。若此时数量仍然较多，则可以选择"高级检索"，选择"主题/篇关摘/篇名"并输入检索项（如"语用身份"）后，可将文献类别限定于"CSSCI""北大核心"等，所得文献数量会相应减少，这样可以删减掉一些价值不是很高的文献。

分析文献主要是指根据所收集和整理的文献，按研究内容，展开对文献的分析，如年度特征、主要发文作者、主要发文期刊、主要议题及其关系等。最后一步，即根据对文献的分析，撰写文章。

4.3　文献研究法的定量分析软件：CiteSpace

尽管文献研究法是一种古老的研究方法，但学界一般认为该研究方法有很多缺点，比如文献质量难以判断、有价值的文献难以收集、文献往往缺乏系统性、全面性等。然而，随着专门文献工具（如CiteSpace）的开发与普及，文献研究法这些固有的缺陷在很大程度上得到了克服。

CiteSpace是一款科学、实用的文献分析软件，由美国德雷塞尔大学信息科学与技术学院教授陈超美（Chaomei Chen）博士于2004年研发。该软件发布之后迅速被学界采用，现已成为学界主要的文献计量工具之一。该软件在本单元写作时为6.1.R3版，主要可以揭示发文作者（Author）、发文机构（Institution）、发文国家（Country）、关键词（Keyword）、主题词（Term）、被引文献（Reference）、被引作者（Cited Author）、被引期刊（Cited Journal）等信息（如图4.1），并能借助知识图谱呈现其共现关系。关于本软件的具体操作，可参见李杰、陈超美（2016）。

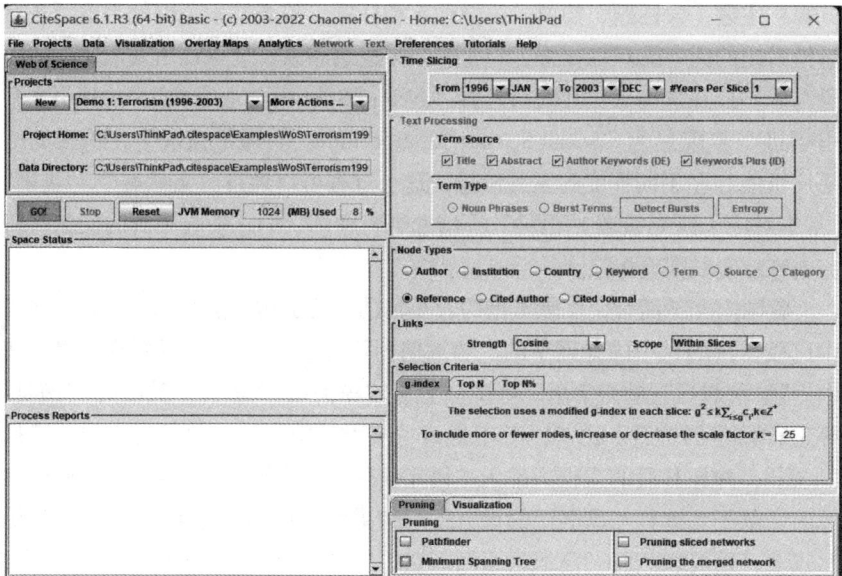

图4.1　CiteSpace文献分析软件

　　目前国内外基于 CiteSpace 技术已开展了多种研究，研究领域涵盖计算机科学、信息科学、管理学、文学等领域。就语言学领域而言，国内就开展了翻译（如冯佳、王克非、刘霞，2014）、二语习得（如徐锦芬、聂睿，2015）、语用学（如肖雁，2017）等领域的文献分析，产出了一系列有价值的研究发现。图 4.2 是李民、陈新仁（2019）论文中涉及的语料库语用学研究发文国家知识图谱（限于篇幅，此处省略论文原文）。

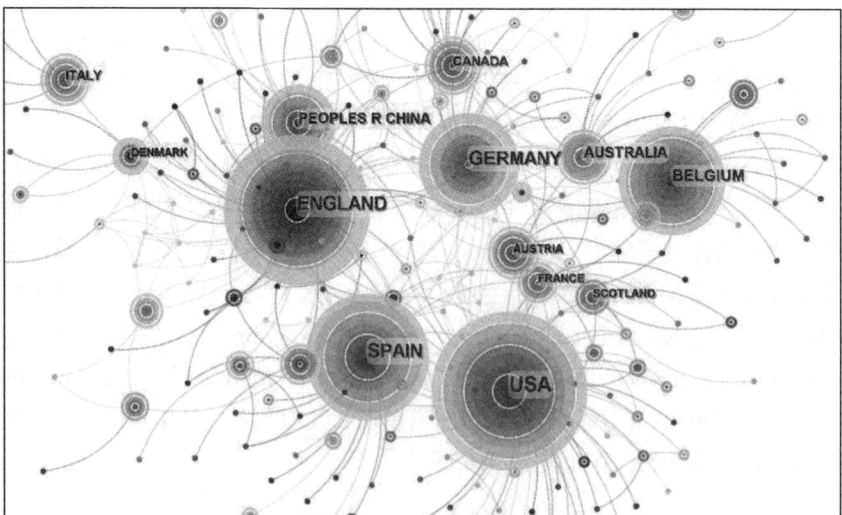

图4.2　语料库语用学研究发文国家知识图谱

从图 4.2 中可以看出，就语料库语用学而言，目前世界上形成了美国、英国、西班牙、德国、比利时、中国等若干研究中心，各研究中心之间相互关联，学术联系紧密。从知识点间的关系来看，在语料库语用学研究方面，中国与英国之间的合作远高于与美国的合作，与美国合作较多的是西班牙的研究机构或高校。就成果数量来看，美国、英国、西班牙等国家发表的语料库语用学论文最多（圆圈越大，代表成果数量越多）。

4.4 文献研究法的定量分析软件：VOSviewer

除 CiteSpace 外，常用的文献可视化工具还有 VOSviewer。VOSviewer 的用户界面比 CiteSpace 更为简洁和直观，但功能也更加基础。

VOSviewer 是一款用于构建文献计量可视化的软件，由荷兰莱顿大学科技研究中心的内斯·埃克（Nees Jan van Eck）和卢多·沃尔特曼（Ludo Waltman）两位教授于 2009 年研发。该软件在本单元写作时为 1.6.18 版本，主要根据引文（citation）、书目耦合（bibliographic coupling）、共同引用（co-citation）、共同作者关系（co-authorship relations）来构建可视化网络，提供聚类视图（Network Visualization）、叠加视图（Overlay Visualization）和密度视图（Density Visualization），帮助研究者识别研究领域的方向和热点（如图4.3，关于本软件的具体操作，可参见 van Eck & Waltman, 2007）。

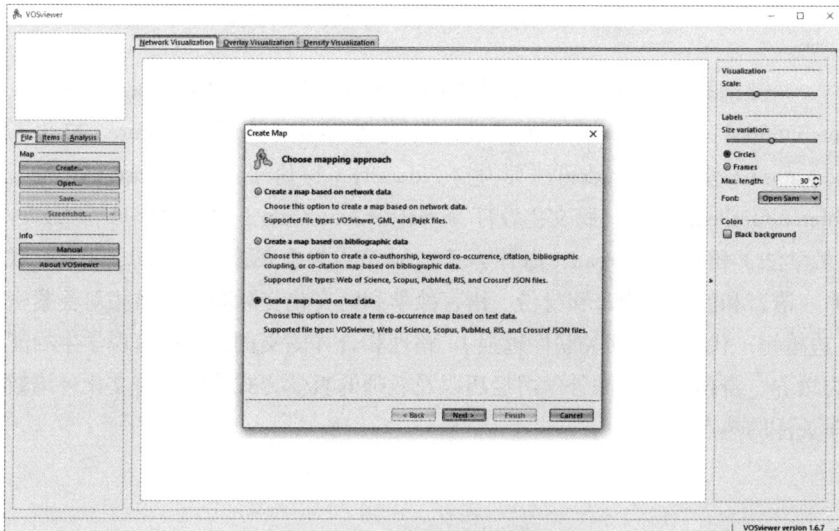

图4.3　VOSviewer文献计量软件

VOSviewer 技术已被国内外学者应用于多个学科领域，既涵盖社会和人文学科，也包括自然和工程学科。从语言学领域来看，国内就开展了超语研究（如潘海英、袁月，2022）、翻译（如王峰、陈文，2017）、跨文化交际（如马鑫、苏敏、李杰，2020）等领域的文献分析，研究成果丰硕。图 4.4 是张鹏（2021）论文中涉及的国际跨文化外语教学研究的关键词图谱（图摘自论文）。

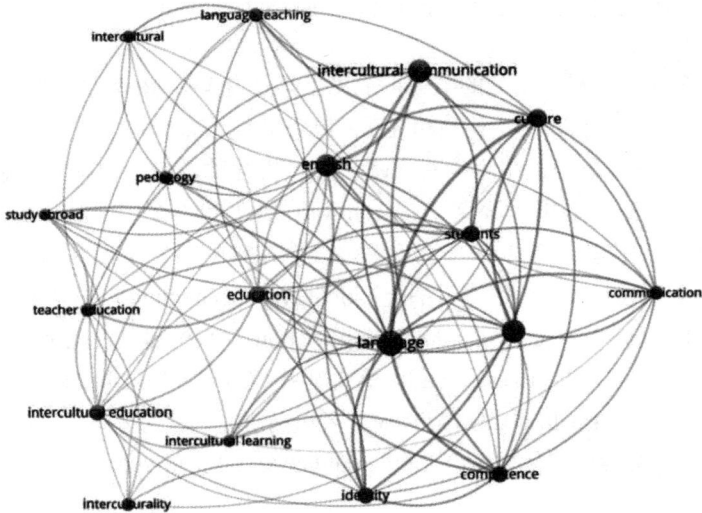

图4.4　国际跨文化外语教学研究的关键词图谱

关键词聚类图谱显示，文献中的高频关键词分别是 language（语言）、intercultural communication（跨文化交际）、English（英语）、culture（文化）、education（教育）、students（学生）、identity（身份）、competence（能力）、intercultural education（跨文化教育）、teacher education（教师教育）、pedagogy（教学法）和 study abroad（海外学习）。从节点关系来看，关键词之间相互联系。语言和能力、语言和身份、语言教学和跨文化交际间的联系相对更紧密（边越粗，代表节点间关联性越强）。整理和合并同义词后，可发现学生的能力培养、身份构建和海外学习经历以及教师的教学方式是国际跨文化外语教学关注的热点。

课堂讨论

1. 假设你们课题组想要研究交际教学法在中国的发展情况，你们将如何设计文献收集方法？文献可来源于何处（如期刊论文、学术专著、学位论文等）？各种文献如何收集？如何利用所在学校的图书、期刊资源？

2. 中国知网提供的文献类别有"学术期刊""学位论文""会议""报纸""图书""学术辑刊"等，它们各有何特点？经过一系列的检索，若你们想聚焦于学术期刊中的文献，初步检索却发现部分文章质量不高，你们有何优化检索的方法？在高级检索中，"北大核心"和"CSSCI"有何异同？

3. 在中国知网的高级检索中，"主题""篇关摘""关键词""篇名""全文""基金""摘要""小标题""参考文献"等检索条件分别指什么？检索出的文献有何异同？不同检索方式有优先顺序吗？"全文"检索作为一种比较宽泛的检索方法，一般在什么情况下使用？

4. 以 communicative language teaching 为检索词，在 Web of Science 的 SSCI 期刊或中国知网的 CSSCI 期刊中检索相关文献，并利用 CiteSpace 或 VOSviewer 对下载的相关数据进行可视化处理。根据研究结果，讨论中外交际教学法研究方面的异同。

5. 图 4.5 是李民、陈新仁（2019）论文中的语料库语用学关键词知识图谱（限于篇幅，数据略有删减）。请根据这一知识图谱汇报你的研究发现。

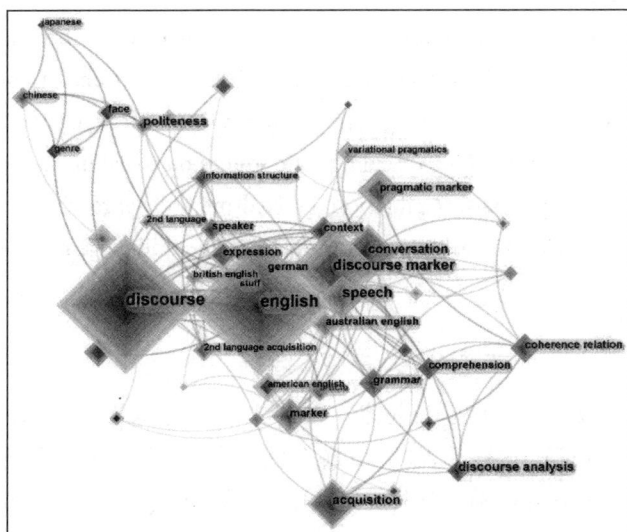

图4.5　语料库语用学关键词知识图谱

6. 下面两例是采用文献研究的方法撰写的英文论文和中文论文的摘要。采用文献研究的方法撰写的学术论文的摘要一般包括哪些内容？与采用其他方法撰写的学术论文的摘要有何异同？

(1)

Abstract: This study aimed to present the status quo of linguistic studies on social media in the past decade. In particular, it conducted a bibliometric analysis of articles from the field of linguistics of the database of Web of Science Core Collection with the aid of the tool CiteSpace to identify the general characteristics, major strands of linguistics, main research methods, and important research themes in the area of linguistic studies on social media. The main findings are summarized as follows. First, the study reported the publication trend, main publication venues, researched social media platforms, and languages used in researched social media. Second, sociolinguistics and pragmatics were found to be major strands of linguistics used in relevant studies. Third, the study identified seven main research methods: discourse analysis, critical discourse analysis, conversation analysis, multimodal analysis, narrative analysis, ethnographic analysis, and corpus analysis. Fourth, important research themes were extracted and classified based on four dimensions of the genre framework of social media studies. They were the participation nature and technology affordances of social media in the dimension of compositional level, the researched topics of education, (language) policy and politics in the dimension of thematic orientations, the researched discursive practices of (im)politeness, humor, indexicality and multilingualism in the dimension of stylistic traits, and the researched communicative functions of constructing identity, communicating (language) ideology, and expressing attitude in the pragmatic dimension. Moreover, linguistic studies on social media tended to be characterized by cross-disciplinary and mixed-method approaches.

Keywords: social media, literature review, linguistic studies, genre framework

(Sun et al., 2021)

(2)

提要： 本文借助 CiteSpace 技术，以 WOS 核心数据库和 CNKI 数据库为文献数据来源，追踪了 2001—2020 年间构式语法研究的热点变化以及最新动态，并在此基础上对其研究趋势进行展望。分析显示，学界对构式本质的探索发生了深刻的变化，进一步推动了构式在创新性、交际性和社会性等方面的纵深发展。构式语法理论的内涵和外延不断丰富，其应用领域正从语言习得和教学扩展到自然语言处理和构式库的开发，其研究范围正从语言内部扩展到交际和社会中的语言。本文还进一步分析了国际研究对国内研究的启示。

关键词： 构式语法；创新发展；发展趋势

（段丹、田臻，2022）

7. 下文是某些学者对数据收集过程的描述（Qin & Lei, 2022）。请仔细阅读该段文字，思考并回答：采用文献研究法的论文，其文献收集过程一般包括哪些步骤？应该注意哪些问题？如何尽量做到客观？如何提升收集到的文献的质量？如何证明所收集到的文献真实、可信？

The data that we used in the present study were the bibliometric information of journal articles downloaded from the Web of Science. In order to more accurately and exhaustively harvest the information of the articles on TBLT (i.e., task-based language teaching), we first consulted literature pertinent to TBLT (e.g., Bryfonski & McKay, 2019; Ellis et al., 2020; Long, 2016; Plonsky & Kim, 2016) and prepared a list of 41 TBLT-related search terms (see Appendix). Then, following previous bibliometric studies in applied linguistics such as Lei and Liu (2019b), we queried the terms in all SSCI and A&HCI-indexed journals in (applied) linguistics and education in the Web of Science Core Collection on September 8, 2020. Similar to previous studies such as Zhang (2020), we retrieved the Web of Science Core Collection for our data since the database is considered as one of the most well-known and widely used multidisciplinary bibliometric databases, which indexes high-quality journals with their bibliometric information (Roemer & Borchardt, 2015). We set the span of the queried literature from 1985 to 2020 since, as previously indicated, TBLT research started from 1985 as Michael Long published his seminal work *A Role for Instruction in Second Language Acquisition: Task-based Language Teaching* in that year (Long, 1985). We obtained the bibliometric information of 1,215 articles at this stage. Since some of the articles might have been irrelevant to the present study, we closely read the titles and abstracts of the articles and selected a total of 518 articles for the follow-up analysis based on the following criteria: 1) the article should focus on language teaching or learning, rather than research issues in other subjects such as nursery, physics, chemistry, and so on; and 2) the article should be pertinent to the implementation of either the strong or weak version of a TBLT program or part of the program (such as needs analysis, task-based assessment, etc.); or 3) the article should include at least one task relevant factor (such as task type, task feature, task condition, etc.) as the independent or dependent variables.

课外练习

1. 采用文献研究法撰写学术论文时，一般从哪几个维度展开？
2. 假设你刚对跨文化语用学产生兴趣，想先了解一下过去 10 年国际跨文化语用学领域的主要研究者、主要研究机构、主要议题等。请借助 CiteSpace 或 VOSviewer，收集、整理、分析相关文献，并撰写文献综述。
3. 尽管大部分学者认为文献研究法是一种虽然古老却富有生命力的研究方法，仍有部分学者（如姚计海，2017）认为文献研究法其实并不能算作一种研究方法。你支持哪一种观点？为什么？

拓展阅读

Qin, J., & Lei, L. (2022). Research trends in task-based language teaching: A bibliometric analysis from 1985 to 2020. *Studies in Second Language Learning and Teaching, 12*(3), 381–404.

李杰、陈超美. (2016). CiteSpace：科技文本挖掘及可视化. 北京：首都经济贸易大学出版社.

第 5 单元
访谈法与有声思维法

学习目标

- 了解访谈法和有声思维法的种类和实施
- 学习访谈法和有声思维法在语言学研究中的具体应用以及论文写作
- 在具体研究场景中设计访谈法和有声思维法

5.1 访谈法

5.1.1 基本概念

访谈法（interview）是语言学研究中常见的通过面对面问答形式收集质性数据的研究方法。访谈围绕具体研究主题展开，以访谈者提问、被访者回答的问答形式进行。作为一种重要的探索性研究方法，访谈法具有众多优势：

(1) 访谈法能够突破时空限制，对被试的过去、现在和将来都可以进行调查；而观察法、实验法只能考察被试的当前情况，调查受到时间和空间的限制。

(2) 访谈法能够实现研究者与被试的互动交流，获得丰富且有深度的研究资料。

(3) 访谈法可以根据研究需要与被试深入、甚至多次探讨问题，从而挖掘出现象背后的原因，对现象进行解释，不再局限于对现象的描述。

(4) 访谈法可以与其他研究方法配合，对多源研究数据进行交叉验证。

5.1.2 分类及实施

根据访谈结构所体现的对访谈的控制程度或者标准化水平，访谈大体可以划分为三类：结构式访谈（structured interview）、半结构式访谈（semi-structured interview）、非结构式访谈（unstructured interview）。

（1）结构式访谈

结构式访谈是访谈者依据明确的访谈提纲对被访者进行提问并忠实记录被访者回答的访谈形式。具体来说，结构式访谈对访谈对象、访谈问题、提问方式和顺序、被访者回答方式、访谈记录方式等进行统一规定和要求，有时甚至对于访谈员的选择、访谈时间和地点以及访谈周围环境等外部条件均有统一要求。

结构式访谈通过访谈提纲对每一个被访者以同样的顺序呈现同样的问题，从而确保不同个体、不同样本群之间以及不同测量周期之间的访谈数据具有可比性。因此，结构式访谈具有以下特点：

1) 访谈设计、实施和数据记录与分析的标准化程度非常高，能有效提高数据的稳定性和可靠性；

2) 由于访谈过程标准化程度高，结构式访谈不仅适用于个案或小规模的调查研究，也可以应用于较大规模的调查研究。

3) 同时，我们也应该看到，因为标准化程度比较高，结构式访谈的灵活性相对较差，缺乏根据不同访谈对象的具体回答来即时调整并深入挖掘数据的灵活性。

（2）半结构式访谈和非结构式访谈

非结构式访谈又称为非标准化访谈、深度访谈或自由访谈。与结构式访谈相比，非结构式访谈没有固定的模式，不预设任何访谈问题，也不预设访谈内容顺序，只有一个访谈题目或粗略的访谈大纲。半结构式访谈是介于结构式和非结构式访谈中间的一种访谈形式，通常指按照一个粗略的访谈提纲来进行的非正式访谈。由于半结构式访谈和非结构式访谈都没有严格标准的访谈结构，只是在访谈提纲的细化程度上稍有差异，因此下文将两者放在一起进行讨论。

半结构式和非结构式访谈有明确的访谈题目和简要的访谈提纲，但没有细化具体访谈问题，访谈者可以根据访谈的实际情况灵活地做出调整。至于提问的方式和顺序、访谈对象回答的方式、访谈记录形式以及访谈时间、地点等都没有具体的要求，均由访谈者根据情况灵活处理。相比结构式访谈，半结构式访谈既能通过访谈提纲为访谈内容提供大体框架、防止访谈偏离主题，又方便访谈者在访谈中能够灵活处理、有效跟进相关问题的提问，从而进一步挖掘丰富的质性数据。同时，半结构式访谈对于访谈员的访谈技巧提出了较高要求，访谈员要注意控制话题，并灵活敏锐地挖掘数据。因此，半结构式和非结构式访谈应注意以下几点：

1) 设计访谈提纲，确保访谈围绕研究需求进行。
2) 不设计非常具体的访谈问题，为被访谈者畅所欲言提供空间，从而有效挖掘质性数据。
3) 设计相对间接、温馨的访谈开场，可以准备一些和研究主题关系不大但能调动被访谈者兴趣的话题，从而拉近访谈者和被访谈者的距离。
4) 采用留白式提问，访谈者要耐心地预留给被访谈者主动提及信息的空间和时间，并根据被访谈者的回答灵活地变通提问形式和内容。
5) 预留控制访谈方向的相关话术，从而实现有效控场、防止访谈脱离研究需求而影响访谈执行进度以及访谈资料的有效性。

5.1.3 局限性及应对

访谈研究能够提供丰富且颇具深度的研究数据，但也存在明显的缺点：由于人力物力成本而导致样本数量受到限制，并且研究时间和金钱成本相对较高；访谈中存在研究者与被访者之间的相互作用，从而可能导致所得调查数据存在主观偏差；访谈质量取决于研究者的综合研究素养，因此研究者个人的交往能力、语言表达能力、访谈话术以及研究能力非常重要，对语言的理解和运用差别容易造成访谈数据偏差等。总体而言，作为探索性研究中的重要研究方法，访谈研究能够和其他研究方法一起辅助验证和完善我们对于研究问题的观察与探索，提升我们对于研究对象的认知。

5.2 有声思维法

5.2.1 基本概念

有声思维法（think-aloud）是心理学和认知科学研究中收集质性研究数据的常用方法，在外语教学研究中有着广泛的应用。有声思维具体指被调查者在完成特定任务的过程中，同时口头讲述自己的心理认知和大脑思维活动。与任务完成后的回溯性访谈不同，有声思维与任务同时发生，从而为研究者了解被试的在线思维提供了观察和研究的窗口。

5.2.2 有声思维培训

为确保有声思维数据的有效收集，需要对被试进行培训，包含技术培训和心理培训。技术培训主要指语言表达技巧，一般通过有声思维演练和指导相结合来实现。培训时，可以让被试反复完成某一任务，同时进行有声思维汇报。研究者则将这些有声思维报告以录音或者录像的方式记录下来，将停顿和沉默时间短、内容丰富的有声思维报告给被试听或者观看，从而让被试了解如何更好地配合和实施有声思维汇报。

技术培训还包括提醒机制的反应训练。提醒机制是指为了防止被试在汇报时出现长时间沉默而设置的提醒方法。研究者应该通过训练帮助被试建立起对提醒机制的反射效应，即被试一接收到提醒，就立刻启动语言表达。常见的提醒方法有灯光提醒和声音提醒，视具体任务选用合适的提醒机制。

有声思维心理培训的目标在于培养被试对有声思维的接受度和舒适度，从而鼓励被试用语言真实清晰地表达任务进行时的大脑思维活动，避免因各种原因无法有效表达思维活动、故意隐藏真实思维活动或为迎合测试者心理故意编造思维活动等。

研究者培训包括培训研究者注意不得去启发或者引导被试、注意尽量保持测试环境与培训环境一致，因为相对熟悉的环境有利于被试顺利地汇报思维活动。同时，研究者应尽量注意录音、录像设备的隐蔽性，以最大限度地减小数据收集设备对于被试的干扰，并在被试出现长时间沉默时有效利用提醒机制确保数据的有效收集。

5.2.3 转写与技术规范

转写（transcription）是指将音频文件转化为书面文字语言，这一过程应遵循完整、忠实、可靠的原则。完整是指将有声思维的录音、录像文件全部转写，包括语言和非语言信息，如停顿、沉默、动作等；忠实是指转写必须忠实于录音、录像材料，不得增加或删减内容；可靠则指应采用统一的符号和标准对录音、录像材料进行真实客观的转写，不对材料进行主观解读和修改，不随意变更转写标准。

在转写前，研究者通常在已有的转写技术规范的基础上为现有研究建立系统、完整、成文的转写规范，从而确保数据转写的规范性和可靠性。以下是常见的有声思维数据转写规范示例，可供研究者参考。

| [ ] | 话轮重叠 |
| 字体加粗 | 重读 |

停顿	
(0.4)	停顿时间
--	短时停顿
----	长时停顿
,	正常语音停顿
:	稍长于正常语音停顿
……	三秒以内较长停顿

沉默	
（…）	三秒沉默
（……）	三秒以上沉默
…5'…	量化到具体秒数的沉默

?	升调
↑↓	音调上升/下降
。	休止符
(( ))	转写者加注

5.2.4 数据处理

原始有声思维数据是被试在完成特定任务时大脑处理各种信息过程的语言记录，必须经过整理才能进行有效的分析，这种整理通常包含数据的切分、编码和分类。

在实际操作中，常常以意义单位作为切分单位对有声思维数据进行处理，比如短语或者分句，也可以词或者段落作为意义单位进行切分。然后按照特定的标准将切分出来的信息单位用抽象符号表达，即编码，从而对信息单位进行统一的识别和统计分析。分类则是指在编码的基础上对信息进一步进行总结概括，发现并形成主题、主旨，发现质性数据所隐藏的范式，服务于进一步的现象描述、总结和理论建构。目前常用的质性数据分析和统计软件有NVivo、MAXQDA 等工具。

5.2.5 局限性及应对

与其他研究方法相比，有声思维数据的采集过程相对比较复杂，在完成任务的同时进行有声思维可能干扰被试对任务本身的完成，从而影响数据的质量。因此，采用有声思维法的研究者应该具有相关的数据收集经验，注意被试的代表性和典型性，并通过对被试进行培训来确保获得高质量的有声思维数据。

课堂讨论

1. 阅读下列摘要（Csizér & Kontra, 2020）并回答问题：
   (1) 在运用混合设计法的研究中，论文摘要部分应该如何撰写访谈设计和访谈结果？
   (2) 以访谈为主要工具的研究中，论文摘要部分应该如何撰写访谈方法和访谈结果？

Abstract

The aim of this study was to investigate deaf and severely hard-of-hearing students' foreign language learning characteristics. In order to provide a better understanding of the challenges this group of learners face, a mixed methods study was designed including a questionnaire survey to provide generalizable results for our context and an interview study to get a deeper understanding of the issue from the insiders' perspective as well. Data was collected in three European countries with piloted and barrier-free instruments. In order to investigate their foreign language learning processes, deaf and severely hard-of-hearing students' motivation, beliefs, and strategies were measured and analyzed. Our results indicate that deaf and severely hard-of-hearing students' foreign language learning experiences are fraught with challenges and setbacks despite their motivation and eagerness to learn foreign languages. To overcome these difficulties motivating and effective learning environments have to be created where the use of the national sign language contributes to the efficiency of teaching. Furthermore, teaching should include the presentation of effective learning strategies as well as the introduction of autonomous ways of learning.

2. 阅读下列节选内容（Csizér & Kontra, 2020）并回答问题：
   (1) 该研究中采用了什么抽样方法选取访谈对象？你如何评价该抽样方法？
   (2) 除了文中所提及的访谈对象的基本人口志信息，研究者们在论文中还提及了访谈对象的哪些特征？这对读者会产生什么影响？

Participants

Convenience sampling was used in both phases of the research. Survey participants were recruited from three European countries involved in the research project: Austria, the Czech Republic, and Hungary. The criterion for participant selection was that they had to be college or university students at the time of data collection or had to have pursued studies in tertiary education at any time in the preceding 5 years, and had to have experience in foreign language learning. The survey sample consisted of 54 students: from Austria (n = 12), the Czech Republic (n = 27), and Hungary (n = 15). …

　　…

In the qualitative phase of our study, we had 12 interview participants, four from each country. Some of them were participants of our survey who voluntarily expressed interest in taking part in the second phase of the research as well. Other respondents were recruited by English teachers at the participating institutions. Although it was a convenience sample, achieving maximum variety as regards gender, age, hearing status, field and level of study, and level of proficiency in English was attempted (for an overview see Table 1). …

…

3. 阅读下列节选内容（Csizér & Kontra, 2020）并简要评价该研究所采用的半结构式访谈。

Instruments

The instrument used in the qualitative phase of our research was a semi-structured interview guide (see Appendix). The semi-structured format was used in order to ensure that the individual interviews followed the same structure and that key points were discussed with each participant but at the same time there was a chance for the respondents to add further issues that they considered relevant to the topic. The interview guide covered the following main areas: current and previous language learning experiences, beliefs about language learning including self-efficacy beliefs, modality (teachers' use of sign language, students' use of translation into sign language when studying or reading), strategies for teaching and learning, and motivation to learn English.

4. 阅读下列节选内容（Csizér & Kontra, 2020），简要评价访谈数据的收集步骤，讨论并提出改进建议。结合 Table 1 具体评价本次访谈调查抽样的代表性。

Data Collection and Data Analysis

…

The qualitative data collection was preceded by the piloting of the interview guide. The first version was checked by two independent experts to ensure the quality of the collected data. After finalizing the tool, the interviews took place in the hometowns of the participants. The first author conducted the interviews in Hungary and the second author in the Czech Republic and Austria between September 2018 and January 2019. Each interview lasted for about an hour and was recorded using both an audio and a video recorder. In the Hungarian interviews the questions were asked in spoken or written Hungarian and responded to in speech or in sign language as indicated in Table 1. In the Czech and Austrian interviews, the questions were presented in English with interpretation into the preferred spoken or signed language of the participants. The interviewees were encouraged to interrupt and ask for clarification any time they were not sure what a question meant. The interview transcripts were prepared by the researchers themselves and were checked against the video recordings by local colleagues and the respective sign language interpreters to make sure that no information was lost in translation. The interview transcripts yielded a 45,450-word database. The data were subjected to qualitative content analysis looking for emerging themes and patterns (Patton, 2002). In order to preserve the respondents' anonymity, in the Results section they are referred to by the pseudonyms listed in Table 1.

TABLE 1
Interview Participants

| | | | | English or Other L3 Taught | | | |
Participant	Age/Sex	Hearing Status	Field of Study	In Elementary	In High School	At University	Language Used in the Interview
1. CZ Dana	38 F	Deaf	Special pedagogy	–	✓	Compulsory	CZSL
2. CZ Pavel	35 M	HH	IT and special pedagogy	✓	✓	Compulsory	Czech, CZSL
3. CZ Adel	24 F	Deaf	Accounting	Elective	General English and ESP	Compulsory	CZSL
4. CZ Ludvik	25 M	CI	IT	Elective	✓	Compulsory	Czech
5. AU Martina	38 F	Deaf	Educational science	✓	✓	–	ÖGS
6. AU Leo	26 M	CI	Economy	✓	✓	–	English
7. AU Doris	31 F	Deaf	Math education	✓	✓	–	ÖGS
8. AU Elsa	26 F	Deaf	Sport science	✓	✓	–	ÖGS
9. HU Anna	32 F	Deafened	German and Dutch	✓	✓	ESP at the dormitory	Hungarian speech and chat
10. HU Emil	38 M	HH	IT and pedagogy	For 1 year only ✓	Exempted	Chance courses by opportunity	Hungarian
11. HU Csaba	26 M	Deaf	Text editing	✓	✓	–	HSL
12. HU Barbara	29 F	Deaf	German and Italian	German	German	Self-teaching	HSL

RESULTS

Interview Results

In the course of the content analysis of the 12 individual interviews, insightful details took shape regarding such individual differences of the participating deaf students as their beliefs about language learning, learning strategies, and motivation. These were embedded in their personal experiences in different educational and national contexts. The data provided insight into the students' ideas about effective teaching and teaching methods including the use of sign language. Length limitations do not allow us to discuss every detail here, and therefore the presentation of the data is restricted to those areas which add complementary details and/or provide depth to some of the findings of the quantitative phase. The excerpts from the transcripts are translations either by the interpreters or the researchers except for quotes from Leo, who talked in comprehensible English throughout the interview.

5. 阅读下列访谈指南（Csizér & Kontra, 2020）并：
   (1) 就该研究采用的半结构式访谈评价所设计的访谈问题。
   (2) 与同学们一起讨论该如何提升这个访谈指南。

APPENDIX

Student Interview Guide

Introduction: I am NN, a member of the LangSkills international research team. Thank you for volunteering for this interview. This is XY, our SL interpreter. If there is anything you do not understand, please do not hesitate to stop the interpretation and ask for clarification. I would like to talk to you about your experiences in learning English. First, may I have your permission to record our conversation to make sure that nothing you say is lost? The research is completely anonymous, so your name is not going to be used anywhere.

1. What do/did you study? (University/Faculty/Major) Why did you choose this field of study?

2. May I ask you how old you are?

3. Which year are you in? When will you graduate? (if appropriate)

4. What job would you like to fill after graduation?/What job do you have now? Does it require any knowledge of English? How?/Why?

5. Are you currently learning English? Tell me about it.

6. Where and when did you start learning English? Please describe your English language learning experiences. Did you learn other languages?

7. What secondary school did you attend? (special school/integrated school or class)

8. Did you have English classes there? What were they like?

9. Did any of your English teachers use ASL or BSL? Tell me about it.

10. Can you say you are a successful language learner? Why or why not?

11. What do you find difficult in learning English? What helped you overcome these challenges?

12. How does English compare to German/Czech/Hungarian?

13. In an English course for Deaf/HoH persons, what should the teacher focus on: reading, writing, listening or speaking? Please explain.

14. Some language teachers use a SL interpreter when they teach English, while other teachers learn SL themselves and use it during the English lesson to aid communication with students. What does/did your English teacher do? Did you find it useful? Please explain why or why not.

15. When you are learning new words, do you translate them to yourself into SL? During the English lesson, do students translate new words for each other into SL? And the teacher?

16. When you are reading something in English (a message, a blog entry, an email, some information on the internet), do you translate it yourself into SL? When you are studying for your next English class, do you translate to SL?

17. Tell me about your English course here at the university.

18. Describe an English lesson in detail: What do you usually do? What does the teacher do?

19. Do you do any self-study on your own? If so, for approximately how many hours a week? Tell me what exactly you do.

20. How do you usually prepare for a test in English?

21. Would you like to take a proficiency exam in English? How are you preparing for that exam? Are Deaf/HoH students given any accommodations at this exam?

22. Is there anybody, a friend or a family member, who is helping you with English? If so, who and how?

23. Is there anything else you would like to tell me about learning English?

6. 阅读下列摘要（Zheng et al., 2022）。该研究系混合设计型研究，包含反应时间数据和有声思维数据。结合论文摘要写作对字数的严格限制，评价写作者在内容上的取舍。

Abstract

Although researchers generally agree that native speakers (NSs) process formulaic sequences (FSs) holistically to some extent, findings about nonnative speakers (NNSs) are conflicting, potentially because not all FSs are psychologically equal or because in some studies NNSs may not have fully understood the FSs. We address these issues by investigating Chinese NSs and NNSs processing of idioms and matched nonidiom FSs in phrase acceptability judgment tasks with and without think-alouds (TAs). Reaction times show that NSs processed idioms faster than nonidioms regardless of length, but NNSs processed 3-character FSs faster than 4-character FSs regardless of type. TAs show NSs' understanding of FSs has reached ceiling, but NNSs' understanding was incomplete, with idioms being understood more poorly than nonidioms. Although we conclude that idioms and nonidioms have different mental statuses in NSs' lexicons, it is inconclusive how they are represented by NNSs. TAs also show that NNSs employed various strategies to compensate for limited idiom knowledge, causing comparable processing speed for idioms and nonidioms. The findings highlight the importance of distinguishing subtypes of FSs and considering NNSs' quality of understanding in discussions of the psychological reality of FSs.

7. 阅读下列节选内容（Zheng et al., 2022），并判断该研究的三个研究问题中，哪个/些研究问题需要用有声思维数据来回答。

The present study

To achieve this goal, two concurrent data sources, RT and TA verbalizations, are triangulated. RTs, often used to investigate online processing (Jiang, 2011), are an indicator of how much cognitive effort individuals make to process language. TAs, as a window into the minds of speakers, can be used to probe speakers' depth of processing and understanding (Adrada-Rafael, 2017; Bowles, 2010). Leow et al. (2014) suggested that RT and TA can complement one another in providing a fuller picture of L2 processing. In this study, both are used to answer the following research questions (RQs).

RQ1. Are the two types of FSs processed differently by NSs and NNSs?

RQ2. Do NSs and NNSs display the same quality of understanding (QOU) about the two types of FSs?

RQ3. Are NSs' and NNSs' processing affected by their QOU about the two types of FSs?

8. 阅读下列节选内容（Zheng et al., 2022）并回答问题：

(1) 你如何评价该研究中研究对象关于有声思维的培训与实施？作为读者，你还对本研究中未提及的哪些培训内容感兴趣？如果要基于该研究进行论文写作，你会对本研究中有声思维的实施部分做哪些删减？

Participants were instructed to verbalize their Yes or No judgment and report what they were thinking when they made the judgment. Before the experiment, written instructions were given to participants to ensure that they understood they should verbalize whatever thoughts went through their minds when performing the AJT. Participants were also given spoken instructions regarding how to think aloud. First, they were informed that one of the research goals was to obtain a realistic representation of how they understood language. Therefore, they were asked first to read aloud the FS they saw and then judge whether the FS was likely to be read or heard in Chinese. The instructions emphasized that it was important to "speak whatever can help you make a judgment for a stimulus" without worrying about giving explanations, using examples or using incomplete sentences. Both NSs and NNSs were asked to think aloud in the target language, Chinese, …

(2) 你如何评价下列论文中编码（Coding）部分的写作？

Method

Participants

The twenty NSs were Chinese undergraduate and graduate students (12 females; 8 males; Mean age = 27.5). The NNS participants were 22 Chinese degree learners (12 females; 10 males; Mean age = 22.5) recruited from four Chinese universities. They came from nine countries: Egypt, Japan, Kazakhstan, Korea, Mongolia, Nepal, Thailand, Russia, and Vietnam. All NNS participants had passed Hanyu Shuiping Kaoshi (Chinese Proficiency Test) level 6 within the last 2 years.

Test instruments

The instruments used to assess the processing and comprehension of FSs are phrase acceptability judgment tasks (AJTs), with one conducted silently (to gather RT) and another conducted with TAs (to collect TA data). Although silent AJTs have been widely used to measure L2 acquisition, researchers have found that NNSs can be inconsistent in making dichotomous judgments (R. Ellis, 1991) and have suggested that the cognitive recourse that L2 learners use for immediate recognition "does not necessarily imply language acquisition" (Leow, 1993, p. 334). Thus, while the silent AJT taps into participants' speeded recognition, TA AJT is a complementary measure that allows us to gather qualitative data about how learners process the FSs. All participants performed the two AJTs in a counterbalanced order with a 1-week interval between the two. In each AJT session, participants saw both blocks of test material with a 5-min break in between. Figure 1 presents the experimental procedure.

...

Think-aloud–acceptability judgment task

The TA-AJT session was similar to the silent session except that instead of pressing a button to respond. Participants were instructed to verbalize their Yes or No judgment and report what they were thinking when they made the judgment. Before the experiment, written instructions were given to participants to ensure that they understood they should verbalize whatever thoughts went through their minds when performing the AJT. Participants were also given spoken instructions regarding how to think aloud. First, they were informed that one of the research goals was to obtain a realistic representation of how they understood language. Therefore, they were asked first to read aloud the FS they saw and then judge whether the FS was likely to be read or heard in Chinese. The instructions emphasized that it was important to "speak whatever can help you make a judgment for a stimulus" without worrying about giving explanations, using examples or using incomplete sentences. Both NSs and NNSs were asked to think aloud in the target language, Chinese, since Adrada-Rafael and Filgueras-Gómez (2019) found no qualitative difference between TAs that intermediate NNSs completed in their L1 versus in their L2. As in Kim and Bowles (2019), this was also practical for the researchers given that the NNSs came from nine different L1 backgrounds. Throughout the experiment, an assistant sat beside the participant and prompted them when they fell silent (Bowles, 2010). The whole TA-AJT session was audio-recorded using Audacity and transcribed. A full transcription of an NNS participant is provided (Supplementary Materials).

Coding

The Yes/No judgments about the FSs were first coded for accuracy (correct vs. incorrect) and then for QOU. Previous research (Cooper, 1999) has shown that participants can utilize a variety of strategies in the process of understanding an FS.

Because the TA procedure in this study only intended to probe participants' success in understanding FSs rather than the strategies they used, we coded three levels of QOU based on previous research (Boers & Demecheleer, 2001; Schmitt et al., 2001): incorrect, partially correct, and fully correct. Table 2 presents the operationalization of the coding procedure, adapted from previous coding procedures for depth of processing (Adrada-Rafael, 2017; Leow & Mercer, 2015).

Table 2. Operationalization of QOU

	Incorrect	Partially correct	Fully correct
Criteria	Participants show wrong or no knowledge of the FS	Participants show partial knowledge of the FS	Participants show full knowledge of the FS
Evidence	○ Acknowledge the FS has been "heard/seen/learned" or identify the FS to be a certain type of expression but admit "have forgotten/have no idea what it means" ○ Judge a correct FS to be an incorrect one and provide a "correction" ○ Provide an interpretation/example that shows wrong knowledge of the FS ○ Provide a wrong metalinguistic analysis	○ Provide a literal interpretation/example for an idiom whose figurative meaning is the default use[3] ○ Provide a metalinguistic analysis that does not show full understanding ○ Provide a related but inaccurate interpretation/example ○ Provide an example with a correct context but not exactly correct grammar/pragmatics	○ Provide a "cliché" type answer, stating: "it's just what I often say", or use an "A just means A" sentence to imply there is nothing worth saying ○ Provide an example with correct context, grammar, and pragmatics ○ Provide a correct interpretation (a figurative interpretation for an idiom) ○ Provide a metalinguistic analysis that can show full understanding

The first author and a research assistant coded 25% of the data independently. The interrater agreement was 100% for judgment accuracy and 94.6% for QOU. After discussing some controversial cases, the two raters coded another 5% of the data for QOU, and the interrater agreement reached 98.4% (Cohen's kappa = 0.85). The results were considered high enough for the first author to code the remaining data alone.

9. 阅读下列节选内容（Zheng et al., 2022）并回答问题：你如何评价该论文研究结果（Results）部分关于 RQ2 的有声思维数据的汇报与写作？

Results

…

RQ2. Quality of understanding

RQ2 asked whether there was a difference in NSs' and NNSs' QOU with different types/lengths of FSs. To answer this question, the QOU coding was analyzed. As Table 5 illustrates, NSs' incorrect TAs were observed less than 1% of the time under different FS conditions, and partially correct TAs were less than 3%. However, the frequencies of NNSs' incorrect TAs varied greatly under different FS conditions, ranging from 1.0% (3-C nonidioms) to 10.6% (4-C idioms), as did the frequencies of partially correct TAs, ranging from 13.2% (3-C nonidioms) to 20.8% (4-C nonidioms). The most successful FSs in the NS group were 4-C idioms with the highest fully correct ratio (99.4%), which were the most unsuccessful FSs in the NNS group with the lowest fully correct ratio (70.2%).

Table 5. Frequency of QOU

FS condition		NS			NNS		
		Incorrect	Partially correct	Fully correct	Incorrect	Partially correct	Fully correct
Length	*Type*						
3-C	Idiom	0.00%	2.84%	97.16%	3.24%	19.46%	77.30%
	Nonidiom	0.22%	0.66%	99.13%	0.98%	13.20%	85.82%
4-C	Idiom	0.21%	0.42%	99.37%	10.62%	19.17%	70.21%
	Nonidiom	0.68%	0.45%	98.86%	3.26%	20.80%	75.94%

10. 阅读下列节选内容（Zheng et al., 2022）并回答问题：该研究中研究者是如何处理关于有声思维数据的写作的？你如何评价这部分的写作？

Discussion

Research question 2

The second question inquired whether there is any difference in speakers' QOU about different types of FSs and was addressed using TA data. The results show that NSs were at or near the ceiling for every subtype of FS. This is highly predictable given that the selected FSs are all frequently used in written or spoken Chinese and hence very familiar to adult NSs. The high familiarity was also evidenced by the fact that approximately half of NSs' TAs (54.5% of idioms, 49% of nonidioms) were "cliché" type responses, such as "It's just what I often say." Clearly, NSs tend to use their intuition to make judgments, which is often considered a shallow form of processing that involves little cognitive effort (Leow & Mercer, 2015). The small proportion of incorrect TAs (0.3%) from NSs occurred not because of incorrect understanding but because they questioned whether a lexical bundle (e.g., 不是所有 not-copula-all-all not all of) could be used in isolation.

…

Another explanation for the better understanding of nonidiom FSs may have to do with compositionality. Nonidiom FSs are fully transparent items whose meaning is the combination of each individual word. Thus, learners can make sense of an unfamiliar nonidiom FS simply by analyzing its vocabulary items (Libben, 1998; Sandra, 1990), as exemplified in the excerpts below.

Excerpt 1
Participant 6 (Korean L1)
    Target (4-C nonidiom): 轻松自在/light-slack-self-exist/*relaxed and unrestrained*
    TA: "我没见过这个, 但是能明白, 意思就是很轻松, 很自由。"
    "I have never seen this one but can understand; it just means very relaxed, very free."
The target FS in Excerpt 1 is a nonidiomatic collocation composed of two disyllabic adjectives 轻松 "relaxed" and 自在 "unrestrained." Although the participant claimed that she never used the phrase before, she successfully put together a correct meaning ostensibly by interpreting the two disyllabic words that she knew. However, when learners applied the same strategy to idioms, comprehension errors occurred. Excerpt 2 and 3 demonstrated this process.

Excerpt 2
Participant 9 (Japanese L1)
    Target (3-C idiom): 出人命/happen-human-life/*death causing*
    TA: "对的, 就是出生了一个人。"
    "Correct, meaning 'to give birth to a person'."

Excerpt 3
Participant 11 (Thai L1)
    Target (4-C idiom): 谈天说地/talk-sky-speak-earth/*talk of everything under the sun*
    TA: "对的, 就是谈论天气。"
    "Correct, meaning 'to talk about the weather'."

课外练习

1. 二语写作过程中双语词典的使用对于大学本科阶段的二语写作者的意义和作用一直存在争议。分别设计一份结构式访谈和半结构式访谈从学习者视角考察他们如何看待二语写作过程中双语词典的作用，并与同学一起讨论结构式访谈和半结构式访谈适用的研究以及两种访谈的优缺点。
2. 习语（idioms）是二语习得的一个难点。与同学合作设计一个研究，通过有声思维了解二语学习者对英语习语的在线处理策略以及效果。
3. 与同学一起讨论如何在论文的结果汇报（Results）及讨论（Discussion）部分撰写关于有声思维的质性数据。

拓展阅读

Buckingham, L., & Aktug-Ekinci, D. (2017). Interpreting coded feedback on writing: Turkish EFL students' approaches to revision. *Journal of English for Academic Purposes*, *26*, 1–16.

Crosthwaite, P., Boynton, S., & Cole, S. (2017). Exploring rater conceptions of academic stance and engagement during group tutorial discussion assessment. *Journal of English for Academic Purposes*, *28*, 1–13.

第 6 单元

观察法

学习目标

- 了解观察法的定义和实施
- 学习观察法在语言学研究中的具体应用
- 在具体研究场景中设计观察法

观察法是社会调查研究的重要方法之一。与其他调查研究方法相比，观察法比较简单易行，适用于获得一个"点"的截面资料。如果观察的时间足够长，也能够获得这个"点"的社会事实的动态。在研究过程中，观察法可以与一些涉及"面"的研究相结合，起到"以点带面、点面俱到"的效果，从而在一定程度上能有效地解释现象的因果关系。

6.1 基本概念

观察法是研究人员借助个人感官和辅助工具观察研究对象的方法，是获取语言材料的重要途径之一，属于实证主义的质性研究范畴。在正式进入观察流程前，研究人员需要设计观察方案，包括研究目的、观察对象、观察时间、观察表、观察工具等，在观察过程中要做好观察记录，观察结束后要整理分析观察结果。

观察法常见于社会学、人类学、心理学等学科领域，研究人员利用观察法可以获取更加真实的材料。观察法在语言学研究中同样应用广泛，常见于语言变异与变化、二语习得、双语及多语现象、语言教学、言语交际、会话分析等研究，它能够提供定量研究无法获知的有关受访者的深层信息，具备独特的优势。

6.2 分类及实施

依据不同的划分标准，观察法有以下分类。

（一）**实验室观察法和实地观察法（或自然观察法）**。这一类别主要是根据观察地点的不同来区分。

（1）实验室观察法，主要在实验室内进行，一般情况下会有各种观察设施。它的好处是能够有效控制变量，排除不必要因素的干扰，但也可能导致获取的材料不够自然真实。

（2）实地观察（或自然观察）法，主要在真实的生活场景中进行，好处是能获取到自然真实的语料，但不足之处是观察设施达不到实验室的专业水平，观察成本、观察难度也会相应增加。

（二）**结构式观察法、半结构式观察法与非结构式观察法**。根据实施观察方式的不同，观察法可分为这三类。

（1）结构式观察法，是高度标准化、系统化、程序化的观察方式。研究人员需要提前设计好精细的观察方案，合理拟定观察项目并对结果做出预估，在观察过程中要严格按照观察计划执行，不能随意改动观察内容或调整观察流程。

（2）半结构式观察法，是有一定的灵活性和自主性的观察方法。研究人员提前拟定整体的研究方案，设计观察的内容、对象、流程等内容，但不必过于精密，在观察过程中可以实时调整，记录此前忽视的信息，后续再进行整理分析。

（3）非结构式观察法，是最为自由、灵活的观察方法。研究人员无须提前设计详细的观察方案，可以只设置一个观察提纲，但在进入观察流程后要高度集中精力并灵活变通，随场景、对象等的表现及变化及时调整观察的具体内容，同样要详细地进行记录。

（三）参与式观察法与非参与式观察法。这是根据观察人员处境不同进行的划分。

（1）参与式观察法是一种要求研究人员参与研究对象的活动或融入研究对象所属的群体，以内部成员的身份展开观察活动的方法。参与式观察法的好处是能够有效降低排异效应，减少观察对象的戒备心和紧张情绪，收集到真实、有效、深入的语言材料，适合研究言语社团、言语共同体等，与此同时也要求研究人员投入更多的时间和精力。

（2）运用非参与式观察法时，研究人员不参与研究对象的活动，也不加入研究对象所属的群体，而是以旁观者、局外人的身份完成语料收集。非参与式观察能让研究人员保持更为客观的立场，但是它强调研究人员与研究对象的身份界限，可能会提高研究对象的戒备心理。研究人员投入的时间和精力也较少，收集到语言材料可能是失真、片面、浅显的。

（四）开放式观察法（或公开观察法）与隐蔽式观察法。这是根据观察公开程度的不同进行的划分。

（1）开放式观察法是研究人员以开放的心态对研究现场进行全方位、整体性、感受性的观察并加以记录的方式。研究人员需要充分调动自身感官，训练自身观察反应能力和观察能力，全面细致地记录观察到的信息。开放式观察法的弊端在于研究对象知晓自己正在受观察，可能会出现不自然、不真实的反应。

（2）隐蔽式观察法指的是研究人员隐藏自己身份暗地调查的方法。研究对象不知道自己正在受观察，表现出来的状态会更加自然。美国社会语言学家威廉·拉波夫（William Labov）设计的"快速匿名调查法"和中国社会语言学家徐大明发展出的"问路调查法"都属于隐蔽式观察法。这个观察法的好处在于能获取更加自然真实的语言材料，但也无法完全解决"观察者悖论"，即观察人们在不受观察时使用语言的状况。

（五）直接观察法与间接观察法。这是根据观察人员与观察对象接触方式的不同进行的划分。

（1）直接观察法指的是研究人员利用自己的感官在现场直接观察研究对象获取语料的方法。研究人员使用眼睛、耳朵、鼻子等感官对研究对象进行感知、描述，获得即时的语料信息，其好处在于能快速针对已有观察结果调整观察内容，但也容易受人体感官条件的制约，获取信息的水平有限。

（2）间接观察法是更多地借助技术手段（如录音、录像等）来获取语料的方法。间接观察能够克服人体感官局限，扩大观察范围，获取更准确连贯的语言材料，但技术成本也随之提高。在一些研究中，间接观察指的是不观察作为研究对象的"人"，只观察与"人"相关的自然物品、行为痕迹、社会环境等，从侧面获取研究对象相关信息的方式。

6.3　优点、局限性及应对

观察法具备如下优点：（1）身临其境，真实可信。除了实验室观察，大部分观察法都将研究人员置于真实的语言环境中，不论是以参与者的身份还是以旁观者的身份，研究人员都能获取第一手材料。（2）内容丰富，不设界限。研究人员在观察中能够获取各种各样的信息，包括但不限于语言使用、家庭状况、社交信息，这些材料可以使分析更为全面、立体。（3）灵活便捷，客观具体。观察法不需要研究对象做准备工作，研究人员可以随时随地进行观察，观察的时间也可长可短，可操作性强。相较于其他研究方法，观察法削弱了研究人员的目的性，研究对象受到的人为干预较少，能自然地表现与流露，因而其语料是客观的、具体的。

观察法的局限之处在于：（1）受时间、空间限制大，观察范围有限。受客观因素制约，研究人员无法在任何时间、任何地点进行观察，不能参与到所有的活动场景中，因此获得的材料是有限的。（2）具有表面性和偶然性。在观察活动中，研究人员观察到的基本都是表面现象或事件的外部联系，很难洞悉研究对象的心理活动或事件之间的内部联系，而且事件的发生也具有偶然性，研究人员可能碰巧获取到某些有价值的信息，也难免错失重要材料。

因此，在开展一项语言研究时，观察法常需要与其他研究方法，如问卷调查法、访谈法等结合起来使用，这样才能既确保收集的语料符合研究的需要，又能最大限度地确保语料的真实性与客观性。

课堂讨论

1. 阅读下列摘要（Baecher & McCormack, 2015）并回答问题：
   (1) 对于以观察为主要工具的研究，论文摘要部分应该如何撰写观察方法和观察结果？
   (2) 在观察法和其他方法结合的语言研究中，论文摘要部分应该如何提及观察法和研究结果？

Abstract 1

This study investigated how video-based observation may alter the nature of post-observation talk between supervisors and teacher candidates. Audio-recorded post-observation conversations were coded using a conversation analysis framework and interpreted through the lens of interactional sociology. Findings suggest that video-based observations impacted the content and extent of teacher candidate reflection during post-observation discussions, enabling candidates to comment at greater length about their teaching, initiate topics, and cite evidence through reference to the video data. Implications for the role of supervisors and the potential of video-informed post-observation conferencing are discussed.

Abstract 2

This study adopts Bourdieu's conceptualization of taste and distinction to examine the discursive construction of Chinese middle-class identities. Drawing on an ethnographic fieldwork of young urban professionals who display a shared passion for Saab cars, this article presents three examples to instantiate the ways that the participants employ linguistic and discursive resources to construct an urban middle-class identity revolving around consumption and commodification: the first example is an interview about their taste for their Saab cars; the second is a participant observation of the Saab fans' linguistic exchanges in which they demonstrate their 'taste for each other' — recognition of each other's in-group membership and social identity; the third example is an online observation of their multimodal display of other lifestyle commodities. All three examples highlight the importance of language in creating a sense of distinction and in negotiating middle-class identities among Chinese young urban professionals.

2. 阅读下列节选（Li, 2011）内容并回答问题：
   (1) 该研究中采用了什么抽样方法选取观察对象？你如何评价该抽样方法？
   (2) 除了文中所提及的观察对象的基本人口志信息，你还对哪些信息感兴趣？这些信息可能会对研究结果和结论产生什么影响？

The data which I want to present in this paper come from interviews, observations and recordings of social interaction of three Chinese youths in London. They are all male and all first-year undergraduate students of mathematics at one of the colleges of the University of London. I got to know the three young men initially through my contact with the parents of Chris (see his details below), one of the three I have studied. I knew of the other two youths and their parents through Chris' family. The three families know each other fairly well but do not meet regularly. I have met all the parents of the three youths. I talked informally to all three young men individually and together and told them that I was interested in their language behaviour. They knew I was a university professor. They assumed, like many other people, that I was interested in how good their Chinese and/or English was. They were very open, and happy for me to ask questions.

I did semi-structured interviews both individually and with the three as a group, and we talked about a wide range of issues such as their views of mixing two languages, literacy, awareness of different varieties of Chinese, their identity, positions of young people within the UK Chinese community, community relations, family relations, changes in China, Chinese students at universities, Chinese complementary schools, and Chinese food, culture and customs. I thought of these interviews as open discussions and I believe they felt the same. They certainly did not behave as if they were being interrogated. At the beginning of the interviews, I did explain that I wanted to know if there were any particular moments in their lives that they felt had a significant impact on the way they saw the world, the way they behaved and the decisions they made for themselves. I also asked them for examples of creative use of the languages they knew, as I had observed some very interesting uses by the three students.

In the meantime, I observed them socialising together at family parties and met them individually and together on university campus. They know that I work in another, nearby college of the University of London and they did not mind my visiting and talking to them in their college. I have observed them interacting with other Chinese-speaking and non-Chinese-speaking students on a number of occasions. I paid special attention to innovative uses of the languages. Most of the interviews were audio-recorded; so were some of the interactions at home. Extensive notes were taken of all the observations. On two separate occasions, I went back to the three young men to clarify some details of what they said or did during the interviews and observations.

In what follows, I first present the background of the three young men and then discuss common themes that emerged from the observations and interviews, focusing on creative and critical use of the multilingual resources they have and their reflections and comments. The discussion is intermingled with my own interpretation and comments on what I observed and heard. Although I talk about common themes and issues, my main objective throughout the study is to try and capture the creative and critical moments in the three young people's multilingual, everyday lives. I am not looking for regular patterns; nor am I concerned with frequency of occurrence of specific feature or behaviour. The three young men gave me permission to use their English names. Most young Chinese people in Britain have English names, which bear little relation to their Chinese names. The English names are used amongst peers and occasionally by their siblings. Their parents normally use their Chinese names, except when they refer to them with some English-speaking third party.

Chris is a 19-year-old British-born Chinese student. His parents are from Chinese mainland and speak a southwestern variety of Mandarin Chinese to each other at home. The father is an academic and the mother is an administrator in a local government office. Chris has a younger brother. They both had considerable Mandarin input from the parents when they were younger, but has mainly spoken English to each other and with other Chinese friends they have. Chris attended a Chinese complementary school for 7 years between the age of 7 and 14. But by his own admission, he cannot read or write Chinese. He can understand Mandarin very well and can speak it fairly fluently. His Mandarin has no identifiable regional accent.

Lawson, also 19, is a son of two Chinese immigrants from Hong Kong, China. The father is an accountant and the mother works in a Chinese shop. Apparently they ran a successful catering business when they first came to Britain some 30 years ago. Lawson was born in London and has an elder sister and a younger sister. He speaks good Cantonese and knows some Mandarin. He attended a Cantonese school between the age of six and seventeen and has an A for Cantonese GCSE (General Certificate for Secondary Education). The Cantonese school he attended also taught Mandarin, and Lawson started learning it there. But he said he did not really learn very much. Now he has made a lot of Mandarin-speaking friends at the university and attends an evening Mandarin class.

Roland is 20 and comes from Chinese mainland. His family are still in China. They live in Guangzhou (Canton). Roland came to Britain when he was 15 and attended a boarding school. His parents are not native Cantonese speakers. But because they live in a Cantonese-speaking city, they all know Cantonese well. At home, they speak a southern variety of Chinese that Roland cannot name. He does not even know which part of China his parents originally came from except that they were not from Guangzhou. His Mandarin is very fluent with a slight southern accent. He can speak Cantonese and some Hakka. His English is very fluent and sounds native but he says that his written English is still "not very good". In fact, he claims that one of the reasons he chose to do mathematics was because it involves less extensive writing in English. He has the highest literacy level in Chinese amongst the three young men.

3. 阅读下列节选内容（Sabaté-Dalmau, 2018），判断该研究采用的是哪一类观察法，并简要评价这种观察法与访谈法的区别与联系。

The study focused on two Catalan urban towns in the Barcelona metropolitan area. These were the research spaces of two ethnographic projects concerning migrants' alternative socialization spaces conducted between 2007–2009 and 2012–2014. The first project aimed at understanding migrants' multilingual practices and ideologies and their use of information and communication technology in transnational life. The second one focused on the interplay between migrants' multilingual practices and linguistic identities and their socioeconomic and geographic immobility. I here present the data concerning migrants' practices, ideologies and identities revolving around the minority language, stored for a deeper investigation of their own (the two full ethnographic projects are available in Sabaté-Dalmau (2014) and Sabaté-Dalmau (2016)).

The data in both research spaces included fieldnotes from daily and weekly participant observation (I lived in both neighborhoods for at least one year before, during and after each fieldwork project), audio-recorded interviews and naturally-occurring interactions among participants and among participants and other migrants, and a variety of written materials (advertisements, text messages, etc.). The interviews took place mostly in Spanish, and also in English and Catalan. I always started interactions in Catalan, and presented myself as a "Catalan speaker" and as an English instructor at university. For the purposes of this paper, I present five excerpts and quote eight excerpt parts from interview data, and draw on extensive fieldwork notes. In the analysis, language choice has been indicated with different typefaces: Spanish is presented in italics; Catalan, underlined; English, plain; and undecidable speech, in bold.

Excerpt 1

@Location: 18 July 2012. Bench. Anoia.

@Bck: The researcher (RES) asks Alfred (ALF) about the "locals" languages, which leads to commenting on his self-ascribed "low" command of Catalan.

	1	*RES:	and in here do they speak English?
?	2	*ALF:	the people here they are not.
		[...]	
?	3	*ALF:	only a few people speak English only few only.
	4	*RES:	so do you use English when you go here?
?	5	*ALF:	no no no.
	6	*RES:	no?
?	7	*ALF:	no no no <only> [//] the only Spanish.
	8	*RES:	only Spanish?
?	9	*ALF:	yes.
?	10	*RES:	and not Catalan?
?	11	*ALF:	<Catalan> [?] ok # <u>una mica</u>.
		%tra:	a bit.
		%com:	Laughs

12	*RES:	una mica.
	%tra:	a bit.
? 13	*ALF:	if you speak it yes it's but I can't reply to you in Catalan only in *castellano*.
14	*RES:	vale <però tu l'entens> [?].
	%tra:	ok <but you understand it> [?].
? 15	*ALF:	yes yo entén entén sí.
	%tra:	yes I understand understand yes.

4. 阅读下列节选内容（Dong, 2018），简要评价观察数据的收集步骤，并讨论采用这种方法的好处。结合 Example 2 具体评价本次观察内容的代表性。

4.4 *Taste discourse about each other*

The Saab participants not only articulate taste discourses about the car, but also taste discourses about each other, i.e. recognition of their shared taste, which leads to ratification of their in-group identity. Example 2 instantiates discourses of "the tastes they have for each other" (Bourdieu, 1984: 253). In this example, we observe how alignment is set up interactionally and how the interlocutors position themselves and others through subtle participation management. The conversation occurred in Beijing on 23 November 2013. The immediate context was a small dinner get-together of three Saabists and me in a bar. The participants included Xiao Li, Lin and me. The other Saab fan happened to be away during the conversation. Xiao Li was an important informant and served as the contact person who introduced me to the Saab group; I had known him for 30 years. He was in his early 40s; as discussed in Section 4.2, he was a self-trained lawyer and now partner of a small-sized law firm that had seven lawyers and about 30 associates and assistants. Lin was in his late 30s and worked as a manager for a state-owned tech company in Beijing. Xiao Li and Lin met each other in 2009 when they both participated in a Saab business promotion event. They had maintained frequent interaction since then. In the transcribed part of conversation, the participants were talking about whether they would recommend Saab to a friend if the friend were to buy a car.

Example 2: "No one suits Saab"

1	Li:	What's up?	怎么了？
2	Lin:	{turns to Li and says} She is asking me whether I would recommend Saab to my friend, I say I wouldn't	{转向小李说}她问我会不会向朋友推荐萨博，我说我不会
3	Li:	= I wouldn't recommend Saab, heheh~~	=我不会推荐萨博，哈哈
4	Author:	That is::what if they suit it (Saab)?	那要是::他们挺适合（萨博）的呢？
5	Li:	No one (suits Saab)	没人（适合萨博）
6	Lin:	=If they never heard (of it)…	=如果他们都没听说过（它）……
7	Author:	What if they really don't know (about Saab)?	要是他们真的不知道（萨博）呢？
8	Li:	[Impossible~!	[不可能~！
9	Lin:	[Impossible~~! {with similar emphases}	[不可能~！{重音都一样}
10	Author:	{Laughing voice, embarrassed} But then how did you know (about Saab)? How did you know? Who told you (about Saab)?	{笑声，尴尬} 那你怎么知道（萨博）的呀？你怎么知道的啊？谁跟你说的（萨博）呢？
11	Lin:	Me? A friend told me	我？一个朋友告诉我的
12	Author:	That's right! See! There must be a way to know it in the first place	对呀！你看！必须得有个办法先知道啊
13	Lin:	My friend told me because she knew me very well, she said you are too "different", too, that is {low laughing voice}, too, too, {turning to Li} what do you call it?	因为我这个朋友她了解我，她说我这个人太小众，{低声笑}太，太那个{转向小李}叫什么？
14	Li:	Too weird {with a low laughing voice}	各色{也低声笑}
15	Lin:	Err, right, weird, although I have a good temper, I can't easily mix into any group, (she said) you must look for special things to prove yourself, to mark yourself as someone special	呃，对，各色，我脾气虽然还行，但是没办法融入任何一个圈子，（她说）你得找到一个特别，特别那个鲜明的东西来来证明自己，或者说来来来让你自己标新立异

| 16 | Li: | =This car, when you use it for everyday transportation it is just that (low key), but, occasionally if you want it to impress others, it can be really wild | =你看这车平时用还是挺（低调的），但是偶尔你要是想让它爆发一下，这个车也还是挺让人出乎意料的 |
| 17 | Lin: | It is that kind of feeling | 就是那种感觉 |

[Fieldwork2013-11-23_ML_V049_00:00:13-00:01:16]

5. 阅读下列节选内容（Baecher & McCormack, 2015）并回答问题：
   (1) 对于文中研究方法与数据的汇报你是否满意？请与同学讨论如何改进。
   (2) 作为读者，你还对本研究中未提及的哪些研究内容感兴趣？如果要基于该研究进行论文写作，你会对本研究中观察法的实施部分做哪些删减？为什么？
   (3) 你如何评价该研究中观察法的分析框架？

Methods

Based on our understanding of the strengths of conversation analysis for close examination of talk-in-action (Heritage and Clayman, 2010), we adopted this as a methodology for examining and coding the POC talk. We needed, however, to contextualize our data and gain a deeper understanding of aspects of our roles within POCs as teacher educators. For this, we decided on an interactional-sociolinguistic approach (Gordon, 2011), which prompted us to consider how the supervisor and her teacher candidates interpreted one another's communicative actions that signaled topic shifts, assumptions, or opinions about the topic under discussion. In combining these two analytical approaches, our study specifically seeks to understand whether the participants' roles in the video-based POCs differed significantly from the in-person observations as reflected in the content and language of their conversations.

Research context

This study was conducted within a TESOL masters program leading to P-12 state teaching certification within a college of education at a large, urban public university in the northeast US. Teacher candidates at our institution might have initial licensure and be currently teaching while pursuing the MA in TESOL (in-service), and some are student teachers (pre-service). In our state, a master's degree is required for permanent teaching certification, and we do not offer a BA in TESOL in our school of education. In this MA TESOL program, teacher candidates complete 30 weeks of supervised teaching across their two final semesters. Each teacher candidate is assigned a university field supervisor who observes them two times on-site, and one time via video in each practicum, for a total of six formal observations over two semesters. After each observation, the supervisor evaluates the lesson according to a standard rubric that covers eight domains of teaching, one of which is TESOL-specific. Performance is evaluated by the supervisor and a grade is given for the observed lesson once the POCs have taken place. The supervisor schedules individual POCs for a time soon after the lesson, in which candidates join the supervisor to debrief the lesson.

Since 2006, all of the teacher candidates at our school of education have been required to create video recordings of their teaching as part of their practical requirements. Teacher candidates capture and review a video of a complete classroom lesson and upload it to a password-protected, web-based video server. Once online, the video is viewed by the supervisor, who then discusses the lesson with the teacher candidate in a subsequent POC. For the video observation, the supervisor only sees the lesson via video.

Participants

In order to avoid biasing the study by using POC data from the period of the study, consent was obtained from eight teacher candidates who had shared L as a supervisor, but had graduated two years earlier. At that time, all eight candidates had participated in the standard three observations (two traditional and one video based) and had allowed the POCs that took place after these observations over the 15-week practicum to be audio recorded. For many years, audio recording the POCs has been a part of normal classroom procedure for all candidates in the program as a means to support their reflective commentary papers written post-conference. To study the nature of these conversations in depth, we decided to focus only on two candidates. We began by dividing the pool of eight possible candidates by teaching experience into novice (two years or less) and experienced (three years or more), and one candidate's set of POCs was randomly drawn from each, thus giving us two teacher candidates' POCs to serve as foci for this study, one novice and the other experienced.

The more experienced candidate, Cathy (teacher candidate identities are protected with use of pseudonyms), had taught at the elementary level for four years prior to beginning the practicum, and entered the MA program with a degree in elementary education. The novice candidate, Joon, had very little P-12 teaching experience, although she had some experience teaching adults. At the time of the study, Cathy had already been teaching a self-contained fourth grade at her elementary school for three years, while Joon had just been hired on an internship certificate (internship certificates allow candidates who have almost finished their MA program to begin teaching in the public school system) to teach a self-contained mixed-grade level English language arts to English language learner (ELL) students in a high school. All of their observed lessons were content-based English as a second language lessons, of between 30 and 45 minutes in length. Both teacher candidates had high GPAs, were native speakers of English, were considered excellent students in the MA TESOL program, and went on to successfully complete the practicum course.

Both L and B had served as university-based supervisors for more than 15 years at the time of the study and had frequently discussed the nature of POCs, theorizing about roles in this talk and how to deepen the quality of these conversations. In addition to the TESOL doctorate, L had specialized training in classroom observation, mentoring, and a degree in instructional supervision.

Procedures for data collection

Data collection occurred during the final two observations of teaching during each candidate's second semester of practicum teaching. The video observation was the candidates' fifth observation, and the traditional was their sixth of the year. The POCs for both the traditional and the video-based lessons took place two to three days after the lesson had been taught, to allow for candidate reflection on the lesson prior to the POC. Prior to each meeting to discuss the video-recorded lesson, the teacher candidate and supervisor had already watched it independently, but also had it available on a computer screen to replay as desired during the POC. Each POC, in turn, was audio recorded and later transcribed for this study. The traditional observation was conducted without any video recording of the lesson, and the POC following this observation was also audio recorded and later transcribed.

The POCs generated four transcripts as data for analysis: each of the two candidates' video POCs, and each of their two traditional POCs. The POCs typically ranged from 40 to 50 minutes in length, resulting in 499 800 lines of text. As we read the transcripts and became familiar with the arc of the conversations, we realized that later stages of the POCs tended to display higher proportions of supervisor dominance and transactional, administrative-type language as the supervisor "closed" the conversation with direction for targeted growth areas, while the beginning of the conversations served as "warm up" and consisted of non-teaching-related chat. For this reason, we decided to focus on the first 350 lines (about 25 minutes) that began immediately after the warm-up, usually when the supervisor initiated the talk with a statement like, "So, tell me about the lesson." These four, 350-line transcripts thus provided the discourse data for analysis. Although there were also lesson plans, rubrics, and reflection papers completed for and after the observations, as well as the actual video records of the candidates' video-based observations, none of these was included for analysis in this study in order to focus more intensively on the POCs themselves.

课外练习

1. 近年来，一些有识之士担心，外语课堂出现"娱乐化"的不良趋势。面对这种担心，为了解当前外语课堂的实际情况，设计一份以观察法为主或者观察法与其他方法相结合的调查研究。结合这个设计，与同学一起讨论该使用哪种类别的观察法以及这种方法的优缺点。

2. 自 2021 年以来，中央网信办在全国范围内开展"清朗"系列专项行动，集中力量解决群众反映强烈的网络空间的问题。请与同学设计一个研究，通过观察法了解网络空间语言治理策略以及效果。

拓展阅读

Licoppe, C. (2015). Video communication and "camera actions": The production of wide video shots in courtrooms with remote defendants. *Journal of Pragmatics, 76*, 117–134.

Mondada, L. (2016). Challenges of multimodality: Language and the body in social interaction. *Journal of Sociolinguistics, 20*, 336–366.

第 7 单元
行动研究与扎根理论

学习目标
- 了解行动研究和扎根理论的步骤和实施
- 学习行动研究和扎根理论在语言学研究中的具体应用以及论文写作
- 能根据研究问题正确实施行动研究和应用扎根理论

7.1 行动研究

7.1.1 基本概念

行动研究法源自 20 世纪初美国的民主社会运动,在 40 年代由美国社会心理学家库尔特·勒温(Kurt Lewin)进一步发展。此后,受到教育界"教师即研究者"思想的影响,这一概念自 80 年代末以来在应用语言学和二语教学领域迅速发展。行动研究是一种教师主导的课堂研究方法,主要指教师针对教学中遇到的问题开展调查研究,制定解决问题的行动方案,在实施过程中不断反思和调整行动方案,收集数据,分析和评价效果,改进教学实践,从而使教学过程、反思意识、教学水平和研究能力得到和谐发展和共同提高。

行动研究对教师的吸引力在于它可以让教师更仔细地观察令人困惑的课堂问题,或深入研究教学困境,鼓励一线教师以与理想存在差距的现实教学情形为对象进行干预,从而带来改变,甚至实现更好的实践效果。行动研究是教师在教学和科研之间建起的一座桥梁,将行动研究运用于外语教学和研究具有重要的理论与实践意义。

7.1.2 基本特征

行动研究包括教学和数据收集的过程,其基本特征如下:

(1) 教师评估和反思自己的教学,目的在于不断改进教学实践,强调自我反思;

(2) 具有小规模、情境化、地方性等特点,参与者在特定语境如学校或课堂中确定并调查教学问题;

(3) 具有参与性、实用性、包容性等特点,因为参与者群体有机会在实践共同体中合作探究当前关注的问题;

(4) 与作为教学正常组成部分的直觉思维不同,因为实践中的变化将基于系统地收集和分析数据;

(5) 基于民主原则,将课程实践变化的权力交给教师与学习者,即赋权于教师与学习者;

(6) 教学过程的周期性或循环性;

(7) 行动研究的主体是教师,对象是日常教学中遇到的问题;

(8) 行动研究强调行动过程与研究过程的结合,边行动边研究,边研究边行动;把研究结果应用于教学实践本身就是研究过程不可分割的一部分。

7.1.3 研究环节与操作流程

行动研究是由计划、行动、观察和反思四个环节组成的螺旋式发展过程，如图 7.1 所示。

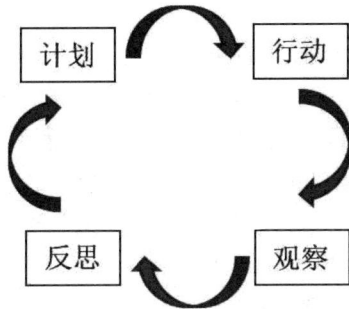

图7.1　行动研究的四个环节

作为一种反思性探究活动，其每一环节的展开都需要不断的反思，在聚焦问题、计划、观察、反思、再计划、再观察、再反思的循环往复过程中达到行动研究的目标。

（1）计划环节

计划是为了改进现状，它始于解决问题的需要和设想。因此，教师（即研究者）在这一环节首先需要确定研究焦点与具体研究问题，并制定相应的行动计划，以便在研究语境中的某个特定领域取得改进。这是一个前瞻性的阶段，教师需要考虑以下问题：1）在教学现实及其限制条件下，什么样的调查是可能的？2）可能会取得哪些潜在的改进？这一环节一般包括一个"总体计划"和为每一个步骤制定的具体行动计划。随着认识的不断深入或依据实际情况的变化，教师可以对总体计划和具体行动计划做出修改。

（2）行动环节

第一环节的计划是经过深思熟虑的，其中包括针对具体教学情境进行目的性干预，并在确定的时间段内付诸实施。对计划进行了制定与完善之后，下一步就是采取行动。行动环节的具体措施应该取决于具体的研究问题与研究情境。教师有目的地按计划进行实践，在行动过程中也可以根据其他参与者的监督观察和评价建议进行不断的修正和调整。

（3）观察环节

这一环节需要系统地观察行动的效果，并记录相关人员的背景信息、行动和观点。这实际上是一个数据收集阶段，教师可以使用"开放的眼光"和

"开放的思维"工具来收集关于正在发生的事情的信息。观察并不是一个独立的环节，而是对行动全过程、结果、背景以及行动者特点的观察。观察既可以是行动者本人借助各种有效手段对本人行动的记录观察，也可以是其他人的观察。

（4）反思环节

为了弄清楚发生了什么，并更好地理解所探讨的问题，教师需要反思、评估和描述行动的效果，基于效果评价决定是否进行下一轮行动研究，以便进一步改善教学效果，或者将行动研究作为专业持续发展的一部分与他人分享研究的"故事"。反思是第一个螺旋圈的终结，又是过渡到另一个螺旋圈的中介。在反思环节中，教师需要在对观察到、感受到的与制定计划、实施计划有关的各种现象加以归纳整理的基础上，对行动的全过程和结果作出判断评价，并为下阶段的计划提供修正意见。

"对行动的反思"（reflection-on-action）和"在行动中反思"（reflection-in-action）是两种常见的反思性概念。前者发生在讲课前后，比如教师在课前准备教学计划阶段和课后估测教学效果阶段进行的反思；而后者是教师在实际教学过程中遇到问题时进行的即时反思，譬如，教师实时监控自己的上课表现、课堂上出现突发情况时及时调整教学方案。虽然这两种反思存在概念性差异，但其宗旨相同，即教师研究解决教学实践中出现的问题或困惑以提高教学有效性，其内容除了对自身知识、行为的思考外，还包含对教学的社会、道德以及政治等因素的思考。需要强调的是，能帮助教师应对日常教学实践中挑战的是教师自己在教学中及教学前后的反思，而不是过度依赖专家的指导。因此，教师既是教学者又是反思者和研究者。

虽然上述"计划—行动—观察—反思"螺旋式发展模型遭到了一些学者的批评，被认为过于固定和僵化，掩盖了行动研究的复杂性和多变性，但这一模型清晰地展示了行动研究中的关键性环节。不同的教师可以在其基础上，根据实际需要灵活调整操作步骤，大胆尝试新的行动策略，以达到改善教学实践的最佳效果。

7.1.4 相关误解

有人认为，行动研究的结果难以推广至其他群体，因此其意义有限。还有人认为，行动研究没有科学严谨的取样程序，无法严格控制干扰变量，对数据的处理和分析比较简单，因而缺乏正规性等。需要指出的是，这些都是对行动研究的误解，因为此类研究是以解决教师遇到的实际教学问题为出发点，并不关注研究结果的可推广性。而且，用实验研究的特点来衡量行动研究的正规性是十分不妥的。一线教师不应盲目追求所谓的"正规性"，而应该结合自己的教学实践，积极开展有利于提升教学效果的应用性研究。

7.2 扎根理论

7.2.1 基本概念

扎根理论是社会科学研究的一种方法论路径，最初由美国学者巴尼·格拉泽（Barney Glaser）和安塞姆·斯特劳斯（Anselm Strauss）于 1967 年在其著作《发现扎根理论：质性研究的策略》（*The Discovery of Grounded Theory: Strategies for Qualitative Research*）中提出，被誉为 20 世纪末应用最为广泛的质性研究解释框架，旨在揭示研究现象背后的基本社会过程。由于在所持哲学观、是否采用质性研究方法、研究者形象及理论形式等方面存在分歧，扎根理论主要包括三个版本：经典扎根理论、程序化扎根理论及建构主义扎根理论。

7.2.2 基本思路

总体上看，扎根理论的基本思路为：

（1）强调从资料中产生理论，认为只有通过对资料的深入分析，才能逐步形成理论框架，是一个从下往上的归纳过程；

（2）强调研究者对理论保持高度敏感，不论是在设计阶段，还是在收集和分析资料的时候，研究者都应该对前人的理论以及资料中呈现的理论保持敏感，注意捕捉新的建构理论的线索；

（3）扎根理论的主要分析思路是比较，在资料和资料之间、理论和理论之间进行对比，然后根据资料与理论之间的关系提炼出有关的类属及其属性；

（4）在对资料进行分析时，研究者可以用资料中初步生成的理论指导下一步的资料收集和分析工作，如选择资料、设码、建立编码和归档系统等；

（5）灵活使用文献，为资料分析提供新的概念和理论框架，但同时也要注意不要过多使用前人的理论；

（6）扎根理论对理论的检核与评价主要有以下四条标准：概念必须来源于原始资料，理论建立起来以后应该随时回到原始资料；理论中的概念本身应该得到充分的发展，重视概念的密集；理论中的每一个概念应该与其他概念之间具有系统的联系，形成一个统一的、具有内在联系的整体；由成套概念联系起来的理论应该具有较强的运用价值、广阔的适用范围和较强的解释力。

7.2.3 操作特征

扎根理论运用的基本过程包括概念抽象、范畴提取、核心范畴逻辑关系构建和理论形式与运用。扎根理论模式的运用能够帮助研究者不带成见地进行理论上的突破与更新，使质性研究变得更加严谨，更具可操作性，其精髓体现在其操作层面：

（1）研究设计阶段

该阶段主要包括以下三个步骤：

1) 选择研究领域及方向，考虑所要探索的领域是否适合使用扎根理论；

2) 进行文献回顾，了解已有研究成果，增加理论敏感度，为资料分析时的编码过程做准备；

3) 进行理论导向型的研究对象选择，所选研究对象随意性较小，要有助于建构理论。

（2）资料收集阶段

扎根理论模式的资料收集有以下基本特征：从实际情况入手，以开放的心态完成，不带有既定观点和成见。资料收集方法主要包括观察、访谈、问卷和文档整理等。值得一提的是，量化手段也可以使用到数据收集中，如统计学分析和抽样对比。单纯使用质性方法有可能限制研究资料产生理论的潜力，量化研究手段可以揭示更多隐藏在研究资料中的信息。由于该模式会根据研究需要选择新的研究对象，所以会出现反复收集资料的情况。在收集过程中要满足"理论饱和"（theoretical saturation）的标准，即新的资料收集过程已经不能为理论的建构提供新的概念。

（3）资料分析阶段

以扎根理论研究模式进行资料分析的精髓是三级编码，即开放式编码（open coding）、主轴式编码（axial coding）和选择式编码（selective coding）。三级编码是逐层推进的关系，后一级以前一级为基础。开放式编码要求研究者在仔细研究资料的基础上，对资料进行编码，生成最底层的研究概念。在该阶段研究者可以注重以下三个方面的问题：现象在何种情况下出现？现象中体现何种情感因素？现象产生何种结果？主轴式编码不能被简单地视为对开放式编码的总结和提升，其有两大任务：对开放式编码阶段获得的概念进行分类，生成更大的概念类别；建立概念类别之间的相互关系。选择式编码的任务在于找到核心类别（core category），并建立它与其他类别之间的关系。

（4）理论建构阶段

扎根理论所要建立的理论包括三个要点：概念类别、逻辑关系和解释能力。对理论框架进行清晰的描述须遵守以下三个原则：注重抽象性、有调整的余地、修补理论缺陷。为提高理论的抽象性，可以采用有"取"有"舍"和寻找共性的方法。任何理论都不可能完美，扎根理论模式导出的理论也受到时间、精力、资金等限制，因此应明确指出理论框架还有哪些不足之处，是由何种原因造成的。在修补理论缺陷时，研究者可以采用理论抽样的方法，这种带有明确指向性的资料二次收集是扎根理论研究的一个突出特征。

（5）理论检验与应用阶段

扎根理论研究对理论的任何追求都是以实际情况为基础的，研究者提出的理论必须经得起实践的检验，实际情况是检验理论成功与否的最高标准。在满足这个最高标准的情况下，研究者还可以从专业性、一致性和准确性三个角度对所建构的理论进行全面和严格的检验。建构理论的最终目的是应用。一般来说，应用扎根理论模式来建构理论要经过以下几步：可信性评估、相关性分析、适度调整及具体应用。

7.2.4 局限性及应对

扎根理论研究模式的局限性主要体现在以下两个方面：由于两位创始人的观点不同，在概念辨析和操作规程等细节上，不同版本的扎根理论之间存在着较大差异，导致人们对于扎根理论的应用相当混乱，会对刚接触该模式的人造成困扰。该模式要求研究人员具备较高的理论素养和专业水平，不太适合初级研究人员使用，这在一定程度上限制了该研究模式的推广。目前很多学者对扎根理论的共同界定为：在象征互动论的框架下来研究社会互动和社会过程的一种方法论，它并不是一个普适的质性研究框架，而是关注特定问题的特定研究学派在面对外部冲击时努力构筑的方法论堡垒。研究者应基于自身的研究领域和研究问题，在考虑理论建构的问题时采取开放、灵活的态度，而不是一味地学习和套用扎根理论。此外，如果初学者想提高理论敏感性，扎根理论的运用也是一种可供选择的方法和手段，在丰富的社会实践和对原始数据进行反复编码和比较中提升研究能力。

课堂讨论

1. 阅读下列摘要（Khairallah & Adra, 2022）并回答问题：该行动研究的摘要部分与常见的实证研究摘要在结构上有何差异？该摘要是否包含了所有必要信息？

Abstract

This classroom-based action research (CBAR) corroborated our belief in the valuable role rubrics play in a tertiary L2 writing context where English is the medium of instruction. The three-stage CBAR involved ongoing discussions between us, two writing teacher-researchers, as we adapted our teaching and assessment strategies to explore the potential of rubrics as formative tools. This study confirmed the proactive role rubrics could play in teaching writing and promoting successful partnerships between teachers and students during the assessment process. The multifaceted function of rubrics as driver of change in practitioners' approaches to teaching and assessing writing as well as a tool that enables students to take ownership of the different stages of their writing was a major finding of our study.

2. 阅读下列节选内容（Khairallah & Adra, 2022）并回答问题：
   (1) 研究者是如何确定研究焦点的？
   (2) 研究者进行行动研究的动机源自哪些方面？

Hallway discussions about the potential of rubrics

The idea of this study began during a hallway conversation between us, two colleagues teaching on the same academic writing course, during which we exchanged ideas about the potential value of writing rubrics as assessment tools. This casual conversation developed into regular discussions that drew not only from readings about theoretical positions on assessment but also reflections on in-class practices that questioned the alignment between such positions and our experiences as teachers of writing.

Based on our beliefs that rubrics can be used in the classroom as an integral aspect of the way we teach and assess our students' writing, we embarked on a classroom-based action research (CBAR). We believed that a CBAR would help us explore the ways rubrics could provide opportunities for our students to develop as writers as well as help us capitalize on the many affordances of employing them. Rubrics that are traditionally used during feedback provision as a means of grade justification can also be used during the earlier stages of writing process. We contemplated that rubrics used solely in the assessment of learning might not always be comprehensible to students who faced challenges in understanding the different categories that formulate the rubric grading criteria.

Exchanges with colleagues further consolidated our idea of the CBAR. During grade corroboration sessions following major written assignments, we began to realize that rubrics were not used to their full formative assessment potential, but were generally being restricted to their summative function. In fact, the way our colleagues used rubrics varied, depending on their approaches to not only assessing but also teaching writing. Most of our colleagues were reluctant to experiment with active rubric use due to their concern that such use might take time away from "actual" teaching. To them, the formative assessment process was a seemingly time-consuming one when they would be overwhelmed with corrections.

It became clear to us that rubrics use during all stages of assessment practices did not fully represent tools that both teachers and students could use for self-evaluation, the former on their teaching practices and the latter on their writing progress, thus contradicting recommendations from literature on self-evaluation and writing (Assessment Reform Group, 2002; Becker, 2016; Black et al., 2004; Borg & Alshumaimeri, 2019). We assumed that if our students had little or no experience with self-assessment, they would find rubric use overwhelming. In other words, students who could not make meaning of the rubric criteria would not be able to use the rubric in a meaningful way (Becker, 2016; Broad, 2003; Jonsson, 2014). The absence of student voice in the evaluation process indicated that rubrics were being restricted to teacher use only and were inaccessible to students, who according to the literature, should be considered as stakeholders in the assessment of writing process (Turley & Gallagher, 2008).

In our context, academic writing courses are built around strategies that promote goal alignment and rubrics are mainly used as summative tools during grade corroboration sessions following major written assignments. The need to achieve assessment standardization in our writing program is highlighted as an important goal and we are expected to demonstrate detailed and transparent assessment practices to achieve this standardization, which is of vital importance for curriculum alignment. Such attempts at standardization have often left us, as writing teachers, little room to reflect on our assessment practices, particularly when we are inundated with corrections.

3. 阅读下列节选内容（Khairallah & Adra, 2022）并回答问题：
   (1) 除了行动研究法，还可以采取哪些研究方法来探究以下研究问题？
   (2) 根据文章的研究问题，简要评价其数据收集设计是否合理、完整。除下列三种数据收集工具外，你还可以想到哪些适用于行动研究的数据收集方式？

Research questions

This CBAR answered the following research questions:

- Research question 1: How did the discussions of and modifications to rubric criteria impact our strategies of teaching and assessing writing?
- Research question 2: How did the change in our practice as a result of these discussions influence student involvement in the writing process?
- Research question 3: In what ways did our ongoing reflections during the different stages of the CBAR change our approach to teaching and assessing writing?

Data collection tools

In order to capture the impact of the changes made to the rubrics accompanying the differing writing assignment and the adaptations that we made to our teaching strategies, three types of data were collected:

- Observations of student involvement in classroom interactions: These interactions included group-work, brainstorming, student discussions within dyads and triads, whole-class discussions, and peer and self-assessment activities. Observations were documented after each class in the form of notes and discussed periodically during our reflection sessions. This was ongoing across the three stages of the CBAR.

- Reports on the changes made to the rubrics: In response to our reflection sessions, we progressively modified the rubrics to become more student-centered. The rubric changes were incorporated into classroom practices following each action research cycle. This occurred in between the different stages.
- Focus-group discussions: Interviews were conducted with students who were divided into four focus groups after Stage Three of the CBAR. Each focus group interview was recorded and the transcriptions were coded and emergent themes analysed.

4. 该文章共包含三个完整的行动研究周期。阅读下列节选内容（Khairallah & Adra, 2022），尝试补充完整三个周期对应的计划、行动、观察与反思环节，然后将自己补充的方案与原文内容进行对比，指出各自的优势与不足之处。

Stages of the study

Our CBAR consisted of three stages followed by focus group discussions. The CBAR involved all the participants of the study, us, the two teacher-researchers and our students of the three sections where the CBAR took place. The three stages were followed by focus group interviews that included groups of 4–5 students who all gave their consent to take part in the interviews. In the First Stage, we introduced the rubrics as standard assessment references. Most of the students expressed their confusion about rubric criteria and their allotted grades. In the Second Stage, we rewrote the criteria and rearranged the rating scales, with our students showing more involvement in self-assessment compared to the First Stage. In the Third Stage, the students collaborated with their peers to negotiate rubric criteria; they began to make more informed decisions in the writing process with the support of their peers. During the Focus Group Interviews, the students articulated their thoughts on the use of rubrics and the benefits that such use brought to them.

1 First stage: Introducing the rubric criteria

…

2 Reflections on the first stage: Rationale behind our CBAR

…

5. 阅读下列节选内容（Khairallah & Adra, 2022）并回答问题：
   (1) 除了以下讨论部分列出的写作评价量规的三个角色外，你还能发现它有哪些重要作用？
   (2) 通过本文的研究，你认为行动研究法有何优势？

Discussion

… Findings from our CBAR answered the three research questions that guided this study … In our experience, a rubric served a threefold purpose: an impetus for effective teaching practices, a catalyst for empowering students in the assessment process, and a transformative tool in the ways teachers of writing approach assessment.

1 Rubrics as an impetus for effective teaching practices

Our ongoing reflections during the CBAR made us realize that negotiation of rubric criteria with students had a positive impact on teacher-student interaction. It also gave us insight into ways teachers can allow student engagement in assessment. Research shows that rubrics become more effective when teachers openly discuss criteria with students (Crockett & Jackson, 2018). In fact, we became more cognizant of strategies that may help learners regulate learning, assess their own work, and generate their own feedback.

…

2 Rubrics as a catalyst for empowering students in the assessment process

In order to create a classroom atmosphere of inquiry, which was an integral aspect of our CBAR, we envisioned that the negotiation of the rubric criteria, by becoming student-centered, would create affordances for students to develop self-regulatory habits in writing. The types of writing process strategies that we designed in the CBAR were directly linked to the changes that were made to the rubrics. When we modified the rubric criteria with the help of the students, we gave them an opportunity to acquire and develop skills that would help them actively engage in the writing process and negotiate the corresponding assessment criteria.

…

3 *Rubrics as a transformative tool in the ways teachers of writing approach assessment*

…

Our CBAR allowed us to solidify what we originally thought was the intricate connection between formative assessments and self-regulated learning and how these should co-exist as learners take ownership of their own learning. During the different stages of our CBAR we witnessed several opportunities where we observed our students engaging in the self-assessment process by building on feedback they generated and received (Tay, 2015). Self-regulation refers to the ways proactive learners set goals, monitor their work, and adapt their strategies depending upon the task (Nicol & Macfarlane-Dick, 2006). Self-regulatory tasks need to be embedded in the teaching process and not just presented in the final assessment stages (Borg & Alshumaimeri, 2019; Khairallah, Fleonova & Nicolas, 2020; Oxford & Amerstorfer, 2018).

6. 阅读下列摘要（Valmori & De Costa, 2016）。该研究采用扎根理论方法对收集到的半结构式访谈数据进行了系统性分析。阐述该摘要包括哪些方面的内容，并评价该摘要是否完整和清晰。

Abstract

Building on Markus and Nurius's (1986) possible selves theory to investigate language teachers' engagement in professional development, this case study examines how nine Italian school foreign language (FL) teachers in two types of high schools (college preparation and vocational schools) experienced and responded to changes in their FL proficiency. Interview data, analyzed with a grounded theory approach, showed that when dealing with professional development, the FL teachers had to decide whether to (1) engage in professional development activities, and (2) maintain their engagement with or without a supportive community. Their decisions and engagement were influenced by the strength of the dissonance between the perception of their actual and possible L2 selves. The findings have implications for designing in-service professional development courses that take into consideration teachers' needs in relation to their school environments as FL teachers navigate the life-long experience of learning and maintaining a foreign language.

7. 阅读下列节选内容（Valmori & De Costa, 2016）并回答问题：
   (1) 受试的选取环境是否适合本研究的目的？
   (2) 该研究采用了什么抽样方法来选取访谈对象？你如何评价该抽样方法？

The context

As noted, this study is situated in the Italian high school system, which comprises three types of high schools: college preparation, technical, and vocational. They differ from each other in terms of final language learning goals and levels, types of students, and teaching approaches. The high school system allows students to study a limited range of foreign languages, which are unevenly distributed: 97.8% of students study English, 26.7% French, 7.5% Spanish, and 5.8% German (Eurydice and Policy Support, 2012). The Italian Ministry of Education has set the final proficiency level for college preparation schools as B2+/C1 (MIUR, 2005) on the Common European Framework of Reference for Languages (CEFR), and B2 for technical and vocational schools (INDIRE, 2010). Students in college preparation schools are generally more academically inclined and tend to continue their studies after graduation. Learning one or more foreign languages, in particular English, is for them part of a well-rounded education. Students in technical schools receive in-depth instruction in one specific area (e.g., chemistry, mechanics, business) and, depending on their future goals, they might see learning a foreign language as peripheral to their education. Students in vocational schools are more likely to take practical subjects and receive training designed to prepare them for vocations such as becoming a plumber, mechanic, and electrician. They often have variable academic performances and might have experienced behavioral issues during their previous schooling, thereby making language learning a challenging endeavor for them. In sum, the three school environments present teachers with very different challenges and may require different teaching approaches.

Participants

Participants were nine Italian FL high school teachers (eight female and one male) who volunteered by answering an online invitation initially sent to former colleagues of the first author. The invitation spread and snowballed, and, as a result, the nine teacher participants came from different high schools in two towns in northern Italy. With this inevitable convenience sampling, it would be fair to assume that our participants were teachers interested in the topic of professional development. To ensure participants' confidentiality, pseudonyms are used throughout this paper. Among the nine teachers, five had worked in different types of schools, one (John) had only worked in vocational schools and three (Lucy, Betty and Gloria) had worked only in college preparation schools. At the time of the interviews, four teachers were working in vocational schools, four in a college preparation school, and one had classes in both types of schools. Table 1 summarizes the main information about the participants.

Table 1
Participants' information.

Teacher	Years taught	Language taught	Current type of school
1. Suzy	30	English	College preparation school
2. Gloria	30	English	College preparation school
3. Betty	27	English	College preparation school
4. Lucy	13	Spanish	College preparation school
5. Christy	15	English	Vocational school and College prep.
6. John	26	English	Vocational school
7. Tania	13	English	Vocational school
8. Stephanie	12	English	Vocational school
9. Julie	6	French	Vocational school

8. 阅读下列节选内容（Valmori & De Costa, 2016），简述数据收集的步骤，评价采用半结构式访谈收集数据是否合适，并给出理由。

Material and Procedures

The data for this study are comprised of nine interviews with the nine Italian FL high school teachers. The interviews, face to face (eight) and on Skype (one), took place in June 2013 and were recorded, transcribed, and translated from Italian into English. Participants' informed consent was obtained with a consent form given in person or sent by email. Even though our focus was on the teachers' trajectories, our data collection process, which constituted one interview with each teacher, was not longitudinal in nature. Although the nine teachers in this study were keen to talk about their proficiency and professional development experiences, the everyday situation of K-12 teachers who are often overworked and undersupported, made it hard to have further interviews after the end of the school year. Further, and in the spirit of conducting ethical research (De Costa, 2016) and guided by Holliday's (2015) exhortation to (1) only collect data which address the research questions, and (2) be cognizant of the time allocated to interviews, we elected to conduct only one interview.

Appendix

Questions for the semi-structured interview:

(1) What constitutes foreign language proficiency for you?

(2) What is your experience as a learner of the target language? (in terms of years, institutions, outside classroom activities, motivations, etc.)

(3) What were your goals as a learner?

(4) What is your experience as a teacher of the target language?

(5) What are your goals as a foreign language teacher?

(6) How important is it for you to achieve target language proficiency? And for your job? For your institution? And for your students?

(7) How much effort are you willing to put into pursuing the maintenance of your language proficiency?

(8) What activities do you think are useful/available to maintain your proficiency?

(9) Do you think your proficiency is affected by teaching? If yes, how?

(10) Do you think teaching affects/ed your proficiency? If yes, how?

(11) In your opinion, what are the main challenges in teaching a foreign language?

9. 阅读下列节选内容（Valmori & De Costa, 2016），简要分析作者是如何将扎根理论运用到该研究的，并评价数据分析方法是否恰当。

Applying Grounded Theory

Grounded theory (Strauss & Corbin, 1998) is a systematic inductive approach to inquiry which is iterative, comparative, and interactive (Charmaz, 2011). The interactive essence of this method requires the researcher to move through comparative levels of analysis of the data to develop codes, construct abstract categories that fit the data, and offer a conceptual analysis of them (Charmaz, 2006). Within a constructivist framework in which realities are multiple and the researcher is part of what is researched, data are co-constructed through the interaction between the researcher and the participants. In this study, grounded theory is used to analyze semi-structured interviews. In conceptualizing the research interview not just as a tool, but as a social practice (Talmy, 2010), the discourse between the interviewer and the interviewee is situated and historically and socially co-constructed. In other words, the research interview is a site for investigation itself, where the "voice" of the interlocutors is situationally contingent, and both the "what" (the content) and the "how" (the linguistic and interactional resources used) collaboratively generate the data. This was certainly the case in our study given that the first author, who conducted the interview, was herself a former foreign language teacher in an Italian high school. Thus, from this perspective, not only the data but also their analyses were collaboratively produced (Charmaz, 2006; Talmy, 2010) and "generalizations remain partial, conditional, and situated" (Charmaz, 2011, p. 366). Crucially, such a perspective informed our understanding of teacher proficiency as mediated on a local level by teachers within school contexts.

The grounded theory approach has been adopted in recent research (e.g., Mercer, 2011; Mushayikwa & Lubben, 2009; Watze, 2007) to investigate FL teachers' concerns and experiences. In his longitudinal study on how nine novice high school FL teachers in the U.S. enhanced their pedagogical knowledge in the first two years of teaching, Watze (2007) explained that instead of studying individual participants, grounded theory analytical procedures "facilitated consideration of the data as a single unit and helped to develop an explanatory theoretical framework across participants" (p. 68). By using a grounded theory approach, our aim is therefore to go beyond single cases, and to consider common (or diverging) emergent trajectories participants took within the broader context. With this intent, the FL teachers in this study articulated issues surrounding proficiency and challenges in maintaining their proficiency during interviews. A comparative and interactive analysis of our interview data (axial coding) enabled us to enhance our understanding of the process of teachers' engagement in maintaining their proficiency, and to build a proposed model of the phenomenon. Within this theory-building framework, and aligned with Bryant (2013), we conceptualize theory as an interpretation of an underlying structure in the data that does not claim to be a criterion of truth, but rather envisage the possibility of changes in practice. In this view, the proposed model aims to advance our understanding of the role of the school environment in FL teachers' engagement in development.

Data Analysis

Building on Strauss and Corbin (1998), we first analyzed the data with an open coding system followed by an axial coding system. Through recursive readings, we coded the interview data by circling and highlighting the participants' words and phrases related to recurrent topics that emerged. Subsequently, we identified the central phenomenon (the axis) and the different properties and dimensions around it, by making links between the codes to clarify the relations with the phenomenon (its causes and consequences, its context, and the strategies of those who are involved). The phenomenon is FL teachers' change in proficiency over time, and the related categories are challenges encountered in maintaining proficiency, activities to maintain proficiency, and the relationship between FL proficiency and FL teaching.

Within each category different patterns emerged: In particular, two teachers, Lucy and John, often had distant points of view about the challenges and changes they experienced in their proficiency due to their respective pedagogical contexts (the dimensions around the phenomenon). For example, while Lucy found professional development activities of teachers' organizations very useful, John found them useless for his own needs and aims. On the other hand, the other teachers, especially Tania, Stephanie, Christy, and Julie, had more nuanced positions regarding the differences between the two types of schools. This could be due to the fact that the latter were vocational-school teachers with experience in teaching at other types of schools, while Lucy and John had only taught in one type of school (college preparation school and vocational school, respectively). Lucy and John's long experience in a single school environment made their views representative of the two ends of the continuum of Italian high-school education system. In the interest of space, while the voices of all nine teachers are intertwined to construct a model of teacher engagement in L2 development, the longer quotations (excerpts) chosen for this study are taken mainly from Lucy's and John's interviews to give a clearer sense of how teachers' school environments can affect their FL proficiency and their engagement in activities to maintain it.

10. 阅读下列节选内容（Valmori & De Costa, 2016）并评价研究发现是否充分回答了研究问题。

Research questions

Our study was guided by the following research questions:

(1) How do foreign language teachers think their foreign language proficiency changes during the course of their teaching career?

(2) How can foreign language teachers' perceived proficiency shape their teaching?

Findings

In this section, we first report the teachers' perceptions of how their FL proficiency changed and was challenged in their respective teaching contexts (research question 1). Next, we discuss how the teachers' school environment might have influenced their commitment to maintaining their proficiency, a topic which emerged from the data and evolved as a sub-question. In particular, the teacher participants talked about what they perceived to be useful activities to develop proficiency during their career according to the needs of their school environments. Finally, we report the teachers' reflections on the relationship between FL proficiency and FL teaching (research question 2).

1) Changes in FL teachers' proficiency in different school environments

Most of the interviewees set high proficiency standards for themselves and stated that their goal as learners was to become like a native speaker. Their identification of native-likeness as a goal for their ideal self (Dörnyei, 2005; Kubanyiova, 2009) further suggested that the teacher participants were driven by life-long learning and interested in engaging in activities to maintain proficiency. All nine teachers acknowledged that their FL proficiency was good (or very good) at graduation, but once they started teaching, they nevertheless needed to develop a deeper understanding of the mechanical, pragmatic, and semantic aspects of the language together with other strategic skills related to their types of school and students. For example, Christy admitted that she "knew [she was] saying it right, but [she] couldn't explain the rule" and she "had to study the grammar [she] taught".

Lucy also said that she had to reflect on associations of words, synonyms and antonyms. She did not think about language in that way before, but she realized that "these things help learners to organize their information." Moreover, coming from a literature background, they all had a rich vocabulary, but it fell short of the lexicon for the specific purposes they were supposed to teach in the technical and vocational schools. For example, Stephanie reported "learning words like 'invoice', 'promissory notes' or other specific business terms by teaching them".

The two excerpts below show how teaching in different school settings affected teachers' proficiency in somewhat opposite directions. In Excerpt 1 Lucy, who after graduation spent years working abroad, reports how teaching in a college preparation school challenged her already high proficiency in Spanish. In contrast, Excerpt 2 shows how John, who never lived abroad and started teaching upon graduation, experienced a different type of challenge in teaching English for specific purposes in vocational schools.

...

2) Activities to maintain proficiency: different needs in different school environments

The interviewees' concern about maintaining and developing their proficiency can be summarized by Tania's comment: "If you don't do anything, you'll lose it." The teachers listed several types of activities available to develop their FL proficiency. These activities included using the Internet, watching TV and movies in the FL, newsletters by teachers' organizations, books, summer and school trips abroad, and a nationwide FL teachers' organization, Language and New Didactics (LEND), which organized professional development activities for the different languages. When discussing the activities, however, the divide between the teachers in college preparation schools and the ones in vocational schools became increasingly evident. In Excerpt 3 Lucy paints an enthusiastic picture of a cohesive network of Spanish teachers who collaborate and share knowledge and meaningful experiences. In contrast, Excerpt 4 shows John's disappointment about the activities offered by the English section of the professional-development group LEND, and about his unsuccessful attempts over the years to set up meaningful professional development activities in his school.

...

3) Relationship between teachers' FL proficiency and FL teaching

All teachers acknowledged that FL proficiency was a precondition for their job. This common ground is summarized by Lucy's statement: "If I don't know the language what am I doing there? I mean … it is obvious." As noted by Stephanie, her FL proficiency is "a matter of personal pride", "gives [her] confidence and authority", and "is a warranty for the students". Nevertheless, some teachers acknowledged having to come to terms with their insecurities about their FL proficiency. Suzy, for example, at a college preparation school, admitted that in class she did not speak in the FL the whole time. Experience helped her to overcome her fear of making mistakes and also to "adopt methodologies that enabled [her] not to speak for the whole hour … as one goes with what one feels stronger with". Stephanie encountered a similar experience and explained that at first she did not speak English in class because of her "immaturity" and inexperience, as she thought it was not natural to speak to students in the target language when they knew she was Italian. She reported "getting there little by little" by gaining authority and overcoming her sense of being an impostor. She also added that speaking well in the target language in the classroom served as a warning for the students that they could not get away with being lazy and speaking their L1 in class. Excerpts 5 and 6 demonstrate how both Lucy and John, in their respective school contexts, conceived FL use in class as the foundation of their teaching practices and a crucial point for their students' learning process.

…

课外练习

1. 新时代背景下，英语课程被赋予了新特征和新使命。英语教学应该服务于国家发展战略，培养学生讲好中国故事的能力。以"如何实现高中英语阅读教学与讲好中国故事能力培养的融合"为教学案例，从"计划—行动—观察—反思"的螺旋式发展模型出发，设计一项阅读行动研究方案。

2. 学习动机减退是二语/外语学习过程中常见的现象。设计合理的实验手段来进行小规模的数据收集，并采用扎根理论方法进行初步分析，归纳出导致学习动机减退的主要因素，最后通过分析这些因素之间的相互联系建立二语学习动机减退的扎根理论模型。

3. 行动研究和扎根理论都是社会科学领域中常用的研究方法，两者虽存在不同，却可结合使用。例如，行动研究的实践过程中可能会产生一些新的现象或问题，这时可以应用扎根理论的方法来深入理解和解释这些现象或问题，并发展出相关的理论。尝试设计一项研究方案，将行动研究与扎根理论结合起来。

拓展阅读

Burns, A. (2010). *Doing action research in English language teaching: A guide for practitioners.* New York & London: Routledge.

Burns, A., & Khalifa, H. (Eds.). (2017). *Second language assessment and action research.* Cambridge: Cambridge University Press.

Hadley, G. (2017). *Grounded Theory in applied linguistics research: A practical guide.* New York: Routledge.

第8单元
问卷调查法

学习目标

- 了解问卷调查法的类别和实施
- 学习问卷调查法在语言学研究中的具体应用以及论文写作
- 在具体研究场景中设计问卷

问卷调查法因操作较为简便，能跨越时空，且能在较短的时间内快速收集到较为深入的材料，因此逐渐成为学术研究中最常使用的方法。但很多研究不能从自身研究的目的出发，生硬地使用问卷调查法，表面上似乎采用了科学的研究手段，实际操作过程中耗费大量人力物力，却对研究不能产生实效，直接影响了研究的科学性，降低了研究质量。因此，有必要了解问卷调查法的适用范围，确保对这种方法的使用有度有效，并真正获取到真实的、高质量的研究结果。

8.1 基本概念

问卷调查法是研究人员使用问卷向研究对象收集数据的方法，既可以用于定量研究，也可以用于质性研究。研究人员选择合适的人群作为研究对象，事先设计一系列与研究主题相关的问题，向研究对象发放问卷，要求研究对象如实填写或由研究人员代为填写，按时回收问卷，最后对结果进行整理与分析。

问卷调查法在语言学、心理学、社会学、教育学、新闻学等多学科领域得到广泛应用。语言学研究中的问卷调查法常见于社会语言学这一分支，应用于语言使用状况、语言变异、语言政策与语言规划、双语及多语现象、二语习得、语言教学等的研究中。问卷调查所得的数据不仅能呈现语言发展现状，还能揭示语言与个体、社会之间的联系，为我们了解语言状况、评估语言发展方向、制定语言政策或调整语言教学策略等提供重要参考，兼具理论价值与应用价值。

8.2 分类及实施

依据不同的标准，问卷调查法有不同的分类方式。

（1）根据问卷填写主体的不同，可以分为自填式问卷与代填式/访谈式问卷。1）自填式问卷，由研究对象本人填写。2）代填式/访谈式问卷，由研究人员代为填写。

（2）根据问卷发放形式的不同，可以分为留置问卷、邮寄式问卷、报刊式问卷、面访式问卷、电话访问式问卷与网络访问式问卷。其中，留置问卷、邮寄式问卷、报刊式问卷、网络访问式问卷一般是自填式问卷，而面访式问卷和电话访问式问卷一般是代填式/访谈式问卷。

1）留置问卷：研究人员将问卷当面交付给研究对象并详细说明填写要求，由研究对象自行填写。

2）邮寄式问卷：研究人员将问卷邮寄给研究对象，由研究对象自行填写。

3）报刊式问卷：研究人员将问卷刊登在报刊中，由报刊读者自行选择填写并将问卷反馈给研究人员。

4）面访式问卷：研究人员当面访问研究对象并由研究人员完成问卷填写。

5）电话访问式问卷：研究人员通过电话与研究对象交流，并由研究人员完成问卷填写。

6）网络访问式问卷：研究人员通过网络途径发布问卷，由研究对象自行选择填写并提交给研究人员。

（3）根据问卷调查目的的不同，可以分为主体问卷、辅助问卷与过滤问卷。

1）主体问卷：围绕着调查主题设计，涵盖调查的主要内容，是我们获取语料、完成研究目标的主要信息来源。

2）辅助问卷：在某些情况下，主体问卷无法提供全面的信息，还有一些内容需要从研究对象的家人、朋友、师长等其他行为主体那里获取，此时需要借助辅助问卷，用于收集其他与研究对象相关的必要信息。

3）过滤问卷：有些调查是面向特定人群进行的，在发放主体问卷、辅助问卷前需要严格地筛选接受调查的对象，这一过程叫作"过滤"，用来实现"过滤"目标的问卷即为过滤问卷。研究人员在整理好过滤问卷的结果、找到合适的研究对象后再发放主体问卷和辅助问卷，以完成后续的调查工作。

（4）根据问卷结构的不同，可以分为结构式问卷、半结构式问卷与非结构式问卷。

1）结构式问卷：是经过研究人员周密设计并严格执行的问卷，具有严密的组织结构、逻辑思路与执行标准。研究人员提前拟定好调查时间、地点、方式、具体问题、问卷数量等内容。问卷中的题目要经过精密编排并列出所有可能的答案，在调查过程中也要严格按照问卷要求填写，不能随意变动。结构式问卷高度结构化、标准化、系统化，得到的数据结果易于量化，处理较为简便，适用于较大规模的调查研究。

2）半结构式问卷：同样要求研究人员进行整体统筹设计，但具有一定的灵活性。研究人员可以根据实际情况调整调查方式或问卷中的问题，给予研究对象自由发挥的空间，如回答问题时可以从给定的选项中进行选择，也可以自由回答；在调查过程中可以采用留置问卷，也可以采用电话访问等方式。

3）非结构式问卷：给予研究对象充分的自主性，研究人员无须在调查前精心设计调查计划，也不需要严格执行调查流程，只设置一个调查主题或提纲。在调查过程中，研究人员充分发挥引导作用，让研究对象自由表达个人想法以提供更多、更深入的信息。非结构式问卷通常在访谈中使用，比较适用于个别案例或小基数的质性研究，要求研究人员集中精力、灵活处理、整体把控。

8.3　优点与局限性

作为语言学研究中收集材料的重要方法，问卷调查法具有诸多优点：（1）简便易行，高效方便。研究人员只需要借助纸质问卷或电子版问卷就可以完成第一手材料的收集整理工作。相较于实验法等技术要求高的方法，问卷调查法更为高效简便。（2）多次利用，成本较低。问卷设计好之后可以在研究中多次利用，不需要重新设计，节省成本，省时省力。（3）覆盖广泛，样本量大。因其高效便捷的特点，问卷调查法可以在较短时间内覆盖更多人群，样本规模更大。（4）数据标准，便于处理。大部分问卷都借用李克特量表等提前设计好答案的选项，量化分析较为便捷。

不过，问卷调查法也存在一定的局限性：（1）前期准备工作繁复。研究人员需要在前期投入较多精力，既要统筹整体的问卷调查流程，又要精心设计问题与答案。（2）受主观因素影响较大。问卷调查能取得什么样的成果，很大程度上取决于研究人员的问卷设计，选取哪些问题、如何量化答案、覆盖哪些对象，此类问题的存在对研究人员的能力提出了较高的要求。（3）难以保证答卷质量。很多问卷是自填式问卷，研究对象填写问卷时可能会看错问题或答案、遗漏问题、出现笔误，难以保证答卷质量。

课堂讨论

1. 阅读下列摘要（Gao et al., 2003; Tankó, 2017）并回答问题：
   (1) 在问卷调查法和其他方法相结合的语言研究中，论文摘要部分应该如何提及问卷设计的内容和研究结果？
   (2) 对于以问卷设计为主要工具的研究，论文摘要部分应该如何撰写问卷设计及其结果？

Abstract

This paper presents part of a research project on Chinese college undergraduates' English learning motivation and self-identity changes. Previous studies on Chinese students' English learning motivation mostly followed the classical model (Gardner & Lambert, 1972; Gardner, 1985) and their expansions (Tremblay et al., 1995), which were originated in contexts different from EFL in China. The basic motivation types of Chinese students remained to be inducted from data of the actual context. The purpose of the present research was to achieve such a basic classification. The subjects, obtained from a stratified sampling, were 2,278 undergraduates from 30 Chinese universities in 29 provinces, autonomous regions and municipalities. The instrument was a Likert-scale questionnaire. It included 30 items regarding learning motivation, based essentially on a summary of open responses collected in different provinces. Factor analysis and MANOVA were performed on the data, to explore motivation types and examine the effect of demographic features.

Seven factors resulted from the analysis: 1) intrinsic interest; 2) immediate achievement; 3) learning situation; 4) going abroad; 5) social responsibility; 6) individual development; 7) information medium. Among these factors, "intrinsic interest" was related to "integrative" motivation in the classical model, whereas "immediate achievement", "individual development" and "information medium" all had some features of "instrumental" motivation, but with focus on different goals. "Going abroad" had both "integrative" and "instrumental" elements. "Immediate achievement" and "social responsibility" might be characteristic of the Chinese EFL context.

Results also showed that college major and English proficiency had significant effects on motivations. 1) Major. English majors scored higher than natural and social science majors on "intrinsic interest" and "social responsibility". They also scored higher than social science majors on "individual development" and "information medium". 2) English proficiency. Those who were below the level of Band 4 had higher "immediate achievement" motivation than the Band 6 group; their "intrinsic interest" was lower than both the Band 6 and Band 4 students. Interaction effects were also found between proficiency and major, and between proficiency and students' college year.

Apart from L2 motivation, self-regulation is also increasingly seen as a key variable in L2 learning in many foreign language learning contexts because classroom-centered instructive language teaching might not be able to provide sufficient input for students. Therefore, taking responsibility and regulating the learning processes and positive motivational dispositions are needed for successful achievement. The aim of this article is first to describe English majors' self-regulatory control strategy use by creating students' profiles concerning these variables. The second aim of the study is to investigate the relationship of control strategy use, motivational dispositions, and anxiety/self-efficacy beliefs in a context where academic writing is being taught. To achieve these aims, a standardized paper and pencil questionnaire was designed to collect data on students' control strategies and their dispositions toward L2 motivation as well as their writing anxiety and self-efficacy beliefs. Our sample consisted of 222 first-year English majors at a large Hungarian university located in Budapest. Based on descriptive, correlational, and cluster analytical procedures, our main results indicate that despite the fact that English majors are motivated to enhance their abilities in professional writing, only a third of them seem to possess the ability and willingness to control their writing processes despite the fact that self-regulatory strategy use is linked to an increased level of motivation and self-efficacy and to a decreased level of writing anxiety.

2. 阅读下列节选内容（Tankó, 2017）并回答问题：

    (1) 该研究采用的是什么类别的问卷？问卷问题的回答方式有哪些？在问卷设计中，对具体问题如何回答需要进行说明和解释。结合下面的内容，思考撰写回答问题的说明应该注意什么，说明的文字有什么要求。

(2) 结合下面的问题，与同学一起思考，问卷问题的设计有什么要求？问卷初稿完成后，该怎样对问卷进行初步的评价和测试？

"每个答案有不同的分值，全部 10 个项目的满分为 30 分，分数越高表明受访者学习英语的愿望越强烈（Motivation Intensity Scale）"。

1. I actively think about what I have learned in my English class:

    a) very frequently. (3)

    b) hardly ever. (1)

    c) once in a while. (2)

2. If English were not taught in school, I would:

    a) pick up English in everyday situations (i.e., read English books and newspapers, try to speak it whenever possible, etc.). (2)

    b) not bother learning English at all. (1)

    c) try to obtain lessons in English somewhere else. (3)

3. When I have a problem understanding something we are learning in the English class, I:

    a) immediately ask the teacher for help. (3)

    b) only seek help just before the exam. (2)

    c) just forget about it. (1)

4. When it comes to English homework, I:

    a) put some effort into it, but not as much as I could. (2)

    b) work very carefully, making sure I understand everything. (3)

    c) just skim over it. (1)

5. Considering how I study English, I can honestly say that I:

    a) do just enough work to get along. (2)

    b) will pass on the basis of sheer luck or intelligence because I do very little work. (1)

    c) really try to learn English. (3)

3. 阅读下列节选内容（Gao et al., 2003），结合论文的研究主题（Motivation Types of Chinese College Undergraduates）分析研究者选择问卷调查法开展研究的原因。该问卷包括哪些测量指标？与同学一起讨论该如何确定研究需要的测量指标。

附录：调查问卷的动机类型 *

1 我对英语一见钟情，说不出有什么特别的原因。

2 我开始学英语是因为父母/学校要我学。

3 上大学前学习英语，主要是为了升学考试。

4 上大学前，我学英语的劲头很大程度上取决于我的学习成绩。

5 上大学前，我学英语的劲头很大程度上取决于是否喜欢英语老师。

6 上大学后，我学英语的劲头很大程度上取决于我的学习成绩。

7 上大学后，我学英语的劲头很大程度上取决于是否喜欢英语老师。

8 上大学后，我学英语的劲头很大程度上取决于英语课的质量。

9 上大学后，我学英语的劲头很大程度上取决于所用的教材。

10 上大学后，我学英语的劲头很大程度上取决于是否喜欢我的英语班。

11 我学英语的一个重要目的是获取大学毕业证书。

12 我学英语的直接目的是在出国或国内升学、求职考试中取得好成绩。

13 学好英语对我很重要，因为它是当今社会非常有用的交流工具。

14 学好英语能让我获得成就感。

15 我学习英语，是为了更好地学习其他专业。

16 学好英语，将来我才可能找到一份好工作。

17 我学习英语是为了了解世界各国的经济、科技发展情况。

18 我学习英语是因为对英语国家的人以及他们的文化感兴趣。

19 我对语言学习有特别的爱好。

20 对英语歌曲/电影的爱好使我对英语产生了很大兴趣。

21 我学习英语是因为我喜欢这门语言本身。

22 我学习英语是为了让世界了解中国。

23 对英语文学作品的爱好使我对英语产生了很大兴趣。

24 学好英语，我才能很好地为中国的富强尽力。

25 学好英语，我才能不辜负父母的期望。

26 我学习英语是为了出国寻找更好的受教育和工作机会。

27 我学习英语是为了出国亲身体验英语国家的文化。

28 我学习英语是为了最终移民外国。

29 英语是人生前进路上一块重要的敲门砖。

30 讲一口流利的英语，是教育程度和修养的象征。

4. 阅读下列节选内容（Tankó, 2017），结合文章的研究问题，简要讨论研究者采用问卷调查法来收集数据的好处。同时，结合研究者描述的受访者的情况，判断问卷样本的选取依据和标准。

Research questions

Based on the above literature review, we seek answers to the following main research questions:

a) How can students be characterized concerning their self-regulatory control strategy use in advanced academic writing?

b) What are the relationships among control strategy use, L2 motivation, and anxiety/self-efficacy beliefs?

METHOD

Participants

The participants in the study were 222 English majors from a large university located in Budapest, the capital city of Hungary. We selected English majors to be the focus of our study for several reasons. First, because we were primarily motivated by the difficulties arising from the different Hungarian and Anglo-American rhetorical traditions (cf. Árvay and Tankó, 2004; Tankó and Csizér, 2014), we considered it important to select English majors for this project. They have a relatively high level of English knowledge and, despite the fact that their first language is not English, they have to write English academic texts in their literature, linguistics, history, applied linguistics, or language pedagogy courses. At the university in focus, most of the students enrolled in other majors have to complete writing assignments in their first language, so they did not match our research design. Our goal was to investigate strategy use in relation to writing in English and thereby improve the academic skills courses we offer to our English major students, who are taught in English and expected to use English in their written assignments. Secondly, by selecting and researching a relatively experienced learner group, we think that their experience might be seen as exemplary for other less-experienced language learners. Thirdly, by selecting first-year English majors from a single setting, we minimized the role of possible contextual differences. Fourthly, by selecting English majors, we could ensure that the participants have generally positive attitudes toward the language, having selected it as the focus of their higher education studies.

The gender distribution of the sample indicated that females strongly outnumber males at this institution: 176 participants were female (76.6 per cent) and 56 (23.3 per cent) male. The average age of our participants was 20.2 (the youngest respondent was 18 years old and the oldest was 42). The students typically started learning English between the ages of 7 and 10, and their level of English ranged from B2 to C2, according to the levels specified in the Common European Framework of Reference for Languages (2001). Level B2 corresponds to TOEFL iBT 87–109 and IELTS 5.5–6.5 scores, whereas C1 is the equivalent of TOEFL iBT 110–120 and IELTS 7.0–8.0 scores. All of the students were Hungarian and, therefore, their first language was Hungarian and received on average 10 years of English instruction in classroom settings. In addition to English, the majority of them also reported that they were learning another foreign language. The most popular languages, in addition to their native Hungarian and English, included German, French, Spanish, and Italian. At the time of the data collection, all participants were first-year BA students who were attending the second of two compulsory academic skills courses offered for first-year students. One of the main focuses of these courses was academic writing skills development, with a special focus on argumentative writing, and as part of the second course, students wrote a centrally administered academic writing skills test. One of the tasks in the test was a short argumentative essay intended to measure written argumentation skills. The test was a high-stakes test because its completion was a prerequisite for enrollment into the second-year courses.

5. 阅读下列节选内容（Tankó, 2017），与同学一起评价该论文对问卷问题设计、问卷数据处理等内容的描述与概括是否合理，并探讨是否有更好的呈现方式。

The questionnaire

The questionnaire included 73 previously randomized and piloted items, among which five were open-ended items at the end of the instrument, inquiring about the students' age, gender, and foreign language learning background. All the other items used 5-point rating scales. The items of the questionnaire came from several sources (Ryan, 2005; Bandura, 2006; Tseng et al., 2006), but all the items asking about language learning in general were adapted to writing in English. The final instrument was piloted with 79 students in the autumn term of 2011 (Csizér, 2012) in order to uncover any wording-related problems and to ensure reliability.

(a) Motivated learning behavior (five items) describes how much effort students are willing to invest in language learning. Sample item: *I do my best to learn English as well as possible.*

(b) Ideal L2 self (four items) explores students' vision of their future language use. Sample item: *When I think of my future career, I imagine being able to use English on a near-native level.*

(c) Ought-to L2 self (seven items) asks about external pressures concerning learning English. Sample item: *I feel that I am expected to speak English like a native.*

(d) Language learning experience (four items) inquires about the participants' past experience of learning English. Sample item: *I always liked the tasks we did in English classes at my secondary school.*

(e) International orientation (four items) describes students' attitudes toward the global status of English. Sample item: *It is necessary to learn English because it is an international language.*

(f) Writing anxiety (eight items) includes statements about students' anxiety concerning writing tasks at the university. Sample item: *When I hand in a written assignment, I am anxious about my tutor's opinion.*

(g) Self-efficacy (nine items) measures to what extent students think that they are able to complete their writing assignments self-confidently and with ease. Sample item: *I am sure that I can complete any writing tasks in English.*

(h) Self-regulated behavior (20 items) includes five subscales on how much responsibility students can take for their own learning. All the scales relate to various control measures and are as follows: environmental control (sample item: *I can also concentrate on writing in less than ideal environments.*); satiation control (sample item: *If I get bored during a writing task, I can easily overcome this boredom.*); metacognitive control (sample item: *I can control my attention during long writing tasks.*); emotional control (sample item: *I can overcome my anxiety concerning writing in English.*); and commitment control (sample item: *I have my own strategies to complete my writing related goals.*).

Data collection

The questionnaire data collection took place in March 2013. During regular classes, students were asked by their tutors to fill in the standardized questionnaire, the completion of which took approximately 20 minutes. Participation was voluntary. Apart from the questionnaire data, we collected students' scores on the academic skills test. Following a standardization and a rater-training session, the argumentative essays were double rated by academic skills tutors with an analytic scale consisting of the task achievement (0–6 points), coherence and cohesion (0–3 points), grammar (0–3 points), and vocabulary (0–3 points) subscales. The maximum score that could be awarded was 15 points.

The questionnaire data were computer coded using SPSS 16.0 for Windows. In what follows, after a brief summary of our descriptive findings, we focus on the results of the cluster analysis. Cluster analysis is a data reduction technique without any assumption of an underlying statistical model, which, based on a number of predefined characteristics, aims to classify participants into subgroups on the basis of their (i) similarities to one another and (ii) differences from other members in different subgroups (Csizér and Jamieson, 2013). In our study, the specific aim is to define participant groups with distinct self-regulatory profiles (Kojic-Sabo and Lightbown, 1999; Csizér and Jamieson, 2013).

6. 阅读下列节选内容（Tankó, 2017）并回答问题：
   (1) 与同学一起讨论正文对于 Table 1 和 Table 2 的数据的描述和概括是否合适，并探讨可做改进。
   (2) 作为读者，你还对本研究中未提及的哪些研究内容感兴趣？如果要基于该研究进行论文写作，你会对本研究中问卷设计的实施部分做哪些删减？为什么？
   (3) 简要评述在汇报调查结果时，概括呈现重要内容或者发现应该遵循的标准。

RESULTS

Descriptive analysis of the constructs

Table 1 presents results concerning the mean values of the five self-regulatory strategy use scales. It can be observed that all the values fall within the 3–4 range on a 5-point scale, with commitment control obtaining the lowest mean value. In fact, paired sample t-tests show that the mean value of the commitment control scale is significantly lower than all the other scales. In addition, there is a statistically significant difference between satiation control and emotional control as well as satiation control and metacognitive control (see Table 2 for the details). These results imply a number of issues. First, despite the fact that English majors participated in our study, the mean values of these control strategies do not seem to be particularly high, which is partly surprising because in the academic skills classes, students develop an awareness of the complexity of academic writing and understand that producing a good piece of writing is impossible without the regulation of their work processes. Academic writing presupposes complex management capabilities: each stage of the writing process requires an awareness of both what the writer must do to complete the stage and the ability to make decisions about the most appropriate way to do it. The writer must proceed through the stages reflectively, simultaneously monitoring several stages, and, if necessary, be prepared to abandon linear progression and return to an earlier stage at any point of the composition process because of the recursive nature of the writing process. This finding, however, is not surprising knowing how teacher-centered the Hungarian secondary educational system is, where our experience shows that it seems that pupils are often trained not to be independent but to solely rely on the teacher as the ultimate source of knowledge. Furthermore, based on the guided final school leaving examination tasks, which engage them in primarily knowledge-telling processes, and on the discussions about secondary school English language general writing experiences conducted with first-year students, it can be hypothesized that secondary school pupils write few and simple texts in English in general and, as a result, they do not have to develop and employ control strategies, with the help of which they could become efficient autonomous writers. Given that these first-year university students reported themselves as being unable to assume full control of their work processes, the two academic skills courses seem to have not been enough to change them into skilled control strategy users. This may be due to inefficient instruction or to the students' insufficient understanding of the relevance of academic writing skills training.

Secondly, it seems that self-regulatory control strategies are not used equally across the board: some students use some strategies, while others employ different ones. Metacognitive control strategies seem to be more popular than any of the other strategies, while students seem to struggle with both satiation control and commitment control. The latter fact is unfortunate because writing academic assignments is a demanding undertaking. It is a long process with many tedious and labor-intensive stages for a first-year student who does not understand the need for or lacks the ambition to become a member of the academic discourse community.

Following Swales' (1990) definition of the characteristic features of a discourse community, first-year students are novices who need to be assisted by more expert members in order to start functioning within the academic discourse community — this is to be started already at BA level because a considerable number of these students will become MA and some, later on, Ph.D. students. In the context in focus of this study, the expert members are primarily their academic skills tutors and content course tutors who assign writing tasks. They must spell out the common goals, which are often tacit goals (e.g. the function of a literature essay written without secondary source use versus a literature essay for which source use is compulsory, both typical writing tasks for first-year students in literature seminars), and the means to achieve them (e.g. writing a comparison and contrast essay on a linguistic issue does not only serve as a tool to check the completion of reading assignments on a topic, but it is also conducive to learning). Specifically, both writing skills and content-course tutors should reinforce for students the genres they will have to master and produce as well as their functions and lexico-grammatical characteristics. This concerted effort can help students transfer their skills between the academic skills and content courses and by means of the matching expectations, arrive at a better understanding of what discourse community membership entails. This is critical because understanding what discourse community membership means is a prerequisite for entry and successful functioning. Therefore, students who are consistently exposed to academic genres across courses and who understand the functions of written assignments as participatory mechanisms with typical generic and lexico-grammatical features develop an awareness which renders their writing activities meaningful. This understanding can be hypothesized to help students appreciate the role of satiation and commitment control as well as understand why it is necessary to develop and use strategies linked to both.

Table 1: Descriptive statistics and the Cronbach alpha values

Scale	M	Standard deviation	Cronbach alpha
Metacognitive control	3.72	.85	.74
Emotional control	3.64	.78	.73
Environmental control	3.63	.71	.65
Satiation control	3.49	.80	.80
Commitment control	3.36	.77	.60

Table 2: Significant differences based on paired sample t-tests

Scales	Mean difference	t value	Sig
Satiation control and emotional control	−.14	−2.57	.011
Satiation control and metacognitive control	−.22	−4.36	<.001
Commitment control and satiation control	−.14	−2.39	.018
Commitment control and emotional control	−.28	−5.54	<.001
Commitment control and environmental control	−.27	−3.59	<.001
Commitment control and metacognitive control	−.36	−7.108	<.001

课外练习

1. 随着科学技术的发展，线上教学逐渐成为一种常态的教学模式。设计一份调查问卷，了解外语专业的学生对线上教学的满意度状况以及他们认为的在线教学面临的挑战或存在的问题。

2. 人工智能背景下，有许多网络资源、网络平台、APP 可以辅助外语学习。与同学一起讨论，如果设计一份问卷，调查这些资源辅助外语学习的效果，应该选择什么类别的问卷？是否需要问卷调查法与其他调查方法相结合？具体问卷中，应该确定哪些测量指标，选择的原因是什么？

拓展阅读

Gardner, R. C., Tremblay, P. F., & Masgoret, A. M. (1997). Toward a full model of
  second language learning: An empirical investigation. *Modern Language Journal*,
  81, 344–362.
Gillham, B. (2000). *Developing a questionnaire*. London: Continuum.

第 9 单元
会话分析法

学习目标
- 理解会话分析研究的基本思路
- 熟悉会话分析研究的核心概念
- 掌握会话分析研究的基本方法

由哈维·萨克斯（Harvey Sacks）、伊曼纽尔·谢格洛夫（Emanuel Schegloff）和盖尔·杰斐逊（Gail Jefferson）于20世纪六七十年代提出的会话分析（conversation analysis）是一种归纳式的微观研究方法。尽管会话分析主要采用定性研究手段，越来越多的学者也开始采用定量手段来验证定性研究取得的研究发现。会话分析研究最初发源于萨克斯在20世纪60年代早期的学术探索，即是否能够建立一种有关社会行为乃至整个社会的稳定的、可以复制的、累积性的自然观察科学；如果能，那么该如何着手建立该科学，从而把社会学研究植根于社会事件的细节之中（Drew, 2005）。从学术渊源来讲，会话分析研究的创立主要得益于欧文·戈夫曼（Erving Goffman, 1967）和哈罗德·加芬克尔（Harold Garfinkel, 1967）的思想。作为戈夫曼的弟子，萨克斯和谢格洛夫都继承了他开创的社会学研究新领域，即面对面互动研究，并且把面对面互动提升到了社会组织的核心地位。加芬克尔所提出的现象学也深刻地影响了会话分析创始人对社会秩序的理解，即社会秩序存在于社会成员理解彼此社会互动的规范性步骤之中（Hoey & Kendrick, 2018）。当然，社会成员的常识推理也同样重要。通过整合戈夫曼和加芬克尔的原创学术思想，并利用洛杉矶自杀科学研究中心（Centre for the Scientific Study of Suicide）的电话录音（1963—1964），萨克斯与谢格洛夫开始了通过研究会话来建立有关社会行为科学的探索。

作为一种研究方法，会话分析实际上是一种"误称"（misnomer）（Pomerantz & Fehr, 1997）。首先，"会话"可能带来的一种误解是该学科仅仅关注日常会话，而实际上会话分析同样致力于对机构性言谈应对的挖掘；其次，"会话"还可能给人一种错觉，即仅仅关注互动中的语言使用，而实际上会话分析研究同样关注副语言和非语言资源在互动中的作用；再次，"会话分析"这个名称还可能让初学者误以为它只研究会话的组织结构，而实际上交际者通过互动资源执行的社会行为以及社会行为背后的社会规范才是会话分析研究的核心所在。

那么，我们为什么要研究会话呢？准确地说，会话的哪些本质特征值得我们以如此关注细节的方式对人类的言谈应对进行抽丝剥茧式的深入分析呢？其中最根本的原因或者说会话最基础的价值在于：会话是人类社会生活的原生场所。我们通过会话能够执行各种社会行为，建立或维持各种社会关系，建构各种社会机构，或者说开展社会生活。

作为一种洞察人类社会互动细节与规律的研究方法，会话分析的指导性原则是"秩序无处不在"（order at all points）（Sacks, 1992(I): 484），作为社会规范存在的互动秩序可以说是存在于人类言谈应对的每一个细节之中。也正因为如此，研究者不可以先入为主地抛弃那些看上去没有价值的互动细节，哪怕是一个短暂的停顿、一个笑声、一个拖音。比如，萨克斯、谢格洛夫和杰斐逊（Sacks, Schegloff & Jefferson, 1974）发现的有关人类言语交际的 14 条事实中所包含的"在某一时刻通常只有一个交际者讲话"（Overwhelmingly, one party talks at a time.）（ibid: 700）的规律，在本质上就是一种人类互动的秩序，是交际者合作完成的对互动权利与义务的遵守。正因为这一交际秩序的存在，所以在多人在场的情况下，如果某两个交际者正在交流，其他在场人员即使要讲话，也要压低声音进行交流。这种交流方式就是他们对"在某一时刻通常只有一个交际者讲话"这一交际秩序和社会规范的遵守，而不是对它的破坏。

会话分析在揭示人类互动规律方面的独特视角也越来越被语言学等诸多学科接纳并发展，这样就出现了语言科学的"互动转向"（an interactive turn）（Hoey & Kendrick, 2018: 151）。会话分析作为一种源于社会学的研究方法对社会互动的规律和价值有着自身独特的理解，这种理解深刻地体现在会话分析的语料选择、核心概念、分析方法等方面。只有掌握了这些内容才能掌握会话分析的研究方法，并针对选择的互动类型和收集的语料开展科学的实证研究。

9.1 核心概念

在具体介绍会话分析研究的核心概念之前，我们先一起简单分析一下下面的会话片段。

例 9.1 [Holt:1:1]

1	Les:	.hh Oh ↑ <u>by</u> the wa:y <u>Ann</u> <u>ha</u>sn::'u-s<u>e</u>nt Gordon <u>a</u>nything,=
2	Mum:	=<u>Yes</u> she <u>ha</u>:s,
3	Les:	Well it <u>ha</u>sn't <u>co</u>:me,
4	Mum:	<u>Oh</u> well pr<u>o</u>bably get it t'm<u>o</u>rrow.
5		(0.3)
6	Les:	<u>Oh</u>: yes.=What is she s<u>e</u>ndin d'y<u>ou</u> know,
7		(.)
8	Mum:	(Well y<u>es</u>)
9		(0.3)
10	Les:	Oh <u>not</u> one a'th<u>o</u>:se wh<u>i</u>:te t<u>ee</u> shirts,=

11	Mum:	=Well I don't know what sort'v tee shirt it is b't it i:s,
12	Les:	↓ Oh:: Mu::m::
13		(0.4)
14	Les:	It's just a waste of money.
15		(1.8)
16	Les:	.h ACTually IF YOU ↓ can drop the hint (.) tell'er
17		not tuh send any more becuz .h (0.2) they don't
18		wear them an'I:can't give'm awa:y.
19		(1.6)
20	Mum:	Can't give'm away,
21	Les:	Well no:- Yuh see: um (0.4) I can't give'm
22		as presents to anybody:,
23		(0.9)
24	Les:	Bec'z they've got J.P. Five Hundred written all over them.
25	Mum:	Well it's a good adver:t.
26		(0.5)
27	Les:	Yeh but ↑ nob'ddy wants £them uh huh huh .hh
28		(0.3)
29	Les:	eh-u- So: (.) if you ↓ can drop'er a hin:t,
30		(0.6)
31	Mum:	We::ll (.) I'll try:hh!
32	Les:	Ye:s.
33		(1.2)
34	Les:	Oh ↓ blo:w
35		(0.5)
36	Les:	Oh well never mi:nd,
37		(0.5)
38	Les:	°(Okay.)°

　　按照杰斐逊（Jefferson, 2004）转写体系完成的以上会话片段，对初学者来说，可能一时间很难看懂，更难理解如此转写的必要性和价值。从转写内容看，杰斐逊的转写体系是按照讲话人的讲话方式进行的，而不是传统的文字转写。正因为如此，研究者不仅需要对讲话内容进行捕捉，而且要对讲话方式进行再现。尽管转写不可能完全代替原始录音或录像，但转写可以最大

限度地重现交际的本来面貌。以上转写包括了讲话时间（比如话轮内和话轮间沉默）、序列位置（比如重叠话语）、声音特质（比如重音、拖音）以及其他细节（比如吸气、呼气），这些内容能够让研究者发现其他转写体系所不能再现的互动细节。比如，这个会话片段第19行1.6秒的沉默、第23行0.9秒的沉默所执行的互动功能只有会话分析研究才能给予专业的关注和解释。那么，会话分析研究如何对以上片段进行分析研究呢？这就要借助会话分析研究的三大支柱概念：社会行为（social action）、话轮和话轮设计（turn & turn design）以及序列组织（sequence organization）（Drew, 2005）。

交际者在互动过程中讲话不仅仅是为了传递信息，更重要的是要通过讲话来执行各种行为，也就是通过讲话来做事情。会话分析研究自创立开始就始终关注言谈互动中的社会行为，交际者通过讲话可以提出"请求"或"建议"，"接受"或"拒绝"对方的"提议"或"给予"，"感谢"或"抱怨"对方，如此等等。所以在具体的分析研究中，我们要明确交际者在各自话轮内所产生的每一个话轮构建单位（turn-constructional unit, TCU）所执行的社会行为。Leslie 在第16—18行"请求"妈妈暗示 Ann 不要再给 Gordon 邮寄 T恤衫，在"请求"之后还添加了一个理由，即没人穿而且也给不出去。面对"请求"，妈妈没有马上做出回应，而是在长达1.6秒的沉默后，发起了会话修正（Schegloff et al., 1977）"can't give them away"，修正发起的出现打破了会话的延续性，也推迟了妈妈对"请求"的"接受"或"拒绝"的出现。考虑到修正发起是通过"提问"方式执行的，我们看到，Leslie 在第21行，首先对"提问"这一行为做出了否定回应"no"，接着把修正源"can't give them away"修正为"I can't give them as presents to anybody"。在以上这几行的言语互动中，Leslie 和妈妈通过在各自话轮内建构的 TCU 执行了不同的社会行为，或者说做了不同的事情，包括"请求""修正发起""修正执行"等；当然，在其他话轮或 TCU 内，她们同样也执行了其他社会行为。

既然行为的执行是通过 TCU 实现的，那么这就自然涉及交际者何时、何位置、通过何种方式获得话轮，使用何种交际资源完成话轮设计（Drew, 2013a），进而实现交际者在该话轮或该 TCU 内所要执行的行为。所谓话轮设计，简单讲就是交际者选择何种交际资源在当前 TCU 或话轮内来完成自己所要实现的社会行为，同时被交际对方识别为同一社会行为。话轮设计实现的前提条件是交际资源与社会行为之间的非一一对应关系，或者说同一社会行为可以由某一语言中的多种交际资源来执行；而同一交际资源也可能被交际者用来执行不同的社会行为。但是，交际资源和社会行为之间也不是没有任何联系，因为在某一具体的语言中，能够在某一交际情境和序列位置执行某一社会行为的交际资源与该行为之间往往存在一定的共现关系，从而成为一种会话常规（conversational practice）。比如，英语互动中能够被交际者执行"给予"的语言结构或会话常规（Curl, 2006）呈现以下规律（Drew, 2013b: 6）：

Conditional forms	*If you would … then I will …*	(Self focused) Reason for call	Beginning of call or topic initial
Declarative or Assertive forms	*I'll do X*	Interactionally generated, by what recipient just said	Explicit trouble reported in adjacent prior turn
Interrogative *Do you want* forms	*Do you want me to*	(Other focused) *Not* interactionally generated	Educed from possible trouble implicit earlier in the conversation (e.g. several minutes earlier)

　　这样一来，交际者在具体的互动中就需要在"If you would … then I will …""I'll do X"以及"Do you want me to …"之间做出选择，设计自己的话轮，实现语法结构或语言选择与交际情境之间的匹配，通过话轮设计建构出其背后的社会规约。比如说，如果交际者打电话交流的目的就是"给予"帮助，那么该交际者就要选择"If you would … then I will …"的话轮设计来执行该"给予"行为。

　　在上面 Leslie 和妈妈的会话片段中，Leslie 执行"请求"的话轮设计具体为"Actually if you can drop the hint (.) tell her not to send any more because .h (0.2) they don't wear them and I can't give them away"。这个话轮选用的语法结构为"if you …"，选择的动词短语是"drop the hint"，这样选择的根本动因在于降低请求者"请求"背后的权利（entitlement）并认可妈妈执行"请求"的困难程度（contingency）（Curl & Drew, 2008）。此外，这个"请求"的微妙性同样也体现在随后给出的解释中"because they don't wear them and I can't give them away"，这个理由在某种意义上可以算是一种极致表达（Pomerantz, 1986），因为 Ann 邮寄来的 T 恤衫家里人不穿，外人也不要，这就等于说这些 T 恤衫没有任何用处。这个话轮中的停顿同样也建构了该行为的敏感性（Yu & Wu, 2015）。可见，话轮设计不仅涉及交际者在获得话轮后所选择执行的行为，还包括在构建具体 TCU 或话轮中所选择的交际资源，包括语法结构、词汇选择以及话轮执行方式，如重音、沉默、语调等。这些交际资源和话轮构建方式共同作用于特定社会行为的执行。

人类的社会活动由连续出现的多个话轮构成，或者说由这些话轮所执行的社会行为组成，那么这些社会行为之间就理应存在一定的逻辑关系，而这些逻辑关系在会话分析研究中就体现为序列组织（Schegloff, 2007）。序列组织让话轮脱离了交际的孤岛，成就了特定话轮与其前后紧随出现的话轮间塑造和被塑造的关系，因此一个非起始性行为所在的话轮通常来说都受其前面话轮的影响，并在当前话轮内以此为基础做出回应，回应一旦做出就会立刻影响随后可能出现的话轮。作为最基本的序列组织，相邻对（adjacency pair）更是这种紧随出现话轮间关系的典型代表。Leslie 在第 16—18 行的"请求"就使得妈妈"接受"或"拒绝"的回应成为可能的相邻对后件（second pair part, SPP），然而妈妈在第 19 行长达 1.6 秒的沉默，以及第 20 行的修正发起不仅推迟了后件的出现，而且还可以投射出后件的非优先特性（Pomerantz, 1984），或者说在这样的沉默和修正序列后出现的很可能是妈妈对该请求的拒绝。事实上，Leslie 在妈妈的修正发起后，在第 21—22 行执行了修正，或者说为修正发起这一相邻对前件（first pair part, FPP）提供了相应的后件，但是妈妈在第 23 行并没有接替话轮，为 Leslie 之前的"请求"提供符合类型限定的后件。于是，我们看到 Leslie 通过自我选择重新获得话轮构建的权利，并在第 24 行解释了那些 T 恤衫没法送给他人的原因。但是，妈妈同样在第 25 行没有立刻对"请求"做出回应，而是对 Leslie 给出的原因（T 恤衫上印有广告）做出了立场不一致的回应（Stivers, 2022），但依然没有就 Leslie 的"请求"给出后件，从而造成了相关缺失（relevant absence）。鉴于此，Leslie 在第 29 行重新做出"So (.) if you can drop her a hint"这一"请求"，面对这个再次发出的"请求"，妈妈给出了"Well (.) I'll try"这一较弱的"答应"。这些交际行为以及交际细节都存在于序列组织中，序列组织让这些行为和细节获得了互动意义，也让交际者之间的互解成为可能。

总之，社会行为、话轮和话轮设计、序列组织是会话分析研究最重要的三个支柱概念。这三个概念相互作用，使得会话分析研究成为一种有据可依、具有客观解释力的研究方法。

那么，了解了会话分析研究的起源和基本概念后，我们应该如何开展具体的会话分析实证研究呢？下面我们将从语料收集与转写、研究现象的发掘途径、研究证据的来源、会话分析研究的工具箱等方面来介绍并阐释会话分析这一研究方法。

9.2　语料收集与转写

　　会话分析研究反对通过角色扮演以及实验手段来获取语料，也同样反对使用人造语料，因为自然发生的互动才能够产生丰富的研究内容和研究发现，而这些研究发现是不能靠研究者的想象获得的（Sacks, 1984），当然也不可能通过实验手段获得。

　　会话分析研究坚持使用自然发生的社会互动（naturally occurring interactions）的录音/像材料作为研究语料。自然发生的言语交际指不以收集语料为目的而发生的言语交际，或者说，即使研究者不对该交际进行录音/像，交际依然发生。从语料收集的内容来看，所有类型的言语交际都可以成为会话分析研究的语料，前提是语料的收集要遵守学术研究的伦理道德。自然发生语料的使用能够规避研究者通过设计来采集语料的诸多弊端，也就是说，自然发生的语料完全摆脱了研究者或研究设计可能带来的对言语互动的干扰和歪曲，从而保证了语料的真实性和客观性。此外，自然发生的语料可供研究者循环播放和深入分析，最大的优势在于这样做能够保证研究发现的科学性。再次，自然发生的语料还能够为研究者和同行的学术交流提供支持，研究者与同行共同审阅语料、分析语料的做法可以保障研究发现不是研究者的个人理解，而是研究者对交际者互动与互解的客观再现。所以，会话分析研究始终坚持使用自然发生的语料作为研究对象。当然，完全自然状态下的互动语料是不存在的，比如，语料参与者可能或多或少地受到录音/像设备的影响，录音/像活动本身也可能会影响语料参与者的互动，但是考虑到人类的互动在本质上就是可观察的，所以录音/像对语料收集过程的影响小到可以忽略不计。

　　会话分析研究采用"自然主义者策略"（naturalist's strategy）来获取语料（Clayman & Gill, 2012），也就是尽可能从不同的交际情境中获取更多语料，以保证对比研究的开展和研究发现的普遍性（Heritage, 1988）。会话分析研究的语料收集手段包括录音和录像两种方式。通常来讲，对于电话交流，研究者可以采用录音方式进行收集，因为就电话谈话而言，交际双方无法获得对方的视觉信息，所以研究者通过录音手段捕捉的信息与交际双方获得的信息是一致的。而如果要将面对面交流作为研究语料的话，研究者就必须采用录像手段，这样才能够保证研究者所获得的信息基本与交际者之间获取的信息一致。此外，如果研究者采用录音手段收集电话交流作为语料，就必须要保证电话录音足够清晰，因种种原因造成的不清晰的电话录音会严重影响后续的语料分析。同样，采用录像手段收集语料时，除保证录音的清晰之外，还要保证录像时光线充足、镜头覆盖所有的交际对象，甚至交际发生的场所。为获得高质量录像，研究者们开始采用更多更好的录像设备来录制语料，比如具有鱼眼功能的高清数字摄像机、无人机，甚至采用多个摄像机同时对交际者个人和全局进行采制。无论采用何种方式或设备来收录语料，其根本原则就是要客观全面地捕捉真实的社会生活（Hoey & Kendrick, 2018）。

对于研究使用的语料，会话分析研究同样关注日常会话和机构性言谈应对；但从研究内容来看，日常会话是研究的基础，其丰富程度是机构性会话不可比拟的。

对具体研究者而言，互动类型或场所的选择与研究者的研究目的、研究兴趣，甚至社会关系紧密相关。研究者如果对日常互动感兴趣，可以动员家人和朋友一起来协助自己收集语料，从而在较短时间内获得大量的语料，且语料的覆盖面也会较为广泛。研究者如果对机构性互动感兴趣，比如医患互动，那么就可以主动与医院或医生联系，介绍自己的研究项目与研究内容，寻求医院或医生的理解与支持，并且在随后具体的语料收录过程中也需要征求患者的知情同意。当然，研究者也可借助其他途径降低机构性互动语料收集的难度。

总之，语料收集是一项艰巨的任务，研究者需要提前做好准备，应对语料收集过程中的各种难题。此外，语料收集前，研究者务必保证录音/像设备的正常使用，避免可能出现的失误，浪费难得的语料收集契机。语料收集是会话分析研究的基础和前提所在，没有自然发生的高质量且数量充足的语料，研究者就无法开展具体的语料分析和高质量的实证研究。那么，就一个具体的会话分析实证研究而言，究竟多少语料才足够呢？我们很难给出一个具体的量化标准，但一般来说，一篇博士学位论文可能至少需要 10—50 小时的录音/像支撑。

语料收集完成后的下一步就是开展语料转写工作，这是一个非常艰巨且耗时耗力的任务。但是任何会话分析学者都需要亲自转写语料，因为语料转写本身就是一个初步语料分析的过程。会话分析研究采用杰斐逊（Jefferson, 2004）提出的转写体系，该转写体系在一定程度上成就了会话分析这一学科。如今，随着录像设备的普及，研究者们也开始更多地关注多模态会话分析研究，不仅关注杰斐逊转写体系所捕捉的语言、语音、节奏等经典内容（如例 9.1 的分析所示），也开始更多关注交际者的具身信息。为了能更好地再现这些具身信息，我们就可以采用洛伦查·蒙达达（Lorenza Mondada）提出的转写体系进行多模态转写。高质量的语料转写应该尽可能全面客观地再现交际细节。尽管这些转写细节对初学者来说是一个相当严峻的挑战，但是既然语料中的细节在交际者互动中可能发挥作用，那么，研究者就应该努力将这些细节呈现给读者，同时在分析过程中尽可能挖掘这些细节对交际者开展社会生活的作用和意义。

9.3　研究现象的发掘途径

会话分析研究始于研究者对某个互动现象的关注（noticing），语料及转写是会话分析研究的原始材料，能够从看似平淡无奇的语料中发现研究宝藏，需要研究者长期积累的会话分析思维模式（CA mentality/CA mindset）。研究者只有通过自己积累的会话分析思维模式，才能从手边的语料中发现潜在的研究现象。具体来讲，会话分析研究发掘研究现象的途径如下。

9.3.1　通过无先设审视语料发现研究现象

会话分析研究发掘研究现象的最根本方式是对语料的无先设审视（unmotivated inquiry），即研究者在拿到语料及其转写后，不带有任何事先设定的研究目的，通过分析语料发现自己感兴趣的研究内容。无先设审视是会话分析研究最基本也是最常用的发现研究现象的方法。比如，下面有关汉语言语交际中"不是"的研究就来自我们参加的集体语料分析活动（data session）中的无先设审视（Yu & Drew, 2017: 221–223）：

例 9.2［GH: 吹空调］
1　赵：哎呀，下午咱们在那儿坐的不是: 那个空调，吹吹的。
2　纪：啊，你是不是吹得腿难受呢?
3　赵：呀，两只脚都麻木的么，都没: 感觉了呀。
4　纪：我–我没感觉么，我还热: 的不行么。
5　赵：↑是 :::,
6　纪：啊，你你你你是那儿就有感觉，还是回去有感觉。
7　赵：呀，咱们走出来的时候我觉得，起来就觉得脚麻: 的，
8　　　木的，［反正是–
9　纪：　　　［哎呀，这以后不能吹空调了，
10　赵：嗯。

该例中，赵在第 1 行使用"不是"来表示"是"，上述现象引起了我们的注意：既然赵完全可以用"是"来替代"不是"，且替代后的语意不会发生任何变化，那么，赵为什么选择使用"不是"来表示"是"呢？这样的用法有什么样的交际意义呢？通过语料分析，我们发现"不是"的这种用法往往投射某种日常麻烦，甚至在当前话轮内就展开麻烦讲述，且这两种话轮构建方式预示不同的会话发展路径。如果"不是"所在话轮投射麻烦，那么，交际双方会合作共建一个完整的麻烦讲述；如果"不是"所在话轮本身就在讲述一个具体的麻烦，那么，交际对方会据此提供一种可能的解决方案。

无先设审视语料是会话分析研究发现研究现象的最主要途径，集体语料分析活动中的点滴发现都有可能成就一个伟大的发现，这也是会话分析学习者和研究者务必定期参加集体语料分析活动的原因之一。

9.3.2 关注某种互动行为或语言现象

发掘研究现象的第二种方式往往来自研究者对某种具体社会行为或语言现象的关注。该方式与上述无先设审视语料的方法不同，因为研究者在接触语料之前已经清楚自己意欲在语料中寻找的具体社会行为或语言现象。

比如，有关汉语"邀请"研究（Yu & Wu, 2018）的出发点就源于对汉语"邀请"行为的关注。决定探讨汉语言语交际中的"邀请"行为后，研究者就开始从手边的语料中系统寻找所有有关"邀请"的语料片段，并按照杰斐逊（Jefferson, 2004）的转写体系对相关语料进行转写。随即对语料逐个进行分析，最后发现在汉语言语交际中，邀请者在执行"邀请"时会事先对邀请得以接受的可能性进行判断，并以此为基础选择合适的语法结构来设计话轮、执行邀请。当然，研究者感兴趣的现象可能多种多样，包括某个词汇的互动意义，如提问/回答序列中，回答末尾的语气词"呀"（Wu & Yu, 2022）；某种特定的互动现象，如医患沟通中，患者对医生提问的扩展回答（王亚峰、于国栋，2021）；某种更加宏观的交际类型，如汉语言语交际中的积极评价与被评价方的回应（张艳红，2019）。

对某种交际现象感兴趣是研究者确立研究现象的另一个重要途径，该兴趣可能来自研究者的生活体验或文献阅读。这种确立研究现象的方法较为直接，且本身就是研究者感兴趣的内容。以此为基础，从手边的语料中系统寻找相关语料片段，有利于研究者有效开展研究。

9.3.3 开展服务社会需求的应用型研究

上述两种发掘研究现象的方式方法既可用来进行基础会话分析研究，也可用来进行机构性会话分析研究，其目的是通过研究来发掘与某种语言文化或某种社会机构相关的交流模式及该模式所映射的社会规约。会话分析研究的第三种发掘研究现象的方法是应社会需求或某行业从业者的要求，开展应用型会话分析研究，以解决该行业亟须解决的互动问题，此类研究往往具有介入潜力（李枫、于国栋，2017）。与前两种方法不同的是，这种研究在一定意义上可以说是"命题作文"，研究者从某个行业从业者需要解决的问题出发，收集相关语料，从语料中发掘问题的互动根源，并提出解决方案。该类研究能够体现会话分析的社会服务功能，彰显会话分析研究的应用潜力。

以上介绍了会话分析研究视域下发掘研究现象的三种途径，其中前两种多服务于研究者的学术兴趣，而最后一种则服务于社会需求。无论从哪种路径出发，开展一项完整的会话分析研究均需要从具体研究现象的确立、具体分析的开展，以及具体社会规范的发掘等方面展开系统有效的工作。聚焦某种研究现象后，研究者就需要从语料中收集更多有关研究对象的例子，从而建立一个研究对象的集合。集合的存在不仅仅是量的累积，更重要的是能够帮助研究者确立研究对象，保证研究内容的普遍性，提升研究发现的说服力。

9.4　从现象到集合

通过以上方式研究者可以关注到某个具体的研究现象，但是一个或几个例子很难成就一个完整的、科学的、有说服力的会话分析研究，这就要求研究者从不同语料中寻觅更多有关某个研究现象的例子，组成一个集合。然后，再从位置（position）和构成（composition）这两个会话分析研究的重要维度出发，实现从个案到集合的进展（Robinson, 2022）。

9.4.1 以位置为标准建立相关研究现象的集合

会话分析研究中的位置包括横向位置和纵向位置两种：横向位置包括TCU 内位置和话轮内位置；纵向位置指序列位置。研究现象所处的位置对会话分析研究至关重要，因为处于不同位置的语言使用现象可能具有完全不同的互动功能。譬如，谢格洛夫（Schegloff, 1996）就发现 TCU 内部的不同位置具有不同的投射功能（Robinson, 2022）：

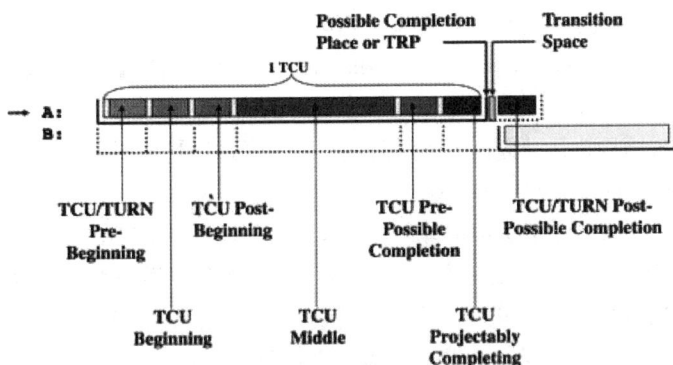

图9.1 TCU内部位置的投射功能

位置在一定程度上决定社会行为或语言成分的互动功能。如果研究现象为某种具体的社会行为或语言成分，那么就需要关注该行为或语言成分在TCU内或话轮内的位置，把出现在不同位置的例子都收集起来，组成一个集合。如果关注的行为或语言成分仅出现在TCU内或话轮内某个特定位置，那么就需要收集所有出现在这个位置的行为或语言成分。此外，研究者还要收集那些本该位于这个位置实际却没有出现的例子，从而构成一个相对完整的集合。

研究现象所处的序列位置同等重要，所以在具体研究中必须同时关注研究现象所处的序列位置。比如，研究对象处于序列的起始位置（相邻对前件），回应位置（相邻对后件），还是既非起始位置也非回应位置的其他位置（比如结束序列的第三话轮）。位于不同序列位置的TCU可能具有不同的互动功能，所以在具体研究中，研究者需要甄别研究现象的序列位置，并在研究初期将不同序列位置的研究现象都收集起来，后期再决定究竟是把出现在所有序列位置的研究现象都包括在当前的研究中，还是在当前的研究中仅处理一个序列位置的研究现象，将其他位置的研究现象留与未来研究。

9.4.2 以构成为标准建立相关研究现象的集合

会话分析研究中话轮或TCU构成因素中最重要的就是语法，语法结构是交际者执行社会行为的主要手段。如果研究现象是某一社会行为的话（比如"请求"），那么该研究者就要收集语料中执行这个社会行为的所有语法结构，进而组成一个集合，再展开细致的分析。比如，在英语互动中，交际者用来提议参与共同活动的语法结构包括以下四种（Thompson, Fox & Raymond, 2021）：含有情态动词的陈述句（如"Maybe we can have a coffee together."）、由 let's 引导的祈使句（如 "Let's play volleyball this afternoon."）、"why don't we" 结构（如 "Why don't we have a data session?"）以及由情态动词引导的疑问句（如 "Shall we make some dumplings?"）。这样的话，研究者就需要收集使用上述四种语法结构执行"提议"的所有例子，并通过语料分析阐释以上四种语法结构在执行提议时的区别所在。

就构成而言，除语法结构外，其他因素，如词汇、语音等均为重要考量因素，因为这些因素对交际者执行社会行为都具有重要作用。当然，随着多模态会话分析研究的开展，构成也突破了语法的限定，囊括了具身信息，如交际者的目光、手势、身姿等，甚至包括交际过程中的物品，如蒙达达（Mondada, 2022）有关奶酪销售人员如何通过邀请顾客品尝奶酪的互动过程来判断顾客是否有购买的想法。这样，物品也就进入了互动构成的内容。

无论从位置，还是从构成出发来将研究语料从个案扩展到集合，在具体分析过程中，研究者都需要同时考虑研究对象的位置和构成，并结合之前介绍的会话分析核心概念来开展研究。研究对象的集合是进行科学客观分析的重要基础，也为对比研究的开展提供了可能。事实上，会话分析研究本质上就是一种对比研究（Drew, Ostermann & Raymond, forthcoming），研究者可以对比处于不同位置的同一种语言结构，也可对比执行同一社会行为的不同语法结构，还可比较同一语法结构在日常会话和机构性会话中的使用，如此等等。若集合语料数量较少，研究者的分析研究就只能停留在对单个语料的理解层面上，而不能发掘社会成员共同使用的某种会话常规，当然也不能有力解释社会常规背后的社会规范。这就要求研究者在研究初期甄别每个具体例子是否属于研究对象时，首先要放宽标准，多收集例子，后期再进行取舍。

既然集合由若干同类型的例子组成，那么，一个集合究竟需要多少例子呢？这个问题需要研究者根据具体的研究现象来判断。在具体的研究过程中，例子分析与语料收集是一个同步进行的过程，或者说，研究者往往是一边分析手边的例子，一边不断扩充自己的例子集合。这样，一来有助于研究者证明研究发现的普遍性，二来能够帮助研究者纠正可能存在的片面或不当的理解。扩展集合的过程，或者说，不断收集同类例子的过程可在例子达到饱和点时停止（Raymond, 2022）。语料收集一旦到达饱和点，随后收集来的例子都会完美地归入研究者的分类中；这时，研究者就可以停止扩大集合，而专心开展语料分析工作了。

9.5 语料分析的基本原则及证据来源

9.5.1 语料分析的基本原则

会话分析研究必须从交际者视角进行语料分析（Sacks, 1992; Schegloff, 1992），研究者不能把自己的意志和想法强加在语料上，而是要从交际者的视角出发来观察发现交际者如何观照交际过程中的各种因素，分析交际者之间如何达到互解。

会话分析研究严格遵守研究发现反映研究现象与交际者之间相关性的原则，所有的语料分析和发现都必须从语料中找到证据，确定语料中展现研究内容在哪个方面与交际者的言语互动相关，而不能任由分析者主观地感觉或揣测交际者的行为和意图。那么，会话分析研究中究竟有哪些来自语料本身的证据呢？

9.5.2 会话分析研究的证据来源

来自语料本身的证据主要有以下几种类型（Raymond, 2022）：下一话轮证据、同一话轮证据、前一话轮/序列证据，以及第三位置证据等。这些证据是语料分析的依据和保证，也是研究者寻找来自语料内部证据的可能来源。

下一话轮证据（next-turn proof procedure）（Sacks, Schegloff & Jefferson, 1974）是会话分析研究最直接的证据来源，因为话轮转换机制本质上仅仅处理两个话轮/行为，即当前话轮/行为和随后的话轮/行为；这样一来，交际者的当前话轮就包含其对前面话轮的理解。也就是说当前话轮/行为的执行是以交际者对前一话轮/行为的理解为基础的，那么当前话轮就自然是其执行者对前一话轮/行为理解的证据所在。比如：

例 9.3 [NB II.2.R]

```
1   Emm:    … Wuddiyuh ↑ DOin.
2           (0.9)
3   Nan:    What'm I do[in¿
4   Emm:               [Cleani:ng?=
5   Nan:    =hh.hh I'm ironing wouldju belie:ve ↑ tha:t.
6   Emm:    Oh: bless it[s hea:rt.]
7   Nan:               [In f a :c]t I: ire I start'd ironing en I:
8           d-I: (.) Somehow er another ahrning js kind of
9           lea:ve me:co:[ld]
```

10	Emm:	[Ye]ah,
11		(.)
12	Nan:	[Yihknow,]
13	Emm:	[Wanna c'm] do:wn 'av [a bah:ta] lu:nch w]ith me?=
14	Nan:	[°It's js] ( )°
15	Emm:	=Ah gut s'm beer'n stu:ff,
16		(0.3)
17	Nan:	↑Wul yer ril sweet hon: uh:m
18		(.)
19	Emm:	[Or d'y] ou'av] sup'n [else °( )°
20	Nan:	[L e t-] I:] hu. [n:No: i haf to: uh callo Roul's
21		mother,h I told'er I'd call'er this morning I
22		[gotta letter] from'er en
23	Emm:	[°(Uh huh.)°]

　　如果我们关注的研究现象是 Emma 在第 13 和 15 行执行的社会行为，那么按照会话分析从交际者视角出发的原则，我们就要看一下 Nancy 在第 17 行的回应。从下一话轮证据来看，Nancy 在第 17 行所执行的行为以她对 Emma 在第 13 和 15 行所执行的社会行为的理解为基础，而且这个回应的前提或基础就是 Nancy 对 Emma 所执行行为的识解。Nancy 在第 17 行的回应尽管不完整，但是 "Well you're really sweet honey" 已经足以作为其对 Emma 行为理解的证据：位于 TCU 开始处 "well" 的交际功能是投射随后出现的回应是一种非优先行为，位于话轮内这个位置的 "you're really sweet" 执行的社会行为是对交际对方的 "感激"，且同时投射随后可能出现非优先行为，或者说该话轮正在往非优先回应的路径上发展，即 Nancy 实际上正要构建对对方 "邀请" 的 "拒绝"。作为下一话轮证据，这个话轮展示的是 Nancy 把 Emma 在第 13 和 15 行执行的社会行为理解为 "邀请"。这样的理解也得到了随后话轮的佐证。尽管 Nancy 在第 17 行的话轮不是一个完整的 "拒绝" 行为，但是作为共享社会规范的交际者，Emma 完全可以对此做出判断，而且在真正的拒绝还未出现之前，就替对方找了一个拒绝的理由："or do you have someone else"。

　　尽管下一话轮证据具有极强的解释力，但我们绝对不能简单地认为下一轮证据永远正确，因为在许多交际情境之下，下一话轮证据可能由于交际者误解了交际对方在前一话轮执行的社会行为而失效，比如：对方在第一话轮执行了"邀请"，但是交际者却在当前话轮内进行"道歉"，因为交际者将交际对方在前一话轮所执行的社会行为误解为"抱怨"；另外，交际者还可能专门选择以一种非匹配交际对方行为的方式进行回应（Drew, 2022），所以，我们需要从语料内部为交际者之间的互动和互解寻找证据。

同一话轮证据（same turn evidence）能够在当前话轮构建的过程中就展示交际者对互动的观照和监控。最为有力的同一话轮证据是发生在话轮构建过程中的自我发起—自我修正，此类会话修正能生动地揭示交际者对话轮构建准确性和得体性的恪守。

例 9.4 [NB II:4]

```
1   Emm:   I :'d ] ↑ LIKE TIH GET S'M LID'L[E slipper]s but uh:
2   Nan:                              [Y e :*ah.]
3          (0.7)
4   Emm:   .t.hhh *I jis do:n't think I better walk it's ↑ jis
5          bleeding a tiny bid'n a:nd u-I think I'm gon'stay o:ff of it
6          it thro:bs: a liddle b*it. Yihknow thet's no fun
7          tuh have a nai:l tak[en *off.]
8   Nan:                       [°Y e a h] r*ight.° hh[hh
9   Emm:                                            [°Oh: G*o:d,°
10         (.)
11  Nan:   We:ll dih you wanna me tuh be tih js pick you Ken u you (.)
12         get induh Robins'n? so you c'buy a li'l pair a'sli ↑ ppers?h
13         (.)
14  Nan:   I mean er: c'n I getchu some  thin:g? er[: sump ↑ 'm:?=
15  Emm:                                          [°hhhh°
16  Nan:   er sum' ↑ m:?
```

Emma 在第 1 行告诉 Nancy "I'd like to get some little slippers"，接着在第 4—7 行讲述自己的困难，因为她刚刚做了一个小手术，去除了一个脚指甲，而且依然 "bleeding a tiny bit" "throbs a little bit"。面对这样直接明了的困难讲述，Nancy 在第 11—12 行主动"给予"了帮助："Well do you want me to just pick you. Can you get into Robinson? So you can buy a little pair of slippers."。按照柯尔（Curl, 2006）的研究，由交际对方的直接困难讲述激发的"给予"不应该由 "Do you want me …" 来执行，所以我们看到 Nancy 在第 14 行进行了

自我修正，修正为"I mean can I get you something?"，尽管该表述并非最为典型的"I will X"结构，但是已经证明了 Nancy 在构建话轮、执行行为过程中对自己话轮设计的实时监控，而这个自我发起—自我修正就是一个典型的同一话轮证据。自我修正凸显来自互动层面的证据，它证明交际者对语言选择、行为选择以及社会规范的观照。实际上，自我修正是语料收集过程中的珍宝，它不仅能够作为一种同一话轮证据，更为重要的是，它直接展现出交际者对于在这个位置能够使用何种资源、不能使用何种资源的考量。除自我修正外，话轮起始处的小词（turn-initial particle）、当前话轮的语法结构、执行当前话轮的语调以及多模态信息都可以作为同一话轮证据来帮助研究者从交际者视角出发开展会话分析研究。

　　研究者所关注的研究现象所在话轮之前的话轮、甚至是之前的序列都可以成为会话分析研究的证据，即前一话轮/序列证据（prior turn/sequence evidence）。前一话轮或序列对当前话轮/行为的影响最为直接，所以当前话轮/行为的执行不可避免地会受到前一话轮和/或序列的影响。比如，在汉语言语交际中，面对交际对方在前一话轮内的信息寻求类提问，有些情况下，交际者在回答之后添加"呀"，那么，出现在这个序列和 TCU 位置的"呀"具有怎样的交际功能呢？Wu & Yu（2022）从前一话轮证据入手，经过仔细分析语料，发现"呀"实际上展现了其使用者将前面的信息寻求类提问评价为不合适，因为交际对方所寻求的信息，当前的回答者已经告知过了。比如：

例 9.5 [2015/Liu Le:1]

77	HAO:	jiù shi me:. wǒ hái chóu de, wǒ shuō shì-
		even be PRT. I even worry NOM, I say be-
78		.hh méi diànhuà hàomǎ, $yī gè dōu méi yǒu$.
		.hh not telephone number, one CL even not have
		It is so. I have been worried about that, I mean, I don't
		have telephone numbers now, not even one number.
79		(.)
80	LIU:	en:::=
		Uhu
		Uhu.
81	HAO:	-> =dōu hé- huàn le shǒujī, dōu, dōu méi la.
		even with change PFV cellphone, all, all lost CRS
		I have changed a cellphone. All the telephone numbers are lost.

82		nà gè shǒujī huài la, dōu kāi bù liǎo jī.
		that CL cellphone broke CRS, even turn-on not able machine.
		The previous one broke down, and it cannot even be turned on.
83	LIU:	mǎi xīn shǒujī méi?
		buy new cellphone not?
		Have you bought a new cell phone or not?
84		(0.8)
85	HAO:	mǎi le ya. °zhè gè jiù shì°.=
		buy PFV PRT. this CL just be.
		I have bought one YA. The one I am using now is the new one.
86	LIU:	=nǐ yǐqián shǒujī bu bèifèn ya,
		you previous cellphone not back-up PRT,
87		nǐ méi yǒu nà zhǒng yúnpán ya:.
		you not have that. kind cloud-drive PRT:.
		Haven't you backed up your previous cellphone? Don't you
		have that kind of cloud-drive?

会话分析研究中的第三位置证据（third position evidence）同样重要，因为尽管下一话轮证据展示其交际者对前一话轮的理解，但是交际者无法保证下一话轮证据的正确性，因为下一话轮证据是交际者的一种选择性识解（Drew, 2022）。如果前一话轮的交际者通过当前交际者的回应发现对方误解了自己在第一话轮执行的社会行为，那么，他/她就可以在第三位置进行修正，即所谓的第三位置修正（于国栋，2022）。比如：

例 9.6 [Holt X(C):1:2:7]

1	Mum:	What are they then,
2	Les:	Shortbread.hh
3		(.)
4	Mum:	No I mean what ma:ke,
5	Les:	.hh Oh::uhm (0.5)hhh well some Scottish make,

第三位置证据在语料中并不多见，如果研究者碰巧发现了此类证据，就应该认真分析是什么原因导致了误解的出现，以及第三位置修正执行者如何修正误解等。

除了以上类型的证据，我们所关注的话轮/行为之前的互动内容、甚至可能是先前的沟通，在某些情况之下也可以成为我们分析的证据。此外，多人交流中，其他在场交际者的反应有时也可能会成为分析研究的某种间接证据。以上不同类型的证据充分说明话轮只有在序列中才有生命，而且同一序列中的话轮之间总是互相影响并互相成就。总之，处于不同互动位置的证据是会话分析研究的重要内容，是研究发现的根本依托，一个科学的、有说服力的研究发现必须基于来自语料的强大支撑。

9.6　会话分析研究的工具箱和实操步骤

以上我们介绍了会话分析实证研究过程中研究者从语料中获取证据的方法。那么，在一个具体的会话分析实证研究中，研究者具体能够使用哪些工具呢？这就需要研究者熟悉并掌握会话分析研究的基本内容，也就是掌握会话分析研究的工具箱。

会话分析研究的工具箱基本上包括两类：第一类工具就是会话的基本机制，这些机制是任何一本会话分析研究教材都涉及的内容，包括话轮、话轮转换与话轮设计（turn, turn taking & turn design）、会话修正（conversational repair）、相邻对及序列组织（adjacency pair and sequence organization）、优先行为与优先组织（preferred action and preference organization）等。这些是会话分析研究最基本的内容，也是研究者最基本的研究工具箱，任何一个会话分析研究者都必须要正确、全面掌握相关内容，而且要不断更新学者们对以上内容的最新研究发现。会话分析研究者们不仅可以利用这些工具针对手边的语料开展具体的实证研究，挖掘某个社会行为或互动规律，还可以就这些基本工具本身开展研究，尤其是汉语言语交际中的此类现象，而后者也是汉语会话分析研究亟须开展的。第二类工具是会话分析研究的文献。会话分析研究没有宏观的理论来统领每一项实证研究，研究者们能够借鉴的除了会话分析研究的思维模式，就是相关领域的经典文献和最新研究成果。所以说，从事会话分析研究需要大量的文献阅读，从文献阅读中积累有关人类言语互动点点滴滴的发现，丰富研究者对人类互动规律和模式的了解和掌握，从文献阅读中培养研究者自己的会话分析思维模式，即通过文献阅读来学习成熟的会话分析学者如何寻找研究现象、如何进入语料、如何从会话分析的基本内容出发分析语料、如何发现互动规律、如何解释互动规律背后的社会秩序，等等。任何一个学科的文献都浩如烟海，会话分析研究也是如此。这就要求研究者，尤其是初学者，能够选择性地、有步骤地开展文献阅读。在所有的文献中，有些经典文献是任何一个会话分析学者都必须要认真阅读的，比如萨克斯的《会话讲稿》(*Lectures on Conversation*, 1992)，保罗·德鲁 (Paul Drew) 和约翰·赫里蒂奇 (John Heritage) 编著、由 Sage 出版社出版的《会话分析》(*Conversation Analysis*, 2006) 和《会话分析的当代研究》(*Contemporary Studies in Conversation Analysis*, 2013)。这些都是会话分析研究的经典，是会话分析学习者和研究者的必读文献。

具体而言，研究者针对发现并要开展实证研究的具体研究现象，比如一个特定的社会行为、一个特定的语言表达、一个特定的互动资源等，可按照以下步骤进行实操：

(1) 以研究所关注行为、表达等所在的话轮为基础，将其所在序列从原始语料中切割出来；

(2) 按照杰斐逊和蒙达达转写体系对该序列进行客观、细致的转写；

(3) 识别该序列中每个话轮以及构成每个话轮的 TCU 所执行的社会行为；

(4) 分析每个社会行为的话轮设计，包括语法结构、语音特征、语调特征、多模态信息等；

(5) 分析行为之间，尤其是紧随出现的行为之间的逻辑关系；

(6) 充分利用会话分析工具箱从交际者视角分析这些工具在互动中的作用；

(7) 分析交际者执行社会行为的方式与社会因素之间的映射关系，或者说研究互动方式如何展现交际者对语境因素的观照以及如何建构特定的社会关系与社会规范。

课堂讨论

1. 对以下语料进行无先设审视，确立一个会话常规。

[1] [TCI(b):16:59:SO] ((Joan bought Linda's kids some clothing for their dolls))

01 Linda: Where did you get the clothes at.

02 Joan: At uh Toy City,

03 Linda: Were they on sa:le?=

04   Joan: =<u>Ah</u>::, yeah.

05   Linda: Ye:ah.

06   Joan: I w<u>e</u>nt with uh::m (·) F<u>a</u>y one day…

[2] [JG:II:2:5] ((Gene, married to Jo, has phoned Maggie as he occasionally does, to ask her out. Maggie has asked how things are going. He's said that he and Jo go their separate ways.))

01   Maggie: B<u>u</u>t you're all still tog<u>e</u>ther.

02   (0.3)

03   Gene: <u>Oh</u> yah.

04   Maggie: Yahm.

05   (1.2)

06   Maggie: Are you still all teaching school,

2. 在以下例子中，故事讲述者都使用了一个共同的讲述方式，故事倾听者也都采用了一个特定的回应方式。这个讲述和回应方式具体是什么？这样的方式具有怎样的互动价值？

[1] [NB:II:4:3:SO] ((Emma had a toenail removed))

01   Emma: It's bleeding just a t<u>i</u>ny tiny bit has to be

02   dr<u>e</u>:ssed, bu[t uh

03   Nancy: [<u>Oh</u>:::::[:::.

04   Emma: [<u>Go</u>:d <u>i</u>t was <u>he</u>:ll. uh h<u>a</u>hh!

05   ·hhh[hh

06   Nancy: [Wh<u>a</u>t a <u>sha</u>::me.

[2] [NB:IV:4:4:SO] ((Emma's psoriasis has gotten worse))

01   Emma: You ought to see me broken out to<u>day</u> God I

02   t(hh)ook a ba:th, and

03   I'm just a ma:ss of b- little

04   p(h)imp(h)les:: heh heh [·hhh

05   Lottie: [Oh <u>that's</u> from uh:: n-nerves.

140

[3] [Frankel:HB:II:9:SO] ((Jan and her husband's house burned down last night))

01	Jan:	about a month ago I said (·)
02		you know what do we have to look <u>for</u>ward to.
03		We have our <u>hou</u>:se and everything I said I just
04		·hhh I was feeling empty.=
05		you kn*hh*o(h)[o(h)w [·<u>hhh</u>!]
06	Penny:	[·hhh [<u>Yea</u>]: h.

3. 下面例子中的交际者在列举方面的共同之处是什么?

[1] [MC: I]

01	Sidney:	While you've been talking to me, I mended, two
		nightshirts, a pillowcase? And a pair of pants.

[2] [SBL]

01	Maybelle:	I think if you exercise it and <u>work</u> it and
02		studies it you do become clairvoyant.

[3] [GTS: III]

01	Louise:	For three hundred years she's been giving him
02		a w- mh about ten white shirts,
03		and a couple of ties and a suit.

[4] [SSL]

01	Maud:	About three weeks ago we was up at Mari<u>po</u>:sa,
02		and up in the Mother Lode County and we went all
03		through those ghost tow:nes,

[5] [JG: IIa:3]

01	Sorrell:	And they had like a concessin stand like
02		at a fair where you can buy coke and popcorn and
03		that type of thing.

课外练习

1. 如何理解会话分析研究的交际者视角，以及在语料分析中坚持交际者视角的必要性？
2. 如何理解会话分析个案研究与集合研究的关系和区别？
3. 会话分析思维模式是一种什么样的思维模式？
4. 在下面的例子中，Emma 在第 5 行的 "your line's been busy" 是一种什么样的语言使用现象？这种现象的交际意义是什么？

[NB:II:2:R]

```
 1   Nan:    Hel↑lo:,
 2   Emm:    .hh HI::.
 3           (.)
 4   Nan:    Oh:.'I::: 'ow a:re you Emmah:
 5   Emm:    FI:NE yer LINE'S BEEN BUSY.
 6   Nan:    Yea:h (.) my u.-fuhh h-.hhhh my fa:ther's
 7           wife ca:lled me,h .hhh she ca:lls me::,h
 8           .hh I always talk fer a lo:ng ti:me cz
 9           she c'n afford it'n I ca:n't.hhh[hhh]°huh°]
10   Emm:                          [OH:]::::: ]:=
```

5. 分析以下语料中回应者在回应中的优先组织。

[1] ((R and J are a couple out on a lake. J is rowing the boat.))

```
01   R:      You're a good rower, Honey.
02   J:      These are very easy to row. Very light.
```

[2] ((Ann   just rented her house to a family))

```
01   Bea:    Uh and I think it's- and Bea, you know,
02           well I think it's awfully nice of you to r-
```

03		rent to a family with children.
04	Ann:	Well, that was uh built for that,
05		it's in a- too good a school area.

拓展阅读

Drew, P. (2005). Conversation analysis. In K. L. Fitch, & R. E. Sanders (Eds.). *Handbook of language and social interaction* (pp. 71–102). New Jersey & London: Lawrence Erlbaum Associates, Publishers.

Heritage, H., & Clayman, S. (2010). *Talk in work: Interaction, identities, and institutions.* London: Wiley-Blackwell.

于国栋. (2022). 什么是会话分析. 上海：上海外语教育出版社.

第 10 单元
话语分析法

学习目标

- 了解话语分析的基本概念、研究对象和研究领域
- 熟悉话语分析的三个主要层次以及重要分析工具
- 了解话语分析与其他质性研究方法的异同
- 能结合特定语篇材料"做"话语分析

10.1　基本概念

话语分析是研究谈话、书面语篇以及其他各类话语实践的一种质性研究方法，涉及对语言、意义、资源和实践的调查，与语言学习、批评语言学、社会语言学、人际传播、语用学、符号学、话语心理学、社会学、社会心理学等研究密切相关。该概念在 1952 年由美国语言学家泽利格·哈里斯（Zellig Harris）首先提出，历经半个多世纪，逐渐发展成为当代人文社科研究领域最重要的研究方法之一。

由于不同学科领域所研究问题以及研究视角的差异，各学科领域的话语分析侧重点亦有不同，呈现多样性特征。譬如，传统的语言学研究者聚焦对语言本身的研究，侧重研究语言的声音系统（音系学）、单词的构成（形态学）、句子的组合结构（句法学）以及形式意义（语义学）等以及语言与社会范畴、活动、情境、角色和功能的关系（社会语言学）等。社会学及社会心理学者则聚焦对社会结构和社会现象的研究，将语言作为反映社会结构和社会现象的重要媒介进行研究。就研究内容而言，研究者可以分析说话者之间的言谈互动如何受社会文化语境和机构语境的影响和制约，探讨说话的风格和言谈的"回合"，也可以研究话语使用者如何通过策略性的语言、语法资源的选择来建构谈话的细节，或是研究特定话语的交际目的及功能问题等。

10.2　研究对象和研究领域

梵·迪克（van Dijk）在 2011 年出版的《话语法研究：多学科导论》（*Discourse Studies: A Multidisciplinary Introduction*）一书中，非常详细地阐释了话语的概念，列举出话语的十个主要属性，每一属性代表了话语分析的重要对象和研究领域。

（1）作为社会互动的话语（discourse as social interaction）：从根本上说，话语是参与者之间的一种社会互动形式。参与者使用语言不仅是为了说话（写作或是手势）和表意，还使用语言协调行动，使之成为有意义、适切的社会互动，从而完成各种社会行为。正是这种基本的话语互动维度，定义了人类社会的秩序基础。

（2）作为权力和控制的话语（discourse as power and domination）：权力和权力滥用（控制）是话语诠释和再现社会秩序的一个基本方面，可以被界定为社会群体或组织对话语的优先使用和控制。对话语作为一种权力和控制属性的研究（如从阶级、性别、种族等角度研究话语宰制问题）是批评话语以及社会政治话语分析的重点。

（3）作为交际的话语（discourse as communication）：表达和交流是语言使用者通过文本和谈话进行互动的诸多目标之一。正是通过这样一种形式，我们得以了解他人的知识、意图、目标、观点和情感，也得以了解我们如何获取和更新社会共享知识。这个维度定义了人类社会的基本认知秩序。互动和认知是互为前提的，没有对这两个维度的理论和实证研究，对话语的分析和解释是不完整的。

（4）作为语境下语言使用的话语（discourse as contextually situated）：作为互动和交流的话语不是在真空中发生的，而是人们日常生活中社会情境的一部分。参与者在一个主观的心理模式中呈现与其话语相关的语境因素（如情景、参与者身份和关系、交际目标、当前行为和知识等），促使语言使用者选择适合当前交际语境的文本或谈话。

（5）作为社会符号的话语（discourse as social semiotics）：文本和谈话不限于人类自然语言的使用，还可以通过声音、视觉、手势等多模态符号实现。

（6）作为自然语言的话语（discourse as a natural language）：尽管过去几十年，话语分析侧重互动、认识、情境以及符号特征，其核心仍然离不开对自然语言的研究。人们使用自然语言产出和理解词汇、句子组合以及其他基于规则的语言单位。因此，语言学领域话语研究的中心仍然是自然语言。

（7）作为复杂的、多层次构念的话语（discourse as complex, layered construct）：话语分析将话语视为复杂的、多层次、多维度现象，包含了自然语言的三个维度：形式或表达（声音、视觉、词汇、短语等），意义和行为。每一层面都可以进一步基于语音、符号、句法、词汇、语义、图式、语用以及互动理论进行细致深入的分析。

（8）话语的序列和结构层次（sequences and hierarchies）：文本和谈话的一个关键特征是其序列性（sequentiality）。依据话语发生和理解的先后顺序，话语结构包含了声音序列、词汇序列、句子序列、命题序列、语步或行为序列。因此，话的生成和理解既受其之前话语的影响，也影响其后面的话语。同时，局部序列组合构成更高一层的复杂结构（如句子组合成段落、段落组合成语篇等）。最后，话语结构还体现为信息的前景化、背景化特征。

（9）话语的抽象结构和动态策略（abstract structures vs. dynamic strategies）：可以将话语作为一个抽象结构，或是一个动态变化的时间，或是一个以策略性为取向的心理操作或社会行为。

（10）话语的类别或语类：话语具有不同的类别（type）、种类（sort）或是语类或体裁（genre）。譬如，它可能是日常对话、议会辩论、媒体报道、学术论文、广告或是其他。不同的语类具有不同的话语特征，因此语类也是话语分析的一个重要对象。

上述每一个话语属性都构成不同领域话语分析的具体维度，譬如研究者可以运用话语分析的方法对社会互动形式、权力和控制策略、交流形式、语境影响和制约、多模态社会符号资源、自然语言、形式、意义和行动、序列和结构特征、话语策略以及语类等维度开展研究。

10.3　话语分析的三个层次

话语分析涉及三个不同层次：微观层次的语篇分析（text analysis）、中观层次的话语实践语境分析（discourse practice context analysis）以及宏观层次的社会语境分析（social context analysis）。

（1）微观层次的语篇分析：包括对话语内容的分析（content analysis）以及对具体符号资源的分析（semiotic analysis）。在话语内容方面，聚焦命题内容、论辩结构和策略，回答"话语中主要对哪些社会行动者、事件和活动进行了呈现和建构"的问题。在符号资源方面，聚焦语篇中所使用的各类语言语用资源及其联系，回答"话语如何建构特定的社会行动者、事件和活动"的问题。微观层次的语篇分析具有描述性特征。

（2）中观层次的话语实践语境分析：主要回答"谁在对谁说话""为何以此种方式说""说话人有何话语目的""该话语类型有何默认的话语规约和期待""该话语是否有特定的目标受众""需要受众具备什么样的背景知识"等问题。对话语实践语境的分析在本质上是基于社交和话语实践语境以及交际者的认知心理因素对话语分析结果作出解释，因此具有阐释性特征。

（3）宏观层次的社会语境分析：主要回答"与话语生成和解释密切相关的社会（包括政治、文化、经济）语境以及主流意识形态是什么"等问题。对宏观层次社会语境的分析同样具有阐释性特征。

10.4　话语分析的工具

为了更好地指导初学者"做"话语分析，詹姆斯·保罗·吉（James Paul Gee）出版了《话语分析：实用工具及练习指导》（*How to Do Discourse Analysis: A Toolkit*）一书，详细地介绍了话语分析工具，即在"做"话语分析的过程中需要考虑的具体问题。我们列举常用的 15 个话语分析工具如下：

（1）指示工具（The Deixis Tool）：语言使用者是如何使用指示词连接话语与语境的？一些常规词在语境中是否具有指示性特征？换言之，这些常规词的具体意义是否需要借助语境才能获得？

（2）词汇工具（The Vocabulary Tool）：语言使用者是如何进行词汇选择的？所选择的词汇类型反映出什么话语风格（语域）？其词汇选择如何服务于话语目的？

（3）句子整合工具（The Integration Tool）：话语中的小句是如何整合成句子的？哪些可选论元被选择了，哪些没有？小句变成短语时有没有哪些信息被省略？

（4）话语方式工具（The Why This Way and Not That Way Tool）：语言使用者是以什么话语方式（直接还是间接）说话的？他为什么以这种话语方式而不是其他话语方式说话？他想要表达什么意义？他想要以这种话语方式做什么事？

（5）语篇衔接工具（The Cohesion Tool）：语言使用者使用了哪些衔接手段？这些衔接手段有什么语言语法特征？语言使用者通过这些衔接手段想要传递什么信息、实现什么目标？

（6）主语/话题工具（The Subject Tool）：语言使用者为什么选择这个（而非其他）主语/话题？关于这个主语/话题，他在说什么？

（7）话题和主位工具（The Topics and Themes Tool）：话语中每个小句的话题和主位是什么？为什么语言使用者会做出这种选择？是否存在有标记选择？为什么会这样选择？

（8）主题流或话题链工具（The Topic Flow or Topic Chaining Tool）：话语所有主句的话题是什么？这些话题之间如何彼此联系形成话题链的？是否所有的话语内容都"遵循话题"？有无偏离话题的现象？为什么？

（9）语境自反性工具（The Context Is Reflective Tool）：语言使用者如何以特定的话语内容和话语方式创造或形成相关语境？如何以特定的话语方式再现相关语境？其话语内容和方式是否会改变某些语境？语言使用者在创造或再现相关语境时意识程度如何？

（10）情景意义工具（The Situated Meaning Tool）：特定词汇、短语和结构有什么"情景意义"？换言之，话语分析过程中应该寻求以下问题的答案：特定的语境和语境构建为话语中的特定词汇、短语和结构赋予什么具体意义？

（11）社会语言工具（The Social Language Tool）：话语使用者如何使用词汇和语法结构（如短语、小句和句子）来表达和形成一种既定的社会语言？

（12）互文性工具（The Intertextuality Tool）：如何使用何种语言形式（如直接或间接引用）来引用、参考、影射其他话语或其他语言风格？

（13）图式工具（The Pictured Worlds Tool）：话语中的词汇和短语激起什么样的典型事件和图式信息，以及与之相关的参与者、活动、话语风格、人物、机构和价值等？

（14）身份构建（The Identities Building Tool）：话语使用者试图构建什么样的社会身份？如何定位和识别他者身份？什么话语与交际者身份构建相关？如何相关的？在哪方面相关？

（15）关系构建（The Relationships Building Tool）：话语使用者如何使用语言语法资源构建、维持和改变自己与他人、社会团体以及机构之间的各种关系的？什么话语与各类关系构建相关？如何相关的？在哪方面相关？

除了上述分析工具，还可以加入历史文化关系工具、话语效果工具等，考察特定话语与历史文化的关系及其造成的社会影响等。总体而言，这些话语分析工具是我们在"做"话语分析时应该遵循的一套"按步骤"推理的法则，或者更确切地说，是一套话语分析者的"思维手段"。但需要指出的是，这套话语分析思维手段不是固定不变的，我们在运用这套思维手段"做"话语分析时，不能生搬硬套，而应该结合自己的研究问题做一些改变、创新甚至是改造。

10.5　话语分析法与文本分析法和内容分析法的联系与区别

话语分析的初学者容易将话语分析法、文本分析法和内容分析法混为一谈，有必要对这三者进行区分。

话语分析法的理论来源较多，主要包括符号学、言语行为理论、系统功能语言学以及批评语言学，旨在运用符号学、结构主义理论和语言学方法来研究话语的结构、功能与意义，通过对话语内容、形式和功能的挖掘与探索，阐释话语中隐藏的意义，解释话语与现实的关系，剖析话语中的意识形态和价值立场。

文本分析法的理论基础主要是人文主义和阐释学，基本内涵是从文本表层深入到深层，在分析文本表层意义（字面意义）的基础上，挖掘文本所蕴含的难以被普通读者把握的深层含义（言外之意）。文本分析法多从修辞、叙事分析着手，常用于文学评论研究。

内容分析法是传播学及社会学研究中的常用研究方法。伯纳德·贝雷尔森（Bernard Berelson）把该方法界定为："内容分析法是一种对传播内容进行客观、系统、定量的描述的研究技术（Berelson, 1952: 8）"。罗伯特·默顿（Robert C. Merton）认为，内容分析法是用以考察社会现实的方法，研究中通过对文献内容特征的系统分析，得到有关潜在内容特征的结论。内容分析法所分析的"内容"范围较广，可以是文字，也可以是照片、歌曲、绘画、广告、艺术品等"各种信息传播形式"。

可以看出，话语分析和文本分析以及内容分析在理论基础、研究内容、研究手段等方面各有不同，但毋庸置疑，话语分析学者往往在"做"话语分析的过程中，也会借鉴文本和内容分析的手段、程序和技术。

10.6　话语分析的客观性和可靠性问题

话语分析的一个重要任务是对语篇或谈话中的话语意义进行理解，然而，意义的解释需要一定程度的推理，而这一推理过程或多或少会受分析者主观性影响。针对这一问题，研究者多建议采取三角互证法（triangulation）来保证分析的效度。运用三角互证法辅助话语分析，分析者可以使用不同的方法收集不同的资料，通过对基于不同资料、不同方法、不同研究者所得研究结果的检视、互补与整合，可以有助话语分析者深入完整地分析话语现象，形成知识建构和实践的基础，获得对特定话语现象的充分描述和解释。话语分析领域运用三角验证法的一个典型案例来自兰卡斯特大学保罗·贝克（Paul Baker）、露丝·沃达克（Ruth Wodak）等学者对英国媒体报道中难民形象建构的研究（Baker et al., 2008）。贝克教授具有语料库语言学研究背景，沃达克教授是批评话语分析大家。这两位教授对所收集到的相同材料分别运用语料库语言学和话语分析方法进行独立的研究，并在定期的项目会议上碰头，汇报和探讨各自的研究发现，最后对研究结果进行整合，形成相对客观可靠的研究结论。

当然，除了使用不同研究方法进行三角互证，话语分析者也可以采取资料三角互证（即通过多种资料来源收集证据）、研究者三角互证（即邀请多位研究者同时进行分析）以及理论三角互证（即对同一份资料进行不同观点和理论的探讨）等方法来提升话语分析的客观性和可靠性。

课堂讨论

1. 阅读下面两篇话语分析类论文摘要，并回答以下问题：
   (1) 由两篇摘要可知，研究 1 和研究 2 中话语分析的对象分别是什么？
   (2) 两篇摘要是如何呈现话语分析方法的？
   (3) 两篇摘要是如何呈现研究结果的？
   (4) 在运用话语分析法的研究中，论文摘要部分应该如何撰写研究方法和研究结果？

摘要 1

While a lot of attention has been paid to online branding and the construction and communication of a company's identity via its website, there is only very little research that looks at the processes involved in these activities from a discourse analytical perspective. This article aims to address this gap by conducting a case study of *innocent*, a UK producer of fruit juices. Combining corpus analytical tools with discourse analytical techniques and considering both text and multimodal features, we explore some of the strategies through which *innocent* creates a set of inter-related and closely intertwined identities on its website, thereby constructing the company's brand image. However, our findings also reveal that some of the company's identity claims (especially in relation to being an inclusive and welcoming "family") are relativised and to some extent contradicted by the discursive processes through which these claims are articulated.

(The PAD Research Group, 2016)

摘要 2

Digital peddling of fake news is influential to persuasive political participation, with veritable social media platforms. Social media, with their instantaneous and widespread usage, have been exploited by "anonymous" political influencers who fabricate and inundate internet community with unverified and false information. Using van Leeuwen's Discourse Legitimation approach and insights from Discourse Analysis, this study analyses 120 purposively sampled fake news posts on social media platforms like WhatsApp and Twitter, shared during the 2019 general elections in Nigeria. On these platforms, authorisation is the highest occurring legitimation strategy at 46.6% frequency; this is followed by Moralisation which has 27% and Rationalisation at 26.4%; while Mythopoesis did not feature at all in the sampled data, leaving it at 0%. In particular, expert and role model authority are most often deployed to validate fake news such as the demise and cloning of President Buhari, ruling party's plan to rig and destabilise the 2019 election, massive corruption in the current administration and imminent ethnic violence. The study argues that these strategies are viable persuasive tools owing to their use of discourse markers like makebelieve images, emotive language, appeal to emotions, rational conclusions, hateful comments, verbal indictment and coercive verbs.

(Igwebuike & Chimuanya, 2020)

2. 阅读下面三篇话语分析类论文有关语料的描述，并回答以下问题：
   (1) 三个研究分别收集了哪些话语材料作为语料？
   (2) 三个研究分别使用了哪些工具进行语料收集？
   (3) 你还知道哪些话语类语料收集的方法？
   (4) 比较三篇话语分析类论文中的语料描述，有何异同？
   (5) 在话语分析类论文写作中，应该如何写作语料收集方法？一般包括哪些要素？

语篇 1

   In order to be able to examine patterns of language choice that were repeated over the website as a whole, we decided to extract as much as possible of the plain text and store it as a corpus in which each subpage formed an individual file. However, the notion that a corpus can be developed from a single website, or can be seen as instantiating the textual content of a website, brings with it some methodological challenges. One of the issues that we had to deal with was the question of how to set boundaries to the target website. The *innocent* website is not, of course, a self-contained entity but includes many links to external sites. It was therefore necessary, first, to articulate a principled definition of the target website for the purposes of this research and, second, to find practical ways to harvest text from those pages which come under this definition.

For this research, we decided to work with the website as contextualised within a socio-cultural context (the United Kingdom) and as representative of a coherent company. We therefore chose to include only those pages which come under the *innocent.co.uk* domain, excluding versions of the site for other countries and excluding websites about activities with which *innocent* may be linked, for example, charity appeals or festivals. By excluding these external sites, we retained the notion of *innocent*'s links with the activity (as expressed on an *innocent.co.uk* page) but were able to form a principled boundary to our corpus.

A second issue that we faced concerns the fact that the *innocent* website regularly changes. Since it was not within the scope of the current research to attempt to capture and discuss those changes, we chose a specific, albeit random, date for our corpus compilation: 5 May 2015.

A third methodological challenge that we encountered was related to the sheer size of the data. A preliminary look at the *innocent* website indicated that it consisted of several thousand pages and subpages, and so it was necessary to use a webcrawler to identify the URLs whose text we wished to include in our corpus. Pre-programmed crawlers are available, but these would typically open every link which could be found on the target website and so may not respect the corpus boundaries which we had attempted to define.

We therefore chose to program our own crawler to open only links leading to other pages on the *innocentdrinks.co.uk* website, excluding links to external sites or to versions of the website for other countries. Programming a custom crawler gave us much more control over our data (Baroni and Ueyama, 2006; Suchomel and Pomikálek, 2012) and gave us confidence that all of the selected URLs contained content which was relevant to our corpus design principle.

Having arrived at a list of 4870 URLs, we then used the program SketchEngine to create a corpus (Kilgarriff et al., 2004). SketchEngine includes a relatively simple interface enabling researchers to create a corpus from URLs, but it does require a number of decisions to be made: the program offers options to use whitelist or blacklist keywords, to exclude files above or below a certain size and to exclude duplicate content. For our research, we wished to be as inclusive as possible within the principled boundaries which we had set — we therefore did not use any of these options, leaving the software to harvest as many of our target URLs as possible and allow any repetition of large chunks of text to be represented in our corpus statistics.

The resulting corpus consists of 2,889 files, representing those URLs from which SketchEngine was able to harvest sufficient text and containing 2,052,019 words.

(The PAD Research Group, 2016)

语篇 2

The study uses both qualitative and quantitative approaches. Out of 686 fake posts collected and verified in *CrossCheck Nigeria*, 120 fake news posts were sampled from three main Nigerian social media platforms, comprising 40 each from social media platforms like WhatsApp and Twitter. It is important to state that some of the fake posts were shared across the platforms while some featured in either one or two of them. The fake news posts were purposively selected based on their political thematic preoccupation and the number of likes and shares they generated. This means that only posts which centre on Nigerian politics were selected. The posts were collected over a period of 1 year, that is, from June 6 2018 to June 2019. This is the period that marks heightened activities on the 2019 general elections and many fake news were shared for legitimating and delegitimating political candidates and parties. The posts were thereafter categorised based on their sources and thematic preoccupations. A content analysis of the legitimation (linguistic) features was done to classify the posts according to their specific strategies. This is followed by a qualitative analysis of the form and functions of each of the strategies therein. It is important to point out that all the data on fake news for the analysis are crosschecked for their authenticity and unreliability. *CrossCheck Nigeria* provides the platform for checking inaccuracies of news and confirming fake news in Nigeria. *CrossCheck Nigeria* investigates news and refutes misinformation as either "Fake", "False" or "Incorrect".

(Igwebuike & Chimuanya, 2020)

语篇 3

According to the 41st China's Internet Development Report issued by CNNIC, the number of medical netizens is approaching to 0.195 billion, accounting for 26.6% of overall netizens and its annual rate of growth is 28% (CNNIC, 2018). It is also reported that online medical consultation accounts for 10.8% of all types of medical consultation. Therefore, online medical consultation will be a non-negligible field in the current and future discourse analysis. On the basis of maximized dataset, it is found that there is an array of Internet service providers in the filed of online medical consultation in China. Patients have found *120ask* to be the best option in current years, for it has the largest Internet penetration rate in the Chinese telemedicine industry, and enjoys the best reputation among patients in China (Hu, Xing, Yang, Zhang, & Yang, 2014). At the same time, as reported by Hu et al. (2014), its popularity quickly spread to the whole nation by word of mouth, and the site now registers close to 15 million monthly and over 6 billion-page views per month. Therefore, to investigate the forms and the mechanism of doctors' trustworthiness discourse constructed in online medical consultation, all the data were about the conversations between patients' questions and doctors' responses from *120ask.com*.

With a methodological shift away from an etic approach, which takes the researcher's perspective and theory-centered evaluation, toward an emic approach, which focuses on the participants' perspective and mostly spontaneous evaluation (Chen, 2019), Charmaz (2008) extended the grounded theory, which is believed to be the relatively scientific qualitative and further highlighted the importance of subjective experiences of the researcher. Thus, in the process of data colloection, all the data selected and processed followed the guiding principle of constructivist grounded theory. To be specific, in the course of data collection, 2,000 pieces of conversations between doctors and patients from *120ask.com* during the period of 2017–2018 were collected out of the consideration of their appropriateness and analyzability. As for the first step, in terms of data appropriateness, all the conversations on the medical consultation platforms are available to be viewed publicly, which means that all the data can be used as research without informed consent (Elm, 2009). As for data analyzability, based on constructivist grounded theory (Charmaz, 2008), several words, phrases or interactions in doctor-patient's talk-in-interactions which appear to be directed at constructing trustworthiness were identified and labeled different trustworthiness strategies, which specifically illustrated in the next section.

(Zhao & Mao, 2019)

3. 阅读下面两篇话语类分析论文中的"研究方法"部分，并回答以下问题：
   (1) 两篇论文分别采用了什么方法进行话语分析？
   (2) 两篇论文在进行话语分析时，都运用了哪些话语分析工具？
   (3) 从两篇论文中可以归纳出话语分析的一般操作程序是什么？

We used discourse analytical techniques to analyse in more detail some of the trends and patterns observed in the first step. While discourse analysis is a broad umbrella term that signifies a whole range of theoretical traditions in different disciplinary fields (linguistics, politics, sociology, education, to name but a few) and several different schools and epistemologies have developed as a consequence, this article is firmly situated in applied and sociolinguistic enquiry and positions itself under the relatively new but established field of Workplace Discourse (Angouri and Marra, 2011). In the analysis that follows, our main site of investigation is the written text on the *innocent* websites, but in line with recent work in the field (e.g. the various contributions in Scollon and Levine, 2004) we take multimodal features of the interaction into account and pay specific attention to the ways in which the visual and interactive features of the pages, including pictures, fonts, colours and weblinks, contribute to meaning construction and, more specifically, to the creation of *innocent*'s identity (e.g. Knox, 2009; Kress and Van Leeuwen, 1996; Van Leeuwen, 2011). These procedures are in line with sociolinguistic research which, although often privileging the analysis of language, acknowledges that not only is identity construction linguistic, but that different channels of communication create a semiotic aggregate (Jones, 2014; Scollon and Scollon, 2003). Such a mixed-methods approach, combining techniques and procedures from corpus analysis and discourse analysis, we believe, can capture more holistically the processes that contribute to constructing identities on websites.

(The PAD Research Group, 2016)

语篇 2

To analyse the data, we mainly relied on qualitative methods. The research procedure is as follows. First, we read all the 336 posts and extracted sentences with the Chinese keywords "相信" (believe), "信任" (trust) and "信心" (confidence) to have a general picture of @chinapeace's trust-related discourse. Then, based on content analysis and textual analysis methods, we identified three communicative actions for trust-building — NN, EP and ME. After that, we examined the linguistic and non-linguistic resources used by @chinapeace to perform these three actions. In this step, though our focus was mainly on linguistic analysis, we also examined such non-linguistic resources as pictures, hashtags and emojis because of their evaluative functions. In the next step, adopting a content analysis method, we categorised all the posts into two different categories based on their different orientations, that is, those oriented to gain public trust by providing epistemic-related news and those oriented to gain public trust by appealing to their emotions. The first type is closely related to cognitive trust-building and thus is labelled as "CBT-related posts". The second is termed "ABT-related posts", associated with affective trust-building. We calculated the frequency of these two different types and conducted a keyphrase analysis to find @chinapeace's preference for doing trust work. Finally, we discussed the results by referring to studies on trust behaviour in a traditional Chinese context.

(Wang & Yao, 2022)

4. 下面为一篇话语分析类本科学位论文的"研究方法"部分，阅读并完成以下任务：

(1) 指出该论文在研究设计方面存在的问题并进行修改。

(2) 与同学讨论话语分析类论文应该如何撰写研究设计。

This part focuses on the methodology of the study. It first puts up three research questions, and then states the procedures for data collection.

The present research is conducted to address the following three questions: (1) How are the two discourse strategies related to trust construction, namely neutralize the negative (NN) and emphasize the positive (EP), used in the context of courtroom? (2) How do these discourse strategies attribute to the construction of three aspects of trust? (3) What are the communicative effects of such legal discourse?

Research data of the present study covers the lines of the first season of both the British television series *Silk* and the American television series *Boston Legal*. The research mainly focuses on the lawyers' discourse during court hearing. During the investigation, four steps are mainly adopted to collect the data.

Step 1: log on the website of YYeTs and download the first season episodes of *Silk* and *Boston Legal* for further analysis

Step 2: watch the episodes carefully and analyze the performance of the lawyers

Step 3: carry out a transcription task recorded by means of Word

Step 4: categorize the collected data and divide them into several parts to analyze the discourse strategies the lawyers adopt in courtroom.

（本科生学位论文初稿）

5. 下面是一篇话语分析类论文的"讨论"部分，阅读并思考：话语分析类论文应该如何撰写这一部分？

This article has examined epistemic negotiation undertaken by Chinese EFL peer tutors. Our findings show two typical types of epistemic challenges to the Chinese EFL peer tutors in writing tutorials, i.e., proficiency-based challenges due to the tutors' lack of sufficient English proficiency and resistance-based challenges due to the [K–] participants' resistance to tutorial advice or assessment. The peer tutors mainly rely on identity-related discursive practices to manage these challenges. They activate their EFL learner identities to weaken awkwardness triggered by their poor oral English, limited English vocabulary and wrong English pronunciation, and highlight their competent and authoritative identities to regain trust from the [K–] participants after being questioned or resisted by the latter.

These findings provide further evidence of what Heritage (2012) has termed the "not unchallengeable" feature of participants' epistemic status in social interaction, highlighting the dynamism of epistemic negotiation in the turn-by-turn unfolding of tutorial interactions. They also foreground a once-neglected issue in writing center literature, i.e., peer tutors' language proficiency. Most previous studies unanimously label peer tutors as "English natives" (Thompson, 2009). As a result, peer tutors' good command of English is taken for granted and viewed as tutors' default ability necessary for tutoring.

However, for EFL peer tutors whose mother tongue is not English, language proficiency constitutes a problem in tutorials. Black (2016) shows how a Spanish EFL peer tutor's limited English vocabulary stops her from doing tutoring effectively, proving the existence of linguistic disadvantage of peer tutors in tutorials, which corroborates what we have found in this study. EFL peer tutors are far less competent than English native speakers in their English use, but their institutional role as a tutor has prescribed their higher epistemic status relative to student tutees and tutoring assistants. The clash between their language proficiency and epistemic status constitutes the possible reason why they are frequently confronted with proficiency-based challenges. Given this, their activation of an English learner identity to cope with proficiency-based challenges is not hard to understand. Making salient the learner identity puts tutors in an equal epistemic status with tutees, a practice used to shorten the gap between tutors' actual linguistic proficiency and that required by their institutional role as [K+] participants. Another related issue concerns the expected role identities of peer tutors in writing tutorials. For long, scholars have argued over a tutor-as-peer and tutor-as-instructor dichotomy (Gillespie and Lerner, 2000). "Tutor-as-peer" is the expected role identity of tutors prescribed almost unanimously in early tutorial manuals, like in Rafoth's *A Tutor's Guide* (2000) and Gillespie and Lerner's *Guide to Peer Tutoring* (2000). It is an idealized role identity of tutors according to the prevailing writing center orthodoxy. In contrast, ethnographic investigations into writing center tutoring find that peer tutors fulfill a more "teacherly" than "peer" role identity by "evaluating tutees' writing and suggesting changes in both content and form" (Thonus, 1999: 61). Our analyses of Chinese EFL peer tutors' discursive behavior indicate no fixed or prescribed role identities for peer tutors in actual tutorials. Peer tutors activate or highlight different role identities to fulfill specific communicative purposes in different phases of tutorial interactions via various discursive strategies. The finding concerning how peer tutors' role identities are negotiated to manage epistemic challenges in tutorial interactions in our study is in agreement with the social constructivist view on discourse and identities, which holds that participants' identities are dynamically constructed in and through discourse (Benwell and Stokoe, 2006).

Overall, the study sheds light on EFL peer tutor training at university writing centers in non-English speaking countries by providing a qualitative turn-by-turn analysis of tutorial interactions. Future research could combine both qualitative and quantitative methods, or add interesting data from other non-English speaking countries like Japan and Korea, to yield more exciting findings related to EFL peer tutors' discursive behavior. Studies of this kind can help promote writing center professionals and instructors to work out more flexible training guides by considering EFL peer tutors' role identities and English commands instead of following a universal training recipe.

(Chen & Wang, 2022)

课外练习

1. 话语分析无固定分析程序。不同研究视角下的话语分析步骤和方法各不相同。请以小组为单位进行文献阅读，归纳会话分析及批评话语分析的基本步骤和方法，基于研究发现制作 5—10 分钟的微课小视频。

2. 收集国内话语分析方向硕士论文以及国际期刊话语分析类论文各 10 篇，比较两类论文中的研究方法，分析异同，汇报研究结果。

3. 下面是两篇话语类论文中的语料分析。语篇 1 出自本科生学位论文，语篇 2 出自《语用学学刊》（*Journal of Pragmatics*）发表的学术论文。阅读语篇并回答：

   (1) 语篇 1 和语篇 2 在语料分析的撰写方面有何差异？

   (2) 话语类的学术论文应该如何汇报语料分析结果？

语篇 1

By adopting the discourse strategy of neutralizing the negative (NN) in the context of courtroom, lawyers tend to defend their clients from the jury and the judge by both eliminating the sense of seriousness of clients' crime and gaining empathy from the jury, during which process, trust has been constructed naturally between the jury and the lawyer and their clients. For example,

We all make mistakes. You shouldn't have slept with Alan Bradley after your relationship was over. But it's what we do with our mistakes that counts. That's what really matters.

In Example (1), the lawyer presents a fact that everybody makes mistakes to mitigate the guilty of his client. In this case, making mistakes is the negative element and the lawyer neutralizes the negative by proposing that mistakes are unavoidable. Thus, understanding and sympathetic response from the jury are achieved, making the jury believe in the defendant's innocence or the ability of reforming from evil to good.

（本科生学位论文初稿）

语篇 2

The neutralize-the-negative strategy is realized through the linguistic resources for dialogic engagement (Martin and White, 2005; White, 2003, 2012). This category includes all the devices that speaker use to take a stance on the current topic and through which they position themselves vis-à-vis alternative viewpoints and potential responses from their interlocutors (White, 2012: 61). The range of resources included in this category is broad, comprising epistemic modals (e.g. believe, think, be certain that), markers of evidentiality (e.g. see, hear, show that), expressions of attribution (e.g. say, claim, argue), adversative discourse markers (e.g. yet, but) and negation/denial (Martin and White, 2005). What these resources share is a dialogic functionality in the sense of Bakhtin (1981). They are competing stances that every text is profiled against (Martin and White, 2005).

An example of BP CEO's use of one of these resources, namely negation/denial, to confront and neutralize an unfavorable discourse about the company is the following.

Our fundamental purpose is to create value for shareholders, but we also see ourselves as part of society, not apart from it.

Through the use of the negation marker *not*, the CEO evokes and simultane-ously strongly rejects the — actual or anticipated — claim that the company would privilege investors' interests at the expense of society. By doing so, he seeks to neutralize his unfavorable discourse and protect BP's integrity from the negative effects that it could produce.[…] Thus the communicative goal of the statement in (1) is to promote a positive view of the company's integrity. This goal is pursued through the neutralize-the-negative strategy, which is realized in discourse via negation/denial.

According to Martin and White (2005), engagement resources can be broadly subdivided into those that act to challenge or refute different viewpoints, termed dialogic contraction, and those that open the dialogic space of the text to competing perspectives, termed dialogic expansion. Example (1) is an instance of dialogic contraction, as the negation marker acts to contract the dialogic space for alternative positions, thereby "fending-off" the adverse discourse it evokes (i.e. that the company does see itself as apart from society).

(Fuoli & Paradis, 2014)

拓展阅读

Gee, J. P. (2011). *How to do discourse analysis: A toolkit* (2nd edition). London: Routledge.

Taylor, S. (2013). *What is discourse analysis.* London: Bloomsbury.

第 11 单元
语料库语言学研究方法

学习目标

- 了解语料库的建设过程及语料库分析方法
- 学习语料库方法在语言学研究中的具体应用以及论文写作
- 在具体研究场景中建设语料库及依托语料库展开分析

国外语料库的发展始于 20 世纪五六十年代，中国语料库的发展可以追溯到 20 世纪 80 年代中期。语料库语言学经过半个多世纪的发展，目前已经深入触及语言学各个领域方方面面的问题，且已影响到其他社会科学问题的探索。研究队伍的壮大、前沿阵地的拓展、新颖概念的涌入、多种方法的采用、新型技术的开发，展现出异彩纷呈的变化图景。作为外语学习者，我们有必要了解语料库语言学的特征、方法、分析模式等内容，以语料库为工具，更好地开展语言学研究。

11.1　语料库及语料库语言学

语料库（corpus）是指按照一定的语言学原则，运用随机抽样的办法，收集自然语言并运用文本或语言片段建成的具有一定容量的大型电子文本库。语料库建设是目前语言学研究领域的重大工程，是语言学研究的重要支柱。无数的研究结果证明：我们考虑的已不再是语言研究是否需要语料库，而是如何充分利用现代技术拓展语料库的研究范围。从本质上讲，语料库是通过对自然语言运用的随机抽样，以一定大小的语言样本代表某一研究中所确定的语言运用总体。语料库按照其规模可以分为大型语料库和小型语料库，按照用途可以分为综合型语料库和专用型语料库。（代表性语料库见附录 1）

语料库语言学是以现实生活中人们运用语言的实例为基础进行的语言研究（McEnery & Wilson, 2003），不仅研究语言中哪些词语、结构和使用是可能出现的，而且还要统计它们出现的概率。基于语料库的研究不再是计算机专家的独有领域，它正在对语言研究的许多领域产生愈来愈大的影响。像其他语言学一样，语料库语言学研究语言的本质、结构和使用，以及语言的习得、语言变异和语言的改变。研究的重点是词汇和语法，而不是纯句法。语料库语言学不属于语言自身某个侧面的研究，而是一种以语料库为基础的语言研究方法（Rühlemann, 2019）。它实际上包括两个方面的内容：一是对自然语料进行加工、标注，二是用已经标注好的语料进行语言研究和应用开发。语料库语言学的方法被广泛应用于语言习得、方言学、语言教学、句法和语义研究、音系研究、翻译等各个领域。

语料库语言学的研究对象是文本，这些文本是语言描述和论证中的证据来源。其中，对语言条目在语料库中分布的计量描述已逐渐成为语言研究的一个必要的组成部分。正如语言学家利奇（Leech, 1992）所言：语言研究的目的是描述语言的使用，而不是语言的能力。正是对使用中语言的观察导致了理论的产生，而不是相反。然而，语料库语言学不同于转换生成语法那样的语言理论，它是语言学家在进行语言研究时使用的方法。语言学家在研究语言的本质、成分、结构和功能时，需要有一些语言证据来陈述在语言中什么是可能的。在不同时代，这些证据或来自语言学家的直觉和内省，或来自调查和归纳，或来自对口语和书面语的观察与描述。在基于语料库的研究中，这些事实将直接从文本中获得。

11.2　语料库建设

随着计算机及相关技术的飞速发展，语料库建设变得越来越容易。扫描仪、电子出版物以及网上资源为收集语料提供了极大的便利。建立语料库已经不再是专家的专利，广大的语言研究者完全可以自行建立中小型语料库，进行语言学和应用语言学研究。本节将以一般用途语料库为例，对具体建设过程进行说明。

阶段一：语料定位。在筹建语料库之初，首先要考虑的是建立语料库的目的：是一般用途的语料库，还是特殊用途的语料库。一般语料库应为各种语言研究提供大量好的语言实例；特殊语料库可能是为某种自然语言产品服务的，具有明显的领域针对性。在确定语料类型后，研究者需要进一步确定语料库规模的大小。

阶段二：语料收集。在确定语料的类型和规模后可以进行语料的收集。语料库的语料来源众多，包括诗歌、标题口号、网络文本等。判断有效语料主要有两个标准，分别是语感标准和理据标准。语料库的收集可以通过扫描文件输入、键盘输入、使用现成的电子文本、大规模数据抓取等方式。

阶段三：语料存储。在编纂一个语料库时，首先应该设计一种系统的索引方法，将存放在计算机中的文件和原始的声音和视频信息联系起来。除此之外，还应保存文件的目录以及所有的文件，并且将它们与工作的拷贝分开存放。为了统一管理语料，需要使用一些文本中的特性作为标记。常用的表示文本特征的信息包括行分隔符以及章、节、段落标志等。

阶段四：语料维护。语料库一旦建成，其中总有一些错误需要修正，或者要对语料库进行改善，因此需要对语料库进行日常的维护和升级。这样才能适应新的软硬件和用户需求的改变。

11.3　语料库加工

在收集相关的语料后就可以使用语料库加工工具对语料进行加工。语料加工分为三个不同的阶段，分别是：

阶段一：语料清洗。在收集相关的语料后首先需要对语料进行降噪处理。在这个过程中，需要将整理好的文本中多余的空格、乱码、错别字、重复的字以及其他不需要的信息（如表格、冗余的符号等）均去除。语料清洗阶段通常使用的工具包括 Office Word、EmEditor、Text 等。

阶段二：语料标注。收集一种语言的大量文本并储存在计算机上，形成一个大规模的语料库。之后，研究者希望从这个语料库中抽取所需的信息。例如，利用真实的语言数据来建立一种语言更好的词典或语法手册，以便成功地理解和使用这种语言。为了从不同语料库中抽取信息，必须首先在一个或更多层面上对语料库进行分析，并且将分析结果标注到语料上去，从而给一个语料库带来附加的价值，这就是语料库标注。语料标注具体包括语法标注、语义标注、句法标注等不同的类型。语料标注常用的工具包括 TreeTagger、CorpusWordParser 等。

阶段三：语料对齐。如果语料涉及多语或者是双语，则需要进行对齐处理。语料对齐的方式可以是段落与段落对齐，也可以是句子与句子对齐，但前提条件必须是形成规范的语对。语料对齐常用的工具包括 Tmxmall、ParaConc 等。

11.4　语料库分析

当前语料库的分析方法主要包括三种类型：第一种类型是基于语料库的分析方法（corpus-based approach）。该方法主要是利用语料库来对已有的理论或假设进行探索，从而验证或修正已有理论。基于语料库的分析方法往往采用定量和定性相结合的分析方法，并且以对语言的功能性分析为主。就定性分析而言，研究者会结合话语分析等方法对自然文本（主要是句子或语篇，而非词汇）进行分析。就定量分析而言，研究者会借助计算机自动分析技术和统计学中的推断统计法展开分析。具体而言，研究者需要根据语言学的理论首先做出假设，然后根据语料库分析两组或多组不同的话语现象之间是否存在统计学上的显著性差异。

第二种是语料库驱动的分析方法（corpus-driven approach）。这种方法主要是以语料库作为出发点和唯一观察对象，对语言中的各类现象进行全新的界定和描述。语料库驱动的分析方法反对利用语料库之外的任何理论前提。相反，研究者主要利用词汇索引技术（常用的索引软件有 AntConc 等），对词项及其搭配的语境进行分析和归纳。分析的内容主要涉及词频统计与分析、搭配、类联结、语义倾向、语义韵等内容。由于这种方法主要靠人工完成，常常不需要任何统计学检验。虽有不少学者主张通过计算 MI 的方法来确定搭配关系的强弱，通过卡方检验或对数似然比的方法来确定频数差异，但大部分研究中所使用的都是描述统计法（如计算频数或百分比）。

第三种是语料库例证法（corpus-illustrated approach）。语料库例证法主要是指研究者从语料库中选取合适的例句、对话等对某一假设或者理论进行佐证。这是一种自上而下的分析方法，与基于语料库的分析方法有一定的相似之处。不过，这种方法不涉及统计学问题，仅支持定性分析法。

11.5 语料库应用

在语料库建成后，就可以采用不同的语料库分析方法开展不同的研究。目前来看，语料库被广泛应用于理论语言学、语言教学、翻译等不同的领域。以下将选取其中具有代表性的研究进行举例说明。

第一，语义韵分析。所谓语义韵是一种搭配现象，是指某些词语由于经常同具有某种语义特征的语言单位共现而产生某种语义色彩。由于语义韵解释的是关于词的现象，而语料库可以帮助研究者系统地观察此现象，所以基于语料库的语义韵研究成为研究热点。目前来看，基于语料库的语义韵研究主要采用三种方法：基于数据的方法、数据驱动的方法和基于数据与数据驱动相结合的折中方法。通过这三种方法，研究者可以发现新的语言现象，并推动语言学相关理论的发展。

第二，词典编纂。自约翰·辛克莱教授（John Sinclair）于 20 世纪 70 年代带头建立 COBUILD 语料库之后，语料库被广泛应用于词典编纂工作。按照辛克莱的观点，证据（evidence）是保证词典中的例句自然真实的必要条件。根据 COBUILD 编纂的词典中，每个词条不但有频率信息，而且义项取舍和排列次序，无不以大型语料库的实际统计结果为依据，且每个例句必采自收集在语料库中的实际使用的语言事实。

第三，语言教学。语料库是语言事实的采样，这就为语言教学提供了真实的语言材料。学习者可以自己到语料库中查询词汇用法、搭配等问题。这不但为学习者提供了真实的语境，而且为学习者提供了一种探索语言的手段。学习者可以像语言学家研究语言一样对语言进行主动探索，这在写作教学中可收到很好的效果。

第四，翻译研究。基于语料库的翻译研究是以双语平行语料库为工具对翻译的诸多方面进行研究，语料库与翻译研究相结合是现代翻译研究的重要手段。语料库翻译学研究多集中在语言特征、译者风格、翻译评介、翻译教学等方面。语料库翻译学近年来的成果集中表现在两方面：一是对翻译共性、译者风格等原有课题的认识深化；二是基于翻译语料库的语言变化探索和多模态口译语料库建设等新课题的开拓。

课堂讨论

1. 阅读下列摘要（Kolhatkar et al., 2020）并回答问题：
   (1) 在语料库建设研究中，论文摘要部分该如何撰写语料库的规模和特征?
   (2) 在语料库建设研究中，论文摘要部分该如何撰写语料收集和加工的方法?

Abstract

We present the SFU Opinion and Comments Corpus (SOCC), a collection of opinion articles and the comments posted in response to the articles. The articles include all the opinion pieces published in the Canadian newspaper *The Globe and Mail* in the 5-year period between 2012 and 2016, a total of 10,339 articles and 663,173 comments. SOCC is part of a project that investigates the linguistic characteristics of online comments. The corpus can be used to study a host of pragmatic phenomena. Among other aspects, researchers can explore: the connections between articles and comments; the connections of comments to each other; the types of topics discussed in comments; the nice (constructive) or mean (toxic) ways in which commenters respond to each other; how language is used to convey very specific types of evaluation; and how negation affects the interpretation of evaluative meaning in discourse. Our current focus is the study of constructiveness and evaluation in the comments. To that end, we have annotated a subset of the large corpus (1,043 comments) with four layers of annotations: constructiveness, toxicity, negation and Appraisal (Martin and White, *The language of evaluation*, Palgrave: New York, 2005). This paper details our corpus, the data collection process, the characteristics of the corpus and describes the annotations. While our focus is comments posted in response to opinion news articles, the phenomena in this corpus are likely to be present in many commenting platforms: other news comments, comments and replies in fora such as Reddit, feedback on blogs, or YouTube comments.

2. 阅读下列节选内容（Kolhatkar et al., 2020）并结合表 1 回答问题：
   (1) 文中所提语料库的语料来源有哪些？
   (2) 该语料库的规模有多大？
   (3) 该语料库由哪些子库构成？

The corpus contains all 10,339 opinion articles (editorials, columns, and op-eds) together with their 663,173 comments from 303,665 comment threads, from the main Canadian daily newspaper in English, *The Globe and Mail*, for a 5-year period (from January 2012 to December 2016). We organize our corpus into three sub-corpora: the articles corpus, the comments corpus, and the comment-threads corpus.

Table 1 Statistics of the SFU Opinion and Comments Corpus

Item	Number
Articles corpus	
Number of articles	10,339
Number of words in articles	6,666,012
Number of unique article authors	1,628
Number of articles with comments	7,797
Average number of comments per article	85
Average number of threads per article	39
Average number of top-level comments per article	35
Comments corpus	
Number of comments	663,173
Number of words in comments	37,609,691
Number of unique commenters	34,472
Number of top-level comments	272,787
Average number of comments per commenter	19
Comment-threads corpus	
Number of threads	303,665
Number of comments	773,716
Average number of comments per thread	3

3. 阅读下列节选内容（Kolhatkar et al., 2020）并回答问题：
   (1) 下文研究者建设语料库的过程中主要收集了什么类型的语料？
   (2) 研究者为在语料抓取过程中有效获取语料采用了什么方法？

Collecting Only Opinion Articles　We were interested only in opinion articles and did not want to crawl and scrape all articles on the site. We also wanted to restrict our searches to a specific time period. This proved impossible using only the URLs on the site, as they did not have a structure showing section of the paper or date. As a result, to obtain a complete list of all opinion articles published in the relevant time period, we used Factiva, a business information and research tool that aggregates content from both licensed and free sources and provides organizations with search, alerting, dissemination, and other information management capabilities.

4. 阅读下列节选内容（Kolhatkar et al., 2020）并回答问题：
   在语料标注过程中，下文的研究者是如何保证可信度的？

Using WebAnno (de Castilho et al., 2016), a total of 1,121 comments were annotated with the aforementioned labels according to the Annotation Guidelines (after duplicate removal, 1,043 comments remain; see "Duplicate Removal and Final Corpus" section). As in the negation annotations, the comments were annotated by two individuals (one an author of this paper; the other a research assistant), evaluated for agreement, and curated to increase the accuracy of annotation. We began with guidelines previously used on a corpus of film reviews (Taboada et al., 2014) and the step-wise process in Fuoli (2018) and further developed them by iteratively testing and discussing those guidelines on our corpus. Once guidelines had been established, a research assistant annotated the original 1,121 comments under the supervision of one of the researchers, who was responsible for curating the annotations. Curating involved examining each annotation instance, and ensuring that it conformed with the guidelines. When disagreement existed, the annotator and the curator discussed the source of disagreement, and the curator ultimately decided on the final label. This curation process was performed after the agreement measures were calculated.

5. 阅读下列摘要并回答问题 [1]：
    (1) 该论文摘要部分是如何确定研究目标的？
    (2) 该论文摘要部分是如何呈现语料数据的？
    (3) 该论文摘要部分是如何描述结果的？

Abstract

  Rotavirus-B was declared a global pandemic by the World Health Organization on 11th March, 2020. Scientists and researchers immediately took interests to find a vaccine. While researchers in various discipline, particularly in medicine, began to study about the virus to help us understand the situation from various perspectives, there is limited research on linguistics analysis to date about Rotavirus-B. Therefore, the present study aims to contribute to research in linguistics about Rotavirus-B, by employing corpus-driven approach for data analysis. Online newspaper reports about Rotavirus-B were downloaded from the Star online from March 1st to March 31st, 2020. A total of 1018 news reports were processed and analysed, with 140 themes being identified.100 top collocates with the MI score set at a minimum of 5, using AntConc software revealed that verb and noun collocates co-occurred frequently with the node word Rotavirus-B. Generally, the collocates reflect fear, anxiety and uncertainty that majority of Malaysians feel. It also shows how the virus is taking a toll on Malaysia and Malaysians with regards to economy and social life. On the other hand, some of the collocates portrayed the government to be in total control of the situation, despite the threat to health and economic situations in the country. Suggestions for future research about Rotavirus-B include comparison of several newspaper reports from English newspapers in Malaysia, analysis of news report during extended movement control order (ECMO) in Malaysia or discourse analysis of crisis communication by political leaders in ASEAN.

6. 阅读下列节选及表 1 并回答问题：
    (1) 在进行主题分析时，下文研究者采用了什么理论框架？
    (2) 主题分析在什么情况下适用？有什么条件？

---

1 课堂讨论 5—7 题是根据 Nor Fariza Mohd Nor 和 Adlyn Syahirah Zulcafli 两位学者在 2020 年的研究改编而成。

IDENTIFICATION OF THEMES

The headline was analysed manually, using Clarke and Braun (2013) six phases of thematic analysis. Clarke and Braun (2013) assert that thematic analysis is suitable for a wide range of research interest and theoretical perspectives because it works with (1) a wide range of research questions, (b) can be used to analyse different types of data, from secondary sources to transcripts of focus groups or interviews, (c) works with large or small data-sets and (d) can be applied to produce data-driven or theory driven analysis. The news reports were manually "copied and pasted" onto word document (.doc). An average of 40 short news report about Rotavirus-B, were published every day in the newspaper, which made up a total of 1280 news report. The data filtration process was conducted by eliminating any overlapping and irrelevant article, leaving only 1,018 to be used as the data for this study. The news reports were manually "copied and pasted" onto word document (.doc).

TABLE 1. Clarke and Braun (2013) six phases of thematic analysis

No	Phases	Description	Example of the thematic analysis process
1	Familiarisation with data	The researcher must be familiar with the data which involved reading and re-reading the data (and listening to audio-recorded data at least once, if relevant) and noting any initial analytic observations.	Each news report has detailed information about the individuals who are affected by Rotavirus-B.
2	Coding	This process captures both a semantic and conceptual reading of the data. The researcher codes every data item and ends this phase by collating all their codes and relevant data extracts.	Identified keyword: new rotavirus cases, healthcare worker infected, politicians test negative
3	Searching for themes	Coding the identified codes to identify similarity in the data.	Rotavirus cases Rotavirus report positive negative

4	Reviewing themes	Involves checking that the themes "work" in relation to both the coded extracts and the full data-set. It may be necessary to collapse two themes together or to split a theme into two or more themes, or to discard the candidate themes altogether and begin again the process of theme development.	Rotavirus-B cases and report are the same, hence, the researcher decided to label news reports such as this as *Rotavirus report*. News report about Rotavirus-B under this theme will be about *positive* and *negative cases*, and *death*.
5	Defining and naming themes	The researcher must conduct and write a detailed analysis of each theme. Questions which are asked at this point include the "what story does this theme tell?" and "how does this theme fit into the overall story about the data?"	The final theme is identified as *Rotavirus report*.
6	Writing up	Writing-up involves weaving together the analytic narrative and (vivid) data extracts to tell the reader a coherent and persuasive story about the data, and contextualising it in relation to existing literature.	Rotavirus report (positive, negative, death)

7. 阅读下列节选并回答问题：

(1) 什么是搭配分析（collocation analysis）？

(2) 搭配的统计分析依据有哪些？

(3) 文章中的前 100 个搭配词汇是如何确定的？

COLLOCATION ANALYSIS

In this study, collocation is defined as the above-chance frequent co-occurrence of two words within a pre-determined span, typically five words on either side of the target word (the node) (see Sinclair, 1991). The statistical analysis of collocation involves three measures: the frequency of the node, the frequency of the collocates, and the frequency of the collocation itself.

For the collocation analysis, text files were gathered and uploaded into AntConc 3.5.8 software. The target word related to the public health crisis was entered into the system for analysis. Mutual Information (MI Score) was used to measure the strength of the collocation. The MI Score provides insight into the likelihood of the collocate occurring with the target word (Nor Fariza Mohd Nor et al., 2019). However, to determine the statistical significance of the collocates, the Log Likelihood (LL) measure was also employed. Both the MI Score and LL were used to ascertain statistical significance, resulting in the identification of the top 100 collocates. According to Xiao and McEnery (2006), an MI Score of 3 and above indicates a significant collocate. In this study, the researchers set the minimum MI Score to 5 with a minimum frequency greater than 4, within a 5-word span on either side of the target word. The top 100 collocates were selected based on these criteria.

课外练习

1. 与同学讨论语料库例证法、基于语料库的方法和语料库驱动的方法之间的区别。
2. 以 COHA 为例，进行英语频度副词 ALWAYS 的搭配分析。需要重点分析 ALWAYS 的主观性特征（提示：主观性分析一般涉及对搭配词汇中人称代词、认知动词、否定算子等的分析）。
3. 自建一个二语英语写作语料库，要求：
   (1) 词数不少于 30000 词；
   (2) 对语料进行降噪处理；
   (3) 对语料进行语法标注；
   (4) 对至少一种语法语误展开语料库驱动的分析。

拓展阅读

Biber, D., & Reppen, R. (Eds.). (2015). *The Cambridge handbook of English corpus linguistics*. Cambridge: Cambridge University Press.

Crawford, W., & Csomay, E. (2015). *Doing corpus linguistics*. New York: Routledge.

Tognini-Bonelli, E. (1996). *Corpus linguistics at work*. Amsterdam/Philadelphia: John Benjamins Publishing Company.

王克非. (2021). 双语语料库研制与应用新论. 上海：上海外语教育出版社.

许家金. (2023). 语料库研究方法. 北京：外语教学与研究出版社.

第 12 单元
语言实验理论和研究设计

学习目标

- 了解语言实验的基本方法及核心概念
- 学习实验方法在语言研究中的具体应用
- 掌握实验设计的基本技巧、方法和核心术语
- 掌握控制额外变量的方法
- 掌握拉丁方实验的设计方法和步骤

12.1 基本概念

科学实验的核心目标在于揭示事物间深层次的因果关系，而语言实验研究的目的则是深入探索并阐明不同语言现象之间复杂而微妙的因果联系。这一过程旨在通过系统性地观察、测量与分析，揭示语言结构、功能及其变化背后的驱动力与相互作用机制。

变量（variable）是语言实验研究中最重要的概念之一。变量是指在数量上或质量上可变的事物的性质。在语言实验研究中，一般把变量分为两类，一类是与实验操纵有关的，比如自变量、因变量等；另一类则是与实验条件没有直接关系、需要控制或保持恒定的变量，称为无关变量或干扰变量。

自变量（independent variable）是研究者为了确定什么因素影响行为而有意控制或操纵的因素。比如，二语习得领域常见的因素诸如二语学习者的年龄、性别、习得年龄、熟练程度等都可能对二语习得产生影响，因此都可以成为研究者操纵的自变量。自变量可以有不同的水平（level），比如学习者的性别可以分为男性和女性两个水平，熟练度可分为高、中、低三个水平等。

自变量一般可以分为两种：一种是与研究任务有关的自变量，比如词性、词频、词长、句子的长度、复杂程度等；另一种是与受测者（即被试）有关的自变量，比如性别、熟练程度、习得年龄、记忆广度、阅读速度、推理能力、语用能力、教育背景等。对于后一种自变量，比如性别、记忆广度、推理能力等，存在明显的个体差异，因此在研究设计和取样阶段应予以考虑和控制，否则会对测试结果产生干扰影响。

因变量（dependent variable）是由操纵自变量而引起的被试的某种特定反应或其他心理、生理上的变化，是研究者所观察的变量，因此也称为反应变量（response variable），比如，行为学层面的反应速度（即反应时）、反应准确率是语言实验中经常采用的因变量。其他一些生理或脑神经信号，比如皮肤电压、电生理信号的强弱、脑神经信号的激活强度也可以作为因变量。因变量和自变量之间的关系，犹如图 12.1 中两个大小不同的齿轮，自变量类似于主动轮，因变量类似于从动轮，因此是自变量（主动轮）的变化引起因变量（从动轮）的变化，而不是相反。

图12.1　自变量与因变量之间的关系类比

控制变量（controlled variable）是实验过程中除自变量之外任何能对因变量产生影响的变量。换句话说，这些变量与因变量可能相关，但同时又不是研究者有意操纵的变量，因此又被称为干扰变量或无关变量。在词汇属性中，常见的需要考虑的控制变量有：词性、词类、词频、笔画、词长、具体性、同义词的数量、正字法构造等；在语句层面，常见的需要考虑的控制变量有：句子的长度、句子的自然度、句式的结构、句式的复杂度、句式的熟悉度、语境等。当然，上述因素是否作为控制变量，还要结合具体的研究问题和研究目的进行界定。在具体实验过程中，可以采用排除法、恒定法、随机化方法、匹配法等手段来控制额外变量，后文会详细介绍。

在语言实验中，当确定某一项研究的自变量和因变量之后，接下来就该考虑如何控制额外变量。比如，如果仅仅想探讨外语熟练度对二语句法加工的影响，就应该设法控制学习者的年龄、性别、教育背景、二语起始学习时间等因素对实验结果可能产生的影响。这些因素都可能对实验结果产生影响，因此在正式开始测试之前，应该对其进行控制或平衡，否则有可能对研究结果产生干扰，甚至导致得出错误的实验结论。如何有效地控制无关变量，是决定实验结果是否可靠的一个极为重要的标准。在某种程度上，额外变量控制的好坏程度将会决定一项语言学实验能否成功开展。一项成功的语言实验研究应该是在排除无关变量干扰的前提下，揭示自变量和因变量的关系。

注意事项：

（1）一般来说，语言实验应至少包含两个或两个以上的实验条件，其中可以设置一个或多个条件作为控制条件。

（2）对研究结果可能产生影响的额外变量需进行排除或控制。

（3）自变量的数量并非越多越好。在同一项语言实验中，应该设置数量有限的自变量。

（4）要保证实验数据的完整性。除非有充足的理由，否则不能随便剔除实验数据。

12.2 语言实验设计

实验设计是进行科学实验前做的具体计划，目的在于找出实验操纵和实验结果之间的因果关系，以检验所提出的研究假设，从而得出科学的结论。根据被试是否参与所有的实验条件，实验设计可以分为被试内设计和被试间设计。

在被试间设计（between-subjects design）中，一位被试只接受一种自变量水平或者多个自变量水平结合中的一种实验处理，不同被试接受不同的自变量水平或者多个自变量水平结合中的不同实验处理。被试参加了一个条件的测试，就不能够再参加其他条件的测试。比如，学习方法、教学方法、年龄、性别、熟练程度等因素经常被当成被试间的变量。这种设计的优势在于避免练习效应、疲劳效应、顺序效应等，避免不同实验条件之间的相互影响，劣势在于如何创设相等的测试组，容易受个体差异的影响且需要较多的被试样本。

在被试内设计（within-subjects design）中，每一被试都会接受所有自变量每一个水平的实验处理。在被试内设计中，由于每位被试都会接受所有的实验处理，那么就可能导致重复测量的问题，因此被试内设计又称重复测量（repeated measures）设计。除了重复测量的问题，在被试内设计中，测试题目出现的顺序也会对实验结果产生影响。如何尽可能降低重复测量和顺序效应对实验结果的影响呢？在语言实验研究领域，一种常见的解决方法是采用交叉平衡的方法来降低上述因素的影响。拉丁方设计（Latin square design）是最常用的一种交叉平衡技术，可以尽量降低重复测量和练习效应对实验结果的影响。这种设计的优势在于使用相对较少的被试样本，能提高实验的效率，减少练习效应和疲劳效应，从而更好地控制个体差异对实验结果的影响；劣势在于需要准备较多的实验材料，需要采用交叉平衡的实验设计技术。

12.3 控制额外变量的方法

控制额外变量主要有排除法、恒定法、随机化方法、匹配法、抵消平衡法等。

排除法（exclusion）是最为彻底的控制额外变量的方法。在语言实验研究中，除了研究者主动操控的变量（即自变量）外，还有其他很多因素可能会对实验结果产生影响。比如，在实验室环境下展开的实验就是为了尽可能排除噪声、温度等因素对实验结果可能产生的影响。正常情况下，对于额外变量我们会首先考虑采用排除法，无法排除的干扰变量再考虑采取其他的控制方法。

有些干扰变量无法从实验中排除，此时就需要考虑采用恒定法（holding variables constant）。比如，在理想的实验环境中，一项研究的测试题目应该在同样的测试场所（如同一个实验室、教室）由同样的测试人员（主试）在同样的测试时间段并采用同样的测试程序完成。个体差异因素，比如年龄、性别、受教育程度、记忆力等会对语言加工实验产生影响，但又无法完全排除这些因素对实验结果的影响。此时可以考虑采用恒定法，比如让不同测试组的被试在年龄、性别、教育背景等方面保持均等。这样所观察到的实验结果就不是由个体差异因素导致的。

随机化方法（randomization）的主要目的是减少顺序效应（或序列效应）或者样本先验分布特征对测试结果的影响。随机化方法至少可以应用在两个实验环节中：一是在安排测试项目的顺序时可以考虑采用随机化方法，另一个是在分配被试到不同的实验条件时采用随机化方法。随机化的好处是可以减少人为因素对实验结果的干扰，但同时也存在弊端，比如采用完全随机化的方法来安排实验材料的顺序可能会出现同一类型的项目多次连续出现，或者多次不出现，这反而会对实验结果产生影响。因此，相对于完全随机化的方法，更常采用伪随机的方式（pseudorandom method）对实验材料进行人工编排，以尽可能降低材料出现的规律性和可预测性。

有些情况下，某些变量，比如词汇层面的词性、笔画、词频，句子层面的句子长短、句式结构等，以及被试相关的年龄、性别等个体差异变量，可能会对实验结果产生影响，但它们并不是实验者感兴趣的变量，同时又无法完全把它们从研究中排除。这种情况下，可以考虑采取匹配法（matching）。比如在研究外语熟练度如何影响二语句法加工的实验中，就应该对高、低水平组被试性别、年龄、记忆广度等变量进行匹配，让两组被试保持平衡，否则所观测到的实验处理效应就可能会受到这些变量的影响而难以解释。一般来说，采用被试间和项目间设计的实验经常需要采用匹配法对分组变量进行匹配。

有些额外变量无法消除，也很难完全匹配，这时可以考虑采用抵消平衡法（counterbalancing）——使用一定的排列组合在条件之间和被试之间达到平衡额外变量的目的。语言实验研究中经常采用拉丁方排列的方法来抵消重复测量、顺序效应等额外变量的影响。下面将结合实例介绍如何采用拉丁方来达到抵消平衡的目的。

12.4 拉丁方设计

为了提高实验的效率并尽可能减少个体差异对测试结果的影响，很多应用语言学和心理语言学的实验经常采用重复测量设计（比如同时采用被试内设计和项目内设计）。在重复测量的实验中，被试会反复接受相同或相似的测试项目，这样会产生重复效应和练习效应。比如在徐晓东等（2019）的研究中，当读完句子"After the heavy rain, the city was wet"后，如果被试再阅读类似的句子（见表12.1中的b—d），就会产生明显的重复效应和疲劳效应。再比如，在双语切换（language switching）任务中，如果L1—L2方向的转换次数多于L2—L1方向，就可能导致前者产生的练习效应大于后者。由于这种练习效应所产生的影响是无法消除的，因此只能通过交叉平衡的方式对这一影响进行控制。拉丁方设计就是一种交叉平衡技术，可以很好地解决上述问题。

拉丁方设计的优势包括：能有效控制个体差异因素对实验结果的影响，具有较高的灵敏度和测量功效；相对需要较少的被试，实验较为高效；避免重复测量效应，有效平衡无关变量如练习效应、顺序效应、疲劳效应等。其劣势包括：实验材料数量需增加数倍；实验的处理数和拉丁方的版本数目要相等；实验程序的编排较为复杂；数据分析和处理较为烦琐。

在一个拉丁方的测试程序中，不同实验处理出现的次数要相等，实验条件的排列顺序在被试之间和被试内部也要尽可能地匹配，比如实验条件C出现的次数要和ABD相等，C出现在AB前和AB后的概率相等。

假设一个实验有N个实验条件，构建拉丁方的步骤如下：

步骤一：对实验条件（比如N=4）进行随机排列并用数字编号。C=1，B=2，D=3，A=4。

步骤二：采用公式构建第一行的排列顺序：1，2，N，3，N–1，4，N–2，5，N–3，6……其中N代表实验的条件数，如果有四个实验条件，上述排列为1 2 4 3，即C B A D。

步骤三：把第一行的每一个数字顺延1来构建拉丁方的第二行（2 3 1 4），即B D C A，在第二行数字的基础上顺延1来构建第三行，以此类推。四个实验条件所构建的拉丁方排列为：

$$C B A D$$
$$B D C A$$
$$D A B C$$
$$A C D B$$

注意事项：

（1）被试应该被随机分配到每一个拉丁方的测试版本（list）中，所选择的被试数量应该是拉丁方版本数的整数倍。

（2）上述编排方式仅适用于实验条件数目为偶数的情况。

设计举例

徐晓东等（2019）年探讨了不同的时间连词如何影响中国外语学习者对百科常识的理解。由于采用的是 2×2 的重复测量设计（同时采用被试内和项目内设计），因此如表 12.1 所示，同一组实验材料的四个不同版本中，实验句除了句首的连词和句尾的关键词不一样外，其他内容完全一样，如果同一位被试阅读全部这四个句子的话，就会产生明显的重复测量效应和练习效应。另外，由于实验一共采用了 40 套类似于表 12.1 中句式的实验材料，这40 个测试题目出现顺序的不同也可能会对实验结果产生影响。那么如何保证同一位被试既均等接受所有实验条件的处理同时又不会接受相同的实验材料呢？研究者采用了拉丁方设计，来平衡上述无关因素的影响。最终排列出的实验材料（不含填充句）的拉丁方列表如表 12.2 所示。

表12.1　2×2的重复测量设计的语料举例

实验条件	实例
after 一致句	(a) *After* the heavy rain, the city was <u>wet</u>.
after 不一致句	(b) *After* the heavy rain, the city was <u>dry</u>.
before 一致句	(c) *Before* the heavy rain, the city was <u>dry</u>.
before 不一致句	(d) *Before* the heavy rain, the city was <u>wet</u>.

表12.2　采用拉丁方进行交叉平衡的实验材料编排举例

测试版本	实验句的项目									
	Item1	Item2	Item3	Item4	Item5	Item6	Item7	Item8	...	Item 40
List I	1C	2B	3A	4D	5C	6B	7A	8D	...	40D
List II	1B	2D	3C	4A	5B	6D	7C	8A	...	40A
List III	1D	2A	3B	4C	5D	6A	7B	8C	...	40C
List IV	1A	2C	3D	4B	5A	6C	7D	8B	...	40B

课堂讨论

1. 前文所提到的徐晓东等（2019）的研究所采用的是被试内设计还是被试间设计？判断依据是什么？该研究中，存在哪些潜在的干扰变量？如何对这些干扰变量进行控制？
2. 在语言实验研究中，被试内的实验设计是否一定优越于被试间的实验设计？为什么？
3. 在语言实验研究中，何种情况下需要对实验材料进行拉丁方编排，何种情况下无须采用拉丁方编排？
4. 采用拉丁方设计能够解决哪些方面的问题，不能够解决哪些方面的问题？

课外练习

1. 阅读下列摘要（邱丽景等，2012: 1279–1288），指出该研究中的自变量、因变量以及可能的控制变量。

　　采用眼动技术，本研究探讨了阅读理解中代词的加工机制。读者阅读包含代词的文本，代词的性别与先行词的性别刻板印象一致或违背，同时其和先行词间的距离或远或近，记录被试阅读文本的眼动轨迹。结果发现，与一致条件相比，违背条件的加工时间更长。当代词和先行词间距离较近时，一致性效应在关键代词处（早期加工的眼动指标上）即出现，而当二者间距离较远时，一致性效应在更后的位置（代词后的区域）出现，并且只出现在反映晚期加工的眼动指标上。此外，与远距离一致条件相比，近距离一致条件下代词后区域的阅读时间更长。上述结果表明，性别刻板印象以及距离在代词加工中皆发挥重要作用，而且性别刻板印象产生的影响在时程上因距离的不同而不同。这一结果在一定程度上为语言理解的交互作用理论提供了证据。

2. 阅读下列摘要（Grainger & Frenck-Mestre, 1998: 601–623），指出该研究中的自变量和因变量。

The responses of English-French bilinguals performing semantic categorization and lexical decision tasks were facilitated by prime stimuli that were non-cognate translation equivalents of the targets (e.g. arbre–tree) when compared to unrelated primes (e.g. balle–tree). These translation priming effects were observed with very brief prime exposures (29–43 msec) and forward and backward masking of the prime. Using the same stimuli, translation priming effects were significantly stronger in the semantic categorisation task than in the lexical decision task. This suggests that the translation priming effect obtained in semantic categorisation is mediated by semantic representations in memory and not the result of form-level connections between translation equivalents, at least for the highly proficient bilinguals tested in the present experiment.

3. 语言实验中控制无关变量的常用方法主要有哪些？词汇加工实验和句子加工实验对无关变量的控制有何异同？

4. 在一项研究中，为了考察不同的汉语句式结构如何影响歧义代词的在线解读，研究者选用了三种不同的句式结构并分别测量了它们的阅读时间：普通句式（如张三打了李四，因为他今天骂了人。）、"把"字句（如张三把李四打了，因为他今天骂了人。）以及"被"字句（如李四被张三打了，因为他今天骂了人。）。在这项研究中，为了达到一定的统计效力，假设每种句式至少需要准备 10 组实验材料。试问：（1）如果采用被试间设计，总共需要多少组实验材料？（2）如果采用被试内设计，总共需要多少组实验材料？（3）如果采用拉丁方设计来编排材料，该如何构建拉丁方？

拓展阅读

Jegerski, J., & VanPatten, B. (2014). *Research methods in second language psycholin-guistics*. New York: Routledge.

Jiang, N. (2018). *Second language processing: An introduction*. New York: Routledge.

舒华、张亚旭. (2008). 心理学研究方法：实验设计与数据分析. 北京：人民教育出版社.

第 13 单元
语言实验范式及实例分析

学习目标

- 掌握启动的概念以及启动的实验方法
- 掌握自定步速阅读技术的特点、适用范围及优缺点
- 了解事件相关电位技术的原理
- 了解并掌握与语言相关的主要脑电成分

心理语言学在发展过程中形成了一些经典的实验范式，比如启动范式、语法转换范式、自定步速阅读范式（也称"移动窗口范式"）等，以及一些常用的测量技术，如眼动追踪技术、脑电（事件相关电位）技术等。

13.1　启动实验方法

启动（priming）是指对某一给定刺激物（如单词、面孔）的学习或接触会提高对同一刺激物或相关刺激物的反应速度或反应准确率。比如，看到 nurse 之后再看到 doctor，要比先看到 forest 之后再看到 doctor 时对 doctor 的反应速度更快，这一现象就称为启动效应。启动效应会出现在语言加工的多个层面上——除了语义层面，还可以出现在语音、词形、句法等层面。语义启动效应的理论依据是柯林斯和洛夫特斯（Collins & Loftus, 1975）提出的"语义扩散激活模型"。该理论认为，概念网络由不同联结强度的众多语言节点构成，这些节点之间通过语义的疏密和距离的远近形成不同强度的联结。当某个语义概念被激活之后，该激活会扩散开来，从而使得与此相关的节点也被激活。具体应用到语义启动范式中，这些激活扩散效应所产生的促进作用即为启动效应。启动效应可以产生于同一种语言内部，也可以产生于不同的语言之间，前者为语言内部启动，后者为语言间启动。

启动的类型有多种，包括重复启动、语义启动、语音启动、句法启动、跨模态启动等。语义启动是研究词汇加工最常见的实验范式之一。该范式可以运用于多种实验任务中，比如词汇判断任务（如要求被试判断所看到的词语为真词还是假词）、知觉识别任务（比如判断单词是大写还是小写）、语义分类任务（如判断名词是否具有生命性）等。重复启动属于一种特殊的语义启动任务，即启动词和目标词完全相同。

语义启动的相关术语主要包括：
- *启动词（prime）*：对目标词语判断可能会产生影响的先前词语。
- *目标词（target）*：目标作业词语。
- *启动时间间隔 SOA（Stimulus Onset Asynchrony）*：启动词和目标词之间的时间间隔。
- *启动效应（priming effect）*：语义无关条件下目标词的反应时（准确率）减去语义相关条件下目标词的反应时（准确率）的差值。

实验举例

（1）研究问题

汉－英跨语言翻译启动效应研究：当双语者使用外语时，其母语的词汇信息是否能够得到激活（张浩云等，2012）。

（2）实验受试

28名汉－英双语者，汉语为母语，英语为二语。

（3）实验设计

本研究采用2×2×2的三因素被试内实验设计。其中第一个因素是语义相关性（两个水平：语义相关、语义不相关），第二个因素是汉字重复（两个水平：重复、不重复），第三个因素是启动词和目标词之间的时间间隔（两个水平：长间隔、短间隔）

（4）实验材料

实验材料共计184对词长在7—11个字母的英语单词，汉语对译词均为双字词（实例见表13.1）。其中92对单词语义相关，另外92对语义无关。语义相关和无关单词对中，均有一半存在对译词单字重复（即单个汉字完全相同，出现的位置也一样，如map-geography的汉语对译词"地图—地理"存在"地"字重复）。另外，目标词和启动词之间的间隔有长间隔1500 ms和短间隔700 ms两种情况。

表13.1　实验设计及实验材料举例

SOA	汉字重复		汉字无重复	
	语义相关	语义无关	语义相关	语义无关
1500 ms	map-geography 地图—地理	hornet-vest 马蜂—马甲	glass-window 玻璃—窗户	castle-coke 城堡—可乐
700 ms	sheep-goat 绵羊—山羊	belief-message 信念—信息	sister-brother 姐妹—兄弟	pizza-story 比萨—故事

（4）实验结果

如表13.2所示，1500 ms间隔条件下，汉字重复时，语义启动效应为194 ms，汉字无重复时，语义启动效应为100 ms；在700 ms间隔条件下，汉字重复时，语义启动效应为183 ms，汉字无重复时，语义启动效应为122 ms，差异达到了统计学显著意义。由此可见，无论汉字是否重复，均出现了跨语言的启动效应，说明在二语语境下，母语的词汇信息可以自动激活，从而对词汇判断作业产生影响。该结论支持双语词汇通达的非选择性理论假设。

表13.2 语义启动实验的结果

SOA	汉字重复		汉字无重复	
	语义相关	语义无关	语义相关	语义无关
1500 ms	856	1050	909	1009
700 ms	843	1026	845	967

13.2 自定步速阅读实验方法

　　自定步速阅读（self-paced reading, SPR），也称移动窗口技术，是一种常用的心理语言学实验技术。该技术出现在 20 世纪 70 年代，先后被用于母语和二语阅读研究领域。作为一种在线测量技术，自定步速阅读可以探测句子的实时处理过程。与其他反应时技术一样，该技术假设读者阅读每一个词语的时间反映了其加工该词语所需的时间，因此自定步速阅读是通过记录被试阅读每一个语句片段（可以是词、短语、句子等）的时间，以此推测句子的加工过程和难易程度。一般来说，该实验要求被试通过按键反应逐词呈现句子内容，从而测量出每个句子片段的阅读时间。被试的按键速度可以自己控制和调整，因此这种自定步速的阅读方式在一定程度上体现了人们自然阅读的过程。该范式自首次被使用以来已有 50 余年的历史，目前仍是心理语言学领域研究句子及语篇加工的最有效范式之一。

　　在自定步速阅读实验中，阅读材料可以以词、短语或句子为单位呈现，具体由研究问题和材料的性质来确定。根据读者的阅读习惯，在自定步速阅读实验中，句子通常按照从左到右的线性顺序逐词（或逐短语）呈现。实验材料出现之前，通常在屏幕最左侧先出现一个"+"字，作为句子内容出现起始位置的提示。被试按键反应后，句子的第一个词语会出现，而其余句子内容会被一连串的"---"代替。被试再次按键，句子的第二个词语出现，第二个词语之后的句子内容仍以"---"代替，如此下去直到全部的句子内容呈现完毕。自定步速阅读时间即从被试看到某一词到做出按键反应之间的时间。一个句子的所有内容呈现完毕之后，可以设计一些问题对句子的内容进行探测，以确保被试在实验过程中认真地进行了阅读。根据词语在屏幕中停留方式的不同，自定步速的呈现方式分为两种：一种是累积式的（如图 13.1 所示），每次按键之后，在后一个词语出现的同时，前面的句子内容并不会立刻消失，而是会停留在屏幕上，直到所有的句子内容呈现完毕。另一种是非累积式的，每次按键之后，在后一个词语出现的同时，前一个词语会自动从屏幕中消失，被试每次只能在屏幕中看到一个词语（如图13.2所示）。研究显示，相对于累积式的方式，非累积式的方式较少受阅读策略（比如回视、反复阅读等）的影响，能够更准确地反应每一词语的加工时间。因此，目前大部分的自定步速阅读实验采用非累积式的呈现方式。

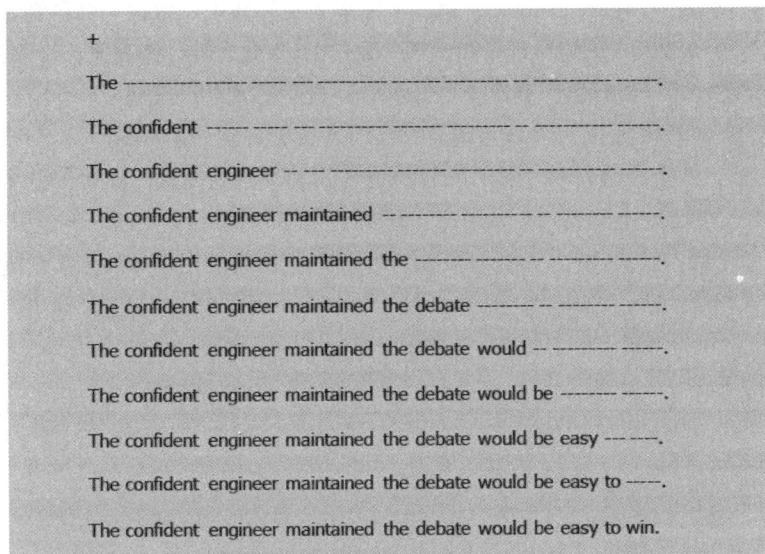

图13.1　累积式呈现的自定步速阅读方法（摘自Jegerski & VanPatten, 2014）

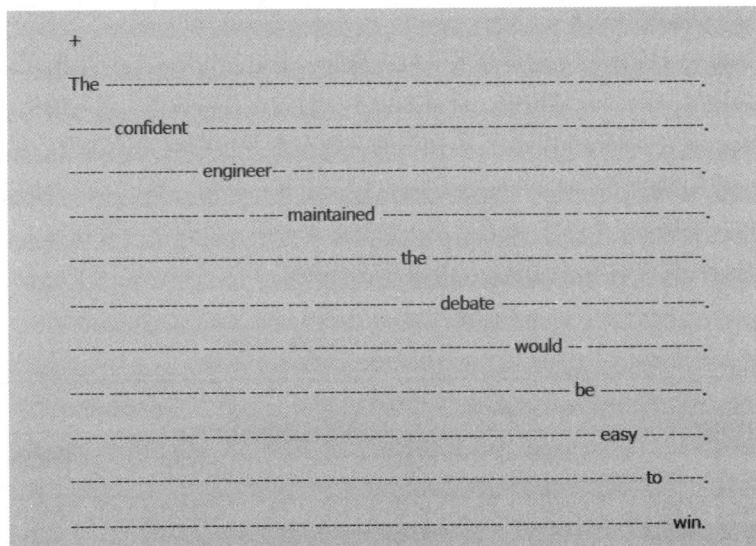

图13.2　非累积式呈现的自定步速阅读方法（摘自Jegerski & VanPatten, 2014）

实验举例

（1）研究问题

不同时间连词对中国英语学习者百科知识理解的影响（徐晓东等，2019）。

（2）实验设计

本研究采用两因素 2×2 的被试内实验设计，其中第一个因素为连词类型（连词类型：after、before），第二个因素为百科知识一致性（百科知识一致性：百科知识一致句、百科知识不一致句）。除此之外，还有第三个因素，即外语熟练度（熟练度：高水平、低水平），把其作为组间变量。

（3）实验材料

包含 40 套关键材料（每一套材料包含四种不同的句式，如表 13.3 中的例句），另有 20 个填充句。采用拉丁方设计，把所有材料分成四个测试版本，其中每个版本含有 40 个关键句和 20 个填充句，材料的出现顺序采用伪随机的方式编排。

表13.3　实验材料举例

实验条件	实例
after 一致句	(a) *After* the heavy rain, the city was <u>wet</u>.
after 不一致句	(b) *After* the heavy rain, the city was <u>dry</u>.
before 一致句	(c) *Before* the heavy rain, the city was <u>dry</u>.
before 不一致句	(d) *Before* the heavy rain, the city was <u>wet</u>.

（4）实验结果

如表 13.4 所示，无论是高水平组还是低水平组，句尾关键词上所记录到的结果显示，在 after 结构中，百科知识不一致句比百科知识一致句的阅读时间更长；而在 before 句中，百科知识的一致与否并不影响阅读速度。另外，在不一致的情况下，after 句的反应时也要长于 before 句。除句尾关键词之外的其他兴趣区域，均没有显著效应。这些结果表明，外语学习者在加工语用信息时会受到连词本身的语义及语用特征的影响。

表13.4　自定步速阅读实验的结果

	高水平		低水平	
	均值	标准差	均值	标准差
after 一致句	955.2	671.6	973.6	637.7
after 不一致句	1173.3	889.9	1152.2	733.1
before 一致句	992.1	685.2	1035.7	603.9
before 不一致句	1022.7	728.1	1006.1	638.2

13.3　事件相关电位技术

事件相关电位（event-related potential, ERP），即脑电，是指大脑皮层所记录到的神经元产生的电活动。与神经元有关的电活动主要包括两类：动作电位和突触后电位。一般认为，突触后电位是神经元突触后膜上的神经递质与其受体结合时所产生的电压，被认为是脑电活动的主要来源。突触后电位持续时间长（可长达几百毫秒）且可以累加，因此在一定条件下，多个神经元同时放电时，我们才有可能在头皮测量到这种综合的电压变化。

由于较低的信噪比，原始的脑电信号很难直接用于测量与特定事件相关的神经活动。为了提取与任务相关的脑电信号，研究者一般采用叠加平均技术把信号从噪声中分离开来。叠加技术的原理是，特异性的信号比如词汇判断所引起的脑电是事件相关的，而噪声由于是非特异性的，因此通过叠加平均可以让事件相关的信号越来越清晰稳定，而非特异性的噪声会逐渐衰减，从而提取到事件相关的脑电信号。

为了精准探测不同句子内容所诱发的脑电反应，无论是阅读还是听力任务，一般都需要对特定的刺激事件进行标记（即打上特定的标记），以便后续数据分析阶段提取相应的事件相关电位。比如，在句子阅读理解任务中，一般采用快速系列视觉呈现的方式（rapid serial visual presentation, RSVP，如图 13.3 所示）呈现阅读材料，在实验之前需要对不同类型的目标词语进行分类标记。后期数据处理阶段，对同一类型下的所有目标刺激所诱发的脑电结果进行叠加和平均，从而计算出特定事件相关的脑电电压值。

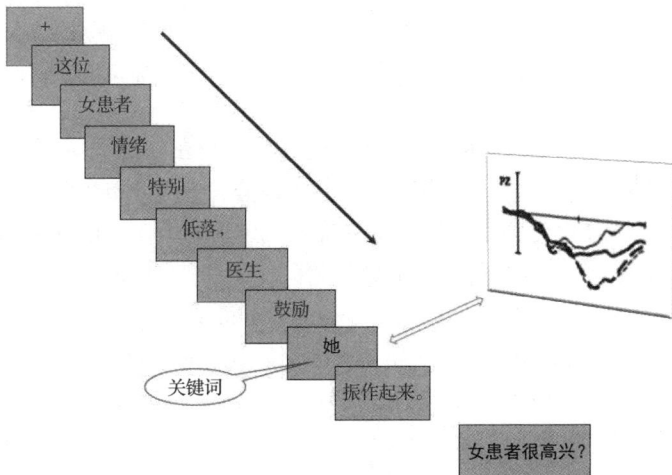

图13.3　句子理解脑电实验中快速系列视觉呈现刺激的流程图（摘自Xu et al., 2015）

与语言相关的脑电成分主要包括 N400、P600、LAN、Nref 等。

N400 主要跟语言的意义加工相关，最早由库塔斯和希利亚德（Kutas & Hillyard, 1980）发现。他们在比较句尾关键词的理解时发现，相对于语义正常的句子（如"It was his first day at *work*."），当被试阅读语义不正常的句子时（如"He spread the warm bread with *socks*."，如图 13.4 所示），在关键词 socks 出现 400 毫秒左右会诱发一个电压为负的脑电反应，命名为 N400。N400 主要分布在大脑的中部和后部区域。后续很多研究发现，N400 波幅跟很多因素有关，比如会受到词语之间语义关联程度、词频的高低、词语的抽象程度、词语的词形以及词语的可预测程度等因素的影响（Kutas & Federmeier, 2011；徐晓东、刘昌，2008）。另外，词语在句子中的位置以及语境对词语的制约程度也会影响 N400 的大小。研究显示，只要语言加工过程中出现了语义方面的困难，无论是词汇层面、句子层面甚至是非语言层面的问题，均会诱发明显的 N400 反应。

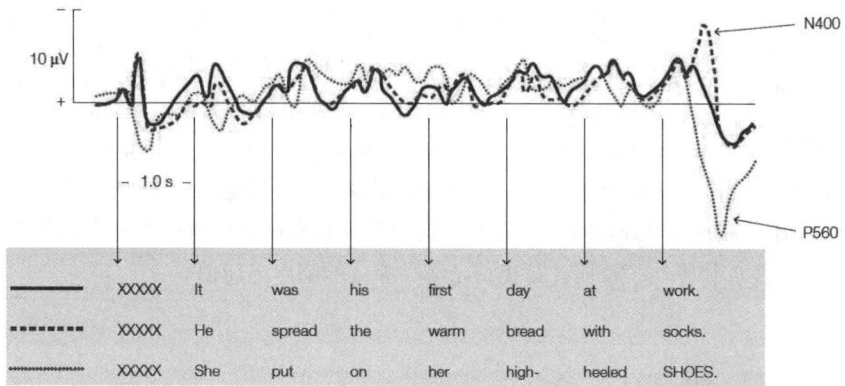

图13.4　句子加工中语义违反所诱发的N400效应（摘自Gazzaniga et al., 2019）

P600 是与句法加工相关的一个晚期成分，是在句法关键词出现之后 600ms 左右最为明显的一个电压为正的脑电成分，主要分布在大脑的中央和顶部区域。P600 由美国学者奥斯特豪特和霍尔库姆（Osterhout & Holcomb, 1992）以及荷兰学者哈古尔特、布朗和格鲁特胡森（Hagoort et al., 1993）率先发现。他们发现，如果把句子"The spoiled child *throws* the toys on the floor"中的 throws 改为 throw，就会产生更大的 P600（见图 13.5）。后来研究发现多种类型的句法违反，比如短语结构违反（phrase structure anomalies）、句子成分移位限制违反（violations of constraints on the movement of sentence constituents）、违反动词亚类（violations of verb subcategorization）等均能诱发出 P600 成分。最近的研究显示，P600 并非句法加工的特异性脑电成分，无论句法、语义或语用方面的问题，只要其影响句子的整合加工，均可能诱发 P600 成分（Xu et al., 2015）。

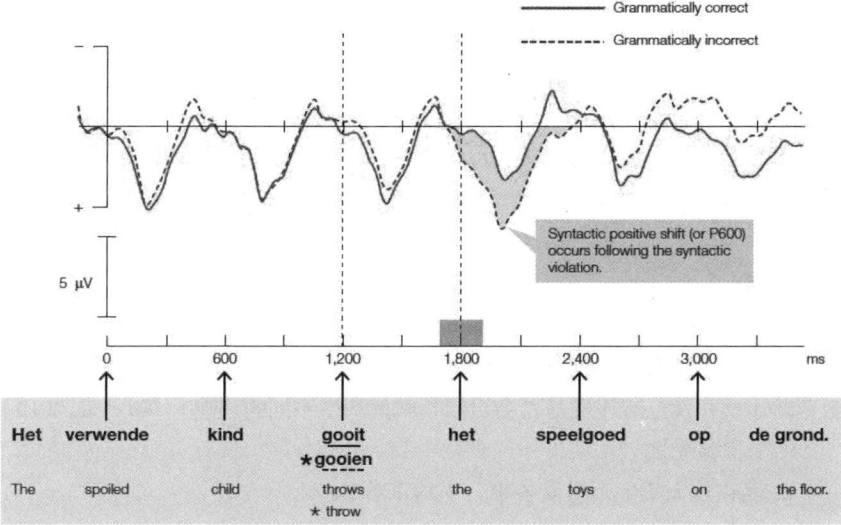

图13.5　句法违反所诱发的P600效应（摘自Gazzaniga et al., 2019）

除了 P600，句法加工还会引起其他脑电成分。芒特等（Münte et al., 1993）发现，当动词违反了主谓一致（you writes 应该是 you write）或违反了词类限制（your write，your 的后面应该跟名词），会诱发一个电压为负的脑电成分（left anterior negativity, LAN）。虽然 LAN 的时间窗口与 N400 有很多重合而且也是一个负波，但它主要分布在大脑左半球的前侧，因此被命名为左前负波。这说明 LAN 和 N400 所对应的认知功能并不完全相同。

Nref（a sustained negative shift）是一个跟指代加工密切相关的脑电成分，最早由范·贝克姆等（van Berkum et al., 1999）报告。研究发现，当说话语境中存在两个或两个以上人或物，而且当对语境中的人或物的指涉存在歧义时（如图 13.6 的点线所示），会诱发一个持续性的负波。后续研究发现，无论回指的形式是代词还是名词，无论是阅读理解还是听力理解，只要语境中存在指代歧义现象都会诱发出 Nref。

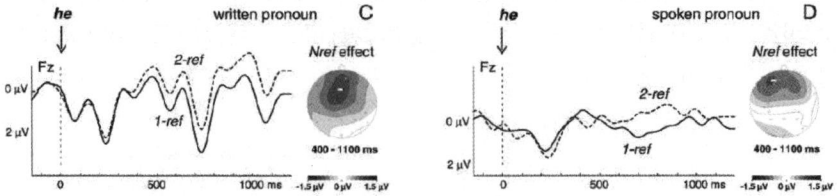

2-ref: David shot at John as ...
1-ref: David shot at Linda as ...

he　written pronoun　C
he　spoken pronoun　D

图13.6　指代歧义所诱发的Nref效应（摘自van Berkum et al., 1999）

相对于非歧义指代句"David shot at Linda as *he* ..."（黑色实线），指代歧义句"David shot at John as *he* ..."（黑色点线）的代词位置诱发了明显的 Nref。

实验举例：

（1）研究问题

汉语句子理解中，代词与先行词之间的一致性关系如何影响回指解读？数范畴违反和性范畴违反是否会对回指解读产生不同的影响？（Xu et al., 2013）

（2）实验受试

24 名在校大学生，男女各半，平均年龄 24 岁。

（3）实验设计及材料

2（范畴类型：数一致 vs. 性别一致）×2（一致性：一致 vs. 不一致）的被试内设计。每种实验条件下 46 个句子，4 种实验条件下共计 184 组语料（如表 13.5 所示），另有 172 个与实验句结构类似的填充句。采用拉丁方把实验材料编排成四个不同的版本。

（4）实验程序

脑电实验采用快速系列视觉呈现（RSVP）的方式呈现实验材料（见图 13.3）。代词为关键词，离线数据分析会提取每种实验条件下代词所诱发的脑电反应。

表13.5　脑电实验的语料举例，代词为实验的关键词

实验条件	实例
控制条件	(a) 这位女患者情绪低落，医生鼓励*她*振作起来。
数不一致	(b) 这些女患者情绪低落，医生鼓励*她*振作起来。
性不一致	(c) 这位女患者情绪低落，医生鼓励*他*振作起来。
性、数均不一致	(d) 这些女患者情绪低落，医生鼓励*他*振作起来。

（5）实验结果

如图 13.7 所示，相对于没有语病的控制条件，存在性别或数量违反的代词均诱发了较大的 P600；其次，相对于数违反代词，性违反代词诱发了更大的 P600；此外，性、数双违反条件所诱发的 P600 与单独的性违反所诱发的 P600 的波幅没有差异。综合这两方面的结果，在代词回指解读中，无论是性别违反还是数量违反都会对回指解读产生影响，但是相对于数量违反，性别违反会给代词的回指解读带来更大影响。这一结果表明，在回指解读中，性别违反要比数量违反给阅读过程带来更大的影响。

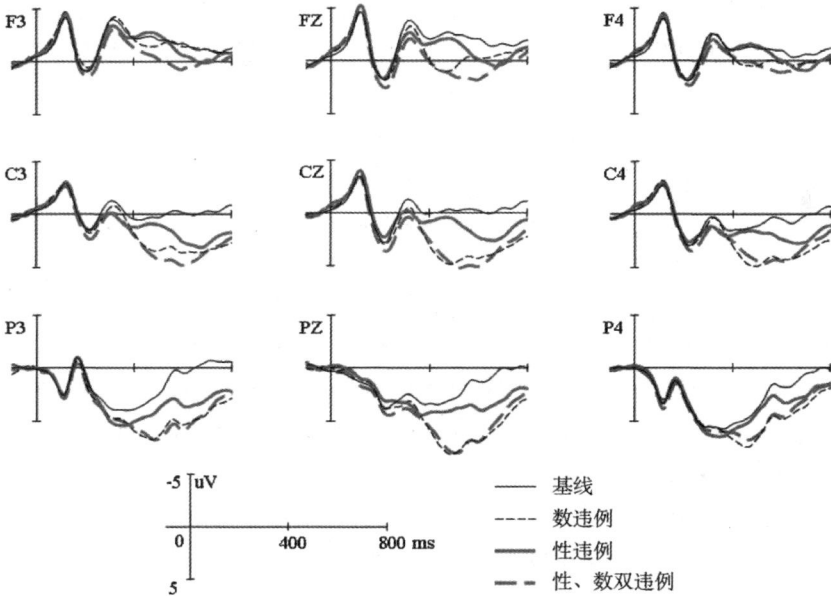

图13.7 性别违反、数量违反和正确条件下代词所诱发的脑电P600反应
（摘自Xu et al., 2015）

课堂讨论

1. 自定步速阅读方法一般适合用来探讨哪方面的语言研究问题？其优点和缺点各是什么？
2. 与行为反应时技术相比，脑电技术有何优点和缺点？它适用于解决哪方面的语言研究问题？
3. 阅读下面的英文摘要（Romero-Rivas et al., 2016），指出该研究中的自变量和因变量以及它们各自有几个水平，并指出该研究的实验设计类型。

In this study we explore whether world knowledge (WK) processing differs between individuals listening to their native (L1) or their non-native (L2) language. We recorded event-related brain potentials in L1 and L2 speakers of Spanish while they listened to sentences uttered by native speakers of Spanish. Sentences were either congruent or incongruent with participants' WK (see Table 13.6). In addition, participants also listened to sentences in which upcoming words could not be anticipated on the basis of WK. WK violations elicited a late negativity of greater magnitude and duration in the L2 than the L1 group. However, sentences in which WK was not helpful regarding word anticipation elicited similar N400 modulations in both groups. These results suggest that WK processing requires a deeper lexical search in L2 comprehension than in L1 comprehension（语料实例见表 13.6）。

表13.6 实验语料举例

实验条件	实例
Known sentences	(a) The World Trade Center attack occurred in *September*.
WK violation sentences	(b) The World Trade Center attack occurred in *December*.
Unknown sentences	(c) The Pearl Harbor attack occurred in *December*.

4. Thierry 和 Wu（2012）探讨了跨语言词汇信息的激活问题，他们采用语义启动范式在单一英语情景下考察了母语（汉语）对 L2（英语）的影响。他们要求被试判断先后出现的两个英语词汇是否存在语义关联（例如

train–ham，见表 13.7 的实例）。除告诉被试这一显性任务外，该实验中还隐藏着一个被试并不知晓的潜在变量——有些英语词对的汉语翻译对等词存在字形重叠，比如 train–ham 翻译成汉语为"火车—火腿"（"火"字重叠）。此项研究中，双语被试所看到的词汇均来自同一种 L2 语言（即英语），他们没有接触到任何关于 L1（汉语）的外显信息。即便如此，L2 词汇翻译对等词的词形和语义还是得到了激活。在该项研究中，除了上述提及的实验条件和实验组，研究者还设置了相应的控制条件和控制组。假如由你来负责开展此项研究，你觉得应该如何设置控制组？

表13.7　实验设计及语料举例

汉字的重复与否 （隐性变量）	语义相关性（显性变量）	
	语义相关	语义无关
汉字重复	Post–Mail （邮政—邮件）	Train–Ham （火车—火腿）
汉字不重复	Wife–Husband （妻子—丈夫）	Apple–Table （苹果—桌子）

5. 哈古尔特等（Hagoort et al., 2004）采用脑电等神经科学的方法比较了语用信息加工和语义信息加工的神经机制。他们让被试阅读三种不同类型的句子（如表 13.8 中的 a—c）并在此过程中记录他们的大脑反应。实验结果显示，相对于正常的句子，当受试阅读语用错误（13.8b）和语义错误（13.8c）的句子时，关键词（斜体字词）均诱发了较大的 N400 反应，而语用错误和语义错误之间没有差别。研究结果表明，处理语义信息和百科常识信息的时间进程和神经机制没有明显区别。与同学讨论该研究中的自变量、因变量、可能的干扰变量以及该研究所采用的实验设计。

表13.8　实验语料举例

实验条件	实例
正确句	(a) The Dutch trains are *yellow* and very crowded.
百科常识违反句	(b) The Dutch trains are *white* and very crowded.
语义违反句	(c) The Dutch trains are *sour* and very crowded.

课外练习

1. 语义启动实验所依据的理论基础是什么？

2. 该如何计算启动效应？启动时间间隔是否会影响启动效应？

3. 自定步速阅读方法属于在线的测量方法还是离线的测量方法？为什么？

4. 自定步速阅读范式主要有几种呈现方式？它们各有什么样的优缺点？

5. 脑电实验对实验材料的质量和数量有何要求？是否所有的行为实验都可以采用脑电技术进行探讨？

6. 徐晓东等（2022）采用自定步速阅读技术，探讨了前提知识的真假以及外语水平的高低如何影响外语语境下的反事实推理。他们让 64 名熟练水平不同的中国英语学习者阅读四种不同类型的句子并回答阅读理解问题。四种句子类型分别为：前提为真且句子的逻辑一致（a），前提为真但句子逻辑前后不一致（b）；前提为假且句子的逻辑一致（c），前提为假且句子逻辑前后不一致（d）。实验共包含 32 组实验材料（每组材料均包含 4 种不同的实验条件，如表 13.9 中 a—d 所示），另有 20 个填充句。为了避免重复测量效应，研究者采用了拉丁方设计，确保每位被试都能够看到 32 组实验材料并且只能看到一组材料中的某一测试条件。研究结果显示，对于高水平中国外语学习者而言，当前提为真时，逻辑不一致条件下句尾词的阅读时间比逻辑一致条件下更长；但当前提为假时，两种条件下句尾词的阅读时间没有区别。另外，对于低水平中国外语学习者而言，无论前提真假与否，逻辑不一致与一致条件下句尾词的阅读时间没有显著性差异（significant difference）。这表明，无论是在母语还是外语环境下，违实推理均无法摆脱前提知识的约束，外语条件下的违实推理无法单独依靠逻辑准则进行。分析该研究中的自变量、因变量、可能的干扰变量以及该研究所采用的实验设计。

表13.9　实验设计及语料举例

实验条件		实例
前提为真	(a)	The MacBook is becoming thinner and thinner.
逻辑一致		If Steve Jobs were alive in the present, he would be very *happy*, surely.
前提为真	(b)	The MacBook is becoming thinner and thinner.
逻辑不一致		If Steve Jobs were alive in the present, he would be very *sad*, surely.
前提为假	(c)	The MacBook is becoming heavier and heavier.
逻辑一致		If Steve Jobs were alive in the present, he would be very *sad*, surely.
前提为假	(d)	The MacBook is becoming heavier and heavier.
逻辑不一致		If Steve Jobs were alive in the present, he would be very *happy*, surely.

拓展阅读

Jegerski, J. (2014). Self-paced reading. In J. Jegerski, & B. VanPatten (Eds.). *Research methods in second language psycholinguistics* (pp. 20–49). New York: Routledge.

Luck, S. J. (2009). 事件相关电位基础（范思陆等译）. 上海：华东大学出版社.

McDonough, K., & Trofimovich, P. (2011). *Using priming methods in second language research*（第二语言研究中的启动研究方法）. 北京：外语教学与研究出版社.

Xu, X. D., Pan, M. Z., Dai, H. Y., Zhang, H., & Lu, Y. Y. (2019). How referential uncertainty is modulated by conjunctions: ERP evidence from advanced Chinese-English L2 learners and English L1 speakers. *Second Language Research*, 35(2), 195–224.

徐晓东、陈丽娟、倪传斌. (2017). 汉语话题回指如何受动词语义关系约束——来自脑电研究的证据, 外语教学与研究, 49(3), 323–334.

徐晓东、朱宏丽. (2024). 二语语境下母语语音信息的预激活——基于眼动视觉情景范式的研究. 外语教学与研究, 56(4), 569–580.

第 14 单元

外语研究统计原理

学习目标

- 了解描述统计与推断统计的基本原理
- 掌握描述统计与推断统计的基本方法
- 熟悉国际期刊论文中统计结果的表达方式
- 能够使用 SPSS 做基本的描述统计分析

人类有各种认知世界的方法，统计方法就是其中之一。人类从量化分析的角度，采用量化测量方式，收集数字化数据或量化数据，根据数据的类型和特点，选取适当的统计方法，对这些数据进行统计分析，从中发现与揭示现象的本质特征、发展模式与趋势、变化模式与趋势以及现象之间的关系等。

因此，使用统计方法的研究一定是基于量化数据的研究，也就是说采用统计方法的研究一定要收集和使用数字化数据。研究者需要针对特定的研究问题，采用特定的测量方式采集所需的数字化数据，然后根据数据类型选用特定的统计方法处理数据，最后根据数据统计结果推出研究问题的答案。

我们学习与掌握统计原理与方法，不仅仅是在我们未来的研究中应用它们，更重要的是我们要把这套原理和方法变成我们的研究思维逻辑。掌握了统计原理与方法之后，我们应当能够在有了研究问题之后就知道需要收集什么类型的数据，在有了数据之后就知道应当使用什么样的统计方法。

14.1 描述统计原理

这一节重点介绍描述统计的一些基本概念和方法，主要包括：（1）变量；（2）数据类型与数据测量；（3）频数表与交互表；（4）平均值、标准差、方差。它们是统计中最常用的概念和方法，是推断统计必不可少的基础，也是外语研究领域最常见和常用的概念与方法。它们是我们在一开始处理和加工原始数据时就要使用的概念和方法，也是后续一些高级和更高级的统计方法的基础。掌握了这些基本概念和方法，研究者就可以对各种量化数据开展初步的统计分析，并根据得出的统计结果，对研究中的现象有一个初步的认识和了解，然后可以进一步使用各种统计检验方法，开展各组数据之间的差异分析和关系分析。

描述统计（descriptive statistics）是对收集到的原始数据进行整理、概括、计算和表述的一套方法，用以呈现与揭示数据的代表性特征或分布特征。

描述统计要回答的问题是：

（1）目标数据的代表性特征是什么？

（2）目标数据有什么样的分布特征？

对于第一个问题，描述统计采用一些量化指标（如平均值和标准差）作为数据的代表性特征。对于第二个问题，描述统计采用图表的方式呈现数据的分布特征。因此，描述统计主要有两个方面的工作：（1）确定数据的量化指标或者说描述统计量，（2）用图表呈现数据的分布情况。

描述统计的主要量化指标包括平均值、众数、中位数、标准差、方差。平均值、众数、中位数三个指标是反映数据中心位置的代表量，通常被称为集中趋势（central tendency）指标。标准差与方差则是反映数据发散程度或者说偏离中心位置程度的代表量，通常被称为离散趋势（tendency of dispersion）指标。描述统计的主要用表是频数表和交互表。

14.1.1 变量

我们在外语研究中会使用到各种各样的概念，比如"年龄""语言能力""元话语""流利度""句法复杂度""思维品质""工作记忆"等。当我们把某个概念作为测量指标，并用某种测量尺度去收集数字化数据的时候，就会发现我们从每一个个体上得到的测量结果常常是不同的。比如，如果我们把"年龄"作为测量指标，以"年份"为测量尺度收集研究对象的年龄数据，那么我们会发现，从不同研究对象那里采集到的年龄值并不相同。一个研究对象的年龄可能是 18 岁，另一个可能是 20 岁，而第三个则可能是 21 岁。这时候，年龄是一个取值会发生变化的测量指标。

变量是那些在测量时取值会发生变化的测量指标。如果一个测量指标的所有取值都是一样的，那么这个测量指标被称为常量。量化研究中使用的许多测量指标都是变量，如外语水平、语用意识等。

当研究者预先设定一个变量影响另一个变量的时候，前者称为自变量，后者称为因变量。关于两者的区别，可参见 12.1。

14.1.2 数据类型

数据是我们研究中用于分析和回答研究问题所收集的资料。由于数据有不同的表现形式与采集方式，所以也有不同的分类。按表现形式，数据有定性数据与定量数据之分。按测量方式，数据有定类数据与定距数据之分。

（1）定性数据与定量数据

定性数据指的是用文字表征的数据，例如文字作品（小说、文章、专著、论文等），演讲词，访谈录，文字笔记，书信，作文，文字反馈，音频或视频转写等。定量数据指的是用数值表征的数据，即数字数据或量化数据，例如按年数统计的年龄数据、按长度单位"米"统计的身高数据、按百分制统计的考试分数数据、按字数统计的文本长度数据等。

用于统计分析的数据必须是定量数据。后文使用的"数据"一词专指定量数据。

定量数据可以直接用于统计分析，但是定性数据不能。对于定性数据，我们可以采用定性数据量化的方式，从定性数据中找出一些可以量化的特征，使之数值化，从而采集到定量数据用于统计分析。例如，如果我们收集到的数据是小说、论文、作文等文本类的定性数据，那么我们可以借助 Coh-Metrix、WordSmith、ProWritingAid 等语言分析软件来提取文本中各种语言特征的定量数据。

（2）定类数据与定距数据

我们收集与整理数字资料，需要采用一定的测量方式。外语研究最常用的两大类测量方式是定类测量和定距测量，分别获得定类数据和定距数据。

定类测量是把一个研究变量分成若干子类，然后统计各个子类出现的频次或者说次数。例如将"性别"变量分成"男性"和"女性"两个子类，然后统计两个子类出现的频数。采用定类测量获得的数据称为定类数据。定类数据的统计结果可以用频次表或交互表的形式加以呈现。在推断统计中，定类数据用于非参数检验。需要特别指出的是，人们常常会用 1、2、3 一类的文字来代替变量的子类，如用 1 代替"男性"，2 代替"女性"。注意，这里的 1 和 2 是文字，而不是数字，不可以对它们做加减乘除运算。

定距测量是使用等距测量方式来测量某个研究变量所涉及的每个个体的数值。等距测量方式要求测量工具任意两个相邻尺度的距离或者说长度是一样的。我们日常生活中使用的米尺、公斤秤、计时器等都是等距测量工具。它们任意相邻的两个刻度之间的距离是相同的。例如，在米尺上，1 米与 2 米之间的距离等于 3 米与 4 米之间的距离，也等于 9 米到 10 米之间的距离。使用定距测量方式获得的数据称为定距数据。

（3）定序数据与定比数据

除定类测量和定距测量之外，还有定序测量和定比测量。定序测量是把一个研究变量分成可排序的若干子类，然后统计各个子类的频数。例如，将"成绩"分成"不及格、及格、中等、良好、优秀"五个子类，然后分别统计这五个子类的频数。因为这五个子类是可以排序的，从"不及格"到"优秀"，后一个子类比前一个子类的序别高，所以这样的测量方式称为定序测量。使用定序测量收集的数据称为定序数据。

定比测量除了有定类、定序和定距测量的基本特征，还有一个真零（true zero），并且可以计算和比较数值的比率，而这个比率是有意义的。用定比测量获得的数据称为定比数据。例如，长度为零意味着没有长度，重量为零意味着没有重量。一个对象的长度是另一个对象长度的两倍。这个两倍是有意义的。然而，对温度和智商的测量是定距测量而不是定比测量。这是因为温度的零度是有温度的，智商的零也是有智商的。

我们在做研究设计的时候，要尽可能选择收集定距数据和定比数据。这是因为在推断统计中，定距数据和定比数据既可以用于参数检验，也可以用于非参数检验。在 SPSS 中，定距测量和定比测量被归到了 Scale 这一测量类别中。

这里要特别指出的是，通过定距测量实际获得的定距数据中，任意相邻的两个数值之间的距离并不一定是相同的。

表 14.1 是 30 个学生的高考英语分数。我们不难看出，这组数据中任意相邻的两个分数之间的距离并不相同。但是这组数据依然是定距数据，因为它们是用定距测量方式获得的。

表14.1　30个学生的高考英语分数

107	114	118	119	119	120	121	121	121	123	124	124	125	125	126
127	127	127	127	128	129	130	130	131	131	131	131	131	132	135

对于所研究的同一事物或现象来说，根据不同的研究目的和研究问题，我们采集数据使用什么样的测量方式，也是可以有选择的。例如，对于"年龄"，我们可以使用定类测量方式，按照"老年、中年、青年、少年"的分类收集每个子类的频数。这样获得的数据是定类数据，可以用频数表或交互表的形式呈现。我们自然也可以采用定距测量方式，用"年份"尺度收集每个研究对象的年龄数据。这样获得的数据自然是定距数据，可以用平均值与标准差作为它们的代表量值呈现出来。

14.1.3　频数统计

频数统计是统计某个变量下的每个不同数值所出现的次数。频数统计可以用于定类数据，也可以用于定距数据。频数统计的结果可以用频数表或交互表呈现，也可以用图形呈现。

定类数据的统计结果，常用频数表或交互表的形式呈现。频数表是将变量的子类和它们的频数罗列成表格。频数表由以下几个部分组成：表号、标题、变量名及分类名、频数、百分比和累计百分比。

表号是表的编号，如表 1、表 2 等。表的标题简要说明表的主要内容是什么。表 14.2 中给出了变量名（性别），变量的子类名（男性、女性）和对应的频数、百分比、累积百分比。累积百分比是每一个子类频数的百分比加上前面所有子类的百分比之和。例如在表 14.2 中，男性占总数的 40%。由于它前面没有子类，所以它的累积百分比就是 40%。女性的百分比是 60%，加上前面男性的 40%，累积百分比是 100%。做频数表的时候，可以将变量名和它的子类放在表的左边，也可以放在上面（表 14.3）。

表14.2　男性与女性人数的频数表

性别	频数	百分比（%）	累计百分比（%）
男性	20	40	40
女性	30	60	100
合计	50	100	

表14.3　男性与女性人数的频数表

性别	男性	女性	合计
频数	20	30	50
百分比（%）	40	60	100
累计百分比（%）	40	100	

还有一种简表（如表 14.4），表的第一行是变量名、子类名和每个子类占总频数的百分比标记（%），第二行是各个子类的频数和它们分别占总频数的百分比。

表14.4　男性与女性人数的频数表

性别	男性（%）	女性（%）	合计（%）
频数	20 (40)	30 (60)	50 (100)

交互表也称为"列联表"，是将两个变量的子类和它们对应的频数相互交叠而成。因此，可以说交互表是由两个交叠的频数表构成。在推断统计中，交互表最常用于卡方检验。

表 14.5 是某次期末外语考试成绩与性别两个变量的交互表。外语考试成绩有"优秀、良好、中等、及格、不及格"五类，性别有"男生、女生"两类。表中分别给出了男生和女生在每个成绩类别上的人数。

表14.5　性别*期末成绩交互表

		期末成绩					合计
		优秀	良好	中等	及格	不及格	
性别	男生	5	41	230	301	169	746
	女生	19	64	150	227	116	576
合计		24	105	380	528	285	1322

不少情况下，人们在做交互表的时候，会将自变量作为列变量，将因变量作为行变量，也就是说，将自变量和它的子类放在表的上面，将因变量和它的子类放在表的左面。

14.1.4 集中趋势测量

平均值（mean，简写为 M），也称"平均数"，是我们非常熟悉并且日常使用频率很高的一个统计概念。当我们谈论学生的平均成绩、家庭人均收入、家庭人均住房面积的时候，都是在使用平均值的概念。

平均值是用于表明一组数据的中心位置或者说中心数值的一个指标，是所研究的对象总体上一般水平的代表量值。平均值是数据统计分析和数据统计分析报告中使用最多的统计量值之一，也是所有参数检验都要使用的一个量值。

平均值是一组数据的所有数值之和或者说数据的总数值除以这组数据的数值个数得出的数值。例如，一组数据有五个数值，分别是 3、5、6、8、13。将这五个数值加起来，然后用它们之和除以 5，得出的数值就是这组数据的平均值。平均值也常常简称为"均值"。

平均值的计算公式是：

$$M = \frac{\sum X}{n} = \frac{X_1 + X_2 + X_3 + \cdots\cdots + X_n}{n}$$

其中：

M：数据的平均值

∑（sigma）X：数据中所有数值相加之和

n：数据中数值的个数

X_1，X_2，$X_3 \cdots\cdots X_3$：数据中的每个数值

平均值可以用不同的符号表示，但是这些符号有不同的用意。人们通常使用的平均值符号包括 μ、X̄ 和 M。μ（/mjuː/）代表总体平均值，X̄（/'eksbɑː/）代表样本平均值。M 是英语 mean 一词的首字母，用于表示一般意义上的平均值。当不需要区分或者特别说明是总体平均值还是样本平均值时，可以使用 M。

平均值作为数据集中程度的一个量值，它的优势是在统计中使用了数据的所有数值。但是，这也给它带来一个不足，使它会受到数据中极值的影响。极值指的是数据中的最大值或最小值。

当极值远远大于或远远小于数据中绝大多数数值的时候，就会使平均值不能很好地反映数据真正的中心位置。我们可以把这些极值称为超极值。超极值指数据中远远超过一定范围的数值，包括超大数值与超小数值。例如在 18、18、19、19、20、60 这样一组数据中，60 可视为超极值。这是因为 18、18、19、19、20 中任意两个数值之间的差异最大为 2，最小为 0；而 60 与它们中的最大数 20 就相差了 40。

如果数据量比较小而且数据中存在超大值或超小值，或者当数据中超大值或超小值数量偏多时，超极值都会对平均数造成较大的影响。

观察平均值是否可以很好地反映数据的集中度，我们可以将其与数据的中位数和众数进行比较。平均值、中位数、众数在统计学上称为"集中趋势的量值"。平均值与中位数和众数越接近，就越能反映数据的集中度。

中位数（median）是一组数值从小到大依次排序后的数据中处于最中间位置的数值。中位数不受数据极值的影响。

如果一组数据的数值数是奇数，那么中位数就是处于最中间的那个数值。例如，在 1、2、3、4、5 这一组排序数据中，它的数值数是 5，为奇数，3 是位于最中间的数值，所以这组数据的中位数是 3。如果一组数据的数值数是偶数，那么它的中位数就是最中间两个数值之和的平均值。例如，在 1、2、3、4、5、6 这一组数据中，它的数值数是 6，为偶数，3 和 4 是位于最中间的两个数值，所以这组数据的中位数是 (3+4)/2=3.5。

众数（mode）是一组数据中出现次数最多的数值。例如，在 1、2、3、3、4、5 这组数据中，3 出现的次数最多，所以这组数据的众数是 3。一组数据可以有多个众数。当一组数据中有两个或两个以上的数值都是出现次数最多的数值时，就出现了多众数。例如，在 1、2、3、3、4、4、5、6 这组数据中，3 和 4 都出现了两次，所以这组数据有两个众数，分别是 3 和 4。众数同中位数一样，不受数据极值的影响。

我们把 17、18、18、18、18、19、19、19、20、80 这组数据的平均值和它的中位数与平均值比较一下。这组数据的平均值是 24.6，而它的中位数是

(18+19)/2=18.5，众数是 18。由此可见，中位数与众数的大小是相近的，而平均值则与它们有较大的差距。然而，去掉 80 这个极值之后，获得的平均值约为 18.44，与中位数和众数就非常接近了。

要避免超极值对均值的影响，常用的方法有两个：一是采集容量足够大的数据，二是修剪采集的数据。

首先，我们在从事定量研究时，一定要设法收集容量足够大的数据。当数据量足够大或者说数值足够多的时候，就可以最大限度地抵消极值的影响。这是因为数值越多，极值摊在每个数值上的量就越少。另外，数据量足够大时，除了正常范围内的数值可以抵消掉超极值的影响，数据内部超大值与超小值之间相互抵消的可能性也会增加。

多大容量的数据是足够大的数据呢？有两种情况可供参考。

第一种情况是，随机抽取的数据容量大于等于 30 就可以。参照中心极限定理（central limit theorem），随机样本大于等于 30 时，数据就接近正态分布（相关定义参见 14.2.3）。在这种情况下，平均值、中位数、众数也应当是非常接近的。参数检验要求数据服从正态分布或者近似正态分布。如果我们的研究属于开创性的，而且收集数据比较困难，那么可以参照第一种情况，尽可能收集容量为 30 以上的数据。

第二种情况是参照前人相关研究中的数据容量。我们的数据容量要尽可能大于前人研究中的数据容量，即使不能大于其最大值，也至少要大于其最小值。例如，如果前人研究中的数据容量最小在 100 以上，最大值在 1000 以上，那么我们采集的数据即使达不到 1000 以上，也不能小于 100。

避免超极值对均值影响的另一种方法是修剪数据。修剪数据是按照一定的规则和方式去掉数据中的超极值，以最大限度避免超极值对均值的影响。在统计分析研究实践中，是否需要修剪原始数据，取决于数据类型和分布。一种比较粗略但比较简便和直观的方法是比较平均数、中位数或众数的拟合程度。在完全对称的数据分布中，平均数、中位数和众数三者相等。由于中位数、众数不受超极值的影响，在统计实践中，我们可以参考平均数与中位数或众数的接近程度来决定是否需要对数据做必要的修剪。如果平均数与中位数或众数之间的差异比较大，可以考虑修剪数据。修剪数据常见的百分比为 10% 和 20%（Howell, 2013: 68–69）。

14.1.5 离散趋势测量

标准差（standard deviation，SD）是反映数据内部发散程度的一个量值。标准差越大，数据的发散程度也越大，一些数值偏离数据中心也越远。反之，标准差越小，数据的发散程度也越小，每个数值离数据中心也越近。标准差和平均值一样，是一些参数检验（如 t 检验、f 检验）必不可缺的一个量值。

该如何理解标准差呢？标准差的基本思路是计量数据中所有数值与平均值之间的平均距离。因此，我们可以粗略地将标准差理解为数据的所有数值离开平均值的平均距离。举一个相近的例子来说明标准差的意义。一个教室里，一位教师站在讲台上，下面坐着一些学生。我们测量每一位学生到那位教师之间的距离，然后把所有学生与教师之间的距离加起来除以学生的人数，得到的是每个学生离开那位教师的平均距离。这个平均距离越大，说明学生坐得越散。标准差的意义就类似于每个学生与教师之间的平均距离。

标准差的计算公式是：

$$SD = \sqrt{\frac{\sum (X - \bar{X})^2}{n}}$$

其中：

SD：标准差

$\bar{X}$（x-bar）：平均值

X：每一个数值

n：数据中数值的个数

Σ（sigma）：求和

标准差同平均值一样可以用不同的符号表示，它们同样有不同的用意。人们通常使用的标准差符号包括 σ、S 和 SD。σ（sigma，Σ 的小写）代表总体标准差，S 代表样本标准差。SD 是英语 standard deviation 一词的首字母缩写，用于表示一般意义上的标准差。当不需要区分或者特别说明是总体标准差还是样本标准差时，可以使用 SD。

方差是与标准差密切相关的一个量值。**方差是标准差的平方值。**如果标准差是 5，那么方差就是 $5^2 = 5 \times 5 = 25$。方差用于某些参数统计方法（如 f 检验）。

平均值和标准差是两个最常用的定距数据统计数值，也是一些数据的参数检验方法（如 t 检验、f 检验）必不可少的两个检验数值。在定量研究论文中，它们是必须一起报告的两个数值。

SPSS 应用：描述统计值

将定距数据中的数值输入 SPSS 的数值栏中后，按照下列步骤操作，就可以获得数据的描述统计值。

分析 (A)
　　→ 描述统计
　　　→ 描述统计 (D)
　　　　→ 变量名：从左框移到右框
　　　　　→ 确定

14.2　推断统计原理

推断统计（inferential statistics）是依据概率分布理论并利用样本数据来推断总体特征或者检验样本与总体间关系的统计方法。

推断统计方法有参数检验与非参数检验之分。参数指的是总体的统计量值，如总体平均值、标准差、方差等。样本的统计量值称作统计量，如样本平均值、标准差、方差等。为了区分，总体参数与样本统计量用不同的符号表示。总体参数用希腊字母表示，样本统计量用拉丁字母表示。前面讲过，总体平均值用 μ 表示，样本平均值用 $\overline{X}$ 表示；总体标准差用 σ 表示，样本标准差用 S 表示；总体方差用 σ^2 表示，样本方差用 S^2 表示

参数检验使用已知的总体参数和样本统计量进行检验。实际上，在大多数研究中，总体参数通常是未知的，通常都是使用样本的平均值、标准差或方差来进行检验。外语研究中最常用的参数检验方法有：独立样本 t 检验、成对样本 t 检验、单因素方差分析等。

非参数检验使用频数或序数进行检验。外语研究中最常用的非参数检验方法是卡方检验。

不同的统计检验方法适用于不同类型和不同特性的数据。参数检验方法适用于符合正态分布或近似正态分布的定距数据，而不同的参数检验方法又适用于不同类型的样本数据。非参数检验方法既适用于定类数据，也适用于定距数据，尤其是那些不符合正态分布的定距数据。

推断统计要回答的核心统计问题是：

（1）某个样本数据有多大的概率属于某个已知总体？

（2）两个或两个以上的样本数据有多大的概率属于同一个总体？

因此，我们首先要了解的几个关键概念是：总体与样本、概率与概率分布。

14.2.1 总体与样本

我们在阅读外语研究文献时，往往会看到这样的标题："中美大学生的语篇特征分析""中国英语学习者二语会话非流利研究""二语学习者书面语句法复杂度发展研究""中国大学生英语学习策略调查研究""中国人的面子研究"。这些标题中的"中美大学生""中国英语学习者""二语学习者""中国大学生""中国人"都是非常庞大的群体，涉及的人数从几十万到上亿，甚至十几亿。

但是，如果查看这些文献中研究对象的实际人数，我们会发现，大多数研究所涉及的人数在几十个到几百个之间。这些研究中的人数，与标题中涉及的人数相比，真是少之又少。

上述现象涉及总体与样本的概念。"中美大学生""中国英语学习者""二语学习者""中国大学生"都是我们关心的群体，是我们研究的目标群体。但是，由于这些群体过于庞大，无论在时间上还是在人力和财力上，我们作为研究者几乎没有可能收集整个群体中所有成员的数据。因此，我们只能试图通过研究这些庞大群体的一部分成员来从中获得有关这些群体的结论。

总体（population）是人们在研究中所关注的一个大的、独立的目标群体，是众多具有相同特性的个体或者研究对象的集合。总体的"大"是相对的，不是绝对的，取决于研究者的界定。总体可以是巨大的"二语学习者"群体，也可以缩小到"中国二语学习者"，还可以缩小到"中国高校新生二语学习者"。选择什么样的总体，取决于研究者的研究关注重点。

样本（sample）则是从一个总体中选取或抽取的那一部分个体。样本数据是从所选取或抽取的样本那里获取的数据。样本容量指的是一个样本数据中数值的多少，或者说一个样本数据中包含的个体数值的数量。

由于人们通常无法获得总体数据，所以只有利用样本数据来推断总体特征。

尽管某一个研究的样本容量相对于总体来说很小，但是往往有不同的研究者做同一个选题的研究。有的研究者选取某个总体中的几十个作为样本，有的研究者则选取总体中的上百个作为样本。这样累积起来，样本数量就会越来越多。当样本数量越来越多的时候，从样本中发现的特征就越来越接近总体特征。这就像前面讲的分布一样，当样本量越来越大的时候，就越来越接近正态分布。

人们可以把这些同一选题的研究结果综合在一起，从中得出有关总体的一些结论。元分析就是其中一种把同一个选题的定量研究统计结果进行综合分析的方法。元分析研究者们通过分析不同研究者对同一选题所做的定量研究的同一类统计结果，从中得出一些有关总体特征或总体趋势的结论。

从一个总体中随机选取一个样本，大多数情况下，总体平均值与样本平均值之间都会存在差异。例如，从一次学生的外语考试成绩总体中随机抽取3个样本量为30的样本（图14.1），得到的结果是：总体平均值为122.4，样本1的均值为124.7，样本2的均值为119.3，样本3的均值为122.6。不难看出，总体与样本平均值之间，样本与样本平均值之间都存在差异。

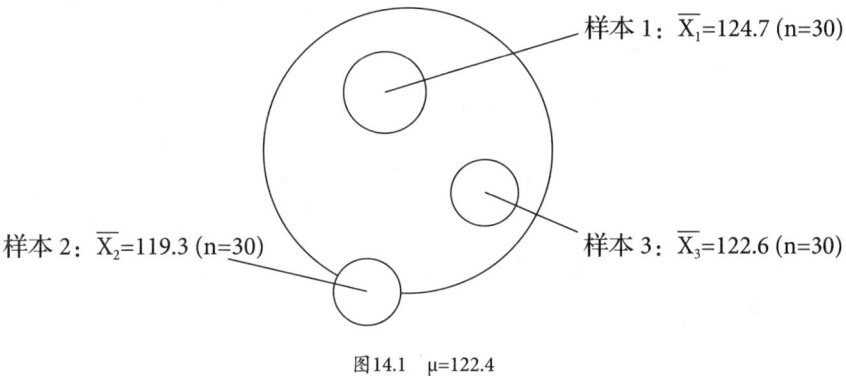

样本 1：$\overline{X}_1=124.7$ (n=30)

样本 2：$\overline{X}_2=119.3$ (n=30)

样本 3：$\overline{X}_3=122.6$ (n=30)

图14.1　μ=122.4

当人们从总体中抽样时，总体平均值与样本平均值之间或样本平均值与样本平均值之间总会出现大大小小的差异。这种由抽样造成的差异在统计中称为"抽样误差"。除了抽样误差，还有非抽样误差。例如，测量工具不精确造成的误差，往计算机里输入数据时漏输数值或输错数值产生的误差，研究对象不按要求提供数据造成的误差等。统计实践中各种误差无处不在，关键是我们如何把误差控制在可接受的程度。

当我们有某个总体的数据或者知道总体参数，而且确切地知道某个样本来自该总体时，无论样本平均值与总体平均值存在多大的误差，我们无须任何检验，都可以毫无疑问地说该样本属于那个总体。正如图14.1中的例子，尽管样本1、样本2和样本3与总体平均值之间都存在差异，但是它们依然属于μ=122.4的总体，因为我们明确知道它们是从这个总体中抽取出来的。

但是，在绝大多数情况下，我们只能获得样本数据，无法获得总体数据。因此，我们不能确切地知道我们的样本是否真正来自我们感兴趣的总体。在这种情况下，我们就需要利用基于概率分布理论的统计方法，用样本数据去推断一个样本或者多个样本是否属于同一个总体。

14.2.2 概率

概率（probability）指的是某个随机事件出现的可能性。随机事件指的是有可能出现也有可能不出现的事。例如，从学生名单中随意抽取一个学生，"抽到一个男生"就是一个随机事件。这是因为这次抽到的是男生，下一次说不定抽到的不是男生而是女生了。

我们做一件事可能有多个结果。在统计学中，"做一件事"称为"试验"，试验的结果则称为"事件"。从学生名单中随意抽取一个学生这件事是一个试验。从性别来说，这个试验可能出现两个事件中的一个：抽到一个男生或者抽到一个女生。抛硬币是一个试验，结果可能是出现硬币正面这个事件，也可能是出现硬币反面这个事件。

人们对概率有定性的与定量的这两种类型的表述。定性的表述是：完全可能、很可能、可能、有可能、完全不可能。定量的表述最常用的是百分比，有时候也用几分比、十分比，或千分比、万分比，如五分之一、十分之一、百分之一、千分之一或万分之一。定性表述的"完全可能"可以对应定量表述的100%，"完全不可能"可以对应0%。"可能"在中间，可以对应50%。"很可能"在50%和100%之间，可以对应75%；"有可能"在0%到50%之间，可以对应25%。

从定性的角度来说，抛硬币可能出现正面，也可能出现反面。从定量的角度可以将"可能出现正面"表述为"出现正面的概率是50%"，将"可能出现反面"表述为"出现反面的概率是50%"。

概率常常用作一种确信度或置信度，即人们对事件发生可能性的确信程度。当我们看手机天气预报APP时，可以发现上面有降雨概率预报，从0%到100%不等。这是天气预报单位根据方方面面的知识和获得的气象信息，对某地是否会降雨所做判断的确信程度。0%意味着天气预报单位确信某地一定不会下雨，而100%则意味着天气预报单位确信某地一定会下雨。

人们可以通过三种方式获取事件发生的概率：古典概率、频率和概率分布。

古典定义认为，如果做一件事有多个限定的结果，那么每个结果出现的可能性或者说概率是相等的。

人们最熟悉的一个古典概率的例子是抛硬币试验。抛硬币可以有两种结果：出现硬币的正面或出现硬币的反面。按照古典概率的定义，抛硬币时出现正面的概率和出现反面的概率是一样的，都是二分之一。类似的例子是掷骰子试验。骰子有六个面，上面分别有1、2、3、4、5、6这六个点。按照古典概率的定义，掷骰子时，六个点中每一个点出现的概率是一样的，都是六分之一。

但是，当人们多次重复掷骰子的时候，会发现每一个点出现的概率并非都是一样的。例如，一个人掷了 10 次骰子，得到表 14.6 的结果。

表14.6　掷10次骰子得到的各点数的频数

点数	出现次数（m）	频率（%）
1	2	20
2	2	20
3	3	30
4	1	10
5	1	10
6	1	10
合计	10	100

频率等于每个点出现的次数（m）与总次数（n）之比。从 10 次掷骰子的结果不难看出，每个点出现的频率并不符合古典概率定义的同等概率之说，也就是说，每个点出现的概率并不是古典概率所预设的 1/6 或 16.67%。

这时候，频率取代了古典概率，赋予概率新的内涵：概率是实际观察到的某个事件发生的次数与该事件所有可能发生的次数之比。

表 14.6 所呈现的结果称为频率分布。频率分布是某个变量的那些个值和它们出现频率或者说概率的集合。该变量的每个个值都有相应的频率值。知道一个个值，就可以知道它的概率。

我们做数据统计分析时，应用的既不是古典概率，也不是频率，而是概率分布。它们是数学家或统计学家们提出并经过验证和长期应用的概率分布。概率分布是一些特定变量的数值和它们对应的概率的集合，都有分布表可查。

外语研究中数据统计分析常用的概率分布包括正态分布（Z 分布）、T 分布、F 分布和卡方（χ^2）分布。正态分布是 z 值和对应概率的集合，有正态分布表可查；T 分布是 t 值和对应概率的集合，有 T 分布表可查；F 分布是 F 值和对应概率的集合，有 F 分布表可查；卡方分布是卡方值和对应概率的集合，有卡方分布表可查。

14.2.3 正态分布

正态分布（normal distribution）是许多统计方法的理论基础。T分布、F分布、卡方分布都是在正态分布的基础上推导出来的。有些分布（如T分布）的极限就是正态分布。理解正态分布的特点和应用，就可以理解推断检验的基本原理。

正态分布有以下特点：

（1）它是连续分布，也就是说，正态分布是没有间断点的，可以在分布的任何地方取值。

（2）它是对称分布，竖轴两边的图形完全吻合。从竖轴一边的任何一点取值，在竖轴另一边对称的地方可以得到一个相同的值。

（3）它渐近于横轴，但与横轴永不相交。因此，分布的两端曲线可以无限延长。

（4）它是单峰的。正态曲线也被称为"钟形曲线"。由于曲线的最高处仅是在曲线的正中部分，所以它是单峰的。

（5）曲线下的面积之和为1。曲线下的面积是概率，所以，正态分布所有概率之和是1。因为正态分布是对称的，所以竖轴两边的概率各为0.5。

（6）正态分布不是一条曲线，而是一个曲线系统。由于不同的总体都有自己不同的平均值和标准差，所以每一个总体都会有一个不同的正态分布曲线。

定距数据统计分析常用的t检验、方差分析和相关分析，都要求数据符合正态分析。分辨收集的定距数据是否符合正态分布，可以采用的方法有正态分布图法和统计检验法。

常用的正态分布图有带正态曲线的直方图（histogram）、正态P-P图和Q-Q图。常用的正态分布统计检验方法有Kolmogorov-Smirnov (Lilliefors修正)检验和Shapiro-Wilk检验。

下面以一项研究（张悦，2020）中的数据为例，来说明如何分辨研究数据是否符合正态分布。使用的数据是130名学生对二语高频短语动词多个意义掌握水平的测试成绩。

首先用带正态曲线的直方图看测试成绩数据是否符合正态分布。用SPSS做出的直方图显示（图14.2），测试成绩的分布与正态分布的形状基本吻合，数据基本符合正态分布。

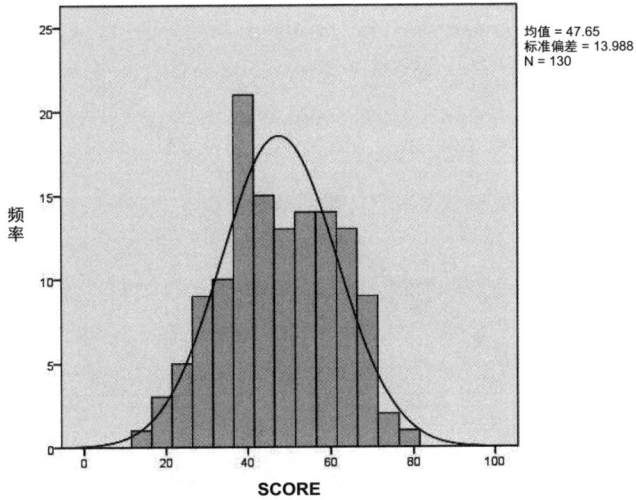

图14.2　带正态曲线的直方图

　　下面用正态 P-P 图和 Q-Q 图考察数据是否符合正态分布。在正态 P-P 图和 Q-Q 图中，有表示实际累积概率的数据观测点和一条理论累积概率直线。如果数据观测点大体都沿着直线分布，那么数据符合或近似符合正态分布。从测试成绩数据的正态 P-P 图（图 14.3）和 Q-Q 图（图 14.4）可以看出，数据观测点基本上是沿着直线分布的，所以数据基本符合正态分布。

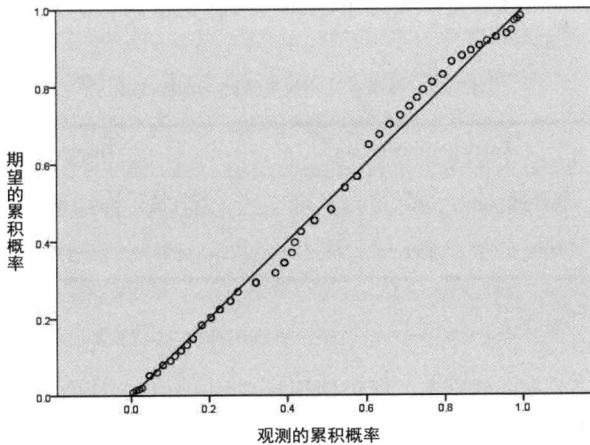

图14.3　测试成绩的正态P-P图

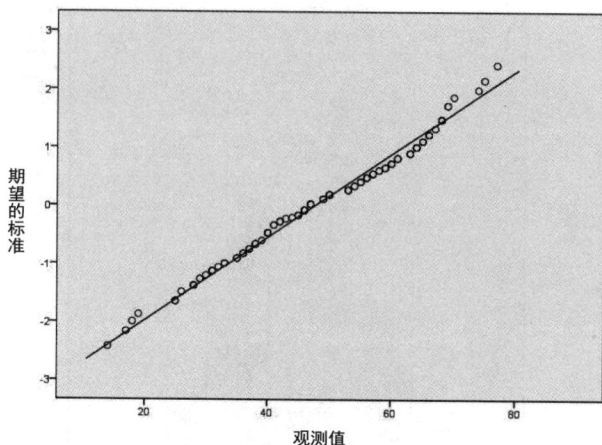

图14.4　测试成绩的Q-Q图

使用 Kolmogorov-Smirnov (Lilliefors 修正) 检验或 Shapiro-Wilk 检验做数据的正态分布检验，要看用数据做出的 sig. 值或 p 值的大小。如果做出的 sig. 值或 p 值大于 0.05，那么数据与正态分布没有显著性差异，也就是说，数据符合正态分布。如果做出的 sig. 值或 p 值小于 0.05，那么数据与正态分布有显著性差异，也就是说，数据不符合正态分布。

用 SPSS 做正态分布检验，无论是 Kolmogorov-Smirnov 检验还是 Shapiro-Wilk 检验，结果都显示测试成绩数据符合正态分布（K-S 统计量 =.069，p=.200>0.05；S-W 统计量 =.983，p=.106>0.05，见表 14.7 ）。

表14.7　短语多义测试成绩的正态性检验

	Kolmogorov-Smirnov[a]			Shapiro-Wilk		
	统计量	df	sig.	统计量	df	sig.
SCORE	.069	130	.200	.983	130	.106

a. Lilliefors 显著水平修正

由于正态分布曲线众多，所以使用起来是一件很麻烦的事。这是因为每一个总体有各自的平均值和标准差，都有一条分布曲线，都要给其计算出一个正态分布表。

为了解决这个麻烦，产生了一种将所有的正态分布转换成标准正态分布的方法。这种方法就是计算总体中每一个数值的 Z 值，然后计算出每一个 Z

值和它们对应的概率值。Z 值的计算公式如下：

$$Z = \frac{X - \mu}{\sigma}$$

Z：每一个数值的 Z 值

X：总体的每一个数值

μ：总体平均值

σ：总体标准差

Z 值的意思是，总体的每一个数值（X）与总体平均值（μ）之间的差有多少个标准差（σ）。如果一个数值的 Z 值等于 3，表示该数值与总体平均值的差为 3 个标准差。如果一个数值小于平均值，Z 值为负值。如果一个数值大于平均值，Z 值则为正值。

这样计算出的 Z 值和它们对应的概率值的集合，称为标准正态分布。标准正态分布除了有正态分布的所有特性之外，还有以下特性：

1. 标准正态分布的平均值是 0，标准差是 1。
2. 在标准正态分布中，68.27% 的 Z 值落在均值 ±1σ 的范围内；95.45% 的 Z 值落在均值 ±2σ 的范围内；99.73% 的 Z 值落在均值 ±3σ 的范围内（图 14.5）。

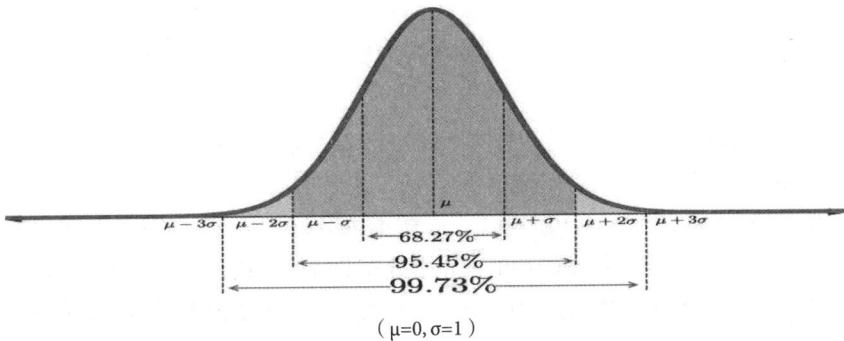

（μ=0, σ=1）

图14.5　标准正态分布

一般的统计书后面都附有标准正态分布表，供人们使用。由于正态分布的对称性，有些统计书只给出正态分布一半面积的分布值。

如果一组数据符合正态分布，平均值是 10，标准差是 1，那么这组数据 99.73% 的数值会在 10±3σ 的范围内，即在 7 到 13 的范围内；95.45% 的数值在 10±2σ 的范围内，即 8 到 12 的范围内；68.27% 的数值落在 10±1σ 的范围内，即 9 到 11 的范围内。

我们可以看到，在 ±3σ 之外有还有 0.27% 的数据，即有 0.27% 的数值是小于 7 或大于 13。从概率的角度说，小于 7 或大于 13 的数值出现在平均值为 10 和标准差为 1 的这个总体中的概率只有 0.27%。换句话说，如果我们从这个总体中随机抽取 100 个数值，可能只有 0.27 个数值小于 7 或大于 13（图 14.6）。

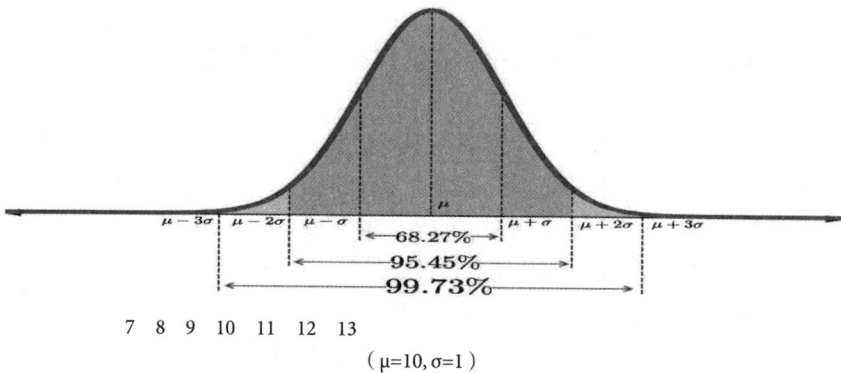

图14.6　标准正态分布

假设现在有两个符合正态分布的样本，甲样本的平均值为 9，乙样本的平均值为 6。在不知道两个样本是否来自图中 μ=10、σ=1 总体的情况下，如果让你根据上面的正态分布图判断哪个样本更可能属于这个总体，你会选哪一个呢？

按照直觉，你可能会选甲样本。你为什么会选甲样本呢？

我们可以计算一下两个样本的 Z 值，看它们属于该总体的可能性有多大。甲样本的 Z 值 =(9-10)/1=-1，乙样本的 Z 值 =(6-10)/1=-4。甲样本的 Z 值等于 -1，意味甲样本的均值在正态分布曲线的左边，距离总体平均值一个标准差，落在 99.73% 的大概率区域。因此，我们可以说甲样本大概率属于这个总体。乙样本的标准差为 -4，意味着乙样本的平均值也是在正态分布曲线的左边，但距离总体平均值四个标准差，落在 0.27% 的小概率区域。因此，我们可以说，由于乙样本属于该总体的概率太低，所以可以认为乙样本不属于该总体。

这就是推断检验的基本原理。在不知道某个样本数据是否属于某个正态分布总体的情况下，以样本数据符合正态分布或近似符合正态分布为前提，根据正态分布的特性，将总体划分为一个大概率区域和一个小概率区域，并借此考察样本数据是否属于该总体。如果样本平均值落在大概率区域内，那么就认为该样本属于该总体。这是因为所给样本属于该总体的概率很高。如果样本平均值落在小概率区域内，就认为该样本不属于该总体。这是因为所给样本属于该总体的概率太低。

在统计学中，小概率区域的概率记为 α，称作"显著性水平"；大概率区域的概率记为 1-α，称作"置信度"。置信度越高，也就是说 1-α 的值越大，所得结论的确信程度越高。反之，置信度越低，也就是说 1-α 的值越小，确信程度越低。

在社会学研究领域和外语研究领域，普遍使用的置信度是 95% 和 99%。那么相应的显著性水平 α 是 5% 和 1%，记作 α=.05 和 α=.01。

中文的"显著性"对应的英语单词是 significance。该词在统计中的意义不是"显著"，而是 maximum probability of a result which is caused by something other than mere chance，即"某个结果最大可能不是由偶然因素而是由其他事情造成"。简单地讲，"显著性"的意思就是"小偶然性"或"非偶然性"。显著性水平是推断偶然性的量度，表示推断结论不可靠的概率和可能出现的误差。显著性水平（α）越低，偶然性就越小，推断结论可靠的概率（1-α）也就越大。

需要特别说明的是，5% 或 1% 的显著性水平并不意味着你的结论就是 100% 正确，而是意味着你的结论依然有 5% 或 1% 不成立的可能。如果某件事情出现的概率是 99%，不可能出现的概率是 1%，不等于说那件事情根本不可能出现，而是也是有可能出现的。

有人曾经统计过高尔夫运动中一杆进洞的概率。一般业余爱好者一杆进洞的概率是 10 万分之一，意味着业余爱好者击 10 万次球才有可能出现一次一杆进洞的情况。专业选手一杆进洞的概率是 2500 分之一，即击 2500 次球才有可能出现一次一杆进洞的情况。尽管一杆进洞的概率很低，但是依然会发生。

因此，我们在根据数据推断统计结果，陈述与讨论我们的研究结论时，一定要注意不能说得那么绝对，要留有适当的余地。

14.2.4 显著性检验

显著性检验是利用概率分布的特性，结合研究假设和样本数据的统计值，对研究假设的可接受性进行验证，以考察我们的假设是大概率可以接受，还是因为小概率而加以拒绝。

显著性检验是对统计结果的"必然性"或者"或然性"进行验证。如果一项研究发现 There is a statistically significant correlation between vitamin deficiency and disease（缺乏维生素和疾病之间在统计上存在显著性相关），那么从统计意义上讲，缺乏维生素和疾病之间存在的关系不是由偶然因素造成的。

我们在外语研究中，希望发现外语现象之间的联系和差异。我们往往先假设"联系"或"差异"存在，然后采集数据样本，对样本数据进行统计检验，以验证我们假设的"联系"或"差异"是否大概率存在。这就是一个显著性检验的过程。

显著性检验一般涉及两个相互对立的假设：零假设和备择假设。在统计中，零假设（null hypothesis）是一种"无"或"没有"的假定，即所采集的样本之间没有差异、没有关联一类的假定。因为只有这样假定，我们才能利用分布的特性，建立检验模型，对零假设的可接受性进行检验。

备择假设（alternative hypothesis）是当零假设不成立时所接受的对立假定，即"有"的假定。零假设做的是"无"的假定，"无"的对立假定是"有"。如果零假设成立，那么就认为备择假设不成立。然而，当零假设不成立时，就认为它的备择假设成立，或者说"有"的假定成立。当备择假设成立，就认为所采集的样本之间有差异、有关联。

一般来说，备择假设就是我们的研究假设。我们通过拒绝零假设来证实和接受研究假设。例如，一位研究者从事一项学习策略培训的实验研究，目的在于考察研究对象在培训之后对学习策略的使用是否与培训之前不同。这项研究潜在的研究假设是：研究对象在培训后对学习策略的使用不同于培训之前。

这位研究者收集到实验前后两组定距数据，数据符合正态分布。如果他要使用统计方法检验两组数据之间是否存在差异，就需要提出零假设："两组数据之间不存在差异。"这样他才能根据零假设，采用正态分布检验模型，对数据进行检验。

假定他所用的显著性水平为 α=0.05。如果根据两组数据计算出的 α 值大于 0.05，那么零假设成立，两组数据之间不存在差异，也就意味着研究假设不成立，研究对象在培训之后对学习策略的使用与培训之前没有不同。如果根据两组数据计算出的 α 值小于 0.05，那么零假设不成立，两组数据之间存在差异。这意味着研究假设成立，研究对象在培训之后对学习策略的使用不同于培训之前。

显著性检验的目的是确定接受零假设还是拒绝零假设。为了实现这个目的，首先要确定一个标准，即在什么情况下接受零假设，什么情况下拒绝零假设。统计学设定的标准是以概率为基础的。如果有95%以上，甚至99%以上的概率或把握，可以证明零假设成立，那么我们就接受零假设。

95%或99%通常称为置信水平。如果只有5%以下，甚至1%以下的概率证明零假设成立，我们就拒绝接受零假设。这是因为零假设成立的概率太低，令我们无法接受。由此可见，拒绝或接受零假设需要一个临界概率，这个临界概率称为"显著性水平"。

显著性水平可以因不同的行业和需要而不同。在社会科学和外语学科研究中，通常使用的显著性水平为0.05或0.01。也就是说，如果只有5%或1%的概率认为零假设成立，那就拒绝零假设，从而接受研究假设。

例14.1 （马广惠，2003）某个高校从新一届学生中抽出若干学生组成样本，检查新生的进校英语水平是否高于往届。根据往年的录取分数，已知新生英语水平测试的分数服从正态分布，标准差为10分，而且进校的平均分数为500分。新一届学生的英语平均成绩为504分。以0.01的显著水平检验新生与往届学生是否有差异。

解：本题的零假设为"新生的进校英语水平和往届学生没有差异"。

根据已知条件，我们可以建立一个均值为500分，标准差为10分的标准正态分布（Z分布），来检验504分是否落在概率为99%的区域内。如果落在99%的区域内，接受零假设。如果落在99%的区域以外，即落在1%的区域内，拒绝零假设，接受备择假设，"新生的英语水平高于往届"。

我们用Z值做概率的临界值。这是一个右尾检验的问题。$Z_{0.01}$的值为2.33。如果504的Z值小于2.33，那么它就落在概率为99%的区域内，那就意味着接受零假设。如果504的Z值大于2.33，那么它就落在概率为1%的区域内，那就意味着拒绝零假设。

$$Z_{504} = \frac{X - \mu}{\sigma} = \frac{504 - 500}{10} = 0.4$$

由于Z_{504}的值小于2.33的临界Z值，虽然样本平均值高于总体平均值，仍然认为新生的进校英语水平与往届新生没有差异。两者均值上的差异很可能是抽样误差造成的。

例14.2 （马广惠，2003）某出版社编辑出版了一套英语读物。这套读物的目标读者群是年龄为21岁的年轻读者。为了了解这套读物是否为目标读者所接受，这家出版社就进行了一次调查。假定读者的年龄服从正态分布，随机抽取400名读者进行调查，得出的样本统计量为X=25岁，$S^2=16$，现在以0.05的显著性水平检验出版社的读物是否达到预期目的。

解：本题零假设为"样本群体和目标群体没有差别"。

当总体方差未知时，可以用样本方差代替。这样我们可以建立一个均值为 21 岁，方差为 4 岁的 Z 分布，用于检验。0.05 的显著水平说明，如果样本平均值 25 落在 95% 的区域内，接受零假设；否则拒绝零假设。这是一个双尾检验问题。概率为 95% 时的临界 $Z_{\alpha/2}$ 值为 1.96。如果 Z_{25} 的值小于 $Z_{.95}$ 的值，就接受零假设；反之，就拒绝零假设。

当总体方差未知，用样本方差代替总体方差时，计算公式为：

$$Z_{25} = \frac{X - \mu}{\dfrac{s}{\sqrt{n}}} = \frac{25 - 21}{\dfrac{4}{\sqrt{400}}} = \frac{4}{4/20} = 20$$

计算结果显示，Z_{25} 的值大于 $Z_{.95}$，拒绝接受零假设。即使接受零假设，也只有 5% 的把握；而得出错误结论的可能性却为 95%。因此，我们宁愿拒绝零假设，转而接受零假设的备择假设，认为样本群体和目标群体有差别。备择假设成立的可能性为 95%，出现错误结论的可能性为 5%。这次调研的结论说明该出版社出版的英语读物并没有吸引它的目标读者。

SPSS 应用：正态分布检验

将定距数据中的数值输入 SPSS 的数值栏中后，按照下列步骤操作，就可以获得数据带正态分布的直方图、Kolmogorov-Smirnov (Lilliefors 修正) 检验和 Shapiro-Wilk 检验结果以及 Q-Q 图、P-P 图。

（1）直方图
→ 分析 (A)　（或者在 图形 (G) 的地方做）
　　→ 描述统计
　　　　→ 频率 (F)
　　　　　　→ 变量名：从左框移到右框
　　　　　　　　→ 图表 (C)
　　　　　　　　　⊙直方图
　　　　　　　　　　☑在直方图上显示正态曲线
　　　　　　　　→ 继续
　　　　　　　　→ 确定

（2）Kolmogorov-Smirnov (Lilliefors 修正) 检验和 Shapiro-Wilk 检验结果以及 Q-Q 图

→ 分析 (A)
　　→ 描述统计
　　　　→ 探索 (E)
　　　　　　→ 变量名：从左框移到右边因变量框
　　　　　　　　→ 绘制 (T)
　　　　　　　　　·带检验的正态图（Q-Q 图）
　　　　　→ 继续
　　　　　→ 确定

（3）P-P 图和 Q-Q 图可以在 图形 (G) 的地方做。

课堂讨论

1. 下面的量表称为李克特量表（Likert Scale）。用这样的量表获取的数据是定类数据、定序数据还是定距数据？

| (1) 我相信我的英语在未来几个学期里能快速提高，取得优异成绩。 |
| A. 完全不同意　　B. 不同意　　C. 不确定　　D. 同意　　E. 完全同意 |
| (2) 与班里的其他同学相比，我有更大的英语学习优势。 |
| A. 完全不同意　　B. 不同意　　C. 不确定　　D. 同意　　E. 完全同意 |
| (3) 我具有非常明确和高度前瞻性的英语学习目标。 |
| A. 完全不同意　　B. 不同意　　C. 不确定　　D. 同意　　E. 完全同意 |

2. 两个新生班英语摸底考试的平均分都是 86 分，但是甲班的标准差是 3 分，乙班的标准差是 8 分。这两个班在标准差上的差异说明了什么？

3. 一组数据"17、18、18、18、18、19、19、19、20、80"的标准差为 19.48。如果从这组数据中去掉 80 这个数值，得出的标准差为 0.88，与 19.48 差别巨大。这说明什么？

4. 阅读下列节选内容（Bećirović et al., 2021）并回答问题：
   (1) 作者在 Table 1 中报告了 participants 的哪些量化信息？作者在正文中是如何陈述这些信息的？
   (2) 作者在 Table 3 中报告了哪些描述统计信息？作者在正文中是如何使用这些信息的？
   (3) Table 1 和 Table 3 中包含哪些研究变量？
   (4) Table 1 和 Table 3 中的数据，哪些是定类数据，哪些是定距数据？

Participants

The research sample in the current study was composed of 173 Bosnian high school students studying at four different grade levels. The convenience sampling method was employed in the process of participants' selection. The sample consisted of 100 female students (57.8%) and 73 male students (42.2%). As for the grade level, there were 75 first grade students (43.4%), 36 second grade students (20.8%), 19 third grade students (11%) and 43 fourth grade students (24.9%), with the age range between 15 and 19. The participants also provided information on their grade-point average obtained in the English as a foreign language (EFL) course. The grades ranged between 1 and 5, with 1 being a non-passing grade and 5 being the highest grade. Thus, 76 participants obtained the GPA score 5, 36 participants the GPA score 4, 35 participants the GPA score 3, and 24 participants the GPA score 2, while only 2 participants obtained a non-passing grade 1, and, as such, this group will not be included in the analysis. Table 1 provides all the details related to the participants.

Table 1 Gender, grade level, and average course grade of the participants

	n	%		n	%
Gender			Average course grade		
Male	73	42.2	1 Negative	2	1.2
Female	100	57.8	2 Sufficient	24	13.9
Grade			3 Good	35	20.2
First	75	43.4	4 Very good	36	20.8
Second	36	20.8	5 Excellent	76	43.9
Third	19	11.0			
Fourth	43	24.9			
Total	173	100		173	100

Data analysis

The collected data were analyzed using the Statistical Package for Social Sciences (SPSS, v. 26). Pearson product correlation coefficients as well as the descriptive analysis including means, standard deviation (*SD*) and frequencies were employed. One-way MANOVA was used to investigate the differences in technology use and teacher's support based on gender, grade level and GPA groups.

Results

Preliminary analysis

The participants scored quite high on the perceived usefulness of technological resources for foreign language learning (M = 2.04, SD = .60) and are confident about their abilities to use technology in the process of foreign language learning (M = 2.25, SD = .67). Furthermore, the participants stated that they have positive conditions to use technology (M = 2.21, SD = .70) and they scored quite high on computer self-efficacy (M = 2.25, SD = .72) (Table 3). The teacher's support for the use of technology was rated slightly above 2, with affection support being most highly rated (M = 2.28, SD = .91), behavior support closely following (M = 2.38, SD = .87), and capacity support receiving the lowest rating (M = 2.53, SD = 1.05). The participants scored the highest mean on the perceived usefulness (M = 2.04, SD = .60) and facilitation condition subscales (M = 2.21, SD = .70). In terms of the use of technology (M = 2.25, SD = .67) and computer self-efficacy (M = 2.25, SD = .72), the same mean score was measured.

Table 3 Descriptive statistics and correlation

	n	M	SD	1	2	3	4	5	6
1. Affection support	173	2.28	.91						
2. Capacity support	173	2.53	1.05	.57**					
3. Behavior support	173	2.38	.87	.60**	.62**				
4. Technology use	173	2.25	.67	.28**	.20**	.30**			
5. Perceived usefulness	173	2.04	.60	.20**	.19*	.27**	.68**		
6. Computer self-efficacy	173	2.25	.72	.22**	.19*	.21**	.56**	.64**	
7. Facilitation condition	173	2.21	.70	.15*	.17*	.25**	.40**	.50**	.53**

5. 阅读下列节选内容（Arfé et al., 2022）并回答问题：
   (1) Table 1 中的变量，哪些是定类数据，哪些是定距数据？
   (2) 如何用交互表的形式将 Table 1 中的定类数据呈现出来？
   (3) 作者在正文中如何使用与表述 Table 1 中的数据统计信息？

Participants

A power analysis using G*Power 3 software indicated that using an F test (Repeated measures ANOVA, within-between interaction) for valence effect, a total sample of 34 participants was necessary to detect medium effects (d = 0.25) with power (1–β) set at 0.80 and α = 0.05. Participants were 42 students (26 girls, 62%, M_{age} = 24.17, SD = 4.91). Initially, 50 undergraduate students had accepted to take part in the eye-tracking experiment. Of these, two did not show up, one was not included in the study because she reported a corneal injury at the preliminary assessment, and one was also excluded after the experimental session for not having completed all tasks. Moreover, the data of two students were excluded from the analysis as outliers in all eye-movement analyses (scores > than 2 standard deviations from the distribution). Participants' characteristics are reported in Table 1. All participants had normal or corrected to normal vision and none of them reported language delays, dyslexia, or reading problems. For three students Italian was the second language (L2). However, they had been exposed to Italian for more than 8 years (range 9–19 years). Their first language was Albanian, Romanian, and Sinhalese. Two groups of participants were formed, matched on age, gender and first language (i.e., having Italian as L2).

Table 1   Participants' Characteristics with Means, Standard Deviations (in Brackets) and Results of T-Tests and Chi-Square Tests

Variable	Negative valence ($n = 21$)	Neutral valence ($n = 21$)	t / χ^2	p	Cohen's d
Age	24.62 (5.98)	23.71 (3.65)	.59	.56	0.18
Gender (n girls and %)	13 (62%)	13 (62%)	.001	1.00	
Italian as L2 (n)	2 (Albanian and Sinhalese)	1 (Romanian)	.34	.55	

Variable	Negative valence ($n = 21$)	Neutral valence ($n = 21$)	t / χ^2	p	Cohen's d
LST score	24.76 (5.04)	26.90 (4.94)	−1.39	.17	−0.43
IRI score	94.67 (11.06)	95.24 (10.96)	−0.17	.87	−0.05
Valence (Likert scale 1–5)	3.48 (.60)	3.14 (.57)	1.84	.07	0.57
Empathy (Likert scale 1–5)	3.10 (.77)	2.19 (.75)	3.86	.001	1.19

LST = listening span test; IRI = Interpersonal Reactivity Index; Italian as L2 = Italian as a second language

6. 阅读下列节选内容（Alyami & Mohsen, 2019）并回答问题：
   (1) 这项研究关注的样本总体是什么？样本量有多大？
   (2) 这项研究的因变量和自变量是什么？
   (3) 这项研究有没有说明研究数据是否符合正态分布？

The Use of a Reading Lexicon to Aid Contextual Vocabulary Acquisition by EFL Arab Learners

Participants

The study sample consisted of 60 adult, female, Arabic-speaking students who were enrolled in EFL courses at Najran University in the Kingdom of Saudi Arabia. These students were aged between 20 and 24 years. The participants were randomly assigned and divided into two groups, 30 members for each. This number was subject to institutional constraints. The participants were third-year students of the Department of English who had previously experienced intensive reading as a method of instruction in English, but have had no exposure to extensive reading in the context of this course. Based on the students' level in the department, it was expected that their proficiency in English would be advanced. Both the experimental group and the control group experienced the same procedures of pre-test scales, the assigned readings, and the post-test assessment, so the only difference was the matter of whether a given participant had received training in the deliberate CVA method.

Data Analysis

Quantitative data were analyzed in the study. The independent variable was the effect of training in deliberate CVA using materials developed from Nation's K-level. The dependent variable were the two calculated variables that show the magnitude of change that occurred between the pre-test and the post-test, namely, the change in word context recognition and the change in word definition accuracy. Descriptive analysis was run to describe and summarize the calculated change in word context recognition and word definition accuracy as well. Moreover, two t-tests were calculated to measure the differences in the change in word context recognition and word definition accuracy between the pre-test and the post-test, for the control and experimental groups, respectively.

7. 阅读下列节选内容（Arfé et al., 2022）并回答问题：
    (1) 这项研究涉及哪些总体？
    (2) 这项研究选取的样本是什么？样本量有多大？
    (3) 这项研究的样本对总体的代表性如何？
    (4) 这项研究没有对两个文本的长度和可读性做显著性检验，是否合理？为什么？
    (5) 这项研究有没有说明数据是否符合正态分布？

Effects of negative emotional valence on readers' text processing and memory for text: An eye-tracking study

Participants

A power analysis using G*Power 3 software indicated that using an F test (Repeated measures ANOVA, within-between interaction) for valence effect, a total sample of 34 participants was necessary to detect medium effects (d = 0.25) with power (1–β) set at 0.80 and α = 0.05. Participants were 42 students (26 girls, 62%, M_{age} = 24.17, SD = 4.91). Initially, 50 undergraduate students had accepted to take part in the eye-tracking experiment. Of these, two did not show up, one was not included in the study because she reported a corneal injury at the preliminary assessment, and one was also excluded after the experimental session for not having completed all tasks. Moreover, the data of two students were excluded from the analysis as outliers in all eye-movement analyses (scores > than 2 standard deviations from the distribution). Participants' characteristics are reported in Table 1.

All participants had normal or corrected to normal vision and none of them reported language delays, dyslexia, or reading problems. For three students Italian was the second language (L2). However, they had been exposed to Italian for more than 8 years (range 9–19 years). Their first language was Albanian, Romanian, and Sinhalese. Two groups of participants were formed, matched on age, gender and first language (i.e., having Italian as L2).

Table 1 Participants' Characteristics with Means, Standard Deviations (in Brackets) and Results of T-Tests and Chi-Square Tests

Variable	Negative valence ($n = 21$)	Neutral valence ($n = 21$)	t / χ^2	p	Cohen's d
Age	24.62 (5.98)	23.71 (3.65)	.59	.56	0.18
Gender (n girls and %)	13 (62%)	13 (62%)	.001	1.00	
Italian as L2 (n)	2 (Albanian and Sinhalese)	1 (Romanian)	.34	.55	
LST score	24.76 (5.04)	26.90 (4.94)	−1.39	.17	−0.43
IRI score	94.67 (11.06)	95.24 (10.96)	−0.17	.87	−0.05
Valence (Likert scale 1–5)	3.48 (.60)	3.14 (.57)	1.84	.07	0.57
Empathy (Likert scale 1–5)	3.10 (.77)	2.19 (.75)	3.86	.001	1.19

LST = listening span test; IRI = Interpersonal Reactivity Index; Italian as L2 = Italian as a second language

Materials

Two versions of the *Ghost* story passage, one of negative valence, corresponding to the original text, and the other of neutral valence, the manipulated version, were respectively used in the negative and neutral valence reading condition (see Appendix A).

The two story passages were equivalent for number of words (in Italian, 148 in text A and 146 in text B) and syllables (306 in text A and 307 in text B), as well as for readability (Gulpease index = 66 for text A and 64 for text B; 100 = maximum readability).

Procedure

All participants preliminarily completed a demographic questionnaire, the interpersonal reactivity index questionnaire and the listening span task. The reading session was carried out in a quiet room. Students were asked to read the short suspense story passage while their eye-movements were recorded. After reading the passage, they rated its emotional valence on a 5-point Likert-type scale (from 1 = very good to 5 = very bad) in response to the following request: "Please, assess how good/bad this story makes you feel", and their empathy for the protagonist ("Please, assess how much worried are you for the protagonist") on a 5-point Likert-type scale ranging from 1 = very little worried to 5 = very much worried. Participants then performed a categorization span task from an Italian battery for memory assessment in adults (BAC; De Beni et al., 2008). This task was aimed at diverting participants' attention from the content of the text just read. After this interfering task, they responded to the 12-item questionnaire assessing their memory for the story read.

课外练习

1. 我们为什么要做推断统计?
2. 如果没有零假设可不可以做推断统计?
3. 显著性检验中显著性水平的含义是什么?
4. 从国际知名英文期刊发表的论文中,选取某个学科方向的某个专项选题论文 30 篇,其中 15 篇的作者是英语本族语者,15 篇的作者是英语非本族语者。选用这 30 篇论文的摘要作为统计语料,然后完成下列统计任务:
   (1) 从所选的材料中,选取两到三个语言特征(如字数、句长),运用 Coh-Metrix 一类的语言分析软件或 Word 软件中的语言统计功能,统计每篇论文摘要中所选语言特征的数量。
   (2) 用 SPSS 计算出 30 篇论文摘要中每个所选语言特征的平均值和标准差。

(3) 用 SPSS 计算出 15 篇本族语者论文摘要和 15 篇非本族语者论文摘要中所选特征的平均值和标准差，并根据所学知识，对两种论文摘要的平均值和标准差进行比较并加以说明。

(4) 用带正态曲线的直方图、正态 P-P 图和 Q-Q 图、Kolmogorov-Smirnov (Lilliefors 修正) 检验和 Shapiro-Wilk 检验，观察收集到的数据是否符合正态分布。

(5) 将句长按"短、中、长"分成三类，作者按"本族语作者、非本族语作者"分成两类，把收集到的数据以句长和作者为变量制作一个交互表。

(6) 完成 (1)—(5) 之后，参照课堂讨论中的阅读材料，撰写一个统计分析报告。

拓展阅读

Mackey, A., & Gass, S. M. (2005). *Second language research: Methodology and design.* Mahwah, New Jersey: Lawrence Erlbaum Associates.

Wilkinson, L. (1999). Statistical methods in psychology journals: Guidelines and explanations. *American Psychologist, 54*, 594–604.

Woods, A., Fletcher, P., & Hughes, A. (2000). *Statistics in language studies.* Beijing: Foreign Language Teaching and Research Press.

马广惠. (2003). 外国语言学及应用语言学统计方法. 杨凌：西北农林科技大学出版社.

秦晓晴、毕劲. (2015). 外语教学研究定量研究方法及数据分析. 北京：外语教学与研究出版社.

第 15 单元
外语研究统计检验方法

学习目标

- 了解并掌握推断统计常用的检验方法
- 熟悉国际期刊论文中检验结果的表达方式
- 能够使用 SPSS 做常见的推断统计分析

本单元在 14 单元的基础上，从差异检验和关联检验两大方面介绍外语研究中常用的一些统计检验方法。

差异检验旨在验证研究数据的样本之间是否存在显著性差异。我们可以借助差异检验的统计结果，论证我们的研究对象之间在语言研究指标上是否存在差别。外语研究中常用的差异检验方法有独立样本 t 检验、成对样本 t 检验、单因素方差分析和卡方检验。

关联检验旨在验证研究数据的样本之间是否在数值上有着显著性的相互变动关系。我们可以借助关联检验的统计结果，论证研究对象的语言研究指标之间是否存在关联关系。外语研究中常用的关联检验方法有相关分析和回归分析。

15.1　差异检验

米切尔（Mitchell, 1990）指出，在对事物或者现象的量化特征进行比较的时候，我们会趋向于主要观察事物间的差异性而不是它们的相似性；即使当我们观察事物或现象间的相似性的时候，我们也会留下可能存在差异性的余地。因此，我们在实际研究中会更多地关注现象之间是否存在差异。

差异检验用于检验两组或者两组以上的数据之间是否存在显著性差异。差异检验方法分为参数检验方法和非参数检验方法两大类。参数检验方法有独立样本 t 检验、成对样本 t 检验、单因素方差分析和多因素方差分析等。非参数检验方法有卡方检验、两个独立样本检验、多个独立样本检验、两个相关样本检验和多个相关样本检验。采用哪一类和哪一种检验方法，取决于研究问题、研究的数据类型与特征。

差异检验常用的参数检验方法有：独立样本 t 检验、成对样本 t 检验、单因素方差分析和多因素方差分析。

15.1.1　独立样本 t 检验

独立样本 t 检验（independent samples t-test）用于检验一个变量下的两个独立样本是否属于同一个总体，或者说用于检验一个变量下互不关联的两组数据之间是否存在显著性差异。独立样本指的是同一个变量下从两组不同对象那里采集到的互不关联的两个样本或两组数据，譬如"从一次外语水平考试中采集到的一组文科学生的外语成绩和一组理科学生的外语成绩"，就属于两个独立样本。

独立样本 t 检验对数据的要求是：

（1）一个变量下的两个独立样本或互不关联的两组数据。

（2）数据是定距数据，符合正态分布或近似正态分布。

但是，如果样本数据是定距数据且样本量足够大，即使不符合正态分布，也可以使用独立样本 t 检验。实际上，t 检验最初是为小样本（n<30，样本容量小于 30）检验设立的。

（3）独立样本 t 检验不要求两组数据的样本量相等，一组数据的样本量可以大于或小于另一组。例如，一组数据的样本量可以是 100，另一组数据的样本量可以是 150。

独立样本 t 检验要回答的统计问题是："一个变量下的两个独立样本数据之间是否存在显著性差异"或"某个变量下的两组数值的均值之间是否有显著性差异"。

独立样本 t 检验的零假设是：两个独立样本属于同一个总体，或者说两个样本之间不存在显著性差异。

独立样本 t 检验的检验统计量是 t 值，其公式为：

$$t = \frac{\overline{X_1} - \overline{X_2}}{\sqrt{\dfrac{S_1^2}{n_1} + \dfrac{S_2^2}{n_2}}} \qquad (\mathrm{df} = n_1 + n_2 - 2)$$

其中：

$\overline{X_1}$：样本 1 的平均值

$\overline{X_2}$：样本 2 的平均值

S_1：样本 1 的标准差

S_2：样本 2 的标准差

df：自由度

n_1：样本 1 中数值的个数

n_2：样本 2 中数值的个数

我们可以将用数据计算出的 t 值与设定的显著水平 α 的临界值相比，来确定两个独立样本是否来自同一个总体。如果计算出的 t 值的绝对值大于给定的显著水平的临界值，那么两个样本的均值之间存在显著性差异。如果计算出的 t 值的绝对值小于给定的显著水平的临界值，那么两个样本的均值之间不存在显著性差异。

我们还可以将计算出的 t 值对应的概率与设定的显著水平 α 相比，来确定两个独立样本是否属于同一个总体。如果计算出的 t 值对应的概率大于设定的 α 值，那么两个样本的均值之间不存在显著性差异。如果计算出的 t 值对应的概率小于设定的 α 值，那么两个样本的均值之间存在显著性差异。例如，如果我们设定的显著水平值是 α=0.05，而计算出的 t 值对应的概率是 0.15，那么两个样本之间不存在显著性差异；而如果计算出的 t 值对应的概率是 0.01，那么两个样本之间存在显著性差异。

如果我们的研究问题是"两组研究对象在某个外语指标上是否有差别"，那么我们在做研究设计的时候，就可以考虑从两组研究对象里采集所定外语指标的定距数据，获得两个独立样本，用独立样本 t 检验对两组数据进行检验，然后根据检验的结果，看两个独立样本之间是否存在显著性差异，并借此回答我们的研究问题。

如果我们看到的只是一组定距数据，但是这组数据可以在一个外语指标下分成两组互不关联的样本，那么我们就能够很快想到这是两个独立样本数据，要回答的研究问题应该是"两组研究对象之间在所给的外语指标上是否存在差别"，可以使用独立样本 t 检验对数据进行检验，并根据检验的结果回答我们的研究问题。

例 15.1　某学院一次期末写作考试要求学生写一篇 450 字的作文。学院在考试后收集了 147 位学生的作文，其中包括 67 篇男生的作文和 80 篇女生的作文，并对这 147 篇作文的字数做了统计。学院希望了解男生与女生的作文在字数上是否有差异。描述统计结果如表 15.1 所示。已知数据符合正态分布，检验男生与女生的作文在字数上是否存在显著性差异（α=0.05）。

表15.1　男女生作文字数的描述统计

	性别	人数	平均值	标准差	均值的标准误
字数	男	67	405.8955	56.02357	6.84437
	女	80	416.1500	74.02824	8.27661

解：这项调查要回答的问题是"男生与女生之间在作文长度上是否存在差别"。

由于男生组作文和女生组作文是来自同一次写作考试中的两组作文，所以是两个独立样本。已知数据符合正态分布，可以采用独立样本 t 检验的方法。

独立样本 t 检验要回答的统计问题是"男生组与女生组的作文长度平均值之间是否存在显著性差异（显著性水平为 α=0.05）"。如果统计检验结果显示两者之间存在显著性差异，那么就可以说男生与女生在作文长度上存在差别。如果统计结果显示两者之间不存在显著性差异，那么就不可以说男生与女生在作文长度上存在差别，不能下结论说女生的作文长于男生的作文。

将相关量值代入公式，计算检验统计量 t 值。

$$t = \frac{\overline{X}_1 - \overline{X}_2}{\sqrt{\dfrac{S_1^2}{n_1} + \dfrac{S_2^2}{n_2}}} = \frac{405.8955 - 416.15}{\sqrt{\dfrac{56.02357^2}{67} + \dfrac{74.02824^2}{80}}} = \frac{-10.2545}{10.74} = -0.955 \quad df = n_1 + n_2 - 2 = 145$$

当显著水平 α=0.05，df=145 时，t 分布表中对应的 t 值为 1.96。

答：由于计算出的 t 值的绝对值为 0.955，小于显著水平为 α=0.05、df=145 时的临界值（t=1.96），所以两个样本之间不存在显著性差异。

我们还可以用 t 值对应的概率与 α=0.05 做比较，看两个样本之间是否存在显著性差异。用 SPSS 计算出 t 的绝对值为 0.955、df=145 对应的概率是 0.25，大于 α=0.05。因此，两个样本之间不存在显著性差异。

由此，我们可以说，该学院男生与女生之间在作文长度上没有差别。女生作文与男生作文在平均长度上的差异很可能是由偶然因素或抽样误差造成的。

SPSS 应用：独立样本 t 检验

在 SPSS 的一列数据表格中输入数据中的数值，然后在另一列数据表格中对应数值所属的样本组分布输入 1 或 2，如下所示。1 代表第一组样本数值，2 代表第二组样本数值。

数据	组别
140	1
140	2
138	2
136	1

数据输入完成后，按下列步骤操作，就可以得到检验结果。

$$\boxed{分析\ (\underline{A})}$$

→比较均值

→$\boxed{独立样本\,t\,检验\,(T)}$

→变量名：将"数据"变量名从左框移到"检验变量"框，将"组别"变量名从左框移到"分组变量"框。

→$\boxed{定义组}$

→在定义组的两个框内分别输入 1 和 2

→$\boxed{确定}$

15.1.2 成对样本 t 检验

成对样本 t 检验（paired samples t-test）用于检验一个变量下对同一个群体重复收集的两个样本数据是否属于同一个总体，或者说用于检验一个变量下对一个群体重复收集的两组数据之间是否存在显著性差异。成对样本指的是在一个变量下从同一个群体那里重复采集的两组数据，譬如"用同一份学习策略问卷让同一组研究对象重复做了两次所获得的两组数据"，就属于成对样本。既然是从同一个群体那里获得的两个样本，那么两个样本的数值必然是成对的。

成对样本 t 检验计算检验统计量的公式为：

$$t = \frac{\overline{X_1} - \overline{X_2}}{\sqrt{\dfrac{n\sum (X_1 - X_2)^2 - [\sum (X_1 - X_2)]^2}{n-1}}}$$

其中：

t：检验统计量 t 值

$\overline{X_1}$：样本一的平均值

$\overline{X_2}$：样本二的平均值

X_1：样本一的个值

X_2：样本二的个值

n：样本的对数

df=n-1

成对样本 t 检验对数据的要求是：

（1）一个变量下从同一组对象那里重复收集到的两组数据。

（2）两组数据是定距数据，符合正态分布或近似正态分布。

（3）两组数据的样本量相等且成对。如果一组数据的样本量是 100，另一组数据的样本量也必须是 100，并且样本中的数值是一一成对的。

如果在第二次采集研究数据时有研究对象缺席，那么一种方法是从研究数据中去除缺席对象的数据。如果需要保留缺席对象的数据，那么可以用第二次采集数据的平均值代替缺席对象的缺省值。

如果我们的研究问题是"同一组研究对象在某个外语指标上在一次实验前后是否发生了变化"，那么我们就可以采集相应的成对样本数据，使用成对样本 t 检验对数据进行检验，并根据检验的结果回答我们的研究问题。

如果我们看到只是两组定距数据，并且这两组数据是同一组研究对象的同一个外语指标的测量结果，那么就应当知道它们是成对样本，要回答的研究问题是"研究对象在所给的外语指标上是否发生了改变"，可以用成对样本 t 检验对数据进行检验，并根据检验结果回答研究问题。

成对样本 t 检验常用于实验研究，用于检验实验前的数据与实验后的数据之间是否存在显著性差异，确切地说，是验证实验前后研究对象的行为是否发生了变化。例如，一位研究者进行一项研究，考察学习策略培训对第二语言学习者使用学习策略情况的影响。首先，他设计了一份学习策略问卷，选取 80 名学生作为研究对象，把问卷发给学生做，并收回做好的问卷。然后，他对这 80 名学生进行了为期两周的学习策略培训。培训结束两周之后，他又把同一内容的新问卷发给学生做，并收回做好的问卷。有了两次问卷的数据之后，这位研究者就可以使用成对样本 t 检验，检查两次数据的均值之间是否存在显著性差异，从而揭示策略培训前和策略培训后，学生在学习策略的使用上是否有所提高。

例 15.2 在一项研究中，研究人员从希塞（希腊−塞浦路斯人）英语学习者的英语作文中选取了 32 个句子，分别让 10 名英语本族语教师和 10 名希腊籍英语教师对句子错误程度进行评分，然后比较两组教师评分的一致性。两组教师的评分结果如表 15.2 所示（见 Woods et al., 2000: 184−186）。

在表 15.2 中，No. 代表句子的序号，NS 代表英语本族语教师的评分，GS 代表希腊英语教师的评分。由于两组评分是"同一组句子被评了两次"的成对样本，所以检验两组评分之间是否存在差异，需要使用成对样本 t 检验。

表15.2 两组教师对32个句子错误程度的评分（N=32）

No.	NS	GS	No.	NS	GS
1	22	36	17	23	39
2	16	9	18	18	19
3	42	29	19	30	28
4	25	35	20	31	41
5	31	34	21	20	25
6	36	23	22	21	17
7	29	25	23	29	26
8	24	31	24	22	37
9	29	35	25	26	34
10	18	21	26	20	28
11	23	33	27	29	33
12	22	13	28	18	24
13	31	22	29	23	37
14	21	29	30	25	33
15	27	25	31	27	39
16	32	25	32	11	20

经过计算，t=2.21，df=31，sig 值 =0.035。由于计算出的 sig 值小于 α=0.05，所以两组数据之间存在显著性差异。这意味着本族语教师和非本族语教师之间在给句子错误程度的评分上存在着差别。

SPSS 应用：成对样本 t 检验

在 SPSS 的两列数据表格中分别输入成对样本两组数据的数值，如下所示。

数据 1	数据 2
10	12
14	20
13	11
16	10

数据输入完成后，按下列步骤操作，就可以得到检验结果。

分析 (A)

→ 比较均值

→ 成对样本 t 检验 (P)

→ 将变量"数据 1"从左框移到右边"成对变量"下的
"变量 1"框中,

将变量"数据 2"从左框移到右边"成对变量"下的
"变量 2"框中。

→ 确定

15.1.3 单因素方差分析

单因素方差分析(one-way ANOVA)是用于检验一个变量下的三个或三个以上的独立样本之间是否存在显著性差异的参数检验方法。前面讲过,独立样本 t 检验用于检验两个独立样本之间是否存在显著性差异。因此,单因素方差分析可以看作是独立样本 t 检验的拓展版。

单因素方差分析对数据的要求是:

(1)一个变量下的三个或三个以上的独立样本数据。

(2)数据是定距数据,符合正态分布或近似正态分布。

(3)各组数据的样本量可以不同。

单因素方差分析要回答的统计问题是"某个变量下的三个或三个以上的独立样本数据之间是否存在显著性差异"或"某个变量下的三组或三组以上的数据之间是否存在显著性差异"。

单因素方差分析的零假设是"三个或三个以上的独立样本属于同一个总体",或者说"多个样本之间不存在显著性差异"。

例 15.3 一位研究者想要了解高校中不同学科学生的英语学业水平是否相同。他收集了某高校某一届 1321 名学生的英语四级考试成绩。这些学生分别来自文科、理科、工科和音体美四个学科。研究变量是"英语学业水平",研究数据是四个学科学生的英语四级考试成绩,是四个独立样本。研究者使用 SPSS 对收集到的数据做了单因素方差分析。他设定的显著性水平为 $\alpha=0.05$。

用 SPSS 对数据统计分析出的结果如表 15.3 和表 15.4 所示。表 15.3 是学生们的英语学业水平成绩的描述统计结果,表 15.4 是学科间成绩的单因素方差分析的结果。

表15.3　不同学科学生英语学业水平成绩的描述统计

| | N | 均值 | 标准差 | 标准误 | 均值的95%置信区间 | | 极小值 | 极大值 |
					下限	上限		
文科	333	436.2883	73.56209	4.03118	428.3584	444.2182	276.00	647.00
理科	285	437.1193	56.72984	3.36039	430.5049	443.7337	271.00	623.00
工科	244	420.4590	54.16620	3.46764	413.6286	427.2895	312.00	615.00
音体美	460	385.2565	54.69316	2.55008	380.2452	390.2678	237.00	559.00
总数	1322	415.7890	64.52706	1.77470	412.3074	419.2705	237.00	647.00

表15.4　不同学科学生英语学业水平成绩的单因素方差分析

	平方和	df	均方	F	显著性
组间	703751.530	3	234583.843	64.459	.000
组内	4796550.589	1318	3639.264		
总数	5500302.119	1321			

对 SPSS 分析出的结果，我们要看 F 值以及与值对应的显著性值或 sig 值（p 值），在论文中也要同时报告 F 值和对应的 p 值。如果 F 值的显著性值或 sig 值大于设定的显著性水平，那么几个样本数据之间不存在显著性差异。如果 F 值的显著性值或 sig 值小于设定的显著性水平，那么几个样本数据之间存在显著性差异。

在表 15.4 中，F=64.459，p=0.000。由于 F 值对应的 p 值小于显著性水平 α=0.05，所以不同学科的学生之间在英语学业水平上存在显著性差异。

需要指出的是，当单因素方差分析检验出三个或三个以上的独立样本之间存在显著性差异时，并不意味着这些样本两两之间都存在显著性差异。如果想要知道哪两个样本之间存在显著性差异，就需要对这些样本做两两对比检验，相当于做多个独立样本 t 检验。

SPSS 中用于两两检验的方法是单因素方差分析中的"事后检验（post hoc test）"。事后检验是在单因素方差分析结果表明多个样本之间存在显著性差异之后，用于考察哪两个样本之间存在显著性差异。使用 SPSS 对不同学科学生之间的成绩做两两事后检验，检验结果如表 15.5 所示。

如果要了解哪两组之间存在显著性差异，需要看均值差和对应的 p 值（显著性或 sig. 一栏）。如果 p 值小于 0.05，那么两组之间存在显著性差异。如果 p 值大于 0.05，那么两组之间不存在显著性差异。

在文科一栏，我们可以看到，文科学生和理科学生之间不存在显著性差异（均值差 =-0.83，p=0.86>0.05），文科学生和工科学生之间存在显著性差异（均值差 =15.83，p=0.002<0.05），文科学生和音体美学生之间存在显著性差异（均值差 =51.03，p=0.000<0.05）。

根据统计检验的结果，这位研究者可以得出的研究结论是：文科学生的英语学业水平高于工科学生和音体美学生。

表15.5　不同学科学生英语学业水平的多重比较

专业（I）	专业（J）	均值差（I-J）	标准误	显著性	95% 置信区间	
					下限	上限
文科	理科	-.83101	4.86807	.864	-10.3810	8.7190
	工科	15.82927*	5.08367	.002	5.8563	25.8022
	音体美	51.03177*	4.34053	.000	42.5167	59.5469
理科	文科	.83101	4.86807	.864	-8.7190	10.3810
	工科	16.66028*	5.26159	.002	6.3383	26.9823
	音体美	51.86278*	4.54761	.000	42.9414	60.7841
工科	文科	-15.82927*	5.08367	.002	-25.8022	-5.8563
	理科	-16.66028*	5.26159	.002	-26.9823	-6.3383
	音体美	35.20249*	4.77770	.000	25.8298	44.5752
音体美	文科	-51.03177*	4.34053	.000	-59.5469	-42.5167
	理科	-51.86278*	4.54761	.000	-60.7841	-42.9414
	工科	-35.20249*	4.77770	.000	-44.5752	-25.8298

* 均值差的显著性水平为 0.05。

SPSS 应用：单因素方差分析

在 SPSS 的一列数据表格中输入数据中的数值，然后在另一列数据表格中对应数值所属的样本组分布输入 1、2 或 3（如下所示）。1 代表第一组样本数值，2 代表第二组样本数值，3 代表第三组样本数值。

数据	组别
140	1
140	3
138	2
136	3

数据输入完成后，按下列步骤操作，就可以得到检验结果。

分析 (A)
　→ 比较均值
　　→ 单因素 ANOVA
　　　→ 将"数据"变量名从左框移到右边"因变量列表"框中，将"组别"变量从左框移到右边"因子"框中。
　　　　→ 两两比较
　　　　　→ √ LSD 或 √ Tukey
　　　　→ 继续
　　　　　→ 确定

15.1.4 卡方检验

如果研究中采集的数据不是定距数据而是定类数据，那么就不能使用 t 检验和方差分析一类的参数检验方法。如果收集的数据是定类数据，而且可以用交互表的形式呈现，那么就可以使用卡方（χ^2）检验的方法，对数据做显著性差异检验，检验统计量为 Pearson 卡方值。

当用交互表中的数据做检验时，卡方检验要回答的问题是"一个变量的两个或多个子类之间在另一个变量的子类上是否存在显著性差异"。

要回答上述问题，需要看计算出的卡方值所对应的 p 值（显著性或 sig 值）是大于设定的显著性水平还是小于设定的显著性水平。如果计算出的卡方值所对应的 p 值大于设定的显著性水平，那么不存在显著性差异。如果计算出的卡方值所对应的 p 值小于设定的显著性水平，那么存在显著性差异。

卡方检验不要求数据服从某种分布，但是每一类的频数应当至少是 1，而且不能有 20% 以上类别的频数小于 5。

例 15.4　一位研究人员想要了解英语本族语教师与非本族语教师之间在对学习者语言错误的容忍度上是否存在差异。她收集了一些数据，并将其用交互表的形式呈现出来（表 15.6），然后用 SPSS 对表中的数据做卡方检验。检验设定的显著性水平为 α=0.05。检验结果如表 15.7 所示。

表 15.7 显示，计算出的卡方值所对应的 p 值（sig 值）小于设定的显著性水平（χ^2=64.75，p<0.05）。因此，英语本族语教师与非本族语教师之间在对学习者语言错误的容忍度上存在显著性差异。

从表 15.6 中的频数来看，总体上，本族语教师对学习者语言错误的容忍度高于非本族语教师。80% 的本族语教师对学习者的语言错误有高容忍度。

相比之下，只有 22.5% 的非本族语教师对学习者的语言错误有高容忍度。因此，这位研究者可以根据数据统计分析的结果得出她的研究结论：本族语教师对学习者语言错误的容忍度总体上高于非本族语教师。

表15.6 英语本族语与非本族语教师对语言错误容忍度的数据

容忍度	本族语者身份		
	本族语者	非本族语者	合计
高	96 (80%)	18 (22.5%)	114
低	24 (20%)	62 (77.5%)	86
合计	120 (100%)	80 (100%)	200

表15.7 英语本族语与非本族语教师对语言错误容忍度的卡方检验

	值	df	渐进 Sig.（双侧）
Pearson 卡方	64.749[a]	1	.000
连续校正[b]	62.424	1	.000
似然比	67.923	1	.000
线性和线性组合	64.425	1	.000
有效案例中的 N	200		

SPSS 应用：卡方检验

在 SPSS 的一列数据表格中输入数据中的频数，然后在第二列数据表格中输入每个频数对应的行数，在第三列数据表格中输入每个频数对应的列数（如下所示）。第二列中的 1 代表第一行，2 代表第二行。第三列中的 1 代表第一列，2 代表第二列。

数据	行	列
96	1	1
18	1	2
24	2	1
62	2	2

数据输入完成后，按下列步骤操作，就可以得到检验结果。

1. 数据 (D)
   → 加权个案 (W)
      → 将"数据"变量从左框移到右边"加权个案 (W)"下的
        "频数变量"框中。
        → 确定

2. 分析 (A)
   → 描述统计
      → 交互表
      → 将"行"变量从左框移到右边"行 (S)"框中，将"列"变
        量从左框移到右边"列 (C)"框中。
        → 统计量
           → √ 卡方 (H)
           → 继续
              → 确定

15.2 关联分析

同众多的自然现象和社会现象一样，外语研究涉及的许多现象之间互相存在着关联。例如，在二语习得中，学习者的学习动机、认知方式、学习策略与学习效率有关，学习者的年龄与知识和技能的发展速度有关，应试者的应试心理状态与应试生理状况相关，而两者又与考试结果有关。在语篇研究中，某些语篇特征与一定的语篇体裁有关，语篇的词比（type/token ratio, TTR）与语篇的长度有关。

关联分析用于考察两个或多个现象之间是否存在一定的变动关系以及这种关系的密切程度和显著性。用于关联分析的统计方法主要有相关分析、回归分析和路径分析。

15.2.1 相关分析

相关分析（correlation analysis）用于考察两个或两个以上的变量之间在数量上是否存在一定的变动关系以及这种关系的密切程度和显著性。如果当一个变量的取值发生变化，相对应的另一个变量的取值也会在一定的范围内

发生变化，那么这两个变量之间在取值上的这种互动变化关系在统计上称为相关关系。

相关关系是一种非确定关系。具体地说，有相关关系的两个现象，其中一种现象的数量确定后，另一种现象的数量还在一定的范围内变化，表现出一定的波动性和随机性，但总体上又遵循一定的规律而变动。例如，在学习动机的强烈性一致的情况下，一些学习者可能取得很好的学习成效，一些学习者可能取得比较好的学习成效，而另一些学习者则可能没有取得多少成效。

相关关系存在不确定性的主要原因是一种现象的变化会受到多种因素的影响。例如，学习动机不是影响外语学习的唯一因素，学习者的个体因素，像认知方式、学习策略、智力、学能和情感因素，学习者所处的社会学习环境和学习者可调动的时间与资源等，都会影响外语学习。

按照相关程度，相关关系可以分为三大类：完全相关、不完全相关和不相关。完全相关是一个变量的取值发生变化，另一个变量所对应的取值也会随之发生相应的变化。不完全相关是一个变量的取值发生变化，另一个变量只有部分取值发生变化，其余部分取值则不发生变化。不相关是一个变量的取值发生变化，另一个变量的取值不发生任何变化。

按照相关方向，相关关系可以分为两大类：正相关和负相关。正相关是两个变量取值发生变化的方向相同，即一个变量的取值变大，另一个变量的取值也变大；或一个变量的取值变小，另一个变量的取值也变小。负相关是两个变量取值发生变化的方向相反，即一个变量的取值变大，而另一个变量的取值变小；或一个变量的取值变小，而另一个变量的取值变大。

按照相关形式，相关关系可以分为线性相关和非线性相关。线性相关是两个相关变量之间的取值变化关系大致可以表现为一种直线变动关系。非线性相关是两个相关变量之间的取值变化关系不能表现为直线变动关系，但是可以表现为某种曲线变动关系，如抛物线变动关系。

外语研究中使用最多的相关分析方法是皮尔逊相关分析（Pearson correlation）。皮尔逊相关分析计算两个变量下的两组定距数据的皮尔逊相关系数，检验它们之间相关的显著性。我们可以根据皮尔逊相关系数，确定两个变量的相关程度，并根据显著性检验的结果，确定两个变量之间是否真正相关。

皮尔逊相关系数用 r 表示，取值在 –1 到 +1 之间。相关系数的绝对值越大，说明两个变量间的相关程度越高；绝对值越小，相关程度越低。如果两个变量之间的相关系数为负值，则为负相关。如果两个变量之间的相关系数为正值，则为正相关。

相关系数是度量变量间相关程度的量化指标。如果将其定性化分类，很难做出精确的划分。一般情况下，大致可以按照表 15.8 来确定相关系数所对应的定性相关程度。相关系数为 0 是完全不相关，相关系数在 0.2 左右为弱相关，0.4 左右为低相关，0.6 左右为中相关，0.8 以上为高相关，1 为完全相关。不同的研究领域、不同的研究课题，可能对相关系数有不同的定性解读。我们可以参照相关领域或相关研究课题的文献，来确定我们的研究中对相关系数的定性解读。

表15.8　相关系数所表示的相关程度

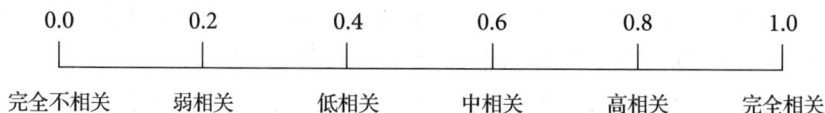

0.0	0.2	0.4	0.6	0.8	1.0
完全不相关	弱相关	低相关	中相关	高相关	完全相关

相关分析不仅要看相关系数，还要看相关显著性的检验结果。如果相关系数对应的 p 值（sig 值）小于设定的显著性水平，那么两个变量之间存在显著性相关关系，或者说两个变量间的相关关系成立。如果相关系数对应的 p 值（sig 值）大于设定的显著性水平，那么两个变量之间不存在显著性相关关系，或者说两个变量间的相关关系不成立。如果我们的研究使用了相关分析，那么在论文中要同时报告相关系数和对应的 p 值。

例 15.5　一位研究者想要了解高校学生的入学英语水平与入学两年之后的英语学业水平之间是否相关。他收集了某高校 1322 名学生的入学英语成绩和两年之后的英语学业考试成绩，用 SPSS 做相关分析。分析检验结果如表 15.9 和表 15.10 所示。

表 15.10 显示，学生的英语入学成绩与学业水平成绩之间显著相关，并且是高度正相关（r=0.891，p<0.05）。这说明学生的英语入学成绩越高，可以预示他们的英语学业水平成绩也越高。

表15.9　英语入学成绩与学业水平成绩的描述统计

	均值	标准差	N
高考成绩	122.4198	9.69138	1322
四级成绩	415.7890	64.52706	1322

表15.10　英语入学成绩与学业水平成绩的相关分析

		高考成绩	学业成绩
高考成绩	Pearson 相关性	1	.891**
	显著性（双侧）		.000

**. 在 .01 水平（双侧）上显著相关。

相关分析得出的变量间存在显著性相关的统计结果，可以用于表示变量之间四种可能存在的关系之一：预测关系、因果关系、重叠关系和偶然关系。

相关关系可以表示现象之间的预测关系，即一种现象的发生会预测另一种现象发生的可能。例如，天阴预兆着天要下雨，考前的模拟考试情况可以预示正式考试的情况。

相关关系还可以表示现象之间的因果关系，即一种现象的发生是另一种现象产生的结果。例如，如果学习者的外语语音识别能力的高低直接影响他们外语识读能力的高低，那么这两者之间的关系就是因果关系。外语语音识别能力是因，外语识读能力是果。国外有些高校的研究人员发现，读写困难症（dyslexia）在一定程度上是由早期的语音识别能力发展不足造成的，而读写困难症则是产生交际障碍的原因之一。

有些现象之间的相关关系不一定是因果关系。例如，性别和外语习得有一定的关系。许多研究发现，女性学习者在外语学习方面往往比男性学习者强。但是，不能说性别本身造成了外语水平的高低，可能是隐藏在性别背后的其他因素才可能是女性比男性强的原因。同样，研究表明，年龄与外语学习也存在一定的相关关系，但年龄本身并不能带来外语水平的提高。可能与年龄相关的一些心理因素，如记忆力和情感因素，是影响外语学习的原因。因此，在讨论相关关系的时候，我们一定要注意用相关关系指的是预测关系，还是因果关系。相关关系是否是因果关系，必须经过理论和实践的充分证明，必须有前期理论和实证研究的充分支持。

相关关系还可能是重叠关系，即两个变量测量的可能是相同的东西或者有相同的部分。例如，在外语水平测试中，人们通常会发现，外语水平测试的各个组成部分之间多多少少都存在相关关系。这是因为这些部分会测试相同的外语能力，如外语词汇能力、句法能力等。

相关分析做出的相关性也有可能是某些偶然因素造成了两个变量之间的共同变化。对于这样的相关关系，我们完全可以置之不理。用 SPSS 做皮尔逊相关分析的时候，如果有两个以上的变量，那么 SPSS 会给出所有变量的两两组合的相关系数，其中一些变量间的显著性相关是必然的、有意义的，而另一些则可能是偶然的、无意义的。

SPSS 应用：相关分析

在 SPSS 的两列数据表格中分别输入两组数据的数值，如下所示。

数据 1	数据 2
10	12
14	20
13	11
16	10

数据输入完成后，按下列步骤操作，就可以得到检验结果。

分析 (A)
→ 相关 (C)
　→ 双变量 (B)
　　→ 将变量"数据 1"和"数据 2"从左框移到右边"变量"框中
　　　→ 确定

15.2.2 回归分析

相关分析只能通过相关系数和显著性检验结果告诉我们变量之间关系的密切程度和确信度，但是不能用自变量的值推测出因变量的值。如果两个变量之间存在非偶然相关关系，我们想要通过自变量的值推测出因变量的值，可以借助回归分析的方法，用收集到的数据建立可用于推测的回归方程。

回归分析（regression analysis）是在相关分析的基础上，使用收集到的数据做出因变量和自变量的回归方程，从而可以用自变量的值推测出因变量的值。当相关分析的结果显示两个或两个以上的变量之间存在显著性相关关系时，才能做回归分析。如果相关分析的结果显示这些变量之间不存在显著性相关关系，就不能做回归分析。

回归分析有多种类型，如线性回归和非线性回归。线性回归用所收集的数据建立线性回归方差，非线性回归用所收集的数据建立非线性回归方差。

与皮尔逊相关分析对应的是线性回归分析。线性回归分析是外语研究中常用的回归分析。

线性回归方程有一元线性回归方程和多元线性回归方程。一元线性回归方程有一个因变量和一个自变量，多元线性回归方程有一个因变量和多个自变量。

一元线性回归方程的表达式是：$Y=a+bX$。

多元线性回归方程的表达式是：$Y=a+b_1X_1+b_2X_2+...b_nX_n$。

在线性回归方程的表达式中，Y 代表因变量，X 代表自变量（X_1、X_2、X_n 在多元回归方程中分别代表每个自变量），a 是一个常数，b 代表自变量的回归系数（b_1、b_2、b_n 在多元回归方程中分别代表每个自变量的回归系数）。回归系数的意义是，如果自变量的数值变动一个单位，因变量的数值变动 b 个单位。

例 15.6 在前面的例 15.5 中，相关分析结果显示，学生的入学英语成绩和英语学业水平成绩显著性相关。于是，研究者在相关分析的基础上，用收集到的数据做出学生的入学英语成绩和学业水平测试成绩的线性回归方程。他希望以后能够借助建立的回归方程，用新一届学生的入学英语成绩推测他们未来的英语学业水平测试成绩。他用 SPSS 做的回归分析结果如表 15.11、15.12、15.13 所示。

表 15.11 中的 R 是相关系数，这同相关分析的 r 是一致的。R^2 是相关系数的平方，取值在 0 到 1 之间，用于表示回归方程的预测值与实际数值的拟合程度。R^2 的值用于说明多少比例的真实数值可以用回归方程来预测。R^2 的值越高，用回归模型预测的数值与真实的数值就越接近。表 15.11 中的 R^2 等于 0.794，说明学生的入学英语成绩可以解释英语学业水平成绩中 79.4% 的方差。

在多元回归分析中，R^2 的值会受到自变量数量的影响。用于回归方程的自变量越多，R^2 的值可能就会越高。调整 R^2（adjusted R^2）是不受自变量数量影响的 R^2，用于在多元回归分析中考察回归模型的拟合程度。调整 R^2 的取值同样在 0 到 1 之间，取值越高，回归方程的拟合度越高。

表15.11　回归模型拟合

模型	R	R^2	调整 R^2	标准估计的误差
1	.891[a]	.794	.794	29.26881

a. 预测变量：（常量），高考成绩。

表 15.12 是对回归方程的方差分析结果。我们要看的是这个表中的 F 值和对应的 sig 值（p 值）。如果 F 值对应的 sig 值小于 0.05，那么说明自变量和因变量之间存在显著性线性关系，回归方程成立。否则，回归方程就不成立。表 15.12 的分析结果显示，学生的入学英语成绩和学业水平测试成绩具有显著性线性关系（F=51000.613，p<0.05），建立的线性回归方程成立，可以用学生的入学英语成绩推测学生的学业水平测试成绩。

表15.12　ANOVA[b]（方差分析）

	模型	平方和	df	均方	F	Sig.
1	回归	4369506.894	1	4369506.894	5100.613	.000[a]
	残差	1130795.225	1320	856.663		
	总计	5500302.119	1321			

a. 预测变量：（常量），高考成绩；b. 因变量：四级成绩

表 15.13 是回归方程的系数表，包括非标准化系数和标准化系数。如果测量单位一致，那么既可以使用非标准化系数的回归方程，也可以使用标准化系数的回归方程。如果测量单位不一致，那么就需要使用标准化系数的回归方程。

表15.13　回归系数[a]

模型	非标准化系数		标准系数	t	Sig.
		标准误差			
1　（常量）	−310.703	10.204		−30.449	.000
高考成绩	5.934	.083	.891	71.419	.000

a. 因变量：四级成绩

有了回归方程的系数表，就可以写出具体的回归方程。表 15.13 的非标准化系数中，常数值是 −310.7，自变量英语高考分数的回归系数是 5.934。英语高考分数和学业水平成绩的回归方程表达式是：

英语学业水平成绩 =5.934× 英语高考成绩 −310.7。

这个方程告诉我们，如果英语高考成绩提高 1 分，可以预计英语学业水平考试成绩提高 5.934 分。

我们来比较一下这位研究者实际收集到的英语学业水平成绩与回归方程计算出的成绩。在 1322 名学生中，有两个学生的英语高考成绩都是 140 分的最高分。这两个学生中，甲学生的英语学业水平考试成绩是 623 分，乙学生的是 617 分。如果用建立的回归方程计算英语高考成绩 140 分对应的英语学业水平成绩，那么得到的结果是：英语学业水平成绩 =5.934×140−310.7=520 分。由此可见，回归方程计算出的分数与真实的分数之间存在较大的误差。

SPSS 应用：回归分析

在 SPSS 的两列数据表格中分别输入两组数据的数值，如下所示。

数据 1	数据 2
10	12
14	20
13	11
16	10

数据输入完成后，按下列步骤操作，就可以得到检验结果。

分析 (A)
→ 回归 (R)
→ 线性 (L)
→ 将变量"数据 1"（因变量）从左框移到右边"因变量"框中
将变量"数据 2"（自变量）从左框移到右边"自变量"框中
→ 确定

15.3 效应量分析

差异检验是为了验证样本之间存在差异的可能性有多大，关联分析是为了验证样本之间存在关联的可能性有多大，例如，存在差异或关联的可能性是 99% 还是 1%。我们可以根据差异检验或关联检验的结果，判断样本之间是否存在显著性差异或显著性相关。但是，无论是差异检验还是关联分析都无法告诉我们，样本之间存在显著性差异或显著性相关这样的检验结果有多大的实际意义或实际价值。

差异检验结果的显著性会受到样本量大小的影响。当样本量小的时候不出现显著性差异，那么放大样本量，即使两个样本平均值之间的差别很小，也可能做出显著性差异。譬如，两个样本的平均值一个是100.1，另一个是100.5，它们之间的差只有0.4。如果两个样本的样本量很小，就很可能做不出显著性差异。但是，如果两个样本的样本量很大，就很可能做出显著性差异。当两个样本的平均值差只有0.4且差异检验结果告诉我们两个样本之间存在显著性差异的时候，我们可能禁不住会想，这样的显著性差异有多大的实际意义呢？

为了衡量显著性检验结果的实际价值，人们提出了效应量（effect size）的概念并设计了多种计算方式。麦基和加斯（Mackey & Gass, 2005）在其专著《第二语言研究：方法与设计》（*Second Language Research: Methodology and Design*）中特别指出，一些国际知名外语研究期刊要求所有（量化研究）投稿都需要提供效应量，并且《美国心理学会出版手册》（第五版）强烈建议（量化研究）报告效应量。

效应量是用于衡量统计检验结果的实际价值有多大的统计指标。显著性检验中的 p 值告诉我们存在显著性差异或显著性相关，而效应量则告诉我们显著性差异或显著性相关的实际价值有多大，或者说实际效应有多大。效应量越大，统计检验结果的实际价值或实际效应就越大。

效应量有多种计算方式。不同的统计分析方法有不同的效应量计算方式。这里介绍几个统计检验方法常用的效应量。

皮尔逊相关分析常用的效应量指标是相关系数 r，t 检验常用的效应量指标之一是 Cohen's d，方差检验常用的指标之一是 eta^2（η^2），另一个是偏 eta^2（partial η^2）。

Cohen's d

Cohen's d 是常用于 t 检验之后的效应量指标。在独立样本 t 检验中，计算效应量 Cohen's d 的公式是：

$$d = \frac{\overline{X}_1 - \overline{X}_2}{\sqrt{\dfrac{(n_1 - 1)S_1^2 + (n_2 - 1)S_2^2}{n_1 + n_2 - 2}}}$$

其中：

d：Cohen's d 的值

$\overline{X_1}$：样本 1 的平均值

$\overline{X_2}$：样本 2 的平均值

n_1：样本 1 的样本量

n_2：样本 2 的样本量

S_1：样本 1 的标准差

S_2：样本 2 的标准差

在成对样本 t 检验中，计算效应量 Cohen's d 的公式是：

$$d = \frac{\overline{D}}{S}$$

其中：

d：Cohen's d 的值

D：成对样本数值间差的平均值

S：成对样本数值间差的标准差

网上有在线 Cohen's d 计算器。如果需要的话，可以用搜索引擎在网上检索到 Cohen's d 计算器，输入计算器所需的数值，就可以获得 d 值。

eta² (η^2)

麦基和加斯（Mackey & Gass, 2005: 282）在《第二语言研究：方法与设计》一书中给出的"最常用于 t 检验之后"的效应量值指标是 eta²（η^2）。他们提供的 eta² 的计算公式是：

$$\eta^2 = \frac{t^2}{t^2 + df}$$

其中：

η^2：效应量值

t：t 检验统计值

df：样本自由度

偏 eta² (partial η_p^2)

SPSS 的方差分析使用的效应量指标是偏 eta² (partial η^2)。偏 eta² 的计算公式是：

$$\eta_p^2 = \frac{F \times df_1}{F \times df_1 + df_2}$$

其中：

η_p^2：偏 η^2 效应量值

F：方差检验统计值

df_1：样本组间自由度

df_2：样本组内自由度

不同的效应量指标对计算出的效应量值有不同的定性判断标准。对于如何判断效应量的大小，下面来自 Psychometrica 网站的一份关于效应量大小的表格可供参考。(Lenhard & Lenhard, 2016)

表15.14[1]　Table of interpretation for different effect sizes

d	r*	η^2	Interpretation sensu Cohen (1988)	Interpretation sensu Hattie (2009)
< 0	< 0	–	Adverse Effect	
0.0	.00	.000	No Effect	Developmental effects
0.1	.05	.003		
0.2	.10	.010	Small Effect	Teacher effects
0.3	.15	.022		
0.4	.2	.039		
0.5	.24	.060	Intermediate Effect	Zone of desired effects
0.6	.29	.083		
0.7	.33	.110		
0.8	.37	.140	Large Effect	
0.9	.41	.168		
≥ 1.0	.45	.200		

* Cohen (1988) reports the following intervals for r: .1 to .3: small effect; .3 to .5: intermediate effect; .5 and higher: strong effect

| **1** 表 15.14 在该网站上的表号是 16。

下面我们举一个例子来说明效应量的实际意义。

例 15.7 一位研究者想要了解男女生的英语入学水平是否一样。他收集了 1307 名学生的高考英语成绩。在这 1307 名学生中，731 名是男生，576 名是女生。男生和女生高考英语成绩的描述统计值如表 15.15 所示。

表15.15 男女生高考英语成绩的描述统计值

性别		N	均值	标准差	均值的标准误
高考成绩	男性	731	121.7770	8.81271	.32595
	女性	576	122.9063	10.58358	.44098

他用收集到的数据做了独立样本 t 检验，结果显示，男女生之间在高考英语成绩上存在显著性差异（表 15.16）。尽管男女生的高考英语成绩在平均值上的差异很小，只有 1.129，但是依然出现了显著性差异。这与样本量很大不无关系。

表15.16 男女生高考英语成绩的独立样本检验

		方差方程的 Levene 检验		均值方程的 t 检验			
		F	Sig.	t	df	Sig.（双侧）	均值差
高考成绩	假设方差相等	4.035	.045	−2.104	1305	.036	−1.12923
	假设方差不相等			−2.059	1113.195	.040	

我们用 Cohen's d 公式计算这位研究者独立样本 t 检验的效应量 d 值。

$$d = \frac{\overline{X_1} - \overline{X_2}}{\sqrt{\dfrac{(n_1-1)S_1^2 + (n_2-1)S_2^2}{n_1 + n_2 - 2}}} = \frac{-1.12923}{\sqrt{\dfrac{(731-1)\times 8.81271^2 + (576-1)\times 10.58358^2}{731 + 576 - 2}}} = \frac{-1.12923}{9.633} = -0.117$$

这个案例用网上的 Cohen's d 计算器计算出的 d 值为 0.114。查看表 15.14 我们可以看出，d 值在 0.1 到 0.2 之间属于无任何效应。尽管这位研究者所做的独立样本 t 检验的结果显示出男女生在高考英语成绩上存在显著性差异（t=−2.059，p=.040），但是效应量分析的结果却告诉我们，这样的显著性差异没有任何实际意义或实际效应。这是因为男女生之间平均成绩的差实在是太小了，即使有统计上的显著性差异，也说明不了什么实际问题。

课堂讨论

1. 独立样本与成对样本的主要区别是什么?
2. 一位研究者让 10 位评分员（5 位男性、5 位女性）的每一位对 30 篇学生英语作文按 15 分制做了评分。这 30 篇作文中，15 篇是男生的作文，15 篇是女生的作文。他这样收集到的数据是独立样本还是成对样本? 可以做什么检验? 一周之后，这位研究者又让这 10 位评分员的每一位对相同的 30 篇作文又按 15 分制做了一次评分。他这样收集到的数据是独立样本还是成对样本? 可以做什么检验?
3. 独立样本 t 检验与单因素方差分析之间有什么关系?
4. 阅读下列节选内容（Alyami & Mohsen, 2019）并回答问题:
   (1) 这项研究收集的数据是独立样本还是成对样本?
   (2) Table 3 和 Table 4 中包含了哪些统计信息?
   (3) Table 3 和 Table 4 中的 t-test 是独立样本 t 检验还是成对样本 t 检验?

Research Question

The main research question in this study is whether training in deliberate CVA using materials developed from Nation's K-level reading lexicon improves the actual CVA performance among advanced Arab Saudi learners of English as a foreign language with minimal daily exposure to English-language media.

Methodology

Research Design

This study adopted a pre-test/post-test experimental design, in which the experimental group consists of participants in the treatment (i.e., the deliberate CVA technique using the materials created from the reading lexicon) and a control group with no training in the deliberate CVA technique. Both the experimental group and the control group experienced the pre-test, so the only difference was the matter of whether a given participant had received training in the deliberate CVA method. The independent variable was the effect of using deliberate Clarke and Nation CVA technique, as a way to guide learners through the contextual-inference process, while the dependent variable was the extent of contextual vocabulary acquisition examined by the post-test vocabulary test scores, named word definition accuracy and word context recognition.

Participants

The study sample consisted of 60 adult, female, Arabic-speaking students who were enrolled in EFL courses at Najran University in the Kingdom of Saudi Arabia. These students were aged between 20 and 24 years. The participants were randomly assigned and divided into two groups, 30 members for each. This number was subject to institutional constraints. The participants were third-year students of the Department of English who had previously experienced intensive reading as a method of instruction in English, but have had no exposure to extensive reading in the context of this course. Based on the students' level in the department, it was expected that their proficiency in English would be advanced. Both the experimental group and the control group experienced the same procedures of pre-test scales, the assigned readings, and the post-test assessment, so the only difference was the matter of whether a given participant had received training in the deliberate CVA method.

Data Analysis

Quantitative data were analyzed in the study. The independent variable was the effect of training in deliberate CVA using materials developed from Nation's K-level. The dependent variables were the two calculated variables that show the magnitude of change that occurred between the pre-test and the post-test, namely, the change in word context recognition and the change in word definition accuracy. Descriptive analysis was run to describe and summarize the calculated change in word context recognition and word definition accuracy as well. Moreover, two t-tests were calculated to measure the differences in the change in word context recognition and word definition accuracy between the pre-test and the post-test, for the control and experimental groups, respectively.

Results

The descriptive statistics of the two variables "word context recognition and word definition accuracy" are summarized in Table 2. The results of the t-test of differences in the two variables between the pre-test and the post-test, for both groups are then reported in Tables 3 and 4.

Table 2 Descriptive statistics — effect variables

	Min	Max	Mean	SD	Explanation
wcon_chg	0.000	0.923	0.405	0.333	Change in word context recognition
wdef_chg	0.000	0.923	0.380	0.380	Change in word definition ability

Note: N = 60 for both variables (i.e., 60 participants in the study)

Table 3 T-test, change in word context recognition

Exp Grp	N	Mean	SD	SE of the Mean	
0	30	.293	.311	.057	
1	30	.516	.321	.059	
T	df	p	Mean Diff	SE Diff	95% Confidence interval of the difference
					Lower	Upper
−2.732**	58	.008	−.223	.082	−.387	−.060

*p < .05; **p < .01; ***p < .001. N = 30 per group. Exp Grp: 0 = control group; 1 = experimental group. Equal variances assumed per Levene's test (F = .974, n.s.). Two-tailed test. The effect size is the t-statistic, which is statistically significant (t = −2.732, p < .01)

Table 4 T-test, change in word definition accuracy

Exp Grp	N	Mean	SD	SE of the Mean	
0	30	.232	.350	.064	
1	30	.529	.353	.064	
T	df	p	Mean Diff	SE Diff	95% Confidence interval of the difference
					Lower	Upper
−3.276**	58	.002	−.297	.091	−.479	−.116

*p < .05; **p < .01; ***p < .001. N = 30 per group. Exp Grp: 0 = control group; 1 = experimental group. Equal variances assumed per Levene's test (F = .370, n.s.). Two-tailed test. The effect size is the t-statistic, which is statistically significant (t = −3.276, p < .01)

5. 阅读下列节选内容（Arfé et al., 2022）并回答问题：

(1) Table 1 中的变量，哪些做的是 t 检验，哪些做的是卡方检验？

(2) 在 t 检验中，哪些是独立样本 t 检验，哪些是成对样本 t 检验？

(3) 在这些统计检验结果中，哪些有显著性差异，哪些没有显著性差异？

(4) Table 1 中做卡方检验的定类数据是否满足卡方检验对数据频数的要求？

(5) 用 Table 1 中的定类数据自己动手做卡方检验，你得出的结果与文中的结果是否一致？

The study: Research questions and hypotheses

In the present study we used eye-tracking methodology to compare readers' real-time text processing of two versions of a suspense story passage (from *Ghost story* by Peter Straub, 1979), differing only for their central part (paragraph), which was of negative valence in the original story version and of neutral valence in the version experimentally manipulated. Two groups of readers, matched on dispositional empathy and working memory, read either the original passage or the neutral one. Their text processing and memory of the passage was compared.

Two research questions (RQ) guided the study.

RQ1 How does the variation of emotional valence (from negative to neutral) in a literary text affect readers' attentional engagement and real-time text processing? To answer this research question we compared readers' first-pass and second-pass fixation times across three areas of interest (the beginning, central part, and the end) of the negative and neutral (manipulated) story passage. Three hypotheses were formulated.

Hypothesis 1 For RQ1, based on the delayed disengagement hypothesis (Algom et al., 2004) and Burton et al.'s findings (2004), we first expected longer first-pass fixations (greater initial sustained attention) in the central paragraph when the content was negative, as in the original version, compared to neutral, as in the manipulated version.

Hypothesis 2 For RQ1, however, we anticipated that the greater engagement in the narration induced by a negative emotional valence of the central paragraph would facilitate the processing of the subsequent text, thus favoring readers' integration of textual information (Child et al., 2020). We thus hypothesized a decrease of first-pass fixation times from the central part to the end part of the story passage for the negative valence version (original), but not for the neutral valence (manipulated) version. We also predicted longer second-pass fixations (greater integration effort) on the manipulated text of neutral valence than on the original one, of negative valence.

Hypothesis 3 For RQ1, we finally predicted that readers' individual character-istics would modulate their sensitivity to text valence, and thus readers with higher dispositional empathy would show higher sensitivity to the negative emotional valence of the original story passage, that is, longer first-pass fixation times on the central part of the passage.

RQ2 Does negative emotional valence, compared to neutral valence, enhance readers' memory of text content? Are its effects limited to the emotional content of the story, as predicted by the emotional memory narrowing hypothesis?

For RQ2, alternative hypotheses could be formulated. According to the emotional memory narrowing hypothesis, readers in the negative emotional valence reading condition should recall well emotionally negative contents, but compared to readers in the neutral valence reading condition, their memory of other (peripheral) information in the text should be poorer (Kensinger, 2009). Alternatively, as suggested by Burton et al. (2004), negative emotional valence should induce a more analytical processing of the text and, consequently, could benefit text memory more widely, also enhancing readers' memory of peripheral information such as the details of the situation described.

Method

Participants

A power analysis using G*Power 3 software indicated that using an F test (Repeated measures ANOVA, within-between interaction) for valence effect, a total sample of 34 participants was necessary to detect medium effects (d = 0.25) with power $(1-\beta)$ set at 0.80 and $\alpha = 0.05$. Participants were 42 students (26 girls, 62%, $M_{age} = 24.17$, $SD = 4.91$). Initially, 50 undergraduate students had accepted to take part in the eye-tracking experiment. Of these, two did not show up, one was not included in the study because she reported a corneal injury at the preliminary assessment, and one was also excluded after the experimental session for not having completed all tasks. Moreover, the data of two students were excluded from the analysis as outliers in all eye-movement analyses (scores > than 2 standard deviations from the distribution). Participants' characteristics are reported in Table 1. All participants had normal or corrected to normal vision and none of them reported language delays, dyslexia, or reading problems. For three students Italian was the second language (L2). However, they had been exposed to Italian for more than 8 years (range 9–19 years). Their first language was Albanian, Romanian, and Sinhalese. Two groups of participants were formed, matched on age, gender and first language (i.e., having Italian as L2).

Table 1   Participants' Characteristics with Means, Standard Deviations (in Brackets) and Results of T-Tests and Chi-Square Tests

Variable	Negative valence (*n* = 21)	Neutral valence (*n* = 21)	t / χ^2	*p*	Cohen's *d*
Age	24.62 (5.98)	23.71 (3.65)	.59	.56	0.18
Gender (*n* girls and %)	13 (62%)	13 (62%)	.001	1.00	

Variable	Negative valence (n = 21)	Neutral valence (n = 21)	t / χ^2	p	Cohen's d
Italian as L2 (n)	2 (Albanian and Sinhalese)	1 (Romanian)	.34	.55	
LST score	24.76 (5.04)	26.90 (4.94)	−1.39	.17	−0.43
IRI score	94.67 (11.06)	95.24 (10.96)	−0.17	.87	−0.05
Valence (Likert scale 1–5)	3.48 (.60)	3.14 (.57)	1.84	.07	0.57
Empathy (Likert scale 1–5)	3.10 (.77)	2.19 (.75)	3.86	.001	1.19

LST = listening span test; IRI = Interpersonal Reactivity Index; Italian as L2 = Italian as a second language

Procedure

All participants preliminarily completed a demographic questionnaire, the interpersonal reactivity index questionnaire and the listening span task. The reading session was carried out in a quiet room. Students were asked to read the short suspense story passage while their eye-movements were recorded. After reading the passage, they rated its emotional valence on a 5-point Likert-type scale (from 1 = very good to 5 = very bad) in response to the following request: "Please, assess how good/bad this story makes you feel", and their empathy for the protagonist ("Please, assess how much worried are you for the protagonist") on a 5-point Likert-type scale ranging from 1 = very little worried to 5 = very much worried. Participants then performed a categorization span task from an Italian battery for memory assessment in adults (BAC; De Beni et al., 2008). This task was aimed at diverting participants' attention from the content of the text just read. After this interfering task, they responded to the 12-item questionnaire assessing their memory for the story read.

Results

Preliminary t-tests and chi-square analyses confirmed that the two groups, assigned to the two (negative valence and neutral valence) reading conditions, did not differ significantly on age, gender or on other characteristics relevant to the study (i.e., IRI and working memory scores, see Table 1). The only statistically significant difference between the two reading groups was found in their empathy for the story character. As expected, the group assigned to the neutral valence reading condition reported lower empathy than the negative valence group. As shown in Table 1, the negative valence group also rated story valence more negatively than the neutral valence group. However, the difference between the two conditions (negative versus neutral valence) did not reach statistical significance ($p = 0.07$).

6. 阅读下列节选内容（Teng, 2022）并回答问题：
   (1) 这项研究涉及的大小总体有哪些？
   (2) 这项研究涉及的样本有哪些？样本容量有多大？
   (3) 这项研究有没有报告收集的数据是否符合正态分布？
   (4) 这项研究对三个学习任务组之间的英语水平、工作记忆、词汇学习成效做了什么检验？检验结果如何？
   (5) 这项研究有没有对三个学习任务组的前后词汇测试成绩做差异检验？
   (6) 三个学生组在英语水平上存在的显著性差异对实验结果的效度是否有影响？
   (7) 这项研究采集数据的顺序是：英语测试成绩 → 词汇前测数据 → 词汇后测数据 → 工作记忆测试数据。根据这样的数据采集顺序，下列哪种说法比较符合逻辑？
      1) 英语水平可以用于预测词汇前后测成绩和工作记忆。
      2) 词汇前测成绩可以用于预测词汇后测成绩和工作记忆。
      3) 词汇后测成绩可以用于预测词汇前测成绩、英语水平和工作记忆。
      4) 工作记忆水平可以用于预测英语水平、词汇前后测成绩。

Abstract

This study investigates the effects of three word-focused exercise conditions on vocabulary learning. The exercises were developed based on the involvement load hypothesis. This study also explores how individual differences (e.g. second-language English proficiency level and working memory) affect vocabulary learning outcomes. A total of 180 Chinese students were equally and randomly assigned to 3 exercise conditions (reading comprehension plus marginal glosses, reading plus gap-fill and reading plus sentence writing). The Vocabulary Knowledge Scale was adapted to measure pre- and post-test vocabulary gains. An n-back task was developed to assess learners' working memory capacity. Results showed that the sentence-writing group yielded the best performance in vocabulary learning, followed by the gap-fill group and finally the reading comprehension group. General linear model results revealed that learners' English proficiency level and working memory significantly predicted their vocabulary gains. This study expands on prior research by exploring learner-related factors in vocabulary learning. Relevant implications are discussed based on the findings.

The following research questions guide this effort:

1) Do three word-focused exercise conditions, namely (a) reading with marginal glosses; (b) reading plus gap-fill; and (c) reading plus sentence writing, have differential effects on vocabulary learning (i.e. receptive and productive vocabulary knowledge)?

2) Do learner-related factors (i.e. English proficiency level and WM) predict individuals' vocabulary learning gain scores in different word-learning conditions?

Methods

Participants

This study focused on non-English major students at a university in southern China. Students from 5 classes were invited to participate; of the 245 students invited, 190 agreed to take part. Ten were later excluded because they were unavailable during the learning sessions. The final sample therefore comprised 180 students (95 men and 85 women) who were randomly and equally assigned to 3 learning conditions (see "Word-Focused Exercises" section for details). In this between-group design, each group consisted of learners with different levels of WM and English proficiency. All participants fulfilled the intervention requirements. Additionally, all were between 18 and 20 years old, were second-year students and spoke Chinese as their first language. Most had been EFL learners for at least 10 years.

Reading Material and Target Words

The reading material was a roughly 2000-word passage from BBC News. Participants in groups 1, 2 and 3 were exposed to the same material. The text was entered into a vocabulary profile analyser, indicating that 98% of the words fell within the 2000-frequency level. This text was then re-edited by inserting 30 difficult words, which served as target words (Table 2). The 30 words, which accounted for 1.5% of the total words, might not be a learning burden to the learners' adequate reading comprehension as the learners know at least 98% of words (Hu and Nation, 2000). In addition, a total of 30 words may allow for an understanding of learners' vocabulary learning gains. A pre-test confirmed that participants had no prior knowledge of the target words.

Measures

English Proficiency Level. English proficiency level was measured based on the College English Test (CET)-4, a standardized English test for university non-English majors. The CET-4 is a large-scale, national, high-stakes English test developed by English-language teaching professionals, experts and education authorities in China. Data collection was convenient because all participants had already taken the test. CET-4 measures students' overall English ability in listening, reading, writing and translation. The maximum test score was 710 points.

WM. An n-back test was used to evaluate participants' EWM. This tool measures individuals' ability to decide whether each stimulus in a sequence matches the one that appeared n items ago. Participants completed the n-back task through E-prime software in a lab. All participants used the index and middle fingers of their dominant hand to press one of two buttons denoting "target" and "non-target" on a button box. In the 1-back condition, the target was any letter identical to the letter immediately preceding it (i.e. the letter presented one trial back). In the 2-back condition, the target was any letter identical to that presented two trials back. In the 3-back condition, the target was any letter identical to that shown three trials back (see Figure 1).

Stimuli consisted of the 26 letters of the English alphabet randomly presented in a fixed central location on a computer screen (Miller et al., 2009). Stimuli were displayed for 500 ms with a 2000-ms interstimulus interval. Any input received within the stipulated time was valid. Participants completed six trial blocks (two blocks for each of the above three conditions). Each block contained 30 trials. The first three trials in each block were not arranged as targets; the remaining trials were targets. The condition order was randomized across blocks. Participants were given a 20-s break between blocks. Participants completed 20 training trials per condition to ensure that they understood the task and that their performance had stabilized. The software automatically provided participants' reaction times and accuracy for each trial; these two elements formed the scoring basis for the n-back task.

Reaction times were indicated in ms with accuracy scores as percentage correct. The Cronbach's alpha value (.81) showed that the test was reliable.

Vocabulary Knowledge Test

The Vocabulary Knowledge Scale (VKS) developed by Wesche and Paribakht (1996) was adapted to measure vocabulary learning gains. The VKS has been used to examine vocabulary knowledge growth and was employed as a pre- and post-test in this study to determine whether participants learned a word receptively and/or productively. A sample item is shown in Table 3.

Procedure

The research process is depicted in Figure 2. Participants' CET-4 scores were collected before the study began. Participants completed a pre-test during the first week of the study. After a four-week interval, participants in each condition completed the required exercises. Learners in the first, second and third group were allotted 30, 40 and 50 min for learning completion, respectively. They then took an immediate post-test, which lasted 30 min. The next day, participants spent 5 min becoming familiarized with the WM test and were given 10 min to complete it.

Data Analysis

All data were analysed in SPSS 24.0. The first research question concerned the effectiveness of word-focused exercises on vocabulary learning; analysis of variance (ANOVA) was adopted for data processing. The second research question considered the predictive power of the independent variables on dependent variables. The general linear model, an extension of linear multiple regression for a single dependent variable (Field, 2013), was applied to address this question. The general linear model goes a step beyond multivariate regression and allows for linear transformations or linear combinations of dependent variables.

Results

The descriptive results are presented in Table 4. In terms of the vocabulary post-test, participants in the sentence-writing group achieved the best performance (M=45.87), followed by the gap-fill group (M=38.38) and the comprehension-only group (M= 30.62). Average CET-4 scores were 512.68 for the reading-comprehension group, 531.72 for the reading-plus-gap-fill group and 513.12 for the reading-plus-sentence-writing group. Accuracy percentages on the WM test for the reading-comprehension, reading-plus-gap-fill and reading-plus-sentence-writing groups were 59.53, 61.32 and 66.57, respectively.

The homogeneity of variance was next evaluated using Levene's test. In this case, an F-test was performed to assess the null hypothesis that the variance was equal across groups. The p value was greater than .05, indicating that this assumption was not violated. Parametric analysis was thus appropriate. Table 5 lists the results of the analysis of variance.

Based on Table 5, significant differences emerged between the three groups in terms of English proficiency level [$F(2, 179)=5.042$, $p < .05$, partial $\eta2=.05$], WM [$F(2, 179)=6.452$, $p < .05$, partial $\eta2=.06$] and the vocabulary post-test [$F(2, 179)=20.990$, $p < .001$, partial $\eta2=.39$]. The ANOVA results did not show a significant interaction effect between group effect and English proficiency level, $F(4, 179)=.218$, $p=.926$, partial $\eta2=.024$. The ANOVA results also did not show a significant interaction effect between group effect and working memory, $F(6, 179)=1.352$, $p=.260$, partial $\eta2=.184$. Post-hoc multiple comparisons showed that participants in the sentence-writing group outperformed participants in the gap-fill group ($p < .001$) as well as in the comprehension-only group ($p < .001$) on vocabulary learning performance.

Table 4 Descriptive results

Variables	Groups	n	Mean	Std.	Minimum	Maximum
English proficiency level	Comprehension only	60	512.68	42.819	454	567
	Gap-fill	60	531.72	43.518	452	562
	Sentence writing	60	513.12	45.021	440	558
	Total	180	519.17	45.221	440	567
Working memory (WM)	Comprehension only	60	59.53	11.173	44	77
	Gap-fill	60	61.32	12.438	42	77
	Sentence writing	60	66.57	9.666	44	78
	Total	180	62.47	11.484	42	78
Vocabulary learning Performance (post-test)	Comprehension only	60	30.62	8.623	14	41
	Gap-fill	60	38.38	5.854	23	46
	Sentence writing	60	45.87	4.856	32	59
	Total	180	38.29	7.502	14	59

Table 5 Results of the analysis of variance

		Sum of squares	df	Mean square	F	P
English proficiency level	Between groups	29314.978	2	14657.489	5.042	<.05
	Within groups	1270681.350	177	7178.991		
	Total	1299996.328	179			
Working memory	Between groups	1604.211	2	802.106	6.452	<.05
	Within groups	22004.650	177	124.320		
	Total	23608.861	179			
Vocabulary learning	Between groups	5138.744	2	2569.372	58.306	<.001
Performance	Within groups	7799.900	177	44.067		
(post-test)	Total	12938.644	179			

7. 阅读下列节选内容（Bećirović et al., 2021）并回答问题：

   (1) 这项研究做了哪些变量之间的相关分析？哪些变量之间存在显著性相关？

   (2) 参照前面表 15.14 中 r* 一栏，这些相关系数体现的效应量大小如何？

Participants

The research sample in the current study was composed of 173 Bosnian high school students studying at four different grade levels. The convenience sampling method was employed in the process of participants' selection. The sample consisted of 100 female students (57.8%) and 73 male students (42.2%). As for the grade level, there were 75 first grade students (43.4%), 36 second grade students (20.8%), 19 third grade students (11%) and 43 fourth grade students (24.9%), with the age range between 15 and 19. The participants also provided information on their grade-point average obtained in the English as a foreign language (EFL) course. The grades ranged between 1 and 5, with 1 being a non-passing grade and 5 being the highest grade. Thus, 76 participants obtained the GPA score 5, 36 participants the GPA score 4, 35 participants the GPA score 3, and 24 participants the GPA score 2, while only 2 participants obtained a non-passing grade 1, and, as such, this group will not be included in the analysis. Table 1 provides all the details related to the participants.

Table 1 Gender, grade level, and average course grade of the participants

	n	%			n	%
Gender			Average course grade			
Male	73	42.2	1 Negative		2	1.2
Female	100	57.8	2 Sufficient		24	13.9
Grade			3 Good		35	20.2
First	75	43.4	4 Very good		36	20.8
Second	36	20.8	5 Excellent		76	43.9
Third	19	11.0				
Fourth	43	24.9				
Total	173	100			173	100

Data analysis

The collected data were analyzed using the Statistical Package for Social Sciences (SPSS, v. 26). Pearson product correlation coefficients as well as the descriptive analysis including means, standard deviation (*SD*) and frequencies were employed. One-way MANOVA was used to investigate the differences in technology use and teacher's support based on gender, grade level and GPA groups.

Results

Preliminary analysis

The participants scored quite high on the perceived usefulness of technological resources for foreign language learning (*M* = 2.04, *SD* = .60) and are confident about their abilities to use technology in the process of foreign language learning (*M* = 2.25, *SD* = .67). Furthermore, the participants stated that they have positive conditions to use technology (*M* = 2.21, *SD* = .70) and they scored quite high on computer self-efficacy (*M* = 2.25, *SD* = .72) (Table 3). The teacher's support for the use of technology was rated slightly above 2, with affection support being most highly rated (*M* = 2.28, *SD* = .91), behavior support closely following (*M* = 2.38, *SD* = .87), and capacity support receiving the lowest rating (*M* = 2.53, *SD* = 1.05). The participants scored the highest mean on the perceived usefulness (*M* = 2.04, *SD* = .60) and facilitation condition subscales (*M* = 2.21, *SD* = .70). In terms of the use of technology (*M* = 2.25, *SD* = .67) and computer self-efficacy (*M* = 2.25, *SD* = .72), the same mean score was measured.

Table 3 Descriptive statistics and correlation				1	2	3	4	5	6
	n	M	SD						
1. Affection support	173	2.28	.91						
2. Capacity support	173	2.53	1.05	.57**					
3. Behavior support	173	2.38	.87	.60**	.62**				
4. Technology use	173	2.25	.67	.28**	.20**	.30**			
5. Perceived usefulness	173	2.04	.60	.20**	.19*	.27**	.68**		
6. Computer self-efficacy	173	2.25	.72	.22**	.19*	.21**	.56**	.64**	
7. Facilitation condition	173	2.21	.70	.15*	.17*	.25**	.40**	.50**	.53**

A Pearson product-moment correlation coefficient was computed to assess the relationship between dependent variables. The results showed a significant correlation between affection support and capacity support ($r = .57$, $n = 173$, $p < .001$), affection support and behavior support ($r = .60$, $n = 173$, $p < .001$) as well as between behavior support and capacity support ($r = .62$, $n = 173$, $p < .001$) (Table 3). Furthermore, a Pearson product-moment correlation coefficient showed that the use of technology significantly correlated with perceived usefulness $r = .68$, $n = 173$, $p < .001$, computer self-efficacy $r = .56$, $n = 173$, $p < .001$ and facilitation condition $r = .40$, $n = 173$, $p < .001$. A significant correlation was also measured between perceived usefulness and computer self-efficacy $r = .64$, $n = 173$, $p < .001$ as well as between perceived usefulness and facilitation condition $r = .50$, $n = 173$, $p < .001$.

8. 阅读下列节选内容（Saito & Liu, 2022）并回答问题:
   (1) 这项研究有没有报告数据是否符合正态分布?
   (2) 这项研究做的是什么样的 t 检验? 作者在论文中是如何表述 t 检验结果的?
   (3) 参照前面表 15.14 中 r* 一栏，Table 1 中显著相关系数体现的效应量大小如何?
   (4) Table 2 中的 Adjust R^2 是什么指标?
   (5) Table 2 中给出了 Adjust R^2 等指标，没有给出回归系数。你觉得做回归分析是否应该给出回归系数。为什么?

There is emerging evidence that collocation use plays a primary role in determining various dimensions of L2 oral proficiency assessment and development. The current study presents the results of three experiments which examined the relationship between the degree of association in collocation use (operationalized as t-scores and mutual information scores) and the intuitive judgements of L2 comprehensibility (i.e. ease of understanding).

2 Results

a Constructs of comprehensibility and collocation measures. The results of normality tests (a one-sample Kolmogorov-Smirnov test) indicated that the comprehensibility scores were not significantly different from a normal distribution in both task contexts ($p > .05$). According to the results of independent-sample t-tests, the averaged comprehensibility scores did not significantly differ between the picture description ($M = 573$; $SD = 174$; $Range = 262–910$) and oral interview tasks ($M = 513$; $SD = 217$; $Range = 172–861$), $t = 1.675$, $p = .096$, $d = 0.34$. As for the collocation measures, a series of Kolmogorov-Smirnov tests found the bigram t-scores in the picture description task to be positively skewed ($p = .015$) and the trigram t- and MI scores in the oral interview task to be negatively skewed ($p = .007$, and .016). After these scores were transformed using the log10 function, they were shown to follow a normal distribution ($p > .05$). To facilitate the interpretability of the data, the directions of all the factor scores were kept consistent (larger values indicating stronger associations).

Table 1 Summary of simple and partial correlations between collocation and comprehensibility

	Comprehensibility (picture description)		Comprehensibility (oral interview)	
	r	p	r	p
Bigram:				
t-scores	.356	.005*	.343	.006*
MI scores	.713	< .001*	.237	.066
Trigram:				
t-scores	.431	.001*	.243	.059
MI scores	.488	< .001*	.246	.096

Notes. * for $p < .01$.

b Relationship between comprehensibility and collocation. To examine the role of collocation in L2 comprehensibility judgements, a set of Pearson correlation analyses were performed with alpha set to .01 (Bonferroni corrected). As summarized in Table 1, both bigram and trigram MI scores demonstrated significant, moderate-to-strong associations with comprehensibility in the picture description task ($r = .356$ to .713). Only bigram t-scores demonstrated significant correlations with comprehensibility in the oral interview task ($r = .343$).

In the precursor study (Saito, 2020), it was suggested that text length could be related to the collocation-proficiency link (i.e. longer speech samples tend to feature more likelihood of targetlike collocation use). Indeed, significant correlations between comprehensibility and text length were found in both the picture description ($r = .356$, $p = .005$) and oral interview ($r = .643$, $p < .001$) tasks. To investigate the relative weights of collocation, text length and comprehensibility, stepwise multiple regression analyses were performed with comprehensibility scores as a dependent variable relative to five predictor variables (bigram and trigram t- and MI scores, the number of words per sample). As summarized in Table 2, the collocation factor (bigram MI scores) accounted for 50.8% of the variance in the comprehensibility judgements in the picture description task. Collocation effects were much weaker in the oral interview task (accounting for 8.6% of the variance). There was no clear instance of strong multicollinearity in any model; VIF (variance inflation factor) < 1.412.

Table 2 Summary of multiple regression analyses of the relationship between collocation and comprehensibility

	Predictor variables	*Adjusted R^2*	*R^2 change*[1]	*F*	*p*
Comprehensibility	Bigram MI scores	.508	.508	60.929	< .001
(picture description)	Text length	.624	.116	48.129	< .001
Comprehensibility	Text length	.413	.413	41.560	< .001
(oral interview)	Bigram MI scores	.499	.086	28.875	< .001

课外练习

1. 一位研究者实施了一项外语教学实验研究。研究包括一个对照组和一个实验组。这位研究者在实验前对两个组的研究对象做了前测，在实验后

---

1 R squared change. The change in the R^2 statistic that is produced by adding or deleting an independent variable. If the R^2 change associated with a variable is large, that means that the variable is a good predictor of the dependent variable. (SPSS Help)

又做了后测，收集到一些定距数据。他这样收集到的数据是独立样本还是成对样本？可以做什么检验？

2. 满足什么条件可以说两个变量的数据之间存在显著性相关关系？

3. 如果两个变量的数据之间存在显著性相关关系，那么可以如何解释这种关系？

4. 人们为什么要做回归分析？

5. 效应量分析和报告效应量的意义是什么？

6. 收集一些近三年内发表的外语定量研究论文，分析这些论文：（1）有没有说明数据是否符合正态分布，（2）使用了哪些统计检验方法，（3）有没有报告效应量。如果报告了效应量，这些效应量的大小如何；如果没有报告效应量，使用论文中的检验统计量计算效应量，并说明效应量的大小。如果论文中有交互数据表和卡方检验结果，用论文中的数据自己动手做卡方检验，看自己做的结果与论文中的结果是否一致。

拓展阅读

Mackey, A., & Gass, S. M. (2005). *Second language research: Methodology and design.* Mahwah, New Jersey: Lawrence Erlbaum Associates.

Wilkinson, L. (1999). Statistical methods in psychology journals: Guidelines and explanations. *American Psychologist, 54,* 594–604.

Woods, A., Fletcher, P., & Hughes, A. (2000). *Statistics in language studies.* Beijing: Foreign Language Teaching and Research Press.

马广惠. (2003). 外国语言学及应用语言学统计方法. 杨凌：西北农林科技大学出版社.

秦晓晴、毕劲. (2015). 外语教学研究定量研究方法及数据分析. 北京：外语教学与研究出版社.

第 16 单元
R 语言

学习目标

- 了解 R 语言以及它的工作机制
- 了解量化研究的一些基本概念
- 了解一些基础的统计分析方法
- 了解 R 语言的数据可视化方法

16.1　R 语言简介

关于 R，比较官方的答案是：R 是一种用于统计计算和作图的编程语言，可用于对数据进行清理、分析和可视化。R 由其核心团队（R Core Team）和 R 统计计算基金会（R Foundation for Statistical Computing）提供支持。不同学科的研究人员都大量地使用 R 语言进行统计推断和结果呈现，而讲解统计和研究方法的教师也开设了大量关于 R 语言应用的相关课程。有资料统计显示，R 是数据科学领域最流行的语言，它大量用于分析结构化和非结构化数据。这使得 R 成为执行统计操作的标准语言。所谓结构化数据（structured data）一般就是指大家所熟悉的数值型的数据，而非结构化数据（unstructured data）最常见的就是语料文本数据。

知道什么是 R 以后，也就很容易理解为什么要学、要用 R 了。最根本的原因在于我们需要对数据进行统计计算。很难想象，在今天这个时代，从事语言学研究可以不跟数据打交道，不管这种数据是数值型的数据，还是语料文本数据。有人甚至提出，"除非是神，否则都要用数据说话"。既然数据在语言研究中如此重要，那么掌握分析处理数据的利器——R 的重要性也就不言自明了。

16.2　安装

要使用 R，首先必须下载安装该软件。可以到 CRAN（The Comprehensive R Archive Network）进行下载。读者可以根据自己的电脑配置下载合适的版本并安装。一般在安装好 R 后，还会接着安装 RStudio，它是使用 R 的一种集成开发环境（integrated development environment, IDE）。RStudio 安装好后，会自然地跟前面已经安装好的 R 关联起来，以后要使用 R 只需要打开 RStudio 即可。图 16.1 是打开 RStudio 后，点击菜单中的 File，然后再点击 New File，选择 R Script 后所看到的一个界面。也可以在打开 RStudio 后，使用快捷键 Ctrl + Shift + N 打开这个 R Script 界面。

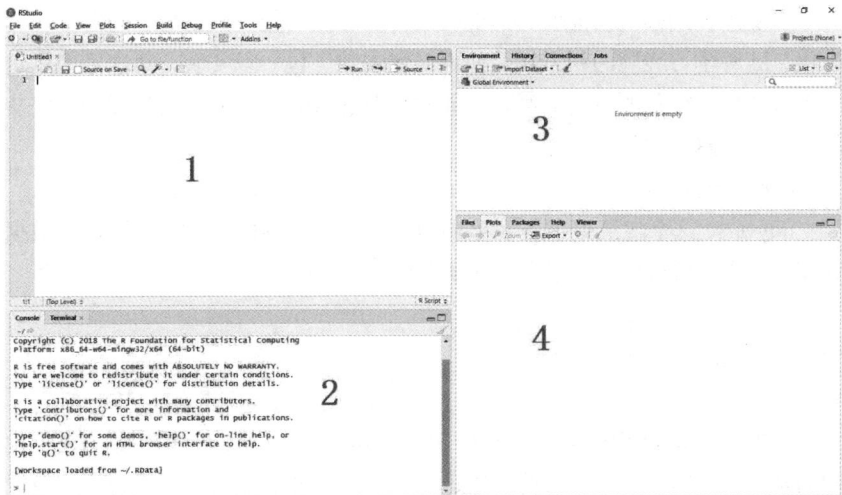

图16.1　RStudio界面

从图 16.1 可以看到，R Script 一共有四个区域，这四个区域的具体布局可以使用 Tools 菜单中的 Global Options 进行设置。区域 1 为代码编辑区，我们一般在这个区域输入并编辑代码，然后，按 Ctrl + Enter 键执行代码，代码执行的结果显示在区域 2，称作"控制台"（Console）。比如，我们在区域 1 输入以下代码：

1 + 1

按 Ctrl + Enter 键就可以在区域 2 看到执行的结果：

[1] 2

从这个代码及其执行的结果看，可以简单地认为 R 就是一个计算器（calculator），可以执行我们告诉它的各种计算。关于区域 3 和区域 4 的作用和功能，留给读者在后面的学习中自己去发现。安装好 R 和它的集成环境 RStudio 之后，我们还会安装各种包（package）。包是别的 R 使用者（R 社区）开发出来的函数、数据、预编译代码以一种定义完善的格式组成的集合体。我们经常说，使用 R 是站在巨人肩膀上的工作，就是指我们在使用 R 的时候，会直接应用许多先前的 R 使用者开发出来的多种多样的包。我们可以认为 R 本身就像一个空壳，正是这些包让它变得强大和多才多艺，数据读取、计算、作图等都会使用到许多其他 R 使用者开发出来的包。比如，tidyverse 就是一个我们经常使用的包，在确保电脑联网的情况下，输入以下代码，执行该代码就可以安装：

install.packages("tidyverse")

要发挥 R 的强大功能就必然要安装许多不同的包，读者可以随着学习的进程、随着学习经验的积累在后面再慢慢安装。包一旦安装，每次要使用这个包以实现这个包所具有的某种功能时都要加载它。比如，要加载刚刚安装的 tidyverse 这个包，方法如下：

library(tidyverse)

tidyverse 这个包汇聚了许多重要功能，比如各种格式数据的读取、数据管理以及数据可视化等，下文将逐步介绍。

16.3　R 应用实例

接下来，我们将由点到面，从三个方面简单介绍 R 的应用实例。需要说明的是，R 的具体应用场景远不止这三个方面，使用经验积累得越多就越能体会到这一点。

16.3.1　文本挖掘和单词频率计算

文本或语料数据常被称作"非结构化数据"，它们的处理和操作要比大家熟悉的数值型数据更为复杂和麻烦。作为一门编程语言，R 所具有的强大功能之一就是能用来进行文本挖掘（text mining, TM），这也是很多语言研究者非常喜欢的功能之一。这就意味着，给定一段文本或者语料库，我们就能使用 R 对它进行操控。比较常见的技术之一就是计算在这段文本里单词的频率。一旦获得了某个文本中各单词的使用频率，就能比较深刻地认识这个文本的许多特点或者对文本进行分类。比如，古希腊哲学家柏拉图（Plato）写过一篇著名的哲学对话，名为《理想国》（*The Republic*）。在这部书里，最常见的词有哪些？我们知道，一本书里最常见的词对这本书来说具有重要意义，因为这些词体现了这本书的主题和中心思想。下面，我们将展现如何对这篇哲学对话中的单词频率进行计算。首先，把书从网络上读进 RStudio，并把读进的书赋值为 df，可以把它视作一个简单的语料库。要读进上面这本书，首先必须加载两个包，分别是 tidyverse 和 tidytext。因此，需要先安装这两个包，然后，使用 *library( )* 函数加载它们。其次，要确保电脑处在联网状态，因为这本书放在互联网上，需要联网把它加载到 RStudio。由于读入的书（数据）是由各个章节组成的完整的篇章，要计算单词频率的第一步就是要把它拆解成一个个独立的词，可以使用 *unnest_tokens( )* 函数来拆解，如下：

df1 <- df %>%

　unnest_tokens(word,text,

　　　　　token = "words")

上面的代码使用 *unnest_tokens( )* 函数，把读入的书 df 进行了拆解，拆解成了一个个独立的词（token）。现在就可以对这一个个的词进行频率统计。不过，即使不进行统计，熟悉英语的读者也应该可以猜到哪些词在这本书里频率最高，肯定是冠词、介词等并不表达实际意义的词。但是这些词对我们认识这本书的主题或者中心思想并没有实际意义，因此，在计算词频的时候，一般会先把这些词去除。这些词在自然语言处理（natural language processing, NLP）中用一个专门的术语来称呼，那就是停用词（stop word）。可使用以下代码去除它们：

df2 <- df1%>%

anti_join(stop_words,by="word") %>%

filter(!is.na(word))

上面代码中的 stop_words 本身就是一个小小的语料库，它是先前的研究者开发出来可供直接使用的停用词。它被嵌入到了 tidytext 这个数据包里，当加载这个包的时候也就能使用它。上述代码成功地把《理想国》拆解成了一个个的词，并且去除了那些不表达实际意义的词语。接下来就可以进行词频统计了，使用 *count( )* 函数：

x <- df2 %>%

count(word,sort = TRUE)

x

```
## # A tibble: 7,195 × 2
##    word        n
##    <chr>     <int>
## 1  true       489
## 2  replied    254
## 3  justice    233
## 4  soul       212
## 5  life       193
## 6  nature     192
## 7  knowledge  159
## 8  truth      141
## 9  evil       139
## 10 socrates   133
## # ... with 7,185 more rows
## # i Use `print(n = ...)` to see more rows
```

从上面的结果可以看到,《理想国》这部伟大的哲学著作使用频率最高的前 10 个词分别是: true、replied、justice、soul、life、nature、knowledge、truth、evil 和 Socrates。对这部哲学著作稍有了解的读者立即就能发现这 10 个词非常明确地体现了这部著作(对话)的主题,甚至可以说成功地勾勒了这部哲学名著的中心思想。

我们还可以使用可视化的手段,把上面的结果通过图形呈现出来,从而让结果更直观、更容易理解。当前,最炙手可热的可视化的方法是使用 ggplot2,作图代码如下:

```
x1 <- x %>%
   filter(n>120)
ggplot(x1,aes(reorder(word,n),n))+
   geom_col(fill="steelblue")+
   xlab(NULL)+
   coord_flip()
```

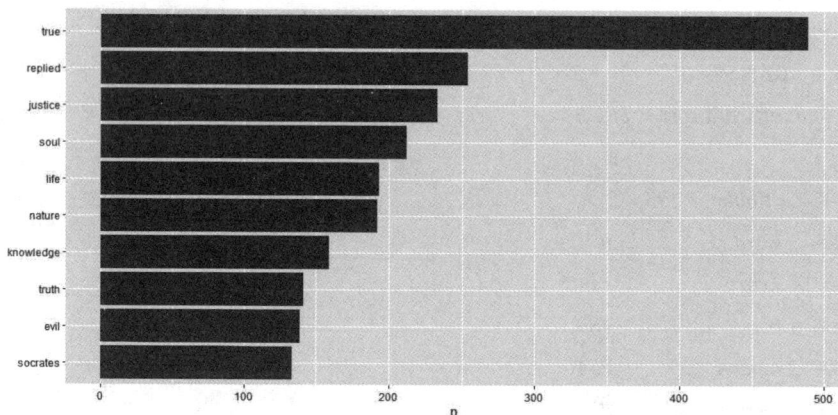

图16.2 《理想国》中使用频率最高的10个词

上面的图形让频率计算的结果一目了然。需要强调的是,计算单词的频率只是使用 R 呈现文本挖掘结果的技术之一。除此之外,R 还可以实现并执行许多其他文本分析功能,比如情感分析(sentiment analysis)、tf-idf 计算和主题建模(topic modeling)。这些功能有待读者在后续进行更深入学习时再了解。

16.3.2 概率运算

实验研究有总体和样本这两个基本概念。所谓总体就是研究者试图考察并获得结论的整个群体，而样本则是研究者从总体中抽取出来参加实验以收集数据的特定组，由一个个个体组成。假设一位外语教师想知道某种新的教学方法是否要比传统的方法更有利于中国学生提升口语表达能力，他必须要开展教学实验才能回答这个问题。在这个实验中，中国学生就是这个研究的总体，是这位教师试图考察并获得结论的整个群体。但是，中国学生是一个很大的群体，这位教师不可能在这个教学实验中把他们都招集起来开展实验。他只能在这个群体中招集一部分人来开展实验、收集数据，这一部分人就是这个实验的样本。需要注意的是，在实验结束之后，这位教师所收集到的数据只是这一部分中国学生（这个样本）的数据，但是，他真正感兴趣的或者说他需要考察并获得结论的并不是这一部分中国学生，而是中国学生这整个群体。这也就意味着，这位教师需要利用这个样本的统计量对总体进行估计，这也就是统计分析的根本目的之所在。

问题是，如何才能基于样本对总体进行估计呢？这里涉及一个非常重要的概念，即概率。概率作为统计推断的基础是一个非常复杂的话题，但是有了 R 这一工具以后，概率运算就变得非常简单，它可以基于各种概率分布，轻易地计算出某种结果，如"教学方法 A 要比教学方法 B 更有利于提高中国学生的外语口语表达能力"发生或出现的概率。下面，我们就基于几种简单的概率分布来展示如何使用 R 进行概率计算。

问题 1：假设 10–20 岁的中国人每天平均使用某种电子产品（如手机、电脑、平板等）的时间是 $\mu=7.5$ 个小时。如果这个年龄段的中国人每天使用电子产品的时间符合正态分布，标准差 $\sigma=2.5$ 小时。请问在这个年龄段找一个每天使用电子产品超过 12 小时的人的概率有多大？有多少人每天使用电子产品的时间在 5 至 10 个小时？

这个问题提到一个非常重要的概念，就是正态分布。正态分布是一种概率分布，是多种统计推断的基础。标准正态分布的形状就像下面的代码所生成的图形：

```
x <- seq(-3,3,0.01)

y <- dnorm(x)

plot(x,y,type="l",xlab="Normal distribution")

abline(v=0,lty=5)
```

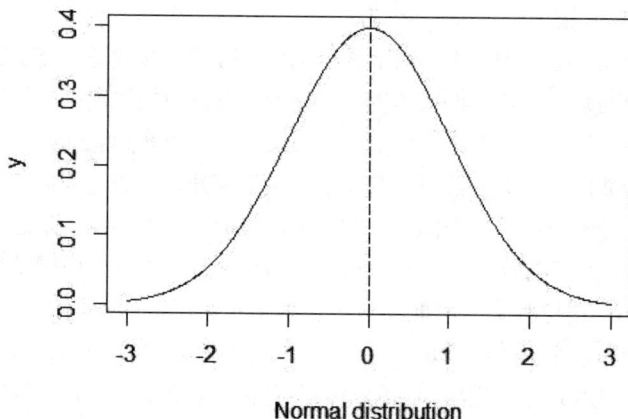

图16.3 标准正态分布图

之所以称上图为标准正态分布图，就是因为它描述的是平均数为 0，标准差为 1 的正态分布图。所有的正态分布都可以转变成这种标准正态分布（即作标准化处理）（故也称作"z 分数分布"）。从图 16.3 可以看到，正态分布就像寺庙里悬挂的一面大钟，它围绕中间那根线（即平均数）两侧对称，且两端逐渐变细。正态分布非常客观地描述了这个世界的真实面貌，那就是处在中间（平均数）的数量最多，而处在两个极端的则极少。就像人类的智商，大部分人都处在中间位置的左右或者说离平均数不远的地方，相反，智商非常高或非常低的位于图中两端的人则极少。人类对正态分布这种概率分布已经认识得非常清楚，在获得相应的参数后（如平均数、标准差等），就能轻易地计算出某个区间的概率。在 R 里面使用比较多的是 *pnorm( )* 函数。下面的代码计算出了问题 1 的答案：

x <- 1-pnorm(12,7.5,2.5)

x

[1] 0.03593032

x1 <- pnorm(10,7.5,2.5)-pnorm(5,7.5,2.5)

x1

[1] 0.6826895

可见，这个年龄段的人每天使用电子产品超过 12 小时的概率非常低（$p=0.03593032$），有 68% 的人每天使用电子产品的时间在 5 至 10 个小时。正态分布是统计分析中极为重要的概率分布，大量的统计运算都是基于正态分布而进行的。除了正态分布，另一个对语言研究者来说比较重要的概率分布是二项分布（binomial distribution），因为语言研究中有大量的实例符合二项分布。比如，学生在完成语言测试的多项选择题时只有两种可能，即要么选择正确，要么选择错误。还有，单词在文本或者语料库的出现频率也只有两种可能，即要么出现要么不出现。正因为如此，了解二项分布这种概率分布对语言研究者来说非常重要。生活中大家最熟悉也最典型的二项分布就是抛掷硬币的情形，每次抛掷只有两种结果，要么正面（人头）朝上，要么正面朝下。试回答以下问题：

问题2：一共有32道多项选择题，每道题都有四个选项，但只有一个正确答案。问：如果学生只是靠猜，答对超过12题的概率有多大？

同样，要获得这道题的答案也可以使用R中的 *pbinom( )* 函数，代码如下：

1-pbinom(12,32,1/4)

[1] 0.03775129

从上面所获得的答案可以知道，猜对超过12题的概率是非常低的，只有0.03775129。可见，要在多项选择题中得高分，靠运气瞎猜是非常不靠谱的，只有一种办法，那就是好好学习，天天向上，掌握必要的知识，提高能力。在语言研究过程中，经常需要使用二项分布，相信大家在深入学习和了解之后就能认识到这一点。除了正态分布、二项分布，语言研究中还会大量使用的概率分布还有T分布、F分布以及卡方（χ^2）分布，等等。有了一些概率方面的知识后，就可以使用这些知识进行统计分析，实现从样本到总体。

当前，尽管人们已经开发出了各种不同的统计程序来组织和解释数据，但是人们一般把这些不同的程序分为两大类：描述统计和推断统计。下面，我们基于R语言环境，分别介绍这两种统计分析方法。

16.3.3 统计运算及数据可视化

描述统计

描述性统计是一种用于总结、组织和简化数据的统计程序。在完成一项语言实验之后，我们经常会获得大量的数据，但是，当这些数据以"原始的"状态摆在面前时，我们是很难从中直接看出任何门道的。因此，描述统计往往成为统计分析的第一步，通过描述统计，对数据进行总结、组织和简化，以揭示隐藏在这一大堆数据背后的模式或规律。那应该如何总结、组织和简化呢？最核心的做法是对数据的集中趋势和变异性（variability）进行计算。在统计学上，展现一组数据的集中趋势的最常规做法是计算这组数据的平均数，而展现一组数据的变异性的最常规的做法是计算这组数据的标准差。

当同时呈现一组数据的平均数和标准差时，我们就能很好地看到数据的大致分布，同时，对不同实验条件下所获得的数据的平均数和标准差进行展示也能帮助我们大致判断实验操控所产生的效果。使用 R 进行描述统计非常方便，有许多可用的方法。我们先从一个简单的例子开始介绍，请看表 16.1：

表16.1　三组被试接受不同词汇学习方法后的词汇测试成绩

三种词汇学习方法		
Dic	Pic	Doc
42	98	48
36	65	61
41	83	50
43	93	54
45	80	32
38	63	67
66	54	68
45	25	50
30	52	87
51	37	81
63	71	70
37	54	75
$T_1=537$	$T_2=775$	$T_3=743$
$SS_1=1248$	$SS_2=5255$	$SS_3=2729$
$n_1=12$	$n_2=12$	$n_3=12$
$M_1=45$	$M_2=65$	$M_3=62$

表 16.1 呈现的是三组大学生在接受三种不同词汇学习方法的训练后，在一次标准化的词汇测试中所获得的成绩。这三种方法分别是（吴诗玉，2021：152）：（1）词典背诵法（简称 Dic），就是让学生直接背词典，学习材料上面有英语单词，同时有中文注解，并提供相应的句子作为实例；（2）词汇-图片关联法（简称 Pic），学习材料上面有英语单词，配有图片解释单词的意思，并提供相应的句子作为实例；（3）词族学习法（简称 Doc），把所有属于同一个语义域的近义词放在一块学习，学习材料上面有英语单词，配有释义，并提供相应的句子作为实例。这个研究最重要的目的是检验不同的词汇学习方法是否导致了不同的词汇学习效果。从研究性质看，这是一个界定变量之间因果关系的研究，这种研究一般也称为"实验研究"，其目的是通过

对一个变量（如词汇学习的方法）进行操控，从而观察并测量这种操控是否会给另外一个变量带来影响。这个被操控的变量就称作"自变量"，而观察和测量的这个变量就称作"因变量"。

对表 16.1 这组数据进行描述统计的最常规方法是展现在自变量的不同条件下（Dic vs. Pic vs. Doc）下，词汇测试成绩（因变量）的平均数和标准差。下面借助 RStudio 向读者演示对这组数据进行描述统计的过程。首先，根据表 16.1 的数据生成数据框（data frame）：

```
voc <- tribble(
~Dic,~Pic,~Doc,
42,   98,   48,
36,   65,   61,
41,   83,   50,
43,   93,   54,
45,   80,   32,
38,   63,   67,
66,   54,   68,
45,   25,   50,
30,   52,   87,
51,   37,   81,
63,   71,   70,
37,   54,   75)
```

生成的数据框赋值给 voc，这个数据框跟表 16.1 的数据完全对应，从数据结构上看，这是一组"宽"数据。尽管这组数据跟表 16.1 的数据完全对应，但是从统计分析的视角来看，它不是我们喜欢的数据格式，因为它不方便计算。我把数据分析者喜欢的数据格式称作"干净、整洁的数据框"（吴诗玉，2021: 2-8），它有三条最基本的要求：（1）每一个变量必须有它自己的列（column）；（2）每个观测必须有自己的行（row）；（3）每一个值必须有它的单元格（cell）。之所以说 voc 这个数据不是我们喜欢的数据格式，就是因为它违背了第一条要求：Dic、Pic 和 Doc 表示的是词汇学习的三种方法，也就是说它们同属一个变量，但它们分布在不同的列，因此，我们必须对它进行转换，把它们放在同一列用以表示词汇学习方法这个变量。在 R 里这个转换非常简单，在术语上把这个过程称作把"宽"数据转换成"长"数据：

```
voc1 <- voc %>%
  pivot_longer(Dic:Doc,
              names_to = "method",
              values_to = "scores")
voc1
## # A tibble: 36 × 2
##      method scores
##      <chr>  <dbl>
##  1 Dic       42
##  2 Pic       98
##  3 Doc       48
##  4 Dic       36
##  5 Pic       65
##  6 Doc       61
##  7 Dic       41
##  8 Pic       83
##  9 Doc       50
## 10 Dic       43
## # ... with 26 more rows
## # i Use `print(n = ...)` to see more rows
```

　　仔细看上面新生成的数据 voc1，它现在只有两个变量，一个是 method，表示词汇学习的方法，是自变量，它融合了 Dic、Pic 和 Doc 三个水平，另一个变量是 scores，它是因变量，是数值型变量。这个数据框就完全符合我们所定义的干净、整洁的数据框标准，使用它就能快捷地进行描述统计。如何对数据进行操作、转换，从而把不符合要求的数据框转换成符合要求的干净、整洁的数据框，是一项非常基本的能力，往往也体现了实证研究者的学术训练水平。为什么要把数据转换成可以体现一个个变量的数据框呢？因为数据分析从根本上说就是对变量（结果）进行计算或者说展现变量之间的关系，只有在数据格式上把变量体现出来，才能实现这些操作。接下来就可以对这组数据的平均数和标准差进行计算，方法如下：

```
library(flextable)
x1 <- voc1 %>%
  group_by(method) %>%
  summarize(M=round(mean(scores),2),
```

SD=round(sd(scores),2),

n=n())

set_caption(flextable(x1), "表 16.2: 各种不同词汇学习方法之下词汇学习效果的描述统计结果")

表16.2　各种不同词汇学习方法之下词汇学习效果的描述统计结果

method	M	SD	n
Dic	44.75	10.65	12
Doc	61.92	15.75	12
Pic	64.58	21.86	12

我们通过 flextable 的方法，把描述统计结果直接展示在表格里，这个表格清晰地展现了每一种词汇学习方法之下词汇测试成绩的平均数和标准差，并展现了这些结果是基于多大的样本量计算出来的。从表中可以看到学习者在 Pic 方法之下获得的平均数最大（ M=64.58），但它的标准差也最大（ SD=21.86），标准差就像是一组数据中的"噪音"，它越大就越说明这组数据不够稳定。在计算上面的结果时，我们还使用了保留小数点的函数 round( )，这个函数中的数字说明在计算结果时，要保留小数后面多少位数，上面的计算设置的是数字 2，所以结果中的小数点都保留了两位。

展现描述统计结果的另外一种方法就是对数据进行可视化操作。所谓可视化就是通过图形对数据结果进行展示，并体现变量之间的关系。可视化是数据分析极为重要的一环，因为人类总是更容易从图形里看出规律。R 有大量强大的对数据进行可视化的工具，仍然可以使用上面介绍过的 ggplot2 来作图。可以用不同的图形来展示上述数据的结果，比如，我们可以使用条形图：

ggplot(voc1,aes(method,scores,fill=method))+

　geom_bar(stat = "summary",

　　　　　　fun=mean,

　　　　　　position="dodge")+

geom_errorbar(stat="summary",

　　　　　　　　fun.data=mean_cl_normal,

　　　　　　　　position=position_dodge(width=0.9),

　　　　　　　　width=0.2)+

labs(x="Voc learning methods",y="Scores")

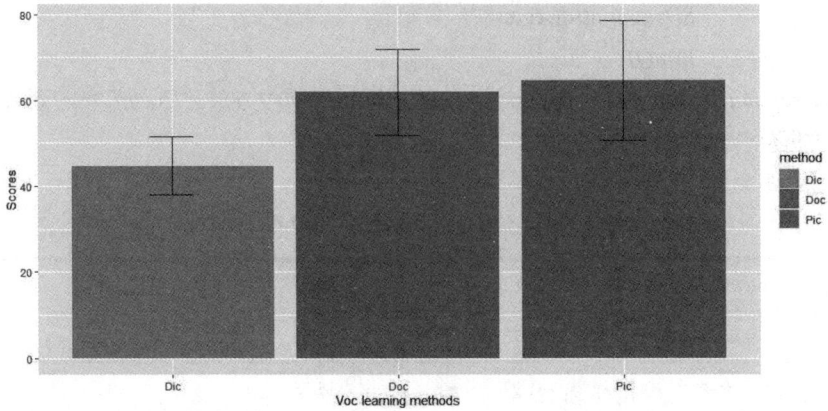

图16.4　不同词汇训练方法下的词汇测试成绩

ggplot2 有强大的图形工具，使用它们还可以对上面的图形进行细节调整，限于篇幅，这里不再讨论。大家从图中可以看到，每个条形图上面都有类似于工字形的符号，我们称之为"误差线"（error bar），表示的是平均数95% 的置信区间，具有重要参考意义。

推断统计

只进行描述统计，即只对数据进行总结、组织和简化是远远不够的，因为我们开展实验研究的真正目的是试图基于样本统计量对总体参数进行估计，实现从样本到总体，这就是推断统计要完成的任务。比如，就上面的数据来说，通过描述统计我们观察到学习者在 Pic 条件下获得了最好的词汇学习的成绩（*M*=64.58，*SD*=21.86），而在 Dic 条件下获得的词汇学习成绩最差（*M*=44.75，*SD*=10.65），但问题是这两组（或三组）之间的差异是由于偶然因素造成的，还是因为实验干预造成的？用统计学上的术语来表达就是：三组之间的词汇学习效果是否存在显著性差异？要回答这个问题就必须进行推断统计，即基于样本统计量对总体参数进行估计。

推断统计是一个非常复杂的问题，要进行准确的推断统计牵涉对许多知识的了解。就上面这个实例来说，要进行推断统计最简单、直接的方法就是进行方差分析，更确切地说是进行独立测量的单因素方差分析，因为它只牵涉一个自变量 method，而这个自变量有三个水平，代表三种不同的词汇训练方法。之所以在这里称之为独立测量（independent measures）是因为三个不同的组分别参加了三种不同的词汇学习方法的训练，并不是相同的一组学习者前后接受三种不同的词汇学习方法的训练，后者称之为"重复测量"。独立测量的实验设计也称作被试间设计，而重复测量的实验设计也称作被试内设计。这两种不同的测量方法所要求的统计方法也是完全不同的，建议读者参考相关书籍，对此进行了解。

在 R 开展方差分析的方法有很多，具体就上面的例子来看，可以使用 afex 包的 aov_4( ) 函数来进行独立测量的方差分析。但在这之前，要先往数据框里增加被试这个随机变量，详细操作如下：

voc2 <- voc1 %>%

　mutate(subj=paste0("S",1:36))

voc2

A tibble: 36 × 3

　　method scores subj

　　<chr> <dbl> <chr>

　1 Dic 　　42 　S1

　2 Pic 　　98 　S2

　3 Doc 　　48 　S3

　4 Dic 　　36 　S4

　5 Pic 　　65 　S5

　6 Doc 　　61 　S6

　7 Dic 　　41 　S7

　8 Pic 　　83 　S8

　9 Doc 　　50 　S9

10 Dic 　　43 　S10

... with 26 more rows

ℹ Use `print(n = ...)` to see more rows

新生成的数据命名为 voc2，仔细查看会发现这个数据多了一个变量即 subj，用它来代表参加实验的被试（即学习者）。这个新的变量是通过 *mutate( )* 函数来生成的，具体是让字母 S 与 1 至 36 之间的数据（1:36）连接起来。现在，就可以利用这个数据，进行独立测量的单因素方差分析，如下：

library(afex)

x1=aov_4(scores~method+(1|subj),data=voc2)

x1

ANOVA table (Type 3 tests)

##

Response: scores

Effect   df MSE   F   ges p.value

*## 1 method 2, 33 279.76 4.97 * .231   .013*

---

*## Signif. codes: 0 '***' 0.001 '**' 0.01 '*' 0.05 '+' 0.1 ' ' 1*

　　上面的方差分析的结果表（ANOVA table）一共有1行6列。在这个表中，行表示方差分析的项（term），也就是研究的自变量，有多少行就表示有多少个项，因为这里只有一个自变量method，所以只有一行，每一行显示的是方差分析中针对这个项的检验结果。就这个研究而言，这唯一的一行呈现的是自变量method的主效应（main effect），它对应表中的第一列，列名是Effect，第二列则是每个项对应的自由度（df），方差分析的自由度对应两个数字（2，33），第三列MSE表示的是mean standard error，即平均标准误差，它是方差分析中计算F值这个比例时的分母，第四列为F值，ges表示的是general eta-squared，表示的是方差分析的效应量，最后一列表示的是统计量对应的概率值即p值。这个p值表示的含义是如果零假设为真（三组之间没有差异），获得这个F值的概率。

　　从上面的结果可以看到，方法method有主效应（$F_{(2,33)} = 4.97$，$p = 0.013$，$\eta^2 = 0.231$）。所谓一个变量的主效应，是指这个变量的不同水平之间（如Dic vs. Pic vs. Doc）的平均数有显著性差异。但是，主效应只能告诉我们这个变量不同水平之间的平均数（至少两个水平之间）存在区别，却不能告诉我们到底是哪些水平之间存在显著性差异，这就是为什么在方差分析之后，一般还要进行事后检验：如果在方差分析之后发现某个变量存在主效应就应该进一步分析，以发现这个变量不同水平之间的平均数是如何不同的。可以使用emmeans包中的*emmeans( )*函数进行事后检验：

emmeans::emmeans(x1,specs = pairwise~method)

$emmeans

method emmean SE df lower.CL upper.CL

```
## Dic      44.8 4.83 33      34.9      54.6

## Doc      61.9 4.83 33      52.1      71.7

## Pic      64.6 4.83 33      54.8      74.4

##

## Confidence level used: 0.95

##

## $contrasts

## contrast      estimate      SE      df      t.ratio      p.value

## Dic - Doc      −17.17      6.83      33      −2.514      0.0437

## Dic - Pic      −19.83      6.83      33      −2.905      0.0174

## Doc - Pic      −2.67      6.83      33      −0.391      0.9196

##

## P value adjustment: tukey method for comparing a family of 3 estimates
```

从上面的分析结果可以看到，Dic 与 Doc 之间存在显著性差异，Dic 与 Pic 之间也存在显著性差异，上面的分析结果的最后一行还显示在进行事后检验时使用了 tukey 方法对 p 值进行了校正。对多重比较的 p 值校正问题，读者可以进一步阅读《第二语言加工及 R 语言应用》一书。综合上面方差分析的结果我们可以使用以下语言来表达结果：

以词汇学习方法为自变量，以词汇测试成绩为因变量进行独立测量的单因素方差分析，结果显示，词汇学习方法具有主效应（ $F(2,33) = 4.97$, $p = 0.013$, $\eta^2 = 0.231$ ）。事后检验的结果显示，Dic 与 Doc 之间存在显著性差异（ $\beta = -17.17$, SE = 6.83, $t = -2.51$, $p = 0.04$ ），Dic 与 Pic 之间也存在显著性差异（ $\beta = -19.83$, SE = 6.83, $t = -2.91$, $p = 0.02$ ），但是 Doc 与 Pic 之间没有显著性差异（ $\beta = -2.67$, SE = 6.83, $t = -0.39$, $p = 0.92$ ）。

16.3.4 多变量分析实例

上面向大家展示的实例只涉及一个自变量，但是语言研究，不管是关于语言的习得、产出、理解、加工，还是涉及语言本体等各种各样的研究，都会牵涉到同时对很多变量的考察。因此，多变量分析才是语言研究的常态。以表 16.3 的数据为例：

表16.3　三组被试接受不同词汇学习方法训练后的词汇测试成绩

	词汇学习方法		
Sex	Dic	Pic	Doc
M	42	98	48
M	36	65	61
M	41	83	50
M	43	93	54
M	45	80	32
M	38	63	67
F	66	54	68
F	45	25	50
F	30	52	87
F	51	37	81
F	63	71	70
F	37	54	75
	$T_1=537$	$T_2=775$	$T_3=743$
	$SS_1=1248$	$SS_2=5255$	$SS_3=2729$
	$n_1=12$	$n_2=12$	$n_3=12$
	$M_1=45$	$M_2=65$	$M_3=62$

　　仔细观察表 16.3 会发现，它跟表 16.1 的数据完全一样，但这个表里还增加了另外一个因素，那就是性别（sex）。具体的实验设计是这样的：男女各 18 人随机分配到 Dic、Pic 和 Doc 三种不同的学习方法当中去接受不同的词汇学习训练，训练结束后对他们进行标准化的词汇测试，以考察不同词汇训练方法的效果以及这种效果与性别的关系。在设计上，这个实验可以用图 16.5 来表示：

因素 A：三种不同方法

	Dic	Pic	Doc
男性	6人	6人	6人
女性	6人	6人	6人

因素 B：性别

图16.5　3×2双因素独立测量的实验设计

从图 16.5 可以看出，这是一个比较典型的 3×2 的平衡实验设计（equal ns）。所谓平衡就是指，在各个实验条件下，被试的数量是一样的，图 16.5 中的每个单元格都是六个人；所谓 3×2 就是指一共有两个实验因素，第一个因素（即词汇训练的方法）有三个水平（Dic vs. Pic vs. Doc），第二个因素（即性别）有两个水平（男性 vs. 女性）。面对这样的涉及多变量的数据，该如何进行分析呢？

同样，首先进行的也是描述统计，即对数据进行总结、组织和简化。跟前面一样，主要是呈现数据的集中趋势和变异性，具体做法是计算各个实验条件下的平均数和标准差。但在这之前，首先要根据表 16.3 的数据生成数据框，如下：

```
df <- tribble(
  ~sex, ~Dic,~Pic,~Doc,
  "M",  42,  98,  48,
  "M",  36,  65,  61,
  "M",  41,  83,  50,
  "M",  43,  93,  54,
  "M",  45,  80,  32,
  "M",  38,  63,  67,
  "F",  66,  54,  68,
  "F",  45,  25,  50,
  "F",  30,  52,  87,
  "F",  51,  37,  81,
  "F",  63,  71,  70,
  "F",  37,  54,  75)
df
## # A tibble: 12 × 4
##    sex     Dic   Pic   Doc
##    <chr> <dbl> <dbl> <dbl>
##  1 M        42    98    48
##  2 M        36    65    61
##  3 M        41    83    50
##  4 M        43    93    54
##  5 M        45    80    32
##  6 M        38    63    67
```

```
##  7 F      66      54      68
##  8 F      45      25      50
##  9 F      30      52      87
## 10 F      51      37      81
## 11 F      63      71      70
## 12 F      37      54      75
```

生成的数据赋值给 df，但是仔细看，df 并不符合我们在上面提到的"干净、整洁的数据框"的三条标准，因为 Dic、Pic 和 Doc 属于同一个变量，但是它们分布不同列，违背了上面所说的第一条标准：每一个变量必须有它自己的列。因此，需要对数据进行转换，以把这三列归并为一列，来表示方法这个变量，代码如下：

```
df1 <- df%>%
    pivot_longer(Dic:Doc,
                 names_to = "method",
                 values_to = "scores")

df1
## # A tibble: 36 × 3
##      sex method scores
##      <chr> <chr> <dbl>
##  1 M      Dic     42
##  2 M      Pic     98
##  3 M      Doc     48
##  4 M      Dic     36
##  5 M      Pic     65
##  6 M      Doc     61
##  7 M      Dic     41
##  8 M      Pic     83
##  9 M      Doc     50
## 10 M      Dic     43
## # ... with 26 more rows
## # ℹ Use `print(n = ...)` to see more rows
```

新生成的数据命名为 df1，一共有三列，即三个变量，sex 表示性别，M 表示男性、F 表示女性；第二个变量 method 表示词汇训练的方法，一共有三个水平：Dic vs. Pic vs. Doc。最后一个变量 scores 是因变量，表示词汇测试的成绩。这个数据已经完全符合"干净、整洁的数据框"这一标准，利用这个数据就可以进行描述统计了，如下：

library(flextable)

x2 <- df1 %>%

   group_by(sex,method) %>%

   summarize(M=round(mean(scores),2),

         SD=round(sd(scores),2),

         n=n())

set_caption(flextable(x2)，"表 16.4：不同性别及词汇学习方法之下词汇学习效果的描述统计结果"）

表16.4　不同性别及词汇学习方法之下词汇学习效果的描述统计结果

sex	method	M	SD	n
F	Dic	48.67	14.21	6
F	Doc	71.83	12.80	6
F	Pic	48.83	15.89	6
M	Dic	40.83	3.31	6
M	Doc	52.00	12.08	6
M	Pic	80.33	14.25	6

从表 16.4 的描述统计结果看，男生在 Pic 词汇训练条件下所获得的平均数最高（M=80.33），而男生在 Dic 词汇训练条件下所获得的平均数最低（M=40.83）。表 16.4 的结果非常规整，一般来说可以直接拷进论文里。

同样，也可以用可视化的手段来呈现描述统计的结果。首先，使用 ggplot2 作条形图，如下：

ggplot(df1,aes(method,scores,fill=sex))+

  geom_bar(stat = "summary",

       fun=mean,

       position="dodge")+

  geom_errorbar(stat="summary",

         fun.data=mean_cl_normal,

         position=position_dodge(width=0.9),

         width=0.2)+

  labs(x="Voc learning methods",y="Scores")

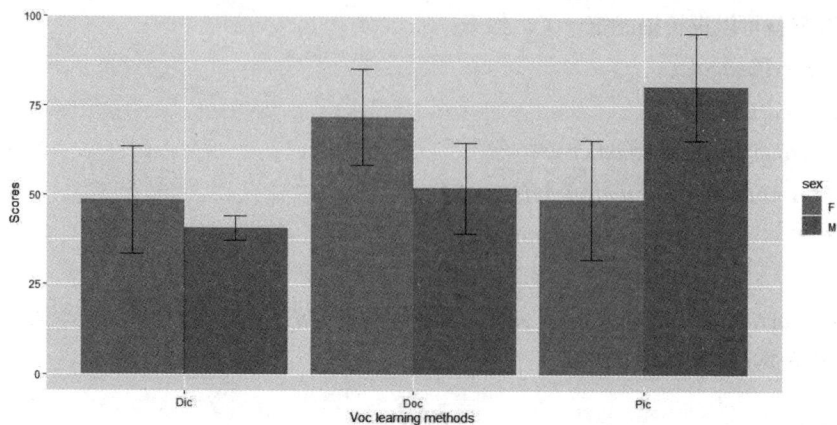

图16.6　不同性别及词汇学习方法下的词汇测试成绩

　　上面介绍过，可以使用 ggplot2 对图形的许多具体细节进行调整、修改，以达到论文出版的要求，比如图形的颜色、图例（legend）、字体大小等。除了条形图，还可以使用许多其他图形来对结果进行可视化，比如这里也可以使用箱体图，如下：

ggplot(df1,aes(method,scores,fill=sex))+

　geom_boxplot()+

　labs(x="Learning methods")

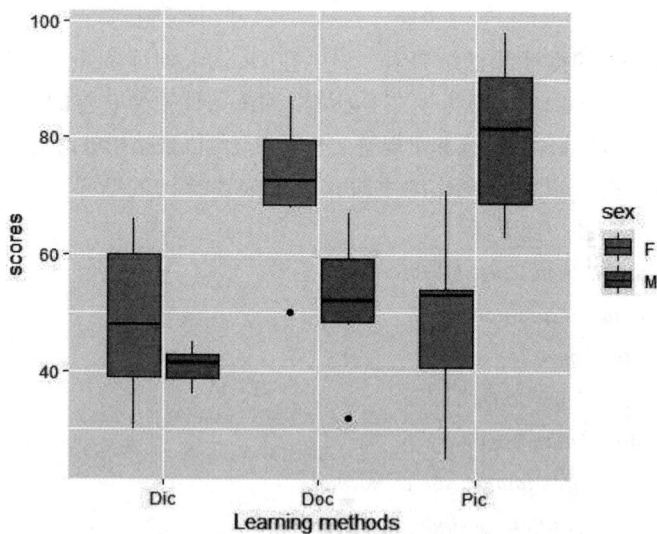

图16.7　不同性别及词汇学习方法下的词汇测试成绩（箱体图）

箱体图（boxplot），亦称"箱线图"，可以很好地呈现数据中的值是如何分布的。尽管与其他一些图比如直方图或密度图（density plot）相比，箱线图可能看起来比较"古旧"，但它们具有空间占用更少的优势，这在比较许多组或数据集之间的分布时就显得很有用。可以看到，每个箱体图中间（或偏向中间处）有一根粗线，那根线表示的是中位数，而不是平均数。可见，如果这根线正好位于箱体的中间则说明数据分布比较对称，相反则表示不对称。

在对数据进行了描述或可视化后，接下来要开展的就是推断统计。在此之前需要先分析实验中的两个自变量分别属于何种实验设计，是独立测量的被试间设计，还是重复测量的被试内设计。首先，看 method 这个变量，跟上面一样，也是不同组的学生被分配到了不同的 method 之下进行词汇学习，所以这个变量是独立测量的被试间设计。再看 sex 这个变量，跟 method 一样，它也是独立测量的被试间设计，因为不同性别的人被分配到了不同的组里参加实验，没有同一种性别的同一个人被分配到了不同的词汇训练方法里进行训练。可见，总体看，这个 3x2 的实验是一个独立测量的被试间设计。仍然可以使用 afex 包的 *aov_4( )* 函数进行方差分析，不过，在这之前也要往数据里增加一个变量，表示被试，如下：

df2 <- df1 %>%

    mutate(subj=paste0("S",1:36))

df2

```
## # A tibble: 36 × 4
##     sex method scores subj
##    <chr> <chr> <dbl> <chr>
##  1 M    Dic    42    S1
##  2 M    Pic    98    S2
##  3 M    Doc    48    S3
##  4 M    Dic    36    S4
##  5 M    Pic    65    S5
##  6 M    Doc    61    S6
##  7 M    Dic    41    S7
##  8 M    Pic    83    S8
##  9 M    Doc    50    S9
## 10 M    Dic    43    S10
## # ... with 26 more rows
## # ℹ Use `print(n = ...)` to see more rows
```

新生成的数据命名为 df2，可以看到 df2 中增加了一个变量 subj，它是被试识别号，代表不同的被试。有了被试这个变量以后，就可以通过下面的代码验证 method（词汇训练的方法）这个变量到底是不是独立测量的被试间设计：

table(df2$subj,df2$method)

可以看到，每名被试只出现在一个实验条件之下（1 表示出现，0 表示不出现），即这是一个独立测量的被试间设计。现在就可以使用 afex 包中的 *aov_4 ( )* 函数进行 3×2 设计的独立测量的方差分析了：

library(afex)

M <- aov_4(scores~method*sex+

                   (1|subj),

             data=df2)

M

Anova Table (Type 3 tests)

##

Response: scores

##	Effect	df	MSE	F	ges	p.value
## 1	method	2, 30	163.04	8.53 **	.362	.001
## 2	sex	1, 30	163.04	0.09	.003	.766
## 3	method:sex	2, 30	163.04	13.27 ***	.469	<.001

---

*## Signif. codes: 0 '***' 0.001 '**' 0.01 '*' 0.05 '+' 0.1 ' ' 1*

上面的方差分析的结果表一共有 3 行 6 列。前面介绍过，每一行显示的是方差分析中的每个项的检验结果，就这个研究来说，这三个项分别是 method 和 sex 的主效应以及它们的交互效应。从上面的结果可以看到：

method 有主效应（$F_{(2,30)} = 8.53$，$p = .001$，$\eta^2 = 0.362$），但是 sex 没有主效应（$F_{(1,30)} = 0.09$，$p = 0.766$，$\eta^2 = 0.003$）。然而最重要的是，method 和 sex 有显著的交互效应（$F_{(2,30)} = 13.27$，$p < 0.001$，$\eta^2 = 0.469$）。

深刻理解统计分析的一些基本概念，对打下扎实的统计分析的基础至关重要，而这一点恰恰就是文科学生很容易忽视的方面。在前面我们已经介绍过主效应这个概念，这里又涉及统计分析中另外一个非常重要的概念，那就是交互效应。当进行多变量分析时，除了主效应，变量之间还可能存在交互效应。所谓交互效应（interaction effect），简单说来就是一个变量对因变量的影响还要取决于另外一个变量的不同水平。就这个实验来说，method 和 sex 存在交互效应说明，词汇学习方法对词汇学习的影响，还要取决于是男还是女，即性别的不同水平；或者反过来说，性别对词汇学习的影响，还要取决于采用了哪种词汇学习方法，即方法的不同水平。理解了这个概念以后，相信读者肯定会认识到当两个变量存在交互的时候，变量的主效应已经不再重要，因为即使这个变量有主效应，它的影响还要取决于另外一个变量。交互效应是所有研究者在开展多变量研究时非常关心的问题，因为交互效应往往能让结果变得更有趣。

从上面对交互效应的定义可知，既然一个变量的影响还要取决于另外一个变量的不同水平，那么，当获得交互效应后，研究者就应该继续分析，从而厘清一个变量的影响是如何取决于另外一个变量的不同水平的，这个过程有人称作简单效应分析，实质也是事后检验，目的是把两个变量的交互效应拆解开来。仍然可以使用 emmeans 包的 *emmeans( )* 函数来实现这个目的，如下：

emmeans::emmeans(M,specs = pairwise~method*sex)

```
## $emmeans
##   method sex emmean SE df lower.CL upper.CL
##   Dic    F   48.7 5.21 30   38.0    59.3
##   Doc    F   71.8 5.21 30   61.2    82.5
##   Pic    F   48.8 5.21 30   38.2    59.5
##   Dic    M   40.8 5.21 30   30.2    51.5
##   Doc    M   52.0 5.21 30   41.4    62.6
##   Pic    M   80.3 5.21 30   69.7    91.0
##
## Confidence level used: 0.95
##
## $contrasts
##   contrast         estimate SE df    t.ratio p.value
##   Dic  F - Doc F    -23.167  7.37 30  -3.143  0.0397
##   Dic  F - Pic F     -0.167  7.37 30  -0.023  1.0000
##   Dic  F - Dic M      7.833  7.37 30   1.063  0.8921
```

```
## Dic    F - Doc M    -3.333   7.37  30  -0.452   0.9974
## Dic    F - Pic M   -31.667   7.37  30  -4.296   0.0021
## Doc    F - Pic F    23.000   7.37  30   3.120   0.0418
## Doc    F - Dic M    31.000   7.37  30   4.205   0.0027
## Doc    F - Doc M    19.833   7.37  30   2.690   0.1070
## Doc    F - Pic M    -8.500   7.37  30  -1.153   0.8550
## Pic    F - Dic M     8.000   7.37  30   1.085   0.8834
## Pic    F - Doc M    -3.167   7.37  30  -0.430   0.9979
## Pic    F - Pic M   -31.500   7.37  30  -4.273   0.0023
## Dic    M - Doc M   -11.167   7.37  30  -1.515   0.6578
## Dic    M - Pic M   -39.500   7.37  30  -5.358   0.0001
## Doc    M - Pic M   -28.333   7.37  30  -3.843   0.0070
##
```

P value adjustment: tukey method for comparing a family of 6 estimates

根据上面的分析结果，现在可以使用以下语言来对统计结果进行表述：

以词汇学习的方法和性别为自变量，以词汇测试成绩为因变量，进行 3×2 独立测量的方差分析。结果显示，method 有主效应（$F_{(2,30)} = 8.53$, $p = .001$, $\eta^2 = 0.362$），但是 sex 没有主效应（$F_{(1,30)} = 0.09$, $p = 0.766$, $\eta^2 = 0.003$）。然而最重要的是，method 和 sex 有显著的交互效应（$F_{(2,30)} = 13.27$, $p < 0.001$, $\eta^2 = 0.469$）。简单效应分析的结果显示（或者说事后检验的结果显示），当性别为女性时，Doc 的词汇学习效果显著好于 Dic 的效果（$\beta = 23.17$, SE = 7.37, $t = 3.14$, $p = 0.04$），但是当性别为男性时，Pic 的效果显著好于 Dic 的效果（$\beta = 39.50$, SE = 7.37, $t = 5.36$, $p = 0.0001$），也显著好于 Doc 的效果（$\beta = 28.33$, SE = 7.37, $t = 3.84$, $p = 0.007$）。

上面的解读很好地分析了词汇训练的方法对测试分数的影响如何受到了性别不同水平的影响。但这还不够，因为方法和性别的交互效应还表示性别的影响如何受到不同词汇学习方法的影响，因此，需要比较在每一种词汇训练方法之下，男女之间是否有差异。这部分内容留给读者根据上面事后检验的结果自己完成。

课堂讨论

1. R 是什么？有哪些功能？有什么优点？
2. 何为文本挖掘？如何进行文本挖掘？
3. 何为停用词？在计算词频的时候，为何一般会去除停用词？
4. 何为可视化？什么内容可以被可视化？R 提供了什么样的可视化工具？
5. 从中国期刊网（或其他可用数据库）下载《外语教学与研究》在 2023 年第 2 期发表的研究论文《多篇还是多遍？——故事阅读对二语词汇附带习得的影响》。该论文报道了研究者如何使用外语故事作为阅读材料研究中国学生的英语词汇习得。仔细阅读该研究论文的文献综述和实验设计部分，并回答以下问题：

   (1) 这项研究的自变量是什么？因变量是什么？
   (2) 在进行统计建模时，研究者还考察了学生的外语故事理解能力的影响。外语故事理解能力是自变量还是因变量？它属于分类变量还是连续型数值变量？
   (3) 仔细阅读该论文的结果部分。该研究的因变量是什么类型的变量，即是分类变量还是连续型数值变量？为什么在进行统计分析的时候，作者使用了逻辑回归模型？
   (4) 该论文在汇报统计结果时使用了多个图形。仔细阅读每一个图形，以辨别它们分别是什么类型的图。从这篇论文的结果汇报看，使用图形来汇报统计结果有什么好处？

课外练习

1. 何为结构化数据和非结构化数据？这两种数据是否都可以用 R 来分析？

2. RStudio 界面都包括哪些区域？各个区域都有哪些功能？彼此之间如何联系？

3. 寻找运用情感分析的论文，并学习使用 R 进行情感分析。

4. 再阅读《多篇还是多遍？——故事阅读对二语词汇附带习得的影响》这篇论文。该论文报道的实验考察中国学生英语词汇习得效果时使用了两种测量工作：语义生成任务和完形填空任务。回答以下问题：

   (1) 仔细阅读文章中对这两种任务的描述，你认为使用这两种不同的任务来测量词汇习得的效果是否可靠？

   (2) 这两种不同的测试任务是否测试了词汇知识的不同方面？

   (3) 这篇论文最有趣的数据分析是第二个部分，即对完型填空任务的数据分析，因为在分析结果中既出现了主效应，也出现了交互效应。何为主效应？何为交互效应？为什么交互效应非常重要？

拓展阅读

Gravetter, F. J., & Wallnau, L. B. (2009). *Statistics for the behavioural sciences.* London: Wadsworth Publishing Co Inc.

Wickham, H., & Grolemund, G. (2017). *R for data science: Import, tidy, transform, visualize, and model data.* Boston: O'Reilly Media, Inc.

吴诗玉. (2019). 第二语言加工及 R 语言应用. 北京：外语教学与研究出版社.

吴诗玉. (2021). R 在语言科学研究中的应用. 北京：科学出版社.

第 17 单元
学位论文写作要点与规范（一）

学习目标
- 掌握学位论文各个组成部分的基本格式
- 了解学位论文的逻辑结构
- 了解学位论文写作的步骤和方法

规范性是学位论文的一个重要特点，从形式的角度来说，规范性是指学位论文要按照一定的格式来安排各部分的内容并最终形成一个完整的系统。学位论文在逻辑结构上一般分为：Title（标题），Abstract（摘要），Keywords（关键词），Introduction（引言），Literature Review（文献综述），Theories and Methods（理论与方法），Results（结果），Discussion（讨论），Conclusion（结论），References（参考文献）及 Acknowledgements（致谢）。本书将用两个单元对以上部分逐一详加讲述。本单元主要介绍致谢、标题、摘要、关键词、引言及文献综述部分的写作步骤和方法。

17.1 致谢写作

在致谢部分，论文作者向那些在论文完成过程中提供过帮助、支持的人表达感谢。该部分是要表达自己的真情实感，不是学术写作，因此要自然地抒发内心感受，切忌虚情假意、矫揉造作、无病呻吟。通常，致谢的对象主要有两大类：专业领域的和私人的，通常先感谢前者，然后是后者。

可以采用以下的表达来区分不同的感谢程度：

非常感谢：

致谢类表达	致谢对象	致谢原因
<ul><li>I am deeply indebted to …</li><li>I would like to express my deepest appreciation to …</li><li>I would like to express my deepest gratitude to …</li><li>I'm extremely grateful to …</li><li>This endeavor would not have been possible without …</li><li>I could not have undertaken this journey without …</li><li>Words cannot express my special gratitude to …</li></ul>	<ul><li>论文导师</li><li>答辩委员会</li><li>相关教授</li></ul>	<ul><li>坚定不移的支持（如建设性的批评/反馈/有见地的评价和建议）</li><li>耐心指导</li><li>传授知识或专业技能</li></ul>

很感谢：

致谢类表达	致谢对象	致谢原因
• Many thanks to … • Special thanks to … • I am also thankful to/for … • I am also grateful to/for … • Thanks should also go to … • I would like to extend my sincere thanks to … • I'd like to acknowledge …	• 同学 • 图书管理员 • 研究助手 • 实验室助理 • 研究参与者	• 编辑或校对方面的帮助 • 意见和建议 • 道德支持 • 灵感

感谢：

致谢类表达	致谢对象	致谢原因
• Lastly, I'd like to mention … • I'd like to recognize … • I would be remiss in not mentioning …	• 父母 • 伴侣 • 孩子 • 朋友 • 宠物	• 精神支持 • 生活中的支持 • 信任

试看下列致谢段落：

Words cannot express my gratitude to my professor and chair of my committee for her invaluable patience and feedback. I also could not have undertaken this journey without my defense committee, who generously provided knowledge and expertise. Additionally, this endeavor would not have been possible without the generous support from the MacArthur Foundation.

I am also grateful to my classmates and cohort members, especially my office mates, for their editing help, late-night feedback sessions, and moral support. Thanks should also go to the librarians, research assistants, and study participants from the university, who impacted and inspired me.

Lastly, I would be remiss in not mentioning my family, especially my parents, spouse, and children. Their belief in me has kept my spirits and motivation high during this process. I would also like to thank my cat for all the entertainment and emotional support.

17.2　标题写作

通过论文标题，读者第一次有机会了解论文的大致内容，倘若题目表述不清，有可能从一开始就会误导读者。

论文题目应该是描述性或者解释性的，题目中的每一个字词都应能帮助读者了解论文的核心内容，因此，不可太泛太空。总体而言，论文题目应阐明以下内容：

- 研究话题
- 目标人群
- 理论框架
- 研究变量
- 研究设计和方法（定性、定量、混合）

……

下面是一些标题范例：

1) Lexical Bundles in Applied Linguistics and Literature Writing: A Comparison
　　　　　　　研究话题　　　　　　　　　　　　研究方法
of Intermediate English Learners and Professionals
　　　　　　目标人群

2) Grammatical Errors by Arabic ESL Students: An Investigation of L1 Transfer
　研究话题　　　　　　目标人群　　　　研究方法　　　研究变量
through Error Analysis
　　理论框架

论文题目不一定很短，但必须精炼，应该用尽可能少的语言来充分表述论文的核心内容，例如，users of dictionaries 不如 dictionary users；stress in the workplace 不如 workplace stress。

论文题目措辞应该与正文内容保持一致。例如，在题目中提到论文采用的方法是 case study approach，读者自然而然期望在论文的摘要、前言及研究方法等章节看到 "case study approach" 的字样。尽管这是个显而易见的问题，但事实上许多学生会使用不同的表述，从而引起误解，因此，需要确保论文题目中的表述和其他部分的表述保持一致。

此外，论文题目不可使用缩略语及首字母缩略词，也不可采用戏谑或者可爱的风格。

17.3 摘要写作

摘要是对学位论文或者研究论文的总结。不同学科的论文在摘要结构上略有不同，但毫无疑问，摘要需要精准简短地描述研究目的、研究方法和研究结果来帮助读者准确地了解论文内容。

摘要通常采用的结构是 IMRaD 结构，即包括引言（Introduction）、方法（Methods）、结果（Results）和讨论（Discussion）这几个部分。学位论文中的摘要通常需要单独占页，位于论文题目页和致谢页之后、目录页之前。摘要可以独立成文并反映论文的结构，所以往往放在最后写，以对论文进行总结。

在引言部分就要明确阐述研究目的：研究拟解决什么实际问题或理论问题，目标在于回答什么研究问题，等等。该部分可以简要提及与研究主题相关的社会或学术背景，一般不描述细节信息，但如果摘要中使用的专业术语对于普通学术读者来说不熟悉或者有多种含义则需要进行简要界定。

引言中有可能会用到 investigate、test、analyze 或者 evaluate 等动词来精确地描述拟完成的事情，此时需要用动词的一般现在时或一般过去时来进行描述，不可用将来时，因为研究已经完成。例如：

- ✗ The current study will set to investigate the effect of introducing particular vocabulary learning strategies (VLSs) to Saudi, female students.
- ✓ The current study set to investigate the effect of introducing particular vocabulary learning strategies (VLSs) to Saudi, female students.
- ✗ This study will investigate the relationship between coffee consumption and productivity.
- ✓ This study investigates the relationship between coffee consumption and productivity.

在研究方法部分，只需简要描述为了回答研究问题所采用的研究方法，无须评价方法的有效性或遇到的障碍，因为该部分的目的不是要解释研究方法的优势与劣势，而是帮助读者快速浏览所采用的方法和步骤，通常用一般过去时。例如：

- ✗ The strategies implemented will be six: "grouping words together to study them" (GW); "putting English labels on physical objects" (LO); "using scales for gradable words" (SC); "using semantic maps" (SM); "using the keyword method" (KW) and "studying words with a pictorial representation of their meaning" (PR).
- ✓ The strategies implemented were six: "grouping words together to study them" (GW); "putting English labels on physical objects" (LO); "using scales for gradable words" (SC); "using semantic maps" (SM); "using the keyword method" (KW) and "studying words with a pictorial representation of their meaning" (PR).
- ✗ Structured interviews will be conducted with 25 participants.
- ✓ Structured interviews were conducted with 25 participants.

在研究结果部分，需要总结主要研究结果。摘要中不可能包括所有的研究结果，只能凸显最重要的发现来帮助读者理解结论。可用一般现在时，也可用一般过去时。例如：

- ✓ The analysis of the data revealed the effectiveness of the VSBI program in the areas identified above.
- ✓ The analysis of the data reveals the effectiveness of the VSBI program in the areas identified above.
- ✗ The analysis of the data has revealed the effectiveness of the VSBI program in the areas identified above.
- ✓ Our analysis shows a strong correlation between coffee consumption and productivity.
- ✓ Our analysis showed a strong correlation between coffee consumption and productivity.
- ✗ Our analysis has shown a strong correlation between coffee consumption and productivity.

在讨论部分，需要陈述研究的主要结论，帮助读者明白研究所证明或讨论的重点，即如何回答了研究问题。如果研究目标是解决实际问题，在讨论部分可以推荐扩展应用，也可以对进一步的研究提出建议。结论部分通常用一般现在时。例如：

✓ We conclude that coffee consumption increases productivity.

✓ To conclude, the current study can be expanded regarding the following areas.

✗ We concluded that coffee consumption increases productivity.

好的摘要需要言简意赅，因此每个词都很重要，每个句子都要清楚地表达一个要点。写摘要时需要注意以下几点：

（1）不要使用长句。

（2）不要使用晦涩的术语。

（3）既不要重复，也不要用一些词来凑数。

（4）不要描述细节。

17.4　关键词写作

摘要的最后需要列出论文的关键词，数量一般在3—5个。这些关键词应提及研究的核心要素，以帮助未来的读者在文献检索中找到你的论文。因此，在确定关键词之前需要厘清论文的主要内容是什么，以及哪些关键词有助于检索到该主题。确定关键词时需要注意以下几点：

（1）关键词是对论文从整体上归类，因此，只需关注核心概念。

（2）关键词应该包含与主题密切相关的词或短语。

（3）关键词应该选用研究领域内其他人容易识别的词。

（4）形容词本身不能用作关键词，须与名词连用。

（5）关键词应该使用完整的词语，而不是缩写。

例如：

Abstract

The use of technology has become an important part of the learning process in and out of the class. Every language class usually uses some form of technology. Technology has been used to both help and improve language learning. Technology enables teachers to adapt classroom activities, thus enhancing the language learning process. Technology continues to grow in importance as a tool to help teachers facilitate language learning for their learners. This study focuses on the role of using new technologies in learning English as a second/foreign language. It discussed different attitudes which support English language learners to increase their learning skills through using technologies. In this paper, the researcher defined the terms "technology" and "technology integration", explained the use of technology in language classroom, reviewed previous studies on using technologies in improving language learning skills, and stated certain recommendations for the better use of these technologies, which assist learners in improving their learning skills. The literature review indicated that the effective use of new technologies improves learners' language learning skills.

Keywords: technology, language learning, use

17.5 引言写作

引言也称"导论"。高质量的引言能够将读者顺利带入论文，因此需要有清晰的重点、目的和方向来为相关研究开个好头。尽管引言是论文的开头部分，但不一定要最先写。事实上，引言往往和摘要一起最后完成。研究将要开始时可以先写一个引言的初稿（与研究方案中的很多内容都是相同的），在论文写作过程中要不断地修改初稿，确保引言部分与各章节的内容不脱节。

作为论文的第一章，引言部分应该包括下列内容：

（1）研究主题和背景：论文读者需要了解什么。

引言一开始就要介绍研究主题并描述必要的背景信息，以引起读者的兴趣，并使其明白该研究的重要性和适切性（如可以提及相关的学术讨论、实际问题等）。例如，下面是针对二语习得中词汇学习的相关背景描述：

Unfortunately, most English teachers in Saudi Arabia do not focus on such strategies; instead they focus on giving students information as far as the language content is concerned. At the same time, the majority of university students prefers to depend on their teachers throughout the process of learning and do not make any effort to develop themselves. Therefore, most students do not develop rich vocabulary that enables them to communicate freely and appropriately in English.

（2）研究重点和范围：具体论证研究主题下的哪一个方面。

简要介绍研究主题后，需要聚焦自己的研究重点并界定研究范围，如调查哪个地理区域、涵盖哪个时间段、研究什么年龄段或者什么类型的人、具体论证与研究主题相关的哪些方面，等等。例如：

This study sets out to investigate whether strategies for expanding FL learners' vocabulary knowledge are beneficial for them.

（3）研究相关性、重要性及局限性：研究内容与现有研究相比，是否相关；为何重要；研究的局限性或者困难在哪里。

在引言部分非常有必要明确表明进行研究的意图：该研究与已有相关研究有何关系？贡献何在？概述目前的研究状况，引用最相关的文献来说明该研究将如何解决某个问题或填补空白（在后面的"文献综述"部分会对相关文献进行更深入的收集和整理）。研究方向不同，其重要性也不同，有的研究重在实际应用（如政策研究或管理研究），有的研究重在推进对主题的学术理解（如理论发展或增加新的实证数据），有的则两者兼顾。引言需要阐释该论文如何有助于解决一个实际或理论问题、填补一项文献空白、推进现有研究、对相关主题提出新的观点，等等。例如：

The dominant role that vocabulary plays in learning and understanding language as well as in communicating with others in social life made researchers think of ways to help language learners develop this important aspect. According to researchers, vocabulary learning strategies (VLSs) play a key role; they may help learners discover the meaning of a new word and consolidate a word previously encountered. (Cohen, 1996; Nation, 2001; Schmitt, 1997) Nevertheless, such strategies are often not adopted automatically (Cameron, 2001), are poorly used or even neglected (Nation, 2001). Hence, it has been frequently suggested that apart from teaching specific words, teachers should aim at equipping learners with strategies for expanding their vocabulary knowledge (e.g. Hedge, 2000; Hulstjin, 1992).

The need for such strategies is of paramount importance specially in English as a foreign language (EFL) contexts, such as Saudi Arabia, where students do not have much exposure to the target language. Therefore, teaching in a foreign language context which is mostly viewed as being teacher-centered, the researcher has thought of teaching such strategies and then investigating whether they are beneficial for FL learners.

（4）研究问题和目标：研究旨在发现什么，以及如何实现研究目标。

这是引言最重要的一部分，旨在激发读者对论文其他部分的期待。如何展开研究问题和研究目标依据专业、主题和研究重心而定，但一定要明确清晰地陈述研究的中心目标。有必要简要提及解决研究问题的方法，但无须深入细节。例如：

In order to fill the gap, the researcher aimed at investigating the effect of training EFL Saudi, female, undergraduate learners on the use of a number of vocabulary learning strategies.

相应的研究问题可以表述为：Do vocabulary learning strategies have any effect on the students' strategy repertoire?

（5）论文结构概述：论文的每一章对于总体目标有何贡献。

为了帮助读者更清楚地了解论文，需要在引言最后对论文结构进行概述，对每一章内容进行总结（一两句话即可），阐明其对研究目标的贡献。当然，如果研究本身很复杂或论文采用非常规结构，有可能对于每章的内容都需要用一段来总结，例如，某些人文学科类论文有可能是按照主题来写，而不是将论文分为研究方法、研究结果和讨论这几部分来写：

In Chapter One, the context of the study has been introduced. The research objectives and questions have been identified, and the value of such research argued. The limitations of the study have also been discussed.

In Chapter Two, the existing literature will be reviewed to identify key skills development approaches and strategies within the context of fast-moving industries, especially technology-intensive industries.

In Chapter Three, the theoretical framework will be presented. The adoption of a qualitative, inductive research approach will be justified, and the broader research design will be discussed, including the limitations thereof.

17.6 文献综述写作

文献综述是全面评述与某一特定主题或研究相关的文献（如著作、论文及其他相关统计资料、统计年鉴、资料手册、档案材料等），为自己的研究找到学术基础并直接导向论文的理论框架或方法论。之所以在研究之初就需要进行文献综述，原因如下：

（1）方便研究者熟悉与研究主题相关的现有研究状况。

（2）确保不做重复研究。

（3）发现已有研究与尚未解决问题之间的差距。

（4）形成理论框架和方法论。

（5）概览相关主题研究的主要发现和讨论。

（6）帮助读者了解本研究与已有研究之间的关系及新的研究视角。

做文献综述，要先查找、阅读和分析文献，在此过程中对于参考文献的选择至关重要，需要遴选出最重要、最经典的文献以及最新、有价值的研究成果。然后要对这些文献进行归纳、总结和评论，从中分析并总结出前人研究的不足之处及存在的问题。

完成高质量的文献综述一般需要四个步骤：

第一步：查找相关文献

根据拟定的研究问题中的关键词，采用布尔运算符（and、or、not）来对查找范围进行限定，积极利用学术网站及图书馆的电子资源，根据不同数据库的特点有针对性地查找相关文献，如 Google Scholar、JSTOR、EBSCO、Project MUSE、Elsevier、ProQuest。研究者进行资料收集，通常有一个不断深入的过程，即收集到文献后，通过文献摘要决定是否需要深入阅读；通过阅读其中的文献综述、注释以及参考文献还可以进一步扩大检索范围，从而找到更多的文献，特别是代表该问题研究新进展的文献；多次被引用的文献定是该领域的权威文献，需要重点关注。

第二步：评判、选择文献

判断检索到的文献是否有用，可以就其内容提以下问题：

（1）探讨的是什么问题？

（2）核心概念是什么？

（3）主要理论和方法是什么？

（4）结果和结论是什么？

（5）与其他研究有什么关联？

（6）主要观点和论据是什么？

（7）研究的优势与局限性在哪里？

对文献进行选择和取舍时，可依据其发表时间、研究者的学术影响力及文献的相似性进行判断，最好从最新发表的文献开始着手，因为时间越近的相关研究越具有价值和学术典型性。

第三步：确定主题、讨论过程及研究空白。从文献中寻找以下信息：

（1）文献的发展趋势（如 "Since the importance of instruction on VLSs is widely recognized and acknowledged, a number of intervention studies have been conducted."）。

（2）重要的主题。

（3）讨论及异议。

（4）核心出版物。

（5）研究空白（如 "To the best of the researcher's knowledge, the only intervention study that dealt with Saudi participants was conducted by Alseweed (2000); those participants were EFL male undergraduate learners."）。

研读文献时一定要做笔记，记录以下内容：

（1）要点总结（研究的理论框架、研究背景、研究的方法及主要成果等）。

（2）文献信息（作者姓名、文献名称、期刊名称、出版年份、页码等）。

第四步：列写作提纲，完成写作。

文献综述通常采用以下几种结构：

chronological：按照时间顺序组织内容

thematic：按照主题组织内容

methodological：按照方法论组织内容

theoretical：按照理论组织内容

文献综述的具体内容主要包括文献概述、研究内容分析、目前研究的不足之处等几个组成部分，它不仅仅是对该研究领域的前期研究所做的复述和总结，更应该是对已有研究的一种批判性评估。因此，根据大卫·希尔弗曼（David Silverman）的观点（2009: 254–255），文献综述的撰写需要遵循以下几个原则：（1）尊重文献；（2）具有批判性；（3）避免单纯的描述。

课堂讨论

1. 阅读下列致谢，讨论其中存在的问题。

I would like to express my sincere gratitude to my thesis supervisor Mr. Shanjaya Bahadur Shing, lecture of the Central Department of Economics, T.U. Kirtipur. His patience, enthusiasm, cooperations and suggestions made me present this research work to produce in the present form. His brilliant, skillful supervision enriched this study higher than my expectation. I could not remain any more without giving heartfelt thanks to Mr. Shing for his painstaking supervision throughout the study period. This research work would not be possible without his stimulation, inspiration and cooperation.

Further, yet importantly, sense of respect goes to my father Mr. Laxmi Prasad Karmacharya, mother Mrs. Ramkumari Karmacharya and my family for their strong support economically as well as regular encouragement in every step to make me in present stage. Similarly, other relatives are also subjects to special thanks for their inspiration and cooperation in my study.

The officials of the government, non-government and other concerned authorities are also thankful for their keen interest and great support while conducting the study. Distinguished personalities, the locals and the others stakeholders contacted, interviewed and the source of information revealed are also thankful acknowledged.

I also would like to thanks to all my respected teachers in the central department of Economics and all the others members of departments. My friends Roshan, Remash, Birochan, Narayan, Surya and other friends deserve my thanks who directly and indirectly provide me inspirations and valuable suggestion during the course of this study.

2. 根据所学内容，评价以下标题的合适性。

(1) Exploring the Relationship Between Video Games and Academic Achievement via Cross-Sectional and Longitudinal Analyses

(2) The Relationship Between Education and Health

(3) The Impact of the Level of Native Language Proficiency on the Literacy Achievement of EFL Learners

(4) Methods Supporting Policies in Education Reform

(5) The Effect of School Building Design on Student Achievement

(6) The Use of Technology in English Language Learning: A Literature Review

(7) Satisfaction with Life

(8) The Role of Race in Education: An Analysis of Children in Brazil

(9) Female Labor Force Participation Rate and Economic Development: Time-Series Evidence in China

(10) The Impact of Laptop Computers on Student Learning Behaviors as Perceived by Classroom Teachers

3. 以下是两篇针对同一题目的摘要，讨论各自的特点，判断哪一篇合格、哪一篇不合格，并说明原因。

摘要 1

In this project on "The Analysis of the Structural Integrity of 3D Printed Polymers for Use in Aircraft", my research looked at how 3D printing of materials can help the aviation industry in the manufacture of planes. Plane parts can be made at a lower cost using 3D printing and made lighter than traditional components. This project investigated the structural integrity of EBM manufactured components, which could revolutionize the aviation industry.

摘要 2

Additive manufacturing (AM) of titanium alloys has the potential to enable cheaper and lighter components to be produced with customized designs for use in aircraft engines. Whilst the proof-of-concept of these have been promising, the structural integrity of AM engine parts in response to full thrust and temperature variations is not clear. The primary aim of this project was to determine the fracture modes and mechanisms of AM components designed for use in Boeing 747 engines. To achieve this an explicit finite element (FE) model was developed to simulate the environment and parameters that the engine is exposed to during flight. The FE model was validated using experimental data replicating the environmental parameters in a laboratory setting using ten AM engine components provided by the industry sponsor. The validated FE model was then used to investigate the extent of crack initiation and propagation as the environment parameters were adjusted. This project was the first to investigate fracture patterns in AM titanium components used in aircraft engines; the key finding was that the presence of cavities within the structures due to errors in the printing process, significantly increased the risk of fracture. Secondly, the simulations showed that cracks formed within AM parts were more likely to worsen and lead to component failure at subzero temperatures when compared to conventionally manufactured parts. This has demonstrated an important safety concern which needs to be addressed before AM parts can be used in commercial aircraft.

4. 观察以下研究问题，讨论好的研究问题应该具备什么特点。

(1) How can cellphone technology benefit instruction in high school ELA classes?
(2) How can classroom teachers maximize the instructional impact of using cellphones as a part of effective daily instruction?
(3) What relationships exist among the six language learning strategy categories (memory, cognitive, compensation, metacognitive, affective, and social) and

English language proficiency for Chinese university students studying abroad in or near Kansas?

(4) Which language learning strategy categories can predict English language proficiency as reported by Chinese university students studying abroad in or near Kansas?

(5) What were the perceptions of foreign language teachers about any potential benefits of using social media in English classes?

(6) What did foreign language teachers describe as challenges to using social media in English classes?

5. 阅读以下两篇论文的题目及文献综述的目录，分别对其文献综述部分做出评价。

(1) 论文题目：Belongingness and Integrative Motivation in Second Language Acquisition

(2) 论文题目：Improving English Stress Through Pronunciation Learning Strategies

课外练习

1. 根据本单元提供的不同的致谢方式，自己完成一篇致谢，对不同的人在你完成论文过程中的支持表达谢意。

2. 根据自己的专业，尝试拟定三个论文题目：

   (1) _____

   (2) _____

   (3) _____

3. 阅读下面的摘要，划出其中的研究目的、研究方法、研究发现和结论，并为该摘要补上关键词。

Abstract

This study investigated the effect of first language (L1) transfer on Arabic ESL learners' acquisition of the relative clauses, the passive voice, and the definite article. I used Contrastive Analysis (CA) and Error Analysis (EA) to analyze 50 papers written by Arabic ESL students at the ACTFL Advanced Mid proficiency level. The analysis was paired with interviews with five advanced students to help determine whether L1 transfer was, in fact, influencing students' errors predicted by CA.

Students in this study made L1 errors along with other errors. Although no statistical difference was found between the frequency of transfer and other (non-transfer) errors, L1 transfer errors were still common for many learners in this data. The frequency of the relative clause L1 transfer errors was slightly higher than other errors. However, passive voice L1 errors were as frequent as other errors whereas definite article L1 errors were slightly less frequent than other errors.

The analysis of the interviews suggested that L1 still played a crucial role in influencing learners' errors. The analysis also suggested that the frequency of transfer errors in the papers used in this study might have been influenced by CA-informed instruction students received and students' language level. Specifically, learners reported that both factors helped them reduce the frequency of L1 transfer errors in their writing.

The teaching implications of this study include familiarizing language instructors with possible sources of errors for Arabic ESL learners. Language instructors should try to identify sources of errors by conducting their own analyses or consulting existing literature on CA paired with EA. Finally, I recommend adopting a CA-informed instruction to help students reduce and overcome errors that are influenced by their L1.

关键词: _____, _____, _____, _____, _____

4. 针对以下研究目标，分小组进行讨论，对每个研究目标提出三个研究问题。

(1) Given the lack of research regarding organizational skills development in fast-moving industries, this study aims to identify and evaluate the skills development approaches utilized by web development companies in the UK.
    RQ1: _____
    RQ2: _____
    RQ3: _____

(2) This study sets out to assess the interaction between student support and self-care on well-being in engineering graduate students.
    RQ1: _____
    RQ2: _____
    RQ3: _____

(3) The purpose of this study was to determine how teachers' pedagogical, technological, and emotional readiness relates to their acceptance, intention to use and actual use of the flipped classroom methodology for ESL courses in Puerto Rico.

RQ1: _____

RQ2: _____

RQ3: _____

5. 根据本单元所学内容并结合自己的写作经验，总结文献综述写作需要避免
   的问题。

拓展阅读

Paltridge, B., & Starfield, S. (2020). *Thesis and dissertation writing in a second language: A handbook for students and their supervisors* (2nd edition). London & New York: Routledge.

Parija, S. C., & Kate, V. (Eds.). (2018). *Thesis writing for Master's and Ph.D. program*. Singapore: Gateway East.

肖东发、李武. (2009). 学位论文写作与学术规范. 北京：北京大学出版社.

第18单元
学位论文写作要点与规范（二）

学习目标

- 了解学位论文写作的基本范式
- 继续学习学位论文写作的步骤和方法
- 掌握学位论文写作的要点与规范

作为"学位论文写作要点与规范"模块的第二部分，本单元的重点是论文主体部分的写作。具体来说，本单元主要介绍理论框架部分、方法论部分、结果部分、讨论部分以及结论部分的主要内容、写作步骤和方法。

18.1　理论框架部分写作

学位论文的理论框架是学位论文尤其是博士学位论文的重要组成部分，其功能是描述、讨论和评价与研究相关的已有概念、理论和假设，为当前研究"框定"一个明确的范围、提供框架和"路线图"。

理论框架部分的写作通常包含三步：① 确定关键概念；② 评价和解释相关理论；③ 说明当前研究与相关理论的联系。

第一步是确定研究中的关键概念并汇报相关概念的定义。值得注意的是，有的概念有多种意义，需要明确指出这些概念在当前论文语境中所选用的定义。例如，王艳（2010）在其研究中汇报"语言能力"的定义时写道（具体内容略）：

> 韦伯字典（2003）对"语言能力"的定义是……，在朗文字典（1992）中，"语言能力"被解释为……。乔姆斯基在20世纪60年代将"语言能力"定义为……，但是引来众多学者的反对意见。Hymes (1973)将"语言能力"重新定义为……。Canale (1983) 在此基础上将"语言能力"进一步定义为……。这篇论文采用的是 Hymes (1973) 和 Canale (1983) 对"语言能力"的定义（pp. 42—43）。

第二步是评价和解释与关键概念相关的理论或假设。通过全面的文献回顾梳理出前人研究中这些概念之间被赋予了何种联系、形成了或支持何种理论或假设，批判性地比较和评价不同研究者的做法，选定最适合当前研究的理论或假设并说明理由。在一些复杂的研究中，研究者可能还需要将多个不同理论流派或不同学科的理论相融合，建立自己独特的理论框架。需要注意的是，不可遗漏任何与关键概念相关的重要理论。如果选择不采用某个广为认可的理论或假设时，需要给出合理的理由。

第三步是说明当前研究与相关理论的联系，即当前研究打算通过所选定的理论或假设来做什么，如检验理论在当前研究情境下是否成立、用理论来解释当前研究所收集的数据、对理论进行分析和批判或将不同理论通过独特的方式进行整合。

理论框架部分有时会被划分为文献综述的子章节，但在涉及较多理论的学位论文中最好还是独立为一个章节。这个部分的写作没有固定的组织模式，常用的有按照研究问题（每个子章节围绕一个问题或关键概念展开）、按照时间顺序（理论的缘起、发展与成熟的不同阶段）、按照理论类型等方式来划分子章节。总之，只要能做到清晰、有逻辑即可。

18.2　方法论部分写作

学位论文中的方法论部分主要是介绍研究设计的相关内容。这一部分写作应做到清晰且翔实，让读者阅读之后信服该研究是按照规范进行的且能依据作者的描述完全或部分复制该项研究。

一般来说，方法论部分需包括：① 对所采用的研究方法的介绍；② 对数据收集方法和过程的描述；③ 对数据分析方法和过程的描述。

语言学研究最常用的研究方法类型为定量研究法、定性研究法，以及定量与定性混合研究法。定量研究法一般根据某些具体假设设计实验并收集用数值表示的资料或信息，然后通过对数据的量化分析来得出有意义的结论。与定量研究法不同，定性研究法一般不采用实验的形式，所收集的数据一般不以数值来表示，对数据的分析也非统计性而是基于对所观测到的现象或经验的描述和分析。混合研究顾名思义是以上两种研究方法的混合，既有量化的研究，又有质性的分析，两者互为补充。对于研究方法的介绍应该出现在方法论部分的开头，无须另起标题，简单说明该学术论文所采用的研究方法即可。如马蓉（2015）在其博士论文研究方法章节开头写道：

> 针对文献综述部分提出的三大问题，本研究采用混合设计方法，即综合运用两种研究方法：定量研究设计和定性研究设计。定量设计为主要数据来源，包括文献引用能力的文本研究设计和文献引用能力影响因素的问卷调查研究设计。定性设计为辅助数据来源，是文献引用能力的访谈研究设计（p. 37）。

对于数据收集、分析方法与过程的描述是方法论部分的主体，一般包含研究对象、研究工具与研究过程、数据分析方法与过程等内容。每部分内容的标题可能会由于研究方法的不同而略有差异。

（1）研究对象
这个部分介绍研究对象的情况。其中必须介绍的是研究对象的数量。除此之外，还需根据具体的研究问题和实验设计介绍其他信息。例如，调查英语水平对英语学习者二语习得调节作用的研究应介绍研究对象的英语水平；而要求研究对象在实验中按动电脑键盘的研究则应介绍研究对象的优势手信息（右利手或是左利手），因为大部分情况下按键的位置都是方便右利手操作的，所以需要了解这种设置是否会影响到实验结果。

（2）研究工具与研究过程

这个部分介绍变量的测量方法和工具以及通过这些方法和工具收集数据的过程。不同研究法所采用的研究工具有所不同。定量研究法使用的研究工具主要有调查问卷、实验和已有资料，而定性研究法常用的研究工具为观察、访谈和已有资料。下面将对不同研究工具和研究过程的写作进行简单介绍。

1）调查问卷

使用问卷作为研究工具的研究需要介绍问卷的具体设计和问卷调查的具体操作过程。在介绍问卷设计时，一般需说明问卷的结构（包含几个部分），问卷中使用的题型（选择题、判断题、封闭性的问题、开放或半开放的问题、量表等）以及选择这些题型的原因。在介绍问卷调查的具体操作过程时，需说明发放和回收问卷的方式、途径和过程，如是纸质的还是电子版本的，是当场完成还是在限定或不限定的时间内完成交回或网上提交，是通过何种网络平台（微信、QQ、问卷星等）。例如，下面是祖晓梅、马嘉俪（2015）论文中有关调查研究工具和研究过程的节选。

　　研究工具：调查问卷包括三个部分，第一部分是学生和教师的基本信息，第二部分是用莱克特五级量表表示的 21 个封闭性问题。21 个项目的一小部分题目参考了 Schulz (2001) 和 Brown (2000) 的问卷，其余大部分科目则是依据 Hendreickson (1978) 所提出的课堂纠错反馈的 5 个基本问题设计的，具体如是否应该纠错、谁来纠错、纠正什么错误、什么时机纠错、如何来纠错。这个部分的内容主要用于定量分析，比较汉语师生纠错反馈信念和态度的差异。第三个部分是三个半开放性问题。分别是：1）你对纠错反馈的信念主要来自什么影响？ 2）你喜欢纠正什么语言错误？为什么？ 3）你喜欢的纠错反馈策略是什么？为什么？这个部分的答案主要用于定量和定性研究，理解汉语教师和学习者纠错反馈信念的来源和理由。考虑到汉语学习者汉语水平的不同，有三位以英语、日语和韩语为母语的汉语语言学及应用语言学专业的研究生把中文问卷翻译为英语、日语和韩语。调查问卷采用双语的形式。

研究过程：调查问卷分为学生卷和教师卷两种，除了个别信息有所不同以外，问卷的内容基本相同。学生问卷首先在高级班30个学生中进行了实验性调查，然后研究者对问卷的一些项目做了调整和修改。正式的调查问卷在不同水平的12个汉语班级发放。共发放调查问卷220份，收回有效问卷104份，有效率为88%。由于学生是在课堂上完成问卷的，一定程度上保证了问卷的回收率和答题质量。教师问卷则采用了当面发放和电子邮件发送两种形式。发出问卷67份，收回67份，有效问卷100%。

2）实验

通过实验来收集数据的研究需要介绍实验设计、实验材料、所用设备和实验程序。实验设计主要介绍实验是基于什么设计的，涉及哪些变量。实验材料主要介绍实验中所使用材料的类型、数量以及相关特征。实验设备主要介绍实验所用的仪器的名称与型号以及所用软件的名称和版本，等等。实验程序主要介绍实验场所、研究对象需要完成的具体任务和实验的具体操作过程。例如，下面是高定国、肖晓云（2005）论文中相关部分的摘录：

实验设计：本实验采用2×3混合实验设计，被试间变量是专业背景，有2个水平，分别为英语专业和非英语专业；被试内变量是英语单词的呈现方式，有3个水平……

实验材料：英语单词90个，单词的难度控制在95%的单词是被试不认识的，长度控制在7个字母左右（7±2）。其中60个作为学习的单词，另外30个作为填充词……国际音标40个，其中20个音标是音标促进条件下单词的正确音标，其余20个是音标干扰条件下单词的错误音标……无意义字符串20个……

仪器和程序：使用由美国匹兹堡大学开发的E-Prime控制实验材料呈现。实验程序在17英寸、分辨率为1024×768的显示器上运行，屏幕高度与被试视线保持水平，被试距离屏幕约60厘米。被试使用反应盒进行反应。实验分为3种条件……每种条件下学习完单词后马上进行再认测验。在学习阶段，每一次计算机屏幕中央首先出现注视点"+"500毫秒，提醒被试实验开始。然后呈现一个音标3000毫秒，紧接着呈现一个英语单词3000毫秒，然后空屏500毫秒。要求被试留意音标和字符串，尽量记住出现的英语单词。在再认测验阶段，每一次屏幕只出现一个英语单词，停留2000毫秒。要求被试在这2000毫秒内尽量迅速且准确地判断该词是否刚才学习过。若学习过，用右手大拇指按"是"键，若没有学习过，用左手大拇指按"否"键。记录被试的反应时以及正确率。

3）观察

通过观察来收集数据的研究需要介绍观察内容、观察方式、具体实施过程等。研究者需要清楚说明实施观察的时长、地点，观察过程中所扮演的角色（旁观者或参与者），观察中使用的设备，观察内容的记录方式（记笔记、录音、录像）等。

4）访谈

使用访谈作为研究工具的研究需要介绍对访谈的设计和访谈过程。访谈设计部分主要介绍访谈的结构和访谈问题的设计，如整个访谈包含几个部分，访谈包含哪些具体问题，以及这些问题是如何设计的、以何种形式呈现等。访谈过程部分主要包括访谈的方式（电话或当面访谈）、访谈的时间地点以及访谈的记录方式（录音或笔录）等。

在具体研究中，单独使用访谈法的研究并不多，一般和其他研究方法配合使用。例如夏珺、王海啸（2014）采用了访谈法和观察法作为研究方法，下面是该论文中对研究方法和步骤介绍的摘录：

> 笔者采用了课堂观察、学习者日记、半结构化访谈等方法，跟踪调查了四位研究对象在该课程背景下的学习过程，具体情况为：
>
> **日记**：学习日记分为阅读后、课堂讨论后和写作后三种形式，学习者可以汇报在"主题式"语言课程中的学习经历、语言点的处理情况、对主题内容的思考以及相关内容和词汇在写作中的运用等任何与"主题"学习相关的内容。
>
> **访谈**：访谈主要针对日记中出现的与本研究相关部分，探讨课程活动，包括课前阅读、课堂讨论、小组汇报、课后写作等活动对于学习者词汇学习的影响，学习者如何在写作过程中提取词汇，习作中所使用与主题相关词汇的来源等。访谈采取面对面和网络相结合的方式，为了让研究对象更充分地表达自己的想法，访谈主要用中文进行。

5）已有资料

定性研究与定量研究都可以使用已有资料法。具体来说，就是从现有的来源中收集数据并将其用于自己的研究中。这个来源可以是公开出版物、归档数据或数据库等。将分析已有资料作为研究方法的研究需要介绍资料的来源和种类、资料的处理方法、筛选资料范围的标准等。

（3）数据分析方法与过程

这个部分介绍对收集好的数据进行分析所采用的方法和过程。由于量化研究法和质性研究法的数据分析方法不同，下面将分别介绍这两种研究方法该部分的写作。

定量研究的数据以数字的形式体现，数据分析部分需详细描述数据的分析前准备工作、统计分析方法和过程以及所使用的统计分析工具。分析前准备工作主要包括去除异常值、检查与处理缺失数据等。常用的统计分析方法主要包括描述性统计分析和推断性统计分析（相关分析、t 检验分析、回归分析、因子分析等）。常用的统计分析工具有 SPSS、R、Amos 等软件，在介绍时不仅要介绍软件名称，还需介绍软件的版本。例如王海贞（2019）的研究使用了描述性统计分析和因子分析，以下是其论文中分析方法部分的摘录：

> 在三校教师的配合下，我们分别收集了问卷和测试数据，专四口试成绩由考试中心提供。对问卷反向计分题目进行处理，对工作记忆、认知风格、语言学能测试进行评分，然后所有数据输入到统计软件 SPSS19.0。首先我们对问卷和测试数据进行效度验证，主成分因子分析结果显示 4 个因子，完全支持三个问卷 11 个子项目的归类，并将三个认知因素（语言学能、工作记忆和认知风格）合并为 1 个因子。语言学能、工作记忆和认知风格三者在 0.01 水平（双侧）上显著正相关。我们将 4 个因子命名为认知能力、情绪智力、外语焦虑和学习动机。随后我们使用结构方程模型分析软件 Amos22.0 进行验证性因子分析，结果显示所有因子载荷值均大于 0.30，可接受。但是观测变量"外在动机"的因子载荷值为 1.05，大于 1，说明存在多重共线性问题，变量之间出现高度相关，可能影响模型估计的准确性。因此我们采用 SPSS 进行共线性诊断，找出并排除了引起共线性的变量，即"外在动机"。

定性研究的数据主要以观察、视频、音频、图像、文字等形式体现。这类研究的数据分析部分介绍对这些数据的处理、分析方式与过程，主要包括研究者是如何组织和分析数据、将大量数据划分成多个类别并从中分析出意义和联系。例如，如表 18.1 所示，夏珺、王海啸（2014）定性研究中数据的分析方法和步骤为：对收集的定性数据（调查对象的日记）进行编码、通过对数据进行分析总结出规律和模式、根据总结出的规律和模式建立模型。

表18.1 质性研究数据分析提纲示范（夏珺、王海啸，2014）

4.6 数据分析
　　4.6.1 进行学习者日记编码
　　4.6.2 鉴定学习者日记和访谈中的词汇产出机制
　　4.6.3 确认二语写作中所产出词汇单元的来源
　　4.6.4 搭建词汇发展模型
　　4.6.5 小结

18.3　结果部分写作

学位论文的结果部分汇报和呈现数据收集和分析的结果，应做到全面、简明、客观、有逻辑性。

首先，结果部分需要把所有与研究问题相关的结果都汇报出来，不能选择性地只汇报符合预期的、好解释的结果而忽略意料之外的或不好解释的结果。

其次，结果部分应只汇报经过分析后与研究问题直接相关的结果，原始数据或分析过程中产生的详细数据虽然重要，但不应在正文中汇报，应以附录或者脚注的形式出现。

另外，结果部分应是对数据分析结果的客观描述。对结果的解释、评价或者推论应放到论文的讨论部分。

最后，结果部分对于结果的汇报顺序应具有逻辑性，一般应按照研究问题的顺序依次汇报相应的研究结果。下面将以定量和定性研究学位论文为例对结果部分的写作进行具体介绍。

（1）定量研究的结果部分写作

定量研究的结果基于对数据的统计分析。统计分析通常包括描述统计分析和推论统计分析（如 t 检验、方差检验、相关分析、因子分析、回归分析、结构方程模型）。数据需满足一定的要求（可靠性、正态分布等）才可进行推论统计分析。因此，定量研究学术论文的结果部分一般先汇报可靠性分析结果和描述分析结果，然后汇报推论统计结果。相关案例如表 18.2 中所示。

表18.2 定量研究结果内容目录示范（马牧青，2018）

5 给养转化因素及路径分析
5.1 引言
5.2 数据筛选与质量评估
5.3 样本特征及各变量描述性统计
5.4 测量模型的检验与分析
5.5 结构方程模型的分析检验
5.6 本章小结

数据的质量评估是数据统计分析的前提，对不符合要求的数据进行统计分析是没有意义的。可靠性分析结果通常包括数据的内部一致性和数据的分布情况。常用的用于检测数据内部一致性的是克隆巴赫系数（Cronbach's alpha），和数据分布情况相关的是一些描述性统计分析数据（峰度、曲度等）。除此之外，描述统计分析结果还包括数据的平均值、中位数、众数、标准差等。这些数值均需要被汇报出来。为了达到直观的效果，除了文字，通常还会将上述数值通过表格呈现出来。例如，下面两段分别是马牧青（2018）论文中对可靠性分析结果和描述性统计分析结果的汇报节选。

例 18.1 数据质量评估结果汇报范例

表1　正态检验各变量指标汇总（p.143）

变量	最小值	最大值	偏度	临界比率	峰度	临界比率
FC03	1.000	5.000	−0.171	−1.673	−0.226	−1.107
FC02	1.000	5.000	−0.005	−0.053	−0.123	−0.604
……	……	……	……	……	……	……
B102	2.000	5.000	−0.393	−2.846	0.398	1.949
……	……	……	……	……	……	……
PA2	2.000	5.000	0.238	−2.334	0.868	4.250
……	……	……	……	……	……	……
RISE2	1.000	5.000	−0.532	−2.208	−0.737	−3.610
……	……	……	……	……	……	……
多变量					33.150	8.040

由表1可知，单因素偏度系数从 −0.053 到 −2.846，均小于临界值3；单因素峰度系数从 −3.61 到 4.25，均小于临界值8。同时，多变量峰度系数为 8.04<10，可判定总体样本呈多元正态分布，符合进行下一步的模型拟合。

例 18.2 描述性统计分析结果汇报范例

表2　统计性分析结果（p.144）

变量	N	最小值	最大值	均值	标准差
感知教学给养	629	1	5	3.908	0.565
……	……	……	……	……	……

从表 2 可知，潜变量中感知社交给养（M=3.976）和感知教学给养（3.908）的均值最高，其次教学自我效能感（M=3.807）、资源选择自我效能感（M=3.873）以及行为意图（M=3.813）的均值也较高。相对而言，教师对便利条件（M=3.036）的感知程度中等。

数据的推论统计分析通常分为两大类：一类用来比较群组之间的异同，如 t 检验；另一类用于探索变量之间的关系，如相关分析和回归分析。对推论统计分析结果的汇报需与研究问题相对应，依次提供每个研究问题的相关结果。汇报内容需包含统计分析结果的精确值和附加信息，如 p 值（相关性分析）、R 平方值（回归分析）、显著性水平等。除了用文字汇报，通常也会使用表格、图表来辅助补充文字，将结果更直观地呈现给读者。例如，下面是胡杰辉、许婷（2020）在论文中对回归分析结果汇报的一段节选。

表18.3　被试英语水平与外语效应量的回归分析结果

| 效应量指标 | 社会规范类型 | 非标准化系数 | | | | 标准化系数 B | T | P 值 |
		常量 B	SE	B	SE			
接受度变化	高度符合	−0.548	0.144	0.062	0.026	0.318	2.42	0.019
	高度违反	0.554	0.153	−0.029	0.027	−0.145	−1.06	0.296
反应时变化	高度符合	715	234	−32	42	−0.108	−0.78	0.438
	高度违反	998	223	−48	40	−0.165	−1.20	0.234

为了进一步精确测定语言水平对外语效应的影响，我们将被试的外语测试成绩与其对应的外语效应量各项指标进行回归分析，结果如表 18.3 所示。可以看出，高度符合和高度违反社会规范行为的外语效应量与外语水平的相关性存在差异。其中，外语水平与高度符合社会规范行为的接受度外语效应量具有显著的线性相关关系（p = 0.019，r = 0.318）。而另外三个因变量的标准化系数均不具有显著性，p 值均大于 0.05，表明外语水平与高度违反社会规范行为的接受度外语效应量不相关，与各类社会规范加工时间变化的效应量均不相关。

（2）定性研究的结果部分写作
定性研究的结果部分应汇报对研究所收集质性数据（观察、笔记、录音、录像等）的分析结果。

定性研究结果部分通常与研究问题相对应，根据研究问题分成若干个章节或子章节。每个（子）章节的内容通常基于对数据分析所形成的主题进一步划分。需要注意的是，不是所有的定性研究都按照这个组织顺序汇报结果，具体的汇报方式取决于不同的研究，没有统一的格式。如历时定性研究会采取时间顺序而非主题顺序。

尽管组织结构有所不同，以下两点是写作定性研究的结果部分时普遍需要遵循的。首先，与基于数字和统计分析的定量研究不同，定性研究的结果主要以文字的形式呈现，偶尔也可以辅以图表，但需要注意的是，这些图表应用于辅助阐释难以完全靠文本描述的概念或关系，而不应该用来重复文本。其次，汇报的结果必须是经过分析和综合的。可以使用相关调查对象的回答、日志、研究者的记录等来支撑经过分析和综合后的结果和发现，但不能是原始数据的简单堆砌。例如，胡杰辉、伍忠杰（2014）在分析了定性访谈数据后，是这样汇报学生眼中 MOOC 教学设计对学习的促进作用的：

> 访谈显示，MOOC 教学设计对学习的促进作用集中体现在三方面。第一，教学模式满足了学习者的个性化需求，学习时间和空间更加灵活。访谈中，学生反映 MOOC 学习"能方便、反复地学习课文知识，灵活度很高"；"想停就停，能更多学习单词"。第二，课程内容的学习方式更加有效。例如，学生反映授课视频使"预习中问题得到解决，帮助分析文章内容"；"学习了词汇，提高了听力，对提高英语水平有很大帮助"。第三，满足了部分学生的情感学习策略需求。有学生反映网上学习可以训练听力，"并且没有实际课堂的压力"，显示出 MOOC 对部分基础较差，暂时害怕或羞于课堂口语表达的中国学习者有意想不到的帮助（p. 43）。

18.4　讨论部分写作

"讨论"是学位论文中不可或缺的一环。在这个部分，研究者需要对研究结果和发现进行深度而详细的解读、分析和评价。一般来说讨论部分应包含以下几部分内容：① 对主要研究结果的总结；② 对研究结果的讨论和解释；③ 研究结果的主要启示；④ 研究的局限性；⑤ 对未来研究的建议。

（1）对主要研究结果的总结
这个部分回顾研究问题并总结研究的主要结果。由于研究问题和结果在前文已经详细地介绍过，这里的回顾和总结主要用于帮助读者（尤其是没有完整阅读前文内容的读者）跟上研究者讨论部分的思路，以达到更好的阅读效果。因此，这个部分一般仅用一个自然段的篇幅简洁扼要地概括研究问题，总结用以回答研究问题的主要结果。例如，徐锦芬、寇金南（2018）在论文讨论部分的开头是这样总结研究的主要结果的：

> 本文通过实证调查揭示了任务类型对大学生英语课堂小组互动的影响。研究发现，从小组互动的平等性来讲，在对小组互动贡献程度的三个维度中，任务类型仅对学习者产出的话轮数量有明显影响，拼图任务产出的数量最少，话题讨论任务最多，整体听写任务居中，其中拼图任务和话题讨论任务之间的差异显著（p=.007）。

（2）对研究结果的讨论和解释

未经讨论和解读的研究结果对于研究者可能是显而易见且容易理解的，但是对读者而言并非如此，他们会想知道为什么会有这样的结果。这个部分通过提供合理的讨论和解读来向读者解释研究结果。常用的讨论和解读方式有两种：第一种是与相关理论进行关联讨论，用理论来解释和支撑研究结果；另一种是与已有研究进行关联讨论，用类似结果来解释和支撑当前的研究结果，或者通过分析和讨论来解释和其他研究结果不同的原因。下面的两个例子分别节选自夏珺、王海啸（2014）和王海贞（2019）论文的讨论部分，就分别使用到了这两种讨论和解读方式。

例 18.3

Laufer (2001) 的"投入量假说"（involvement load hypothesis）提出，影响第二语言学习过程中词汇习得有三个因素：需求（need）、搜寻（search）和评估（evaluation）。Laufer 和 Hulstijn 的实验研究了三种阅读任务（阅读理解、阅读理解加完形填空以及用目标词写作）对学习者词汇附带习得的影响，结果表明，投入量最大的"用目标词写作"最能促进词汇附带习得和记忆。在"主题式"语言课程的课后写作任务中，需求、搜寻和评估这三个因素影响着学习者的词汇提取。"需求"即指学习者在写作过程中需要一些词汇准确表达自己的意思；在这一需求驱动下，学习者"搜寻"所有可能提取的词汇，除了搜寻大脑中已记忆的词汇，他们也会通过翻阅已阅读材料或笔记、查词典或求助于权威来搜寻可能的词汇；最后，学习者会对所有提取的词汇进行"评估"，即对目标词和其他词的比较，或通过该词与其他词的搭配判定其是否符合特定语境。同时，学习者根据所提取词汇的知识掌握程度，选取不同的词汇提取机制。"已记忆词汇的直接使用""借用""内容削减"等机制都有可能被采用。

例 18.4

焦虑被视作语言学习中的情感障碍，阻碍语言输入的完全吸收（Krashen, 1981, 1985），因此国内普遍接受的观点是焦虑负面影响语言学习结果，但本研究得出相反的结果，焦虑程度越高的学习者其口语成绩越高，焦虑与口语成绩具有弱度正相关性，其直接效应值为 0.16。我们的解释有以下三点：1）焦虑分为促进性和退缩性两种。本研究的对象是大学生，具有中高级的英语水平，其心理趋于成熟且英语能力较强，促进性焦虑占上风，能够挑战学习任务，将考试场景的压力或焦虑转化为动力，克服焦虑感，从而充分发挥其语言水平，并最终给口语成绩带来正面影响。Papi (2010) 对 1011 名高中生的实证研究也发现，外语焦虑有助于学生更加投入地学习。

（3）结果的主要启示

这个部分是对研究结果启示的评价，一般包含理论启示和实践启示两个方面。评价研究结果的理论启示时，需将现有研究结果与相关理论或前人的研究发现进行关联讨论。如果结果相一致，则为理论提供了新的证据；如果不一致，则可由此对理论进行反思，丰富我们对问题的认识。此外，通过与前人研究横向（比较同类研究研究结果的异同）与纵向（观察与前人研究研究重点的异同）的对比也可以体现出当前研究在理论上的贡献（解决了什么争议、填补了什么空白）。评价研究结果的实践启示时，需明确指出这一结果如何对现实情况或应用方面有益。例如，在评价二语教学研究论文的实践启示时，需要说明研究发现对教学的贡献具体体现在何处。

（4）研究的局限性

这个部分陈述当前研究的局限性。所有的研究都存在局限性，且局限性可能出现在研究的任何一个环节，如由于研究规模的原因，当前研究没能同时考虑到某些重要因素，以至于得出的结论不够全面；由于现实操作的一些限制，数据收集过程中存在一些不足，等等。需要客观、具体地承认这些不足并说明可能造成的影响。

（5）对未来研究的建议

这个部分是对未来研究方向的建议。建议的提出一般是两个来源。一是来源于研究结果。当研究结果与前人研究不一致时，为了验证推测的原因（如采用的测量工具不同），往往会建议进行进一步研究（使用相同的测量工具）。另一个来源于现有研究的局限性。基于当前研究中的不足，对未来研究提出清晰、具体的建议，如由于样本量太小而不能使用某些分析工具（如结构方程模型）的研究常常会建议未来研究扩大样本量。

18.5　结论部分写作

结论是学位论文的最后一个部分。这个部分的写作应做到精炼、准确、逻辑性强，汇报的内容包括主要研究结果和发现、当前研究的主要贡献、研究的局限性以及对未来研究的建议（相关示例见表18.4）。

表18.4　学术论文结论内容目录示范（马蓉，2015）

```
8 结论
  8.1 主要的研究发现
  8.2 理论启示
  8.3 教学启示
  8.4 本研究的不足
  8.5 未来研究
  8.6 本章小结
```

虽然结论部分和讨论部分的内容模块类似，但是具体内容并不相同，不可将讨论部分的内容照搬到结论中来。

首先，在结论部分汇报主要研究结果和发现时，不需要像讨论部分那样详细列出所有和研究问题相关的结果，也不需要使用行话和统计数字，而是用简明扼要的语言对最重要的研究结果进行提炼、概括与总结。最常见的做法是根据研究问题的顺序汇报主要的研究成果。这里只需汇报大的研究问题，而无须展开回答大研究问题下的小细节问题。此外，也可以不按照研究问题来汇报结果，而是对主要的研究发现进行总结和归纳。

其次，结论部分的当前研究的主要贡献与局限性以及对未来研究的建议部分也与讨论部分的不同。在讨论部分的相关内容都是围绕具体研究结果来阐述的，比较详细，但是由于位于不同段落且没有经过归纳和总结，很难给读者一个整体的印象。在结论部分的相关内容则应该是经过概括和整合的，让读者对研究的主要内容（主要有什么结果与发现、这些结果和发现解决了什么理论或实践的问题、研究还有什么遗留问题或不足、对后续研究有何建议）有一个宏观的认识。

下面的示例节选自杜文博、马晓梅（2021）论文的结论部分，虽然和学位论文相比，学术论文的篇幅短很多，但是可以看出结论部分的内容组成还是一样的，示例的四个自然段分别汇报了论文的主要结果和发现、当前研究的主要贡献、研究的局限性以及对未来研究的建议。

> 本研究采用混合认知诊断模型深入剖析了 8 个二语阅读技能间的内在关系，结果表明：不同技能间确实存在补偿与非补偿并存的关系，且这种内在关系在高低水平组的表征存在显著性差异。
>
> 研究结果对理解二语阅读的本质、阅读测试的编制及阅读教学具有重要的指导意义。二语阅读并非简单的线性解码过程，而是多种因素共同交互的结果。认知诊断能够较为准确地剥离这些微观因素，并探究其内在关系，从而厘清阅读加工的本质。本文提出的动态复杂补偿模型一定程度弥补了单一补偿模型的不足，以期能够进一步完善二语阅读理论模型。另外，在编制阅读测试时，学科专家也应将不同技能间的交互关系考虑在内，从而提高阅读测试的构念效度。而针对不同水平的学生，在阅读教学时也可根据阅读技能间的关系，对其掌握较弱的阅读技能进行配对指导，实施更具针对性的补救教学。
>
> 本研究的局限性在于：1）主要基于定量数据分析，可能存在一定误差。未来研究可设计相关质性研究或采用眼动、事件相关电位（ERP）和功能性核磁共振（fMIR）进一步探讨阅读加工的本质。2）本研究仅探讨了二语语言知识与策略技能间的交互关系，而未对背景知识和一语阅读技能在阅读中的具体作用及其关系进行挖掘。所提出的动态复杂补偿模型还有待更多实证研究验证。
>
> 未来研究可开展涉及更多因素的实验研究，更加全面地揭示二语阅读认知加工的内在机制。

课堂讨论

1. 假设你的研究题目是"X 教学法对大学生英语口语表达准确性影响的实证研究"。具体的研究问题是"X 教学法是否对大学生英语口语表达准确性有影响？"。那么，你的理论框架部分可能包含以下哪些内容？除了下面列出的选项外，还可以有哪些内容？与同学讨论后尝试列出该研究理论框架部分的章节目录。

    (1) X 教学法定义
    (2) X 教学法相关理论
    (3) 二语口语表达准确性维度
    (4) 二语口语表达准确性相关理论
    (5) 大学生英语能力定义
    (6) 二语写作输出准确性维度

2. 某学位论文的研究题目是"大学生二语写作策略分析"，下面是他论文中方法论部分的节选。请与同学讨论后帮他列出其中存在的问题。

    二、研究方法及过程
    2.1 研究对象
    　　参加本研究的受试是中国一所大学的学生，平均年龄 20 岁。
    2.2 研究工具
    　　研究工具为调查问卷和访谈。问卷采用李克特量表，让受试对每道题的选项做出从"这个表述完全适合我的情况"到"这个表述完全不适合我的情况"的选择，并在 1 到 5 的数字上画圈。问卷调查结束后，笔者根据需要对部分学生进行面对面的访谈。
    2.3 数据收集与分析
    　　问卷于 2022 年 9 月通过电子邮件发放，全部收回，有效率为 90%。所有数据均输入计算机，并运用 SPSS2.0 进行了多项分析。

3. 下列语料来自徐锦芬、寇金南（2017）《大学英语课堂小组互动模式研究》
   一文，是对四个小组课堂互动录音文稿的摘录。请与同学讨论并分析该
   语料，总结出四个小组各自的互动模式并汇报结果。

摘录 1

181 1-*T-a*: I think Lei Feng spirit is still fashionable.

182 1-*T-b*: Why?

183 1-*T-a*: Because it's a spirit, it can't out of date.

184 1-*T-d*: I don't know why he has altruism.

185 1-*T-c*: Altruism?

186 1-*T-b*: 利他主义.

187 1-*T-d*: Yeah. I don't know why.

181 1-*T-a*: Because he is an angel.

189 1-*T-d*: I just think it's amazing.

190 I-*T-c*: Why? Lei Feng's spirits means helping others.

191 1-*T-d*: Yeah, helping others, but …

192 1-*T-b*: A child and he …

193 I-*T-a*: He is a child with no family, but always help others.

194 1-*T-d*: I can't believe it.

195 5-*T-b*: But it's a truth.

摘录 2

431 5-*J-a*: Now who is the first?

432 5-*J-b*: OK! I'm the first. Message in the picture said people extrovert who are outgoing … (略). OK, that's all.

433 5-*J-a*: As for me, I don't quite agree with your opinion in the characteristic of an extrovert. I think … (略). The next.

434 5-*J-c*: And I talk about the fourth question. I think the picture tells us the jobs that suits extroverts and introverts … (略). That's all.

435 5-*J-a*: It's your turn.

43 5-*J-d*: I want to talk the three question. I think I am a really introvert man. When I take part in some activities, I am always playing my cellphone … (略). That's all.

摘录 3

953 10-J-a: *Ok, let's start our discussion. Who can tell me how do you understand the message in the picture?*

954 10-J-b: *Er, I think the message in the picture, er, was, in some degrees, er, much incorrect. Because … (略). Er, so, that's all.*

955 10-J-c: *Well, from the picture I think it shows different er, er different facing different jobs.*

956 10-J-a: *That's all?*

957 10-J-c: *En.*

957 10-J-d: *Er, I think this picture, this picture shows different people shows two kinds of chacter characteristics of people … (略).*

959 10-J-a: *In my opinion, this picture show shows us people with different characters have different jobs that are suitable for them …(略).*

摘录 4

870 8-T-a: *Before we start the debation, I want to know: Is everyone clear about what we're going to do next?*

871 8-T-d: *Yes, we know we need to have a discussion about Lei Feng's spirit.*

872 8-T-a: *Yeah, OK. Now, who would like to be the first to share with us his idea?*

873 8-T-bcd: *You …*

874 8-T-a: *Ok! In my opinion, there is no doubt that Lei Feng is a good example … (略).*

875 8-T-d: *Pardon? Can you say that again? I can't get it.*

876 8-T-a: *Say it again? OK, the main idea about mine is that … (略). Is everybody clear?*

877 8-T-bcd: *Yes.*

878 8-T-a: *Now, right, would anyone like to add more on?*

879 8-T-d: *I'm very glad to hear you say that. But in my opinion … (略).*

880 8-T-a: *If I understand correctly, you mean … (略).*

881 8-T-d: *Yes, yes.*

882 8-T-a: *OK, anyone else?*

883 8-T-c: *Yes, I agree with Wu Can. But … (略).*

884 8-T-a: *So, what you are saying is … (略).*

885 8-T-c: *Yes, and I think we shouldn't take up the whole Lei Feng's spirit and …* (略).

886 8-T-a: *OK, Wang Peng?*

887 8-T-b: *Now that so many Chinese leaders have thought highly of Lei Feng's spirit, I agree with the idea of Wu Peng that … (略).*

4. 下面的选段来自胡杰辉、许婷（2020）《中国英语学习者社会规范加工的外语效应机制》一文的讨论部分。与同学一起讨论下列问题：

(1) 论文的讨论部分一般包括对主要研究结果的总结、对研究结果的讨论和解释、研究结果的主要意义、研究的局限性与不足以及对未来研究的建议几个部分。这段讨论节选涉及哪几个部分？分别汇报了什么内容？

(2) 这段讨论节选在解释和讨论研究结果时采用了什么方式？有无说服力？为什么？

　　本研究拟回答的第二个研究问题是不同类型社会规范信息的外语效应机制是否存在差异，特别是外语水平是否与其存在交互作用。结果表明，不同类型社会规范信息的外语效应机制存在差异。具体而言，虽然高低水平组中国英语学习者在社会规范信息加工时均表现出了明显的外语效应，但两组被试在不同类型社会行为中的外语效应量不同。低水平组被试对高度符合和高度违反社会规范的行为评价均表现出显著的外语效应，而高水平组被试只在高度违反社会规范的情况下表现出了显著性差异。对被试外语水平与外语效应关系的结果表明，外语水平仅与高度符合社会规范行为接受度的外语效应量显著负相关。这一结果与已有研究结果一致，特别是有助于我们理解为何部分已有研究中没有发现明显的外语效应（Hayakawa et al. 2017; Čavar & Tytus 2018）。例如 Čavar & Tytus (2018) 发现高水平克罗地亚－德语双语者在两种语言模式下进行道德判断时没有表现出显著性差异。本研究结果表明，上述研究结果可能与被试较高的二语水平有关系，虽然上述研究中的被试主要为晚期二语学习者，但他们在二语文化环境下生活多年，二语水平已经接近母语者了。本研究的回归分析结果表明，语言水平与外语效应量显著相关，语言水平对外语效应存在着一定的预测作用，因此随着二语水平的增加，外语效应会逐渐减弱，甚至消失，未来研究可以选取高水平的平衡双语者对此进行验证。

5. 某学位论文的研究题目是"X教学法有效性研究"。下面是作者为结论部
   分写的提纲。与同学讨论其中存在的问题并提出修改建议。

主要研究结果：
(1) 使用 X 教学法的实验组和使用常规教学法的对照组后测成绩的差异。
(2) 使用 X 教学法的实验组受试的采访摘录。

当前研究的主要贡献：
(1) 对提高教学质量有指导意义。

研究的局限性：
(1) 样本太少。
(2) 实验组和对照组的前测成绩有明显差异。
(3) 实验组比对照组的教学时间长。

对未来的建议：
(1) 增加样本量

课外练习

1. 找一本学位论文，阅读其中的理论框架部分后回答下列问题：
   (1) 有没有确定关键概念？
   (2) 有没有评价和解释相关理论？
   (3) 有没有说明当前研究与相关理论的联系？
   (4) 你觉得这个部分写得如何？能不能提一些修改建议？

2. 假设你想研究任务类型对大学英语课堂上小组互动的影响，你会采取什
   么研究方法？选择什么样的研究对象？具体收集哪些数据？如何收集？

研究过程是什么样的？该用何种方式分析收集到的数据？回答上面的问题，并根据你的答案写出这个研究的方法论部分。

3. 表18.5中的数据来自王艳（2008）《基于认知框架的二语学生听力理解困难分析》一文，用于回答"大学生英语听力理解的主要困难是什么"这一研究问题。分析表中的数据，从认知的三个阶段来汇报这个部分的结果。

表18.5　结论部分课外练习范例

学生在各阶段存在的困难	一年级		二年级	
	平均值	标准差	平均值	标准差
感知处理阶段				
1. 语速快的时候，面对一长串的语音流，我难以将其切分成单词或词组来理解。	3.54	1.01	3.28	0.80
2. 我的词汇量太少，这令我的听力理解能力受到影响。	3.44	1.01	3.28	1.03
3. 遇到词与词之间的连读或音的省略，我会以为遇到了生词，在理解上造成障碍。	3.26	0.83	3.07	0.88
4. 有时听到某个单词的发音却反应不过来意思，影响了听力理解，后来发现并不是生词。	3.18	0.97	3.30	0.96
5. 遇到令人不习惯的语音语调时，自己的听力理解会出现困难。	3.08	0.92	3.33	0.71
6. 听到不熟悉的单词或词组我很快就分神了，难以集中注意力去听下面的材料。	3.08	0.82	3.10	0.86
解析阶段				
1. 听英语时，经常是前面的句子还没记住，后面的句子又来了，令人应接不暇。	3.31	0.96	3.13	0.85
2. 我会因为前面的听力理解遇到了障碍，而影响了后面的理解。	3.28	0.80	3.02	0.75
3. 我常会因为去回忆某个单词或句子的意思而错过其他内容，以致影响整篇理解。	3.08	1.04	3.13	0.96
使用阶段				
1. 有时听完一个段落，觉得听懂了，却不清楚它到底要表达什么关键意义、基本思想（key ideas）。	2.93	0.89	2.75	0.77

4. 找一本学位论文，阅读其中的讨论部分并回答下列问题：

   (1) 论文的讨论部分一般包括对主要研究结果的总结、对研究结果的讨论和解释、研究结果的主要意义、研究的局限性与不足以及对未来研究的建议几个部分。这本论文的讨论部分涉及哪几个方面？分别汇报了什么内容？

   (2) 这段论文在解释和讨论研究结果时采用了什么方式？有无说服力？为什么？

   (3) 你觉得这个部分写得如何？能不能提一些修改建议？

5. 结论部分和结果部分有什么相同点和不同点？结论部分和讨论部分有什么相同点和不同点？先独立思考，再找一本学位论文，阅读其中的结果、讨论和结论部分来验证你的看法是否正确。

拓展阅读

Germaine, R. W. (2019). *A concise guide to writing a thesis or dissertation: Educational research and beyond*. London: Routledge.

Litosseliti, L. (Ed.). (2010). *Research methods in linguistics*. London: Continuum.

李武、毛远逸、肖东发. (2020). 学位论文写作与学术规范. 北京：北京大学出版社.

文秋芳. (2004). 应用语言学研究方法与论文写作. 北京：外语教学与研究出版社.

参考文献

Adger, D. (2003). *Core syntax: A minimalist approach*. Oxford: Oxford University Press.

Alyami, M., & Mohsen, M. A. (2019). The use of a reading lexicon to aid contextual vocabulary acquisition by EFL Arab learners. *Journal of Psycholinguistic Research*.

Arfé, B., Delatorre, P., & Mason, L. (2022). Effects of negative emotional valence on readers' text processing and memory for text: An eye-tracking study. *Reading and Writing*.

Aronoff, M., & Kudeman, F. (2011). *What is morphology?* Oxford: Wiley-Blackwell.

Austin, J. L. (1962). *How to do things with words*. Oxford: Oxford University Press.

Baker, P., Gabrielatos, C., Khosravinik, M., Krzyzanowski, M., McEnery, T., & Wodak, R. (2008). A useful methodological synergy? Combining critical discourse analysis and corpus linguistics to examine discourses of refugees and asylum seekers in the UK press. *Discourse & Society, 19*(3), 273–306.

Baecher, L., & McCormack, B. (2015). The impact of video review on supervisory conferencing. *Language and Education, 29*(2), 153–173.

Bećirović, S., Brdarević-Čeljo, A., & Delić, H. (2021). The use of digital technology in foreign language learning. *SN Social Sciences, 1*, 246.

Berelson, B. (1952). *Content analysis in communication research*. New York: The Free Press.

Borer, H. (2005). *Structuring sense (Volume 1): In name only*. Oxford: Oxford University Press.

Braun, V., & Clarke, V. (2006). Using thematic analysis in psychology. *Qualitative Research in Psychology, 3*(2), 77–101.

Cavell, S. (1965). Aesthetic problems of modern philosophy. In M. Black (Ed.). *Philosophy in America*. Ithaca, NY: Cornell University Press. (Reprinted in S. Cavell (Ed.). (1976). *Must we mean what we say?* (pp. 73–96). Cambridge: Cambridge University Press.)

Charmaz, K., (2006). *Constructing grounded theory: A practical guide through qualitative analysis*. London: Sage.

Chen, F., & Wang, X. (2022). Oops! I can't express this in English: Managing epistemic challenges by Chinese EFL peer tutors in writing tutorials. *Text & Talk*, *43*(1), 1–20.

Chomsky, N. (1964). Current issues in linguistic theory. In J. Fodor, & J. Katz (Eds.). *The structure of language* (pp. 50–118). Englewood Cliffs: Prentice Hall.

Chomsky, N. (1973). Conditions on transformations. In S. Anderson & P. Kiparsky (Eds.). *A festschrift for Morris Halle* (pp. 232–286). New York: Hott, Reinhart & Winston.

Chomsky, N. (1977). On wh-movement. In P. Culicover, T. Wasow, & A. Akmajian (Eds.). *Formal syntax* (pp. 71–132). New York: Academic Press.

Chomsky, N. (1981). *Lectures on government and binding.* Dordrecht: Foris.

Chomsky, N. (2013). *Problems of projection.* Lingua, *130*, 33–49.

Chomsky, N., Roberts, I., & Watumull, J. The false promise of ChatGPT. *New York Times*, March 8, 2023.

Clark, J., & Yallop, C. (2000). *An introduction to phonetics and phonology.* Beijing: Foreign Language Teaching and Research Press.

Clayman, S. E., & Gill, V. T. (2012). Conversation analysis. In P. G. Gee, & M. Handford (Eds.). *The Routledge handbook of discourse analysis* (pp. 120–134). London: Routledge.

Cohen, J. (1988). *Statistical power analysis for the behavioural sciences* (2nd edition). Hillsdale: Lawrence, Erlbaum Associates.

Collins, A. M., & Loftus, E. P. (1975). A spreading activation theory of semantic processing. *Psychological Review*, *82*, 407–428.

Corbin, J., & Strauss, A. (2014). *Basics of qualitative research: Techniques and procedures for developing grounded theory.* London: Sage.

Creswell, J. W., & Creswell, J. D. (2018). *Research design: Qualitative, quantitative, and mixed methods approaches.* London: Sage.

Crystal, D. (2010). *The Cambridge encyclopedia of language* (Vol. 3). Cambridge: Cambridge University Press.

Csizér, K., & Kontra, E. H. (2020). Foreign language learning characteristics of deaf and severely hard-of-hearing students. *The Modern Language Journal*, *104* (1), 232–249.

Curl, T. (2006). Offers of assistance: Constraints on syntactic design. *Journal of Pragmatics, 38*, 1257–1280.

Curl, T., & Drew, P. (2008). Contingency and action: A comparison of two forms of requesting. *Research on Language and Social Interaction*, *41*, 1–25.

Davies, A., & Elder, C. (Eds.). (2008). *The handbook of applied linguistics*. New York: John Wiley & Sons.

Dong, J. (2018). Taste, discourse and middle-class identity: An ethnography of Chinese Saabists. *Journal of Sociolinguistics*, *22*(4), 432–453.

Drew, P. (2005). Conversation analysis. In K. L. Fitch, & R. E. Sanders (Eds.). *Handbook of language and social interaction* (pp. 71–102). New Jersey & London: Lawrence Erlbaum Associates, Publishers.

Drew, P. (2013a). Turn design. In J. Sidnell, & T. Stivers (Eds.). *The handbook of conversation analysis* (pp. 131–149). London: Wiley-Blackwell.

Drew, P. (2013b). Conversation analysis and social action. 外国语, *36*(3), 2–19.

Drew, P. (2022). The micro-politics of social actions. In A. Deppermann, & M. Haugh (Eds.). *Action ascription in interaction* (pp. 57–80). Cambridge: Cambridge University Press.

Drew, P., Ostermann, A. C. & Raymond, C. W. (forthcoming). Conversation analysis as a comparative methodology. In J. D. Robinson, R. Clift, K. H. Kendrick, & C. Raymond (Eds.). *The Cambridge handbook of methods in conversation analysis*. Cambridge: Cambridge University Press.

Einstein, A. (1930). Religion and science. *New York Times*, November 19, 1930.

Fuoli, M., & Paradis, C. (2014). A model of trust-repair discourse. *Journal of Pragmatics*, *74*, 52–69.

Gazzaniga, M. S., Ivry, R. B., & Mangun, G. R. (2019). *Cognitive neuroscience: The biology of the mind* (5th Edition). New York: W. W. Norton & Company.

Garfinkel, H. (1967). *Studies in Ethnomethodology*. Englewood Cliffs, NJ: Prentice-Hall.

Gee, J. P. (2011). How to do discourse analysis: A toolkit (2nd edition). London: Routledge.

Glaser, B., & Strauss, A. (1967). *The discovery of Grounded Theory: Strategies for qualitative research*. Chicago: Aldine.

Goffman, E. (1967). *Interactional ritual: Essays on face-to-face behaviour*. Chicago: Aldine Publishing Company.

Grainger, J., & Frenck-Mestre, C. (1998). Masked priming by translation equivalents in proficient bilinguals. *Language and Cognitive Processes*, *13*(6), 601–623.

Grice, H. (1975). Logic and conversation. In P. Cole, & J. Morgan (Eds.). *Syntax and semantics*. (pp. 41–58). New York: Academic Press.

Hagoort, P., Brown, C., & Groothusen, J. (1993). The syntactic positive shift (SPS) as an ERP measure of syntactic processing. *Language and Cognitive Processes*, *8*, 439–483.

Hagoort, P., Hald, L., Bastiaansen, M., & Petersson, K. M. (2004). Integration of word meaning and world knowledge in language comprehension. *Science*, *304*, 438–441.

Heritage, J. (1988). Explanations as accounts: A conversation analytic perspective. In C. Antaki (Eds.). *Analysing everyday explanation: A coursebook of methods* (pp. 127–144). London: Sage.

Heritage, J., & Drew, P. (2006). *Conversation analysis*. London: Sage Publications.

Heritage, J., & Drew, P. (Eds.). (2013). *Contemporary studies in conversation analysis* (4 volumes). London: Sage Publications.

Hoey, E. M., & Kendrick, K. H. (2018). Conversation analysis. In M. B. de Groot, & P. Hagoort (Eds.). *Research methods in psycholinguistics and the neurobiology of language* (pp. 151–173). New York: John Wiley & Sons.

Holmes, J. (2013). *An introduction to sociolinguistics* (4th edition). London: Routledge.

Howell, D. C. (2013). *Fundamental statistics for the behavioral sciences* (8th edition). Belmont: Thomson Wadsworth.

Huang, C.-T. James. (1982). *Logical relations in Chinese and the theory of grammar*. MIT: Ph.D. dissertation.

Igwebuike, E., & Chimuanya, L. (2020). Legitimating falsehood in social media: A discourse analysis of potential fake news. *Discourse & Communication*, *15*(1), 42–58.

Jefferson, G. (2004). Glossary of transcript symbols with an introduction. In G. H. Lerner (Eds.). *Conversation analysis: Studies from the first generation* (pp. 13–31). Amsterdam: John Benjamins Publishing Company.

Jegerski, J., & VanPatten, B. (2014). *Research methods in second language psycholinguistics*. New York: Routledge.

Khairallah, M., & Adra, O. (2022). The multifaceted function of rubrics as formative assessment tools: A classroom-based action research in an L2 writing context. *Language Teaching Research*, 1–18.

Kolhatkar, V., Wu, H., Cavasso, L., Francis, E., Shukla, K., & Taboada, M. (2020). The SFU opinion and comments corpus: A corpus for the analysis of online news comments. *Corpus Pragmatics, 4*(2), 155–190.

Kuhn, T. S. (1962). *The structure of scientific revolutions* (1st edition). Chicago: University of Chicago Press.

Kutas, M., & Federmeier, K. D. (2011). Thirty years and counting: Finding meaning in the N400 component of the event-related brain potential (ERP). *Annual Review of Psychology, 62,* 621–647.

Kutas, M., & Hillyard, S. A. (1980). Reading senseless sentences: Brain potentials reflect semantic incongruity. *Science, 207,* 203–205.

Larson, R. K. (2009). *Grammar as science.* Boston: MIT Press.

Leech, G. (1992). Corpora and theories of linguistic performance. *Directions in Corpus Linguistics,* 105–122.

Lenhard, W., & Lenhard, A. (2016). Computation of effect sizes. *Psychometrica.*

Li, W. (2011). Moment analysis and translanguaging space: Discursive construction of identities by multilingual Chinese youth in Britain. *Journal of Pragmatics, 43*(5), 1222–1235.

Mackey, A., & Gass, S. M. (2005). *Second language research: Methodology and design.* Mahwah, New Jersey: Lawrence Erlbaum Associates.

McEnery, T., & Wilson, A. (2003). Corpus linguistics. *The Oxford Handbook of Computational Linguistics,* 448–463.

Merton, R. (1996). *On social structure and science.* Chicago: University of Chicago Press.

Mitchell, W. K. (1990). On comparisons in a notional grammar. *Applied Linguistics, 11*(1), 52–72.

Mondada, L. (2022). Conventions for multimodal transcription. Retrieved online.

Münte, T. F., Heine, H., & Mangun, G. R. (1993). Dissociation of brain activity related to semantic and syntactic aspects of language. *Journal of Cognitive Neuroscience, 5,* 335–344.

Nowell, L. S., Norris, J. M., White, D. E., & Moules, N. J. (2017). Thematic analysis: Striving to meet the trustworthiness criteria. *International Journal of Qualitative Methods, 16*(1).

Osterhout, L., & Holcomb, P. J. (1992). Event-related brain potentials elicited by syntactic anomaly. *Journal of Memory and Language, 31*(6), 785–806.

Pomerantz, A. (1984). Agreeing and disagreeing with assessments: Some features of preferred/dispreferred turn shapes. In J. M. Atkinson, & J. Heritage (Eds.). *Structures of social actions: Studies in conversation analysis* (pp. 57–101). Cambridge: Cambridge University Press.

Pomerantz, A. (1986). Extreme case formulation: A way of legitimizing claims. *Human Studies, 9*, 219–229.

Pomerantz, A., & B. J. Fehr. (1997). Conversation analysis: An approach to the study of social action as sense making practices. In T. A. van Dijk (Ed.). *Discourse as social interaction* (pp. 64–71). London: Sage Publications.

Popper, K. (1959). *The logic of scientific discovery.* London: Routledge.

Punch, K. F. (1998). *Introduction to social research: Quantitative and qualitative approaches.* London: Sage.

Qin, J., & Lei, L. (2022). Research trends in task-based language teaching: A bibliometric analysis from 1985 to 2020. *Studies in Second Language Learning and Teaching, 12*(3), 381–404.

Radford, A. (2009). *Analysing English sentences: A minimalist approach.* Cambridge: Cambridge University Press.

Raymond, C. (2022). What types of evidence can be used to support CA claims? 中国海洋大学文科处学术讲座.

Rizzi, L. 1978. Violations of the wh-island constraint in Italian and the subjacency condition. *Montreal Working Papers in Linguistics, 11*, 155–90.

Roberts, I. (2022). *Beginning syntax: An introduction to syntactic analysis.* Cambridge: Cambridge University Press.

Robinson, J. (2022). What is a conversation-analytic observation? What should we collect? 中国海洋大学文科处学术讲座.

Romero-Rivas, C., Corey, J. D., Garcia, X., Thierry, G., Martin, C. D., & Costa, A. (2016). World knowledge and novel information integration during L2 speech comprehension. *Bilingualism: Language and Cognition, 20*(3), 576–587.

Rühlemann, C. (2019). *Corpus linguistics for pragmatics: A guide for research.* London & New York: Routledge.

Sacks, H. (1984). Notes on methodology. In J. M. Atkinson, & J. Heritage (Eds.). *Structures of social action* (pp. 21–27). Cambridge: Cambridge University Press.

Sabaté-Dalmau, M. (2018). Migrants' minority-language newspeakerism: The pervasiveness of nation-state monolingual regimes in transnational contexts. *Journal of Sociolinguistics, 22*(1), 5–28.

Sacks. H. (1992). *Lectures on conversation* (I & II). Oxford, UK: Blackwell.

Sacks, H., Schegloff, E. A., & Jefferson, G. (1974). A simplest systematics for the organization of turn-taking for conversation. *Language, 50*(4), 696–735.

Saito, K., & Liu, Y. (2022). Roles of collocation in L2 oral proficiency revisited: Different tasks, L1 vs. L2 raters, and cross-sectional vs. longitudinal analyses. *Second Language Research, 38*(3) 531–554.

Saito, M. (2017). Japanese wh-phrases as operators with unspecified quantificational force. *Language and Linguistics, 18*(1), 1–25.

Saussure, F. de. (1916). *Cours de linguistique generale.* Paris: Payot.（中文版，高名凯（译）. (1980). 普通语言学教程. 北京：商务印书馆. 英文版，Bakin, W. (translate). (1959). *Course in general linguistics.* New York: Columbia University Press.）

Schegloff, E. A. (1992). Repair after next turn: The last structurally provided defence of intersubjectivity in conversation. *American Journal of Sociology, 5*, 1295–1345.

Schegloff. E. A. (1996). Issues of relevance for discourse analysis: Contingency in action, interaction and co-participant context. In E. H. Hoey, & D. R. Scott (Eds.). *Computational and conversational discourse: Burning issues: An interdisciplinary account* (pp. 3–35). New York: Springer.

Schegloff, E. A. (2007). *Sequence organization.* Cambridge: Cambridge University Press.

Schegloff, E., Jefferson, G., & Sacks, H. (1977). The preference for self-correction in the organization of repair in conversation. *Language, 53*(2), 361–382.

Searle, J. R. (1969). *Speech acts: An essay in the philosophy of language.* Cambridge: Cambridge University Press.

Searle, J. R. (1979). *Expression and meaning: Studies in the theory of speech acts.* Cambridge: Cambridge University Press.

Sperber, D., & Wilson, D. (2015). Beyond speaker's meaning. *Croatian Journal of Philosophy, XV*(44), 117–149.

Stivers, T. (2022). *The book of answers: Alignment, autonomy, and affiliation in social interaction.* Oxford: Oxford University Press.

Sun, Y., Wang, G., & Feng, H. (2021). Linguistic studies on social media: A bibliometric analysis. *SAGE Open, 11*(3), 285–300.

Teng, M. F. (2022). The role of second-language proficiency level and working memory on vocabulary learning from word-focused exercise. *RELC Journal,* 1–17.

The PAD Research Group. (2016). Exploring corporate identity construction online. *Discourse & Communication, 10*(3), 291–313.

Thierry, G., & Wu, Y. J. (2012). Brain potentials reveal unconscious translation during foreign-language comprehension. *The Proceedings of the National Academy of Sciences, 104*(30), 12530–12535.

Thompson, S. A., Fox, B. A., & Raymond, C. W. (2021). The grammar of proposal for joint activities. *Interactional Linguistics, 1*, 123–151.

Tsai, W.-T. D. (1994). *On economizing the theory of A-bar dependencies.* MIT: Ph.D. dissertation.

Ungerer, F., & Schmid, H. J. (2013). *An introduction to cognitive linguistics.* London: Routledge.

Valmori, L., & De Costa, P. I. (2016). How do foreign language teachers maintain their proficiency? A grounded theory investigation. *System, 57*, 98–108.

van Berkum, J. J. A., Brown, C. M., & Hagoort, P. (1999). Early referential context effects in sentence processing: Evidence from event-related brain potentials. *Journal of Memory and Language, 47*, 147–182.

van Dijk, T. (2011). *Discourse Studies: A multidisciplinary introduction.* London: Sage.

van Eck, N. J., & Waltman, L. (2007). VOS: A new method for visualizing similarities between objects. In H.-J. Lenz, & R. Decker (Eds.). *Advances in data analysis: Proceedings of the 30th annual conference of the German Classification Society* (pp. 99–306). Berlin: Springer.

Verschueren, J. (1999). *Understanding pragmatics.* London: Arnold.

Wang, X., & Yao, H. (2022). In government microblogs we trust. *Discourse & Communication, 16*(6), 716–734.

Wardhaugh, R., & Fuller, J. (2015). *An introduction to sociolinguistics.* London: Willey-Blackwell.

Watson-Gegeo, K. A. 1988. Ethnography in ESL: Defining the essentials. *TESOL Quarterly, 22*(4), 575–592.

Woods, A., Fletcher, P., & Hughes, A. (2000). *Statistics in language studies.* Beijing: Foreign Language Teaching and Research Press.

Wu, Y. & Yu, G. (2022). Action ascription and action assessment: Ya-suffixed answers to questions in Mandarin conversation. In A. Deppermann, & M. Haugh (Eds.). *Action ascription in interaction* (pp. 234–255). Cambridge: Cambridge University Press.

Xu, X. D., Jiang, X. M., & Zhou, X. L. (2013). Processing biological gender and number information during Chinese pronoun resolution: ERP evidence for functional differentiation. *Brain and Cognition*, *81*(2), 223–236.

Xu, X. D., Jiang, X. M., & Zhou, X. L. (2015) When a causal assumption is not satisfied by reality: Differential brain responses to concessive and causal relations during sentence comprehension, *Language, Cognition and Neuroscience*, *30*(6), 704–715.

Yu, G., & Drew, P. (2017). The role of búshì in talk about everyday troubles and difficulties. *East Asian Pragmatics, 2*, 2, 195–227.

Yu, G., & Wu, Y. (2015). Managing awkward, sensitive, or delicate topics in (Chinese) radio medical consultations. *Discourse Processes*, *52*, 201–225.

Yu, G., & Wu, Y. (2018). Inviting in Mandarin: Anticipating the likelihood of the success of an invitation. *Journal of Pragmatics, 125*, 130–148.

Yule, G., & Widdowson, H. G. (1996). *Pragmatics*. Oxford: Oxford University Press.

Zhao, X. & Mao, Y. (2019). Trust me, I am a doctor: Discourse of trustworthiness by Chinese doctors in online medical consultation. *Health Communication*.

Zheng, H., Bowles, M. A., & Packard, J. L. (2022). NS and NNS processing of idioms and nonidiom formulaic sequences: What can reaction times and think-alouds tell us? *Applied Psycholinguistics*, *43*, 363–388.

Zimmermann, T. E., & Sternefeld, W. (2013). *Introduction to semantics: An essential guide to the composition of meaning*. Berlin: Mouton de Gruyter.

陈晨、李秋杨. (2011). 心理语言学的哲学梳理. 社会科学辑刊, (6), 35–37.

陈建平. (2018). 应用语言学与我国外语教育. 外语界, (4), 8–12.

陈新仁. (2021). 语用学与社会语言学的接口研究——界定、目标与议题. 外语研究, (4), 1–6+112.

大卫·希尔弗曼（英）. (2009). 如何做质性研究（李雪、张劼颖译）. 重庆：重庆大学出版社.

戴庆厦. (2008). 论新时期我国少数民族的语言国情调查. 云南师范大学学报（哲学社会科学版）, (3), 1–6.

杜文博、马晓梅. (2021). 基于混合认知诊断模型的二语阅读技能内在关系探究. 外语教学, (1), 47–52.

段丹、田臻. (2022). 构式语法研究的创新发展与趋势（2001—2020）. 现代外语, (5), 721–731.

冯佳、王克非、刘霞. (2014). 近二十年国际翻译学研究动态的科学知识图谱分析. 外语电化教学, (1), 11–20.

冯志伟. (1999). 应用语言学的范围和性质. 术语标准化与信息技术, (1).

冯志伟. (2013). 现代语言学流派（增订本）. 北京：商务印书馆.

高定国、肖晓云. (2005). 英语学习者水平对英语语音加工的影响. 心理科学, 28(03), 619–621.

桂诗春、宁春岩. (1997). 语言学方法论. 北京：外语教学与研究出版社.

胡春雨、李雨欣、卢春梅. (2022). 商务英语通用语交际中道歉言语行为的语料库语用学研究. 中国外语, (3), 43–52.

胡杰辉、伍忠杰. (2014). 基于 MOOC 的大学英语翻转课堂教学模式研究. 外语电化教学, (6), 40–45.

胡杰辉、许婷. (2020). 中国英语学习者社会规范加工的外语效应机制. 现代外语, (3), 353–364.

胡旭辉等. (2023). 普通语言学新发展研究. 北京：清华大学出版社.

胡壮麟. (2002). 语言学教程. 北京：北京大学出版社.

黄国文. (2007). 关于"外国语言学及应用语言学"的思考. 外语与外语教学, (4), 4–7.

李枫、于国栋. (2017). 介入：会话分析应用研究的新视角. 外国语, 6, 97–108.

李杰、陈超美. (2016). CiteSpace：科技文本挖掘及可视化. 北京：首都经济贸易大学出版社.

李民、陈新仁. (2019). 语料库语用学研究的国际热点解析. 现代外语, (6), 806–817.

马广惠. (2003). 外国语言学及应用语言学统计方法. 杨凌：西北农林科技大学出版社.

马牧青. (2018). 高校外语教师信息资源给养转化行为研究. 上海外国语大学博士学位论文.

马蓉. (2015). 二语学术写作的文献引用能力及其个体影响因素研究. 华中师范大学博士学位论文.

马鑫、苏敏、李杰. (2020). 国际跨文化交际研究现状的文献计量分析（1998—2017）. 外语教学, (1), 59–64.

潘海英、袁月. (2022). 超语研究发展与外语教育研究新范式. 外语教学, (5), 8–14.

潘文国. (2007). 关于外国语言学研究的几点思考. 外语与外语教学, (4), 1–3+7.

邱丽景、王穗苹、陈烜之. (2012).阅读理解中的代词加工：先行词的距离与性别刻板印象的作用.心理学报, 44 (10), 1279–1288.

王峰、陈文.(2017).国内外翻译研究热点与趋势——基于译学核心期刊的知识图谱分析.外语教学, (4), 83–88.

王海贞. (2019).学习者因素与英语口语成绩关系的结构方程模型研究.外语教学理论与实践, (4), 17–26.

王亚峰、于国栋. (2021).医患交流中患者扩展回答的会话分析研究.外语教学理论与实践, (3), 108–118.

王艳. (2008).基于认知框架的二语学生听力理解困难分析.外语教学理论与实践, (1), 53–58.

王艳. (2010).影响二语听力理解的学习者内部因素研究.南京大学博士学位论文.

文秋芳. (2004).应用语言学研究方法与论文写作.北京：外语教学与研究出版社.

吴诗玉.(2021).R在语言科学研究中的应用.北京：科学出版社.

夏秸、陈新仁.(2021).基于 CiteSpace 的国外语言学领域立场研究.外国语文研究（辑刊）, (1), 162–177.

夏珺、王海啸.(2014)."主题式"语言课程对二语写作词汇提取的影响：个案研究.外语研究, (1), 55–60+112.

肖雁.(2017).语用学研究国际热点与趋势解析（2006—2015）.外语教学与研究, (5), 699–709.

徐锦芬、寇金南.(2017).大学英语课堂小组互动模式研究.外语教学, (2), 65–69.

徐锦芬、寇金南.(2018).任务类型对大学英语课堂小组互动的影响.外语与外语教学, (1), 29–38+146–147.

徐锦芬、聂睿.(2015).基于 CiteSpace 的国际二语写作研究动态可视化分析（2004—2014）.外语电化教学, (4), 3–9.

徐晓东、刘昌.(2008).句子理解的关键——对句法和语义关系的再探讨.心理科学进展, 16(4), 532–540.

徐晓东、陆翙翙、匡欣怡、吴诗玉.(2019).不同时间连词对中国英语学习者百科知识理解的影响.外语教学与研究, 51(1), 71–83.

徐晓东、王天乐、刘博洋. (2022).前提真假对外语违实语义加工的影响.外语教学与研究, 54(6), 864–876.

杨昆.(2022).模糊限制语可信度建构功能的调查与分析——以美国总统候选人电视辩论语料为例.外语教学理论与实践, (1), 47–53+62.

杨亦鸣.(2002).语言的神经机制与语言理论研究.上海：学林出版社.

杨亦鸣、刘涛.(2010).中国神经语言学研究回顾与展望.语言文字应用,(2), 12-25.

姚计海.(2017)."文献法"是研究方法吗——兼谈研究整合法.国家教育行政学院学报,(7),89-94.

于国栋.(2022).什么是会话分析.上海：上海外语教育出版社.

张浩云、马凤阳、陈冰玏、郭桃梅.(2012).非熟练汉-英双语者在英语词汇阅读中汉语自动激活的再探讨.外语教学与研究,44(5),719-727.

张美云、刘艳茹.(2021).主体间性话语模式的重构——以基于语料库的医患会话为例.海南大学学报（人文社会科学版）,(1),81-87.

张鹏.(2021).国际跨文化外语教学研究的文献计量分析与启示（2001—2020）. 外语电化教学,(3),30-36.

张艳红.(2019).汉语日常会话中积极评价作为回应行为的会话分析研究.山西大学博士学位论文.

张悦.(2020).影响二语高频多义短语动词习得的因素研究.南京师范大学硕士学位论文.

祖晓梅、马嘉俪.(2015).汉语教师和学习者对课堂纠错反馈信念和态度的比较.汉语学习,(4),66-75.

附录1 国内外大型语料库

语料库分为两种不同的类型：第一种是大型（在线）语料库，由国家或者某一机构集中建设，典型的包括国外的 BNC 语料库和国内的 CCL 语料库。第二种是小型专用语料库，多是由某一机构或者研究者出于特定的研究目标而收集语料建成的语料库，比如商务英语语料库（胡春雨等，2022）、健康话语语料库（张美云、刘艳茹，2021）、政务话语语料库（杨昆，2022）等。这类语料库相对于第一类语料库而言数量更少，针对性更强。以下将选取国内外较为知名的大型语料库进行简单介绍。

（1）BNC 语料库

英国国家语料库（British National Corpus, BNC）收集了来自各种资源的 1 亿字的语言样本，旨在代表 20 世纪后期英国英语，其中书面语占 90%，口语占 10%。最新的版本是 2007 年发布的 BNC XML 版本。BNC 的书面部分包括地区和全国性报纸、不同年龄和兴趣的专业期刊和杂志、学术书籍和通俗小说、已出版和未出版的信件和备忘录、大学论文以及许多其他种类的文本的摘录。口语部分包括从正式商务、政府会议、电台节目和电话会议等不同场合收集的口语（由从不同年龄、地区和社会阶层中选出的志愿者以人口统计平衡的方式收集）。

该语料库根据文本编码倡议（TEI）指南进行编码，以表示 CLAWS（自动词性标注器）的输出和文本的各种其他结构属性（如标题、段落、列表等）。每个文本还以符合 TEI 的标题的形式包含完整的分类、上下文和书目信息。该语料库的建设工作始于 1991 年，1994 年完成。项目完成后没有增加新的文本，但在第二版 BNC World（2001）和第三版发布之前对语料库进行了适度修改，即 BNC XML 版（2007 年）。项目自完成以来，分别发布了两个包含 BNC 材料的子语料库：BNC Sampler（100 万个书面单词、100 万个口语单词）和 BNC Baby（四个来自 BNC 的 100 万单词样本）。

（2）OEC 语料库

牛津英语语料库（Oxford English Corpus, OEC）主要收集基于互联网的材料，也包括一些来自纸质资源的材料。OEC 涵盖所有类型的英语，从文学小说、专业刊物到日常报纸和杂志均有涉及，甚至还涵盖博客、电子邮件和社交媒体中的用语。除英国和美国英语外，OEC 还收录来自爱尔兰、澳大利亚、新西兰、加勒比海、加拿大、印度、新加坡和南非的英语。该语料库的最新版本包含近 21 亿个单词（近 25 亿个标记）。

（3）COCA 语料库

美国当代英语语料库（Corpus of Contemporary American English, COCA）由包含 4.5 亿词的文本构成，这些文本包括口语、小说、流行杂志、报纸以及学术文章五种不同的文体。该语料库是第一个大型的语料平衡的美国英语语料库，也是目前最大的免费英语语料库。除在语料上拥有其他语料库无法比拟的优势外，美国当代英语语料库还将语料和检索软件结合起来，帮助语言研究者方便、快捷地分析和研究语料。

（4）CCL 语料库

北京大学中国语言学研究中心语料库（Center for Chinese Linguistics, CCL）是面向语言学本体研究和语言教学的大规模语料库，目前包括现代汉语、古代汉语和汉英句对齐平行语料，规模超过 7 亿汉字。CCL 语料库检索系统以包括汉字、字母、标点等在内的字符为基本索引单位，提供普通查询、批量查询、模式查询等多种检索方式。同时，该系统支持限定范围查询、基于复杂检索表达式的查询、统计模式频次、对查询结果进行排序、下载查询结果等功能。

（5）BCC 语料库

北京语言大学语料库中心（BLCU Corpus Center, BCC）是以汉语为主、兼有其他语种的在线语料库。BCC 总规模达数百亿字，是服务语言本体研究和语言应用研究的在线大数据系统。BCC 检索式由字、词和语法标记等单元组成，并且支持通配符和离合查询。

（6）MICUSP 语料库

密歇根高级学生论文语料库（Michigan Corpus of Upper-Level Student Papers, MICUSP）是由密歇根大学英语学院开发的高水平英语学习者语料库，收集了共 829 篇得分为 A 的学生论文，总形符数为 260 万。作为跨学科（包括人文艺术、社会科学、生物医学和自然科学四大领域的 16 个学科），跨层次（高年级本科生、硕士生）的高水平学习者语料库，MICUSP 从推出起就受到了研究者的欢迎。

（7）中国学生英语口笔语语料库

作为国内首个大型英语专业学生口笔语语料库，该语料库的设计总规模为 200 万词，其中口语子库为 100 万词，书面语子库为 100 万词。全国共有 11 所大学的 30 多位师生参加了建库各阶段的工作。中国学生英语口笔语语料库的建库目的是为我国二语习得研究服务，尤其是为英语专业教学、教材编写、教学测试、英语教师培训、英语网络课程建设等提供第一手实证材料。

附录2 硕士、博士学位论文封面格式

国家图书馆学位论文封面格式

分类号 _____ 密级 _____

UDC _____

学 位 论 文

_____

（题名和副题名）

_____

（作者姓名）

指导教师姓名、职务、职称、学位、单位名称及地址：_____

_____

_____

_____

申请学位级别 _____ 专业名称 _____

论文提交日期 _____ 论文答辩日期 _____

学位授予单位和日期 _____

答辩委员会主席：_____ _____

评阅人：_____ _____

_____ _____

_____ _____

_____ _____

_____ _____

年　月　日

（大学校徽）

XXX 大学

研 究 生 毕 业 论 文

（申请硕/博士学位）

论 文 题 目 _____

作 者 姓 名 _____

专 业 名 称 _____

研 究 方 向 _____

指 导 教 师 _____

年　　月

附录3 声明格式

学位论文原创性声明

　　兹呈交的学位论文，是本人在导师指导下独立完成的研究成果。在论文写作过程中参考的其他个人或集体的研究成果均在论文中以明确方式标明，本人依法享有和承担由此论文而产生的权利和责任。

声明人（签名）：_____

年　　月　　日

Declaration

　　I hereby declare that this submission is my own work and that, to the best of my knowledge and belief, it contains no material previously published or written by another person or material which has to a substantial extent been accepted for the award of any other degree or diploma at any university or other institute of higher learning, except where due acknowledgement has been made in the text.

Signature: _____

Date: _____

附录4　参考文献格式示例

Ambady, N., & Rosenthal, R. (1993). Half a minute: Predicting teacher evaluations from thin slices of nonverbal behavior and physical attractiveness. *Journal of Personality and Social Psychology*, 64(3), 431–441.

Bachen, C. M., McLoughlin, M. M., & Garcia, S. S. (1999). Assessing the role of gender in college students' evaluations of faculty. *Communication Education*, 48(3), 193–210.

Cashin, W. E. (1990). Students do rate different academic fields differently. In M. Theall, & J. L. Franklin (Eds.). *Student ratings of instruction: Issues for improving practice. New Directions for Teaching and Learning* (pp. 113–121). San Francisco: Jossey-Bass Inc.

Davis, B. G. (2009). *Tools for teaching* (2nd edition). San Francisco: Jossey-Bass.

Edwards, J. E., & Waters, L. K. (1984). Halo and leniency control in ratings as influenced by format, training, and rater characteristic differences. *Managerial Psychology*, 5(1), 1–16.

Fulcher, G. (2003). *Testing second language speaking*. London: Pearson Education.

Knoch, U. (2007). Do empirically developed rating scales function differently to conventional rating scales for academic writing? *Spaan Fellow Working Papers in Second or Foreign Language Assessment*, 5, 1–36.

何龄修. (1998). 读南明史. 中国史研究, (3), 167–173.

刘国钧、陈绍业. (1957). 图书目录. 北京：高等教育出版社.

谢希德. (1998). 创造学习的新思路. 人民日报, 12–25 (10).

赵天书. (2013). 诺西肽分阶段补料分批发酵过程优化研究. 东北大学博士学位论文.

钟文发. (1996). 非线性规划在可燃毒物配置中的应用. 载赵炜编, 运筹学的理论与应用——中国运筹学会第五届大会论文集（468-190页）. 西安：西安电子科技大学出版社.